ROYSTON 1900

A Year in the Life of a Small Market Town

Stan & Jean Ralls

Photographs Les Smith

ISBN 0 9511722 3 9

Published by The Royston and District Local History Society,
Royston Town Hall, Melbourn Street, Royston, Herts. SG8 7DA

Printed and bound in Great Britain
by Burlington Press, Foxton, Cambridgeshire.

CONTENTS

		Page
Introduction	Section 1	5
Thoughts from the Past		6
A Brief Look at 1900	Boer War: Indian Famine: General Election: Labour Party: China: Matters for the Government: Queen Victoria in Ireland: Technology: Sport: Influenza: Coca Cola.	7
Serving the Town	Royston Urban District Council: The Board of Guardians & the Workhouse.	13
Health	Cottage Hospitals: Royston Cottage Hospital: Royston Nursing Association.	22
Essential Services	Water: Gas: Fire Service: Police and the Courts: Post Office: Telephone.	24
Education	British School: National School: Educational Standards: After Elementary School: Miscellaneous Items.	33
Getting About	Railway: Horse: Bicycle: Carriers: Pleasures in Store - The Coming of the Motor Car.	41
After Work	The Churches and their Associations: Royston Military Band: Borrowing Books: Political Groups: The Institute: Sport: Public Houses: The Volunteers: Entertainments: Memories of Royston Fair.	47
Working in Royston	Introduction: List of people at work : Situations Vacant: Miscellaneous Items.	63
This and That	Charities: Cemeteries: Population Statistics: The Haunting of the Old Post Office: Some Residential Addresses: A Wedding: A Prize Winning Dog: Money: A Cause for Sadness: The Absent-Minded Beggar.	77
The News in Brief 1900	Introduction Section 2	85
Calendar for 1900		86
January to December	Month by Month - Reports of routine matters and activities which help to build up a picture of life in 1900 for ordinary townspeople.	87
Bibliography		207
Map of Royston 1900		208

ACKNOWLEDGEMENTS

We should like to thank all those local people and members of Royston and District History Society who have helped in their own way in the preparation of this book. Their assistance has been much appreciated. Special thanks go to the following:

Royston Town Council & the Trustees of Royston Museum and Local History Collection.
Jane Vincent, Curator of Royston Museum, for providing access to items and photographs in the Museum Collection.

Mid-Anglia Newspapers Ltd. and Mrs Dorothy Cooke for permission to reproduce material from past editions of the *Royston Crow.*

Les Smith LRPS who has reproduced and enhanced the old photographs, and provided photographs of relevant items in the Museum Collection.

Robert H. Clark & Son, Royston Golf Club, Douglas Plowman, John Smith, Fred Sillence and Sylvia Beamon for providing articles, assistance with historical detail, proof reading and publishing advice and Freda Wright for providing the picture for the front cover.

Material from the following institutions has also been used and thanks is given for their kind permission to reproduce information, maps and pictures.
Hertfordshire Record Office, Cambridgeshire Record Office, Public Record Office, Kew, BT Archives, Times International, The Bank of England, Spinks & Son, The British Library Board, the Ordnance Survey, Stanley Gibbons, Shire Publications and *History Today.*

INTRODUCTION

This book takes a look at a year in the life of the people in Royston in 1900, one hundred years before we move into a new century.

It has been divided into two sections. The first section deals with various subjects, some of which, though of national and world-wide importance, nevertheless impinged in no small way upon the lives of the town, either because they affected them directly or they read about them in the newspapers, and others which provide background information concerning routine matters and organisation.

This section is enhanced both by copies of photographs taken around 1900 and housed in Royston Museum or by photographs of relevant exhibits in the museum and copies of original documents located in various Record Offices. Unfortunately, none of the photographs in the Museum were specifically dated 1900. However, as those dated a little earlier or later are absolutely typical of 1900 they have been included as they do provide an accurate picture of the time.

The second section deals with specific activities in the town, on a month by month basis, in the year 1900. Most of these were reported in the *Herts and Cambs Reporter (Royston Crow)*. The original articles have been summarised to make them accessible to the modern reader and contain news items, including church activities, education, entertainments, sports results, information on births, marriages and deaths, council matters, letters from the Boer War and details from Petty Sessions, etc. Interspersed throughout this section are copies of advertisements from the newspaper to provide a flavour of the cost of living and items available for purchase.

THOUGHTS FROM THE PAST

The following quote from *The Times*, on January 1st 1901 presents the feelings of one Victorian getting ready to welcome the new century. (The move from the nineteenth century to the twentieth century was not made until 1901 because this year had been officially, and many believe correctly, designated the start of the new century). How have we measured up one hundred years later?

"The twentieth century has dawned on us; and as we float past this great landmark on the shores of time, feelings of great awe and wonder creep over us. What will be the history of mankind in the hundred years whose first hours are even now gliding by? What changes will the new century witness? Will they be mainly for good or for evil? Will the dominance of man over nature increase in the same degree or to a far greater degree than in the age gone by? How the changes will affect the morals and minds of men remains a subject for speculation. Will they be healthier, longer lived, better and more intelligent, or will they remain the same as the people we have known?"

A BRIEF LOOK AT 1900

To state simply in a few sentences what life was like in 1900 is a very tall order, but it may prove helpful to think about a few basic facts. 1900 was to be the last year of the Victorian Age as Queen Victoria was to die in January 1901. Queen Victoria was at the summit of a society which was based on a finely graded hierarchical structure and everyone knew where he or she fitted into it and there was rarely any mixing socially. At the top were the landowners secure in their wealth, power, education and culture, responsive to their public duty with acts of philanthropy. Below them came the middle classes, which were made up of the professionals, the entrepreneurs and wealthy business men who strove to become one of the property-owning classes. They became owners of the detached and semi-detached villas springing up away from the town centres and each household employed at least one servant. Below these came the working classes. This class was made up of a wide grouping of people defensive of their own position in the 'pecking order'. At the top was the skilled worker and at the bottom the simple labourer. They resided in the terrace houses - even these had marks to show status such as bay windows and porches. Below these people came the very poor and wandering unemployed who turned up for assistance to the Union Workhouses. Also at this time religion played a larger part in life than it does today.

For most of Victoria's reign, the aristocracy and gentry dominated the country. They controlled elections and formed the bulk of the Houses of Commons and Lords. Only they could become officers in the armed forces, clergymen in the Church of England, County Government Officers and have access to Oxford and Cambridge Universities. They remained reluctant to remove the causes of inequality in society. However, throughout Victoria's long reign many different groups were formed who were dissatisfied with the inequalities in society. Their calls for reform were persistent and various acts which improved the lot of the lower classes in many fields such as health, housing, voting rights and education were introduced and laid the foundations for increasing state intervention to come.

Technological advances were precipitating previously unimagined changes. When we picture life in 1900, it is life without many items which are integral to our way of life now - they did not exist or were only at an early stage of development and available to the tiniest minority. For the small towns it was a world without mains electricity, radio, telephone, television, motor vehicles, aeroplanes, computers, supermarkets, synthetic materials, central heating, washing machines, microwaves, refrigerators, double glazing, mass holidays abroad, generous annual holidays, etc. In spite of the advent of the railways, the main form of transport between local towns and villages was still the horse and cart with the use of the bicycle gradually increasing.

The population of Royston in 1900 was about one quarter of what it is today but the infrastructure needed to support this relatively small population was made up of a rich diversity of trades and professions. Royston was far from being unique in this matter and it was only later on in this century that such towns lost their need for the local supply of goods. This came with the development of a transport system based upon the railway, motorised road transport and steamships which enabled a much greater variety of goods produced in other parts of the country, the Empire and the world to become generally available.

The spread of mass literacy in the nineteenth century led to the rise of the popular press and forerunners of the modern tabloids. By 1900 the *Daily Mail* (founded in 1896) and the *Daily Express* (1900) had far larger circulations than the old quality dailies like *The Times* and *The Daily Telegraph*. Their articles were kept short and easy to read and were designed to excite and entertain as much as to inform. In the *Royston Crow* a similar pattern can be seen with international news placed in conjunction with the local happenings.

The Boer War

The major event in the world which had a direct effect locally was the Boer War. In October 1899 the long uneasy relationship between Britain and the two Boer Republics of the Transvaal and the Orange Free State had erupted into open warfare. The British saw the beginning of Boer nationalism as a threat to their control of Southern Africa and its recently discovered gold and diamond deposits.

As the year opened, the war was going badly for Britain. On January 23 an attack was launched on the Boer forces besieging Ladysmith. British troops stormed an enemy strong point on Spion Kop and captured it. Defending this position for a day the British lost a thousand dead and had to retreat. Full news about this defeat was kept from the public for many weeks. (There being no radio or television made this a much easier task than it would be now!)

Following this defeat changes had to be made in the British Army. They became more mobile and the traditional red uniforms were replaced by khaki which blended in with the veldt. This strategy worked; Kimberley was relieved in February, quickly followed by Ladysmith, and May saw the relief of Mafeking, the news of which was received with great celebrations in England. In June 1900 Pretoria was taken and by September other chief Boer towns were under occupation and President Kruger of the Transvaal had fled abroad.

The war seemed to be over but the Boers rallied into commando bands and by the end of the year Britain had over 100,000 troops in South Africa. Two more years of guerrilla warfare followed until peace was finally made in 1902 at Vereeniging.

The Boer War intruded considerably into life in Royston in 1900 and much space was allocated in the local press, keeping people informed of the progress of the fighting. Individual correspondence was also printed regularly. Money was collected for the War Fund and parcels were sent out to the troops. During the year Income Tax was raised to 1/- in the £ (equivalent to 5p in the £) and a Tax of 2d. per lb. was levied on tea. (2d. was slightly less than 1p.) Many local men in regular regiments, such as the Suffolk Regiment, the King's Royal Rifles and the Imperial Yeomanry, served time in South Africa and in 1900 some of the Volunteers found themselves in South Africa. This was the first occasion that members of Volunteer Regiments had served abroad.

Local Views on the War

Comments from Surgeon-Lieutenant Col. Balding (Dr. Balding) - _Recently retired from the Local Volunteers._
(Made at the Volunteers' Prizegiving - March 6th 1900, at the Royston Institute.)

"There was never a time when the Army, and the Navy, occupied the thoughts of all British subjects as at the present time. We are now engaged in a war without parallel in the history of the British Empire, and perhaps in the history of the world, and that want of a parallel was in the large number of troops which have been sent out with such extreme rapidity to fight so many thousands of miles away from home. Now great as this war is, and as are the serious issues involved, it came upon this country in one respect unexpectedly. At any rate the greatness and the magnitude has so rapidly developed that it has sprung upon us and found us very little prepared for it. When this became known and that the Government intended to take up the war with vigour it was astonishing how readily the whole country responded to the call - and all loyal subjects at once felt that they were bound to support the Government of the day, and all ranks of the Army at once accepted their responsibilities. Throughout this contest in South Africa, the usual pluck of the British Army has been as well as ever displayed. There has been the greatest desire on the part of all ranks to be as near the front as possible, regardless of danger. That as we know has been the general characteristic of the British Army for ages, and it has never been better exemplified than in this South African War, where all danger has been disregarded and duty has been prominently in the mind of all ranks. If our generals and commanding officers had any difficulty, it had been in preventing their ranks from running into danger from which no good could possibly result. Another quality which has been displayed by our soldiers in the face of reverses and being locked up in sieges day by day, week by week and month by month, has been the quality of fidelity; in the face of disappointments, trials and temptations, they had stuck to their colours and been true to the cause, to their country and the Queen."

"With reference to the Navy, for many years past we have been told that if ever England engaged in a great war, it will be a Naval War. How curiously this War is the very opposite of that! In consequence of the insularity of our opponents the British Navy has had almost nothing to do. But it so happened that in consequence of our want of artillery when our forces landed in South Africa, the Army was obliged to call upon the Navy for all the assistance it could give, and with what result?

The result was that the guns of the Navy, sent out for the purpose of being used afloat, were at once unshipped with a rapidity which astonished some of the generals of our Army, and were landed, transported hundreds of miles and immediately brought into action by the Naval Brigade. As soon as they were brought into action, their use was most efficacious. On more than one occasion it seemed almost to turn the scale in the conflict of the day, much to the surprise of our enemies, the Boers, who found they could not stand against Naval Guns. And the Queen herself, who never seems to forget anything, has not forgotten this and within a few days we had seen that she had telegraphed the Commander in Chief thanking the Naval Brigade for its efficient service on land."

Extracts from comments made by Colonel Longmore of the Battalion
(Guest speaker and invited to award prizes at the Volunteers' Prizegiving)

"The Navy had not had many great opportunities during the present War, but the Admiralty had shown how exceedingly efficient they were in transporting a large Army from one part of the Globe to another. It would be difficult to find in the whole history of the world, an Army of anything like the size of that now being sent to South Africa transported without the slightest mishap................"

He also spoke of the discipline of the troops "................ in the whole history of the British Army there has not been a more splendid specimen of discipline than what had taken place with Sir Redvers Buller's forces in the previous few months. It had been something like attacking one of the strongest fortresses that ever existed; in fact, fortress after fortress for several miles. After an army had met with three reverses, for that army to have such a belief in their General and such implicit obedience as to go on through ten days of hard fighting in that terrible country, the immense value of discipline was shown."

South Africa showing where Royston men fought and died

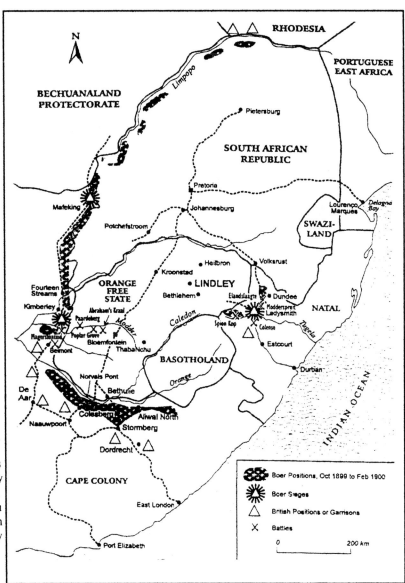

This map is reproduced courtesy of *History Today*. It first appeared in that magazine in the issue of May 1998.

Keeping Royston Informed

Emergency Rations - Boer War

(Royston Museum Collection)

The emergency ration container was divided into two sections. One side contained cocoa and the other side beef extract. The photograph shows the actual size, this being approximately 12 x 6 x 4cm.

The Indian Famine

From the Queen's Speech on February 2nd:

"I have received from the Ruling Chiefs of Native States in India numerous offers to place their troops and the resources of their States at my disposal for service in South Africa. These proofs of their loyalty to myself and of their devotion to the cause of my Empire have afforded me much gratification."

"We regret that owing to the insufficient rainfall in the autumn over a great part of Western and Central India, the harvests have failed so much as to create a famine. Timely measures have been taken by my Government, and by the Rulers of the Native States affected, to relieve suffering and to prevent starvation. We regret to add that the epidemic of plague continues, and that although its severity has not increased since last year, there is at present no prospect of a diminution."

At the end of February, the Viceroy of India presided at a public meeting in Calcutta to inaugurate the fund for the relief of the sufferers of famine. Lord Curzon said that the famine was of unprecedented magnitude, and the pathos and tragedy of the situation were emphasised by the plague at Bombay. He rejoiced to find that the British nation, in the midst of its anxieties and troubles, had opened its purse, and that the Lord Mayor of London was able to help. Whatever the public gave would not affect the extent and character of the State outlay, and no difference would be made between the claim of Native States and British India. He announced that the Queen had become a patron of the fund, and had given £1,000, whilst many other generous donations had been received.

10

General Election

During October 1900 a General Election took place and Lord Salisbury's government (Conservative), which had held office since 1895, remained in office with a clear majority. The successes of the British in South Africa engendered a mood of national patriotism and the Conservatives made full use of this and while the campaign was in progress they disregarded any questions of social provisions or economics. They maintained they were the only party who could bring this conflict to an end with conditions acceptable to England. They were totally opposed to the concept of "peace at any cost" which is what they considered the opposition wanted. As well as this, the opposition, the Liberals, were in disagreement over the war and this made them very unpopular.

"Our brave soldiers in South Africa expect that every voter this day will do his duty.
To vote for a Liberal is to vote for the Boer." A Conservative poster, 1900.

The Conservative victory was helped considerably as the Liberals were deeply divided over the war. Important party members like H. H. Asquith supported it, but David Lloyd George branded it a waste of lives and money. These opposing views ended any possibility of a Liberal victory in the election. When David Lloyd George tried to give his opinion of the war in Birmingham, he was howled down by the audience and had to make a dramatic exit. It appeared that a long period of Conservative government lay ahead. Even in Royston much rowdiness occurred at the Liberal Meeting and elsewhere in the Constituency.

Royston fell into two constituencies; North Hertfordshire (Hitchin Division) and West Cambridgeshire. (Electors included in West Cambs included residents of Kneesworth St., Melbourn St., Back St., The Cross, Baldock St., Melbourn Rd. and The Green). The contest was an interesting one locally in the light of the past history of the West Cambs division which, like North and East Cambs, had favoured both parties in turn. It was first of all won by the late Sir Charles Hall, by a narrow majority over the late Mr. Neville Goodman and after being held by Sir Charles, it was wrested from him at the 1892 election by Mr. Hugh E. Hoare the Liberal Candidate, who was returned with a majority of 398. In turn it was taken from the Liberals in 1895 by Mr. Raymond Greene, who defeated Mr. Hoare with a majority of 420, and retained his seat in 1900.

The Labour Party

In 1884 the vote had been given to all male householders over 21 who paid rates. For the first time many, although not all, working men could vote. At first most of these new votes went to the Liberals, and the tiny socialist parties like the Independent Labour Party received little support. By 1900, it was obvious that social reforms on a large scale would not happen until the working class had its own representatives in Parliament. In 1900 a group of trade unionists and socialists formed the Labour Representation Committee (LRC) to work for the election of MPs sympathetic to the workers' cause. The first secretary was a Scot, Ramsay Macdonald. The LRC attracted little attention initially and in the election of 1900 managed to return only two MPs: Keir Hardie and Richard Bell. Mr. Keir Hardie, speaking at the annual Conference of the Independent Labour Party, said if everything had not been accomplished during the time the organisation had been in existence which ardent supporters might have desired, at least they could claim that the opinion of the people towards Socialism and Labour representation had undergone a complete revolution. He condemned the war in South Africa, which, he said, had for its prime motive the enslavement of black labour and the pauperisation of white labour.

China: Peking: Fifty five days

In 1900 Chinese resentment against 'foreign devils' increased. A secret society called the 'Righteous and Harmonious Fists', nicknamed 'Boxers', vowed to expel all foreigners. In the spring of 1900 the Boxers swept through northern China towards Peking, massacring foreigners. On June 20 they invaded the area of the city where Europeans lived and besieged the foreigners in their compounds. After 55 days the siege was lifted by an international force and this foreign intervention reduced the authority of the Chinese Government.

Other Matters for the Government

As well as the Boer War, the Election and the Indian Famine and the Boxer Rebellion, other subjects were on the agenda in Parliament. The second reading of the Burial Authorities (Cremation) Bill was moved. Its main object was to declare that the powers of a burial authority to provide and maintain cemeteries should be deemed to extend to and include the provision and maintenance of place and the necessary appliances, for burning the bodies of dead persons.

The Government intended to frame a scheme under which adequate provision would be made for the widows and orphans of soldiers killed in war.

A report on the financial aspects of the proposals made by the Select Committee of the House of Commons of 1899 about the aged deserving poor had been presented to Parliament. On the assumption that the pensionable age was fixed at 65, the committee estimated that the annual charge for the United Kingdom would in 1901 be £10,300,000, in 1911 £12,650,000 and in 1921 £15,650,000.

The question of more regulation for the drinks industry and for Public Houses was also on the agenda. Parliament discussed purity of ingredients in the manufacture of beer, the hours of opening of Public Houses and a minimum age for the purchase of alcohol.

The only private members bill to reach the Statute Books prohibited child labour underground.

Income tax was raised to cover war expenses in South Africa and China; 4d. on Income Tax, 1/- on a barrel of beer, 6d. a gallon on spirits, 4d. on tobacco and 2d. a pound on tea.

The Queen visits Dublin

In April 1900, Queen Victoria visited Dublin. She travelled in the Royal Train over the Great Western Line to Wolverhampton and thence by the London and North Western Railway to Holyhead where she embarked on the Royal Yacht for the journey to Kingstown and from there to Dublin. In the city, which was profusely decorated for the occasion, she was given a very enthusiastic welcome. Whilst there she stayed in the Viceregal Lodge in Phoenix Park.

A loyal address of welcome was given, and the Queen replied thanking them, saying she was "deeply gratified that she had been able to revisit the Motherland of those brave sons who had recently borne themselves in defence of her Crown and Empire."

Technology

At the Great Paris Exhibition in the spring and summer the public were able to see some of the great technological advances - an escalator (the first in Europe), X-Rays, wireless telegraph, motor cars and silent movies were some of the items on display. It was the first exhibition to be powered by electricity.

An air ship, named after the German Count Zepplin, completed a succeessful test flight over Lake Constance near the Swiss-German border when it reached a height of 1000 feet and stayed in the air for eighteen minutes lifted by 400,000 cubic feet of hydrogen. It was fitted with a rudder and two petrol engines.

Also, Benjamin Holt, of the USA., invented the caterpillar track; Massachusetts, USA. opened the first fully automated telephone exchange; the oxy-acetylene torch was invented in France and the Brownie Box Camera was first produced in the USA by Eastman-Kodak. It went on sale for $1 and made photography, which had previously been too expensive for most people, a popular hobby.

Sporting News

The Second Olympic games of modern times were held in Paris in conjunction with the Exhibition there. 1300 competitors took part but only 11 were women and some athletes refused to compete on Sundays. An American Business man, D. F. Davis, presented a cup to be awarded to the winners of a knock-out contest for national lawn tennis teams. This is still competed for to-day and is known as the Davis Cup. In 1900 the USA beat Britain in the final.

Influenza Outbreak

Major cities in Britain were hit badly by an influenza epidemic and fifty people a day died in London. There was a shortage of nurses to cope with the epidemic and some wards had had to be closed. There is evidence that Royston was affected but not so badly. A similar epidemic had happened seven years previously.

Coca-Cola

In August Coca-Cola was introduced into Britain. It had already been on sale in the USA for 14 years.

SERVING THE TOWN

Royston Urban District Council

The town was administered by the Urban District Council of twelve members, formed in October 1897, under the provisions of the *Local Government Act, 1894*. This met every 2nd Monday in the month at 6 p.m. in the Town Hall (formerly The Institute). Members served for three years and then could be re-elected.

In 1900 the District Council was a fledgling organisation and a quote from Kingston's *History of Royston* will give us an idea of the chaotic state of the civil administration of the town at the turn of the century before its inception.

" The town of Royston on the passing of the Parish and District Councils Act, in 1894, was probably a unique example of complicated boundaries. Within the township there were set up under the Act six Parish Council areas - Royston, Herts. and Cambs. parishes, and parts of Therfield, Barkway, Bassingbourn and Kneesworth, besides a small part of Melbourn. Six Parish Councils were elected for certain matters through several Joint Committes; the District Councils of the Union had to form a special Joint Committee, and the two County Councils had their Joint Committee, for the town was in Herts. and Cambs. Altogether, the town was for a year or two in the hands of two County Councils, six Parish Councils, and several Joint Committees - upwards of a dozen different authorities! An Urban District Council was vetoed by the Local Government Board, and, after a struggle between the two County Councils of Herts. and Cambs., the question to which county the town should belong was fought out before a Select Committee of the House of Commons, and, the town being generally in favour of Hertfordshire a Provisional Order was made and confirmed by Parliament placing the town entirely in that County as one civil parish, under an Urban District Council of twelve members, and the first Council was formed in 1897. The town still continues in two counties for Parliamentary elections. The area of the civil parish is now practically the area of the ecclesiastical parish which had been previously extended."

Items under discussion during 1900 were wide ranging: the take-over and financing of the Institute for use as Council Offices; the paving of many roads; sewage and the advisability of purchasing their own land for use as a sewage farm instead of renewing a lease; the extension of the sewers themselves; new buildings; the extension for the water main and new reservoir; street lighting and matters applying to public health. Details of some of these discussions will be found in the second section.

Members	
Chairman	Joseph Edward John Phillips
Vice Chairman	George Walters Howard
To retire in April, 1899	Simms Camps; Thomas Goodman; Harry Smith; Alfred Thomas Titchmarsh
To retire in April, 1900	Herbert Ray Archer; Alfred Kingston; Ernest Matthews: Ralph Erskine Sanders
To retire in April, 1901	Daniel Barley Balding; Thomas Luke Gimson; George Walters Howard; Joseph Edward John Phillips
To retire in April, 1902	Simms Camps; Thomas Goodman; Harry Smith; Alfred Thomas Titchmarsh

Officers	
Clerk	Harold Francis John Banham, Kneesworth Street
Treasurer	Francis John Fordham, Banker, High Street.
Medical Officer of Health	Bushell Anningson M.A., M.D. M.R.C.S. Eng. Walthamsal, Barton Road, Cambridge
Surveyor and Collector	James Smith, Melbourn Steet 1899: Thomas W. Witt, Rates Office, Town Hall 1902
Sanitary Inspector - Inspector of Nuisances	William James Webb appointed Sept 1899 after resignation of Mr. Woodward

Other Public Officers

Assist.Overseer & Collector of Land, Assessed & Income Tax
James Smith, Melbourn Street 1899
Edwin Haywood, High Street 1902
Coroner for Royston Division of the County of Herts.
Daniel B. Balding, Melbourn St. 1899
Wm. B. King, High St. 1902
Deputy Coroner. Herbert Ray Archer, Melbourn St.

Clerk to Commissioner of Taxes H. Dalton Nash, High St.
Inspector under Contagious Diseases(Animals) Act for Odsey & Buntingford Divs: Fred Hewson(MRCVS), The Roystons
Town Crier: Willam Stamford, 6 Sun Hill 1899
Alonza Barron 1902
Certifying Factory Surgeon: C. W. Windsor MA, Melbourn St.
County Council Main Road Surveyor for Buntingford Division
Walter Gregory, Gower Rd., Royston.

Men who served Royston in 1900

Although this photograph was taken in 1897, it is an excellent record of the men serving the town in 1900.
Photograph R. H. Clark (Royston Museum Collection)

<table>
<tr><td>

Back Row

John Phillips
George Walters Howard
William T. Rowley
Ellis Wilkerson
Rev. T.H. Lomas
Alfred Kingston
Ernest Matthews
Thomas Luke Gimson
Walter C. Titchmarsh

</td><td>

Arnold J.Jacklin
Charles Warren

Sitting

Rev. J. Harrison
Joseph E. Phillips
Frederick N. Fordham
Francis J. Fordham
Dr. Herbert Ray Archer
Harry Smith

</td><td>

Front Row

Henry S. Tuke
Alfred Thomas Titchmarsh
Simms Camps
Alfred Cheshire

George Cautherley
Thomas Goodman

</td></tr>
</table>

Board of Guardians - Royston Members.

Chairman of the Board of Guardians J. E. Phillips.
Clerk to the Guardians Arthur Sharpe.
Treasurer Frederick Nash Fordham, Bank, High Street
Collectors to the Guardians and Relieving Officers
   Royston District; Edwin Davies, Radnor House
   Melbourn District; John Davies, Gower Road.
Medical Officers
   No. 1 District: Herbert Ray Archer, Melbourn Street
Public Vaccinator   Daniel Barley Balding, 1899
                 Herbert Ray Archer, 1902.
Vaccination Officer H.N. Woodward, Barkway Road 1899
                 W. J. Webb, Melbourn Road 1902

Superintendant Registrar
Thomas Shell, High Street 1899:
Deputy, Frederick Shell, Melbourn Street 1899
Arthur Sharpe, 1900: deputy, Edwin Haywood 1902.
Registrar of Births, Marriages and Deaths
Royston District: Edwin Davies, Radnor House
Deputy, James Smith, Royston 1899. Ebenezer Henderson 1902
Melbourn District: John Davies, Gower Road
Deputy, Francis Cane, Mill Road
School Attendance Committee
Meeting at conclusion of meeting of the Board.
 Clerk -   Thomas Shell 1899 (Died 1900)
           Arthur Sharpe 1900

The Board of Guardians and the Workhouse

On the Baldock Road, where the Downlands estate now stands, was to be found the Union Workhouse. In the year 1900 the workhouse had already been overlooking the Heath for many years. Called the "Union" and viewed with expressions of apprehension if not fear by the residents, it was to survive nearly 140 years until its demolition in 1971. In its later life it was called Heath Lodge.

Until 1834 the only social service available for the alleviation of distress to the destitute had been administered by individual parishes. The view of the government was that the situation was out of hand and as a result there were too many layabouts living on the rates and too much idleness and indiscipline. The solution was to make any help an uncomfortable and unpleasant business, so that poor people would feel better off if they did not apply for relief at all.

By the *Poor Law Amendment Act* passed in 1834 the Government had the power to amalgamate parishes into unions administered by a Board of Guardians. These boards could utilize the combined income from the poor rates to build and run workhouses. In 1835, parishes were amalgamated to form the Royston Union (some of which lay in the present day Cambridgeshire) and a representive was appointed from each parish to the Board of Guardians. The Union comprised the following parishes in Hertfordshire: Ashwell, Barkway, Barley, Hinxworth, Kelshall, Nuthampstead, Reed, Royston and Therfield and in Cambridgeshire: Abington Pigotts, Barrington, Bassingbourn, Great and Little Chishill, Fowlmere, Foxton, Guilden Morden, Heydon, Kneesworth, Litlington, Melbourn, Shepreth, Shingay, Steeple Morden, Thriplow, Wendy and Whaddon.

After due negotiations and opposition from the parishioners involved, who descended upon Royston to try to demolish this new building, a workhouse for 244 paupers was eventually erected at a cost of £6,744 and opened in 1836.

Life inside the workhouses was harsh and uncomfortable and tasks of work were expected in exchange for board and lodging such as picking oakum, tilling ground, stone breaking, 'more irksome than ordinary labour', so that the destitute would not be tempted to continue it longer than necessary. The guardians resolved that, "for the future no relief either in kind or money should be furnished to any able-bodied male pauper or to any part of his family out of the workhouse". The effect of this decision, to give relief only within the workhouse, was to create a bitter hatred and loathing for the system which lasted well into the twentieth century.

From the time of their beginnings to the end of the century, the workhouses slowly changed. A central Poor Law Board had been set up with a bureaucracy of inspectors attached to it. Revelations of what went on in some of the workhouses during the 1860s led to gradual improvements. However, the system was cost effective, and no other state in Europe took such an interest in provision for the poor. Nevertheless, within the workhouses the sexes were separated, uniform worn and strict discipline maintained and the fact remained that they came to symbolise an ultimate degradation, the loss of any status within society.

That new developments had been incorporated into the procedures of the Royston Union is obvious in the reports of the meetings of the Board of Guardians which took place every other Wednesday at 11a.m. in the Board Room of the workhouse itself. At these meetings, chaired by J. E. Phillips and attended by representatives from the parishes included in the Union, many issues concerning procedures and the health and welfare of the inmates were aired. At each meeting of the Guardians financial statistics were presented as was a record of the numbers catered for in each category of inmate.

During 1900 several matters arose for discussion during the Guardians' meetings: boarding out for children in a system of foster-care supervised by appointed visitors, responsibility for bathing of vagrants, the eventual employment of a nurse to take charge of the Sick Wards, Lying-in Ward and the Children's Nursery after the difficulty of finding suitable people, the installation of a new water supply, treats for the inmates, costs to the parishes of the Poor Relief, tenders for food and clothing for both indoor and outdoor relief, and repainting of the workhouse. A visiting inspector had attended one of these meetings and had expressed his satisfaction with the running of the workhouse and of the efficiency of the 'working cells'. As the Guardians declined to pay for the services of a resident chaplain, services were held in the Workhouse on alternate Sundays by the Vicar and Nonconformist Ministers. There were some Nonconformists who were allowed to attend their own church if they so wished.

A Medical Officer (Charles William Windsor - appointed in Sept 1899 at a salary of £45 to replace Dr. Balding) visited daily and a night-nurse for the infirmary was employed as required. In addition there were 'receiving wards' and a mortuary.

Children from the workhouse attended local schools (in 1900 5 boys and 6 girls). From 1870 the emphasis was to place the pauper child as far as possible in a normal environment mixing with other children. Hence to the reformers of the period the state schools provided an ideal answer, while for the Boards of Guardians, it was increasingly cheaper than employing their own teachers and equipping their own schoolrooms. However, it must not be forgotten that the uniformity of clothing and the regulated lifestyle of the pauper child often continued to distinguish them from their fellow pupils.

By the turn of the century a different kind of destitution, which had not been considered fully at first had become apparent, that of the aged and the mentally sick. The aged poor were placing a greater burden on the Poor Law. By the mid-1890s many workhouses had over half their inmates in this category. 20% of those aged 65-69 were paupers, whereas 40% of those over 75 were in receipt of poor relief. However, the aged were united in their opposition to the workhouse and they were prepared to accept considerable hardship rather than become inmates. This is possibly due to the stricter regime, introduced with the campaign against outdoor relief, which made the position of the aged worse in workhouses where they were simply classed with the able-bodied. The customary discomfort was supported by the uniformity of the standard diet and rigid timetable, ill-suited to the aged, or indeed the mentally sick. In such institutions the grievances were increased by the feeling of being rejected by family.

It was thought that outdoor relief should be the normal provision of poor relief to the aged and it should be adequate in amount and where resort to indoor relief was needed, it was felt there should be improvements in accommodation. Thus by the mid 1890s there was an increasing belief that the aged should be regarded as a more deserving category of pauper and a less disciplined environment evolved for them.

Vagrants, casual workers and their families were also housed when it was impossible to find work and their treatment was much harsher. They were housed in cells ('casual wards') separated from the other inmates, and required to carry out some work in return for lodging. Numbers varied considerably due to need at different periods of time. These could vary from year to year. In July 1900, the Master of the workhouse reported that the number of vagrants relieved during the half-year ended Midsummer had been 278 as against 607 for the previous year, a reduction of 329.

The accompanying dietary chart, a copy of one found in the workhouse before its demolition, is not actually dated but it shows the typical food provided to casuals at the turn of the century and the tasks they were required to perform. In fact one item (stone-breaking) is not mentioned but later in the monthly reports we find the might of the law descending on a man who refused to do stone-breaking.

A Typical Meeting of the Board of Guardians

Members were present from Royston and from the other parishes in the Union

Present

Mr. J. E. Phillips (Chairman), Rev. R. Hines, Rev. J. S. Butcher,
Messrs. J. C. Wilkerson, T.W. Russell, J.T. Jackson, W. P. Stockbridge, J. G. Fordham, J. Wallis, J. J. Balding, T. G. F. Pigott, W. W. Clear, J. Hart, S. P. Bullen, H. J. Gibbs, T. L. Gimson, J. M. Coleman, A. Coningsby, J. G. Russell.
Clerk Mr. A. Sharpe.

Relief Statistics

Royston District: The amount of out-relief granted during the fortnight was £59 2s. 3d.; corresponding figure 1899, £61 18s. 2d.

Melbourn District: The amount of out-relief granted during the fortnight was £56 11s. 3d.; corresponding period 1899, £55 19s. 7d.

Inmates

The number of inmates in the Workhouse for the week was : men, 49 (none able-bodied); women, 32 (none able-bodied); children 17; Total 98

Corresponding period in 1899: men, 62 (none able-bodied); women, 30 (none able-bodied); children; 23; Total 115

Vagrants

The number of vagrants relieved during the fortnight was - first week 9, second, 17.

DIETARY OF CASUALS

FIRST SCHEDULE

DIETARY
of Casuals who are inmates of the Casual Ward

1. Subject as hereinafter provided the dietary for casuals shall be in accordance with the following Dietary Tables.

CLASS	DESCRIPTION	SUPPER, BREAKFAST	DINNER
1	**Men and Boys** 12 years or over	Bread ----8oz. Margarine or Dripping -- 1oz. Hot Tea, Coffee, Cocoa or Broth- 1 pint	Bread--------8oz. Cooked or Tinned meat---2oz. Cheese---2oz Potatoes (hot) 4oz. Salt, a sufficiency
2	**Women and Girls** 12 Years old or over	Bread----6oz. Margarine or Dripping------1oz Hot Tea, Coffee, Cocoa or Broth 1 pint	Bread-------6oz. Cooked or Tinned Meat--------2oz. Cheese------2oz. Potatoes(hot) 4oz Salt, a sufficiency
3	**Children** under 12 years	Such meals as , subject to the approval of the Council, be prescribed by the Medical Officer	

In addition to the above, some vegetable other than potatoes shall be provided at one meal in each day

2. The dietary of the casual who is sick or infirm shall be such as may be prescribed in writing by the Medical Officer.

3. The master may, if he thinks fit in any case, give to a casual an additional allowance (not exceeding 4oz.) of bread at any meal, and in each case he shall record his action in the Admission and Discharge Book.

4. In the case of an infant suckled by his mother the allowance for the infant may be given to the mother instead of the infant

5. In the case of each child under twelve years of age the matron will cause the allowance of food prescribed in respect of each meal to be prepared in such manner and to be given at such times and in such a way as shall be suitable to the child.

6. Where milk is prescribed, it shall be new milk, whole and undiluted: provided that the unsweetened condensed whole cream milk or dried whole cream milk may be substituted for new milk in the proportion to each half-pint of four ounces of condensed milk or one and a half ounces of dried milk, with a proper addition of hot water.

MIDDAY MEAL
for Casuals discharged from the Casual Ward

7. The midday meal to be provided for each casual on the day of his discharge from the Casual Ward shall be in accordance with the following Dietary Table:-

CLASS	DESCRIPTION	RATION
1	**Men and Boys** 12 years old or over	Bread, 8oz.; cheese, 2oz.
2	**Women and Girls** 12 years old or over.	Bread, 6oz.; cheese, 2oz.
3	**Children** 8 years old or over, but under 12 years old	Bread, 4 oz.; butter, 1oz.
4	**Children** 3 years old or over, but under 8 years old.	Milk, ½ pint; bread, 3oz.; butter, 1oz.
5	**Children** 10 months old or over, but under 3 years old.	Milk, ½ pint; sugar, ½ oz,; bread 2oz
6	**Children** under 10 months	Milk, ½ pint; sugar, ½ oz.

8. Unless other arrangements have been made for the provision of a midday meal, that meal shall be handed to the casual on his taking his discharge.

9. If in any case the master has reason to believe that a casual does not require to be provided with a midday meal and does not provide him with the meal or with the requisite authority for obtaining it, he shall enter a note of his reasons in the Admission and Discharge Book

10. On Christmas Day, or on some other day near thereto, the Dietary Tables may be suspended and special directions may be given for the dieting of the Casuals.

****

SECOND SCHEDULE

TASKS OF WORK FOR CASUALS
The task of each day of detention shall be:

MALES
*Eight hours' work in gardening or digging or pumping, or chopping or sawing or bundling wood, or carrying coal, or washing or scrubbing or cleaning.

FEMALES
Eight hours' work in washing, or scrubbing or cleaning or needlework.

Original in Royston Museum.   **(Eight hours has been crossed through in pencil and THREE substituted)*

The Master and Matron of a Workhouse

The *Poor Law Officers' Manual* provides an interesting insight into the qualities required by the Master and Matron of a workhouse. Excerpts follow:

"The Master of the Workhouse is the most important officer engaged in the administration of the relief of the poor. He requires the possession of more qualifications than any other officer, and in most Unions attracts the greatest amount of public notice.............

The Master of the Workhouse should be a man possesing a calm and steady temper; he should be firm, authoritative and vigilant, but, at the same time, gentle and considerative towards the poor and distressed objects who come under his care.

He should be prudent and decorous in his conduct as respects all, but particularly as regards the females, and he should be guarded and temperate in his language and demeanour. He should be sober in his diet, cleanly in his person, and orderly in his behaviour.

He must ever be active in his supervision of the Workhouse and the inmates, careful in watching the various incidents and accidents which occur in it, preserving order and sobriety of conduct among the inmates, keeping them employed, as far as practicable in useful labour. He should be attentive and soothing to the sick, and should provide for the peaceful end of the dying and their decent burial.

He should prevent all attempts to disturb the regularity of the house by unseemly visitors, or disorderly conduct in the apartments provided for himself and other officers.

At the same time that he exercises calm and judicious control over these officers, he should avoid all captious, overbearing or oppressive conduct towards them.........

He must be careful and judicious in his reports as to the stores...........and he must be economical in the expenditure of the stores entrusted to his charge. He must bear in mind that he has no authority to order goods to be supplied........

Books of account are required to be accurately kept by him...........In his dealings with the tradesmen who supply the Workhouse, he must abstain from all attempts to obtain personal advantage............. He must scrupulously demand the due execution of the orders of the Guardians,......... and he should abstain from familiar intercourse with any Guardians.

Sometimes his office require him to have a knowledge of gardening and simple farming so far as to be able to superintend the cultivation of the Workhouse garden............. which serves for the employment of the pauper inmates.

No person who has a family of young children or has private affairs to attend to which require his frequent care and consideration, is proper to undertake the office, because the whole of his time and thoughts must be engaged in the discharge of his duties.

The discharge of the duties of Master requires that he should be in the possession of full vigour of health in mind and body. When these fail he ceases to be fit for the office, and if he continue to hold it, mischievous results may be expected to follow............... Such a failure is now met whereby a superannuation allowance may be granted."

Much of what has been expressed above is applicable to the Matron. In addition:

"She should be active and vigilant in her supervision of the wards, so as to secure cleanliness throughout all of them, and should be careful to preserve order in the female part of the establishment.

She must be watchful over the sick and young children, and use her utmost endeavours to prevent the growing up girls from intercourse with the vicious and disorderly inmates of their own sex...............

She should be plainly but neatly dressed, and should avoid all finery unsuitable to her position. She should rise early, be constantly engaged in the supervision of the House, and not merely by fits and starts.

She must understand household work and domestic cookery .... and must exercise economy and restrain waste. Sometimes she is required to be skilled in the management of a dairy.. .... She should be competent to superintend the cutting out, the making up and the proper marking and preserving of linen and garments for use in the Workhouse."

"The posts were, legally distinct and separate but in practice, so intimately connected that they cannot be treated separately. Though these officers need not be husband and wife, yet they usually are so; and much benefit results from this provision."

In 1900 Mr and Mrs John Wesson were the Master and Matron of Royston Workhouse.

Poor Law Officers' Manual (Hertfordshire Record Office).

During 1900, 122 admissions were made into the workhouse from all the villages that made up the Royston Union. The following table from the Religious Creed Register lists only those from Royston. *(The complete register is housed in Royston Museum.)*

THE RELIGIOUS CREED REGISTER
Royston Union

J. W. Wesson

Master (or Matron) of the Workhouse.

Date of admission	NAME Chritian and Surname	Religious Creed	Name of Informant	Discharged or Dead	
6. 1. 1900	Elizabeth Rayment	Ch. Eng.	Herself		10. 1. 1900
6. 1. 1900	John Woods	Ch. Eng.	Himself		30. 4. 1900
24. 1. 1900	Ann Janeway	Congr.	Herself	Died	14. 4. 1903
31. 1. 1900	Geo. Stanley Giffen	Ch. Eng.	His mother		3. 3. 1900
31. 1 1900	Elizabeth Rayment	Ch. Eng.	Herself		17. 3. 1900
21. 3. 1900	Rachel Holloway	Chapel	Herself		7. 5. 1900
21 3. 1900	Her daughter, Rosa	Chapel	Her mother		7. 5. 1900
28. 3. 1900	William Kingston	Ch. Eng.	Himself	Died	23. 4. 1900
15. 4. 1900	Joseph Collier	Ch. Eng	Himself		23. 4. 1900
5. 5. 1900	Joseph Collier	Ch. Eng.	Himself		14. 5. 1900
8. 5. 1900	Rachel Holloway	Congr.	Herself		7. 5. 1900
8. 5. 1900	Rosa Holloway	Congr.	Her mother		7. 5. 1900
10. 5. 1900	John Horall	Ch. Eng	Himself	Died	20. 3. 1901
15. 5. 1900	Elizabeth Rayment	Ch. Eng	Herself		10. 6 1900
1. 7. 1900	Patrick Preston	R. Catholic	Himself		18. 7 1900
4. 8. 1900	Martha Coe	Ch. Eng	Herself		8. 10. 1900
11. 8. 1900	Rachel Holloway	Congr.	Herself		4. 9. 1900
11. 8. 1900	Rosa Holloway	Congr.	Her mother		4. 9. 1900
15. 8. 1900	Elizabeth Rayment	Ch. Eng.	Herself		22. 8. 1900
25. 8. 1900	Elizabeth Rayment	Ch. Eng.	Herself		21.12. 1900
22. 9. 1900	Rachel Holloway	Congr.	Herself	Died	22. 1. 1900
22. 9. 1900	Rosa Holloway	Congr.	Her mother		26. 3. 1900
21 10.1900	Wm.Pywell Fewkes	Congr.	Himself		23.10. 1900
18.11.1900	William Baines	Ch. Eng	Himself		30.11 1900
21.11.1900	John Woods	Ch. Eng.	Himself		3. 6. 1907
6.12.1900	Elizabeth Rayment	Ch. Eng.	Herself		28.12. 1900
29.12.1900	William Barker	Wesleyan	Himself		22. 1. 1901

Some extracts of correspondence with the Local Government Board *(Public Record Office - MH12/ 4657)*

".......ask your sanction to the payment of one pound ten shillings to the Matron of the Workhouse (Mrs J. E. Wesson) and to the porter (Mr. E. W. Cleak) for four weeks extra services during the absence of a Cook at the Workhouse." (January 1900)

".......I am directed by the Guardians to inform you that arrangements have been made for the imbeciles to have a bath once every week and not more than two persons to be bathed in the same water. ..... I am also directed to inform you that arrangements are being made for a better water supply for the bathing."(February 1900).

".......ask for your sanction to the payment of the sum of one guinea to Mr. E. F. Bindloss, District Medical Officer in respect of assistance, which it was necessary for him to obtain, in connection with the administration of Chloroform to Emily Sharp aged 12, the child of Alfred Smith, of Whaddon, in the removal of postnasal adenoid growths and tonsils." (December 1900)

WORKHOUSE.

REPORT of Visit made by the Commissioners in Lunacy, pursuant to
Act 53 Vict., ch. 5, s. 203.

(x)—78557 -1000-2-97

County.	Union or Parish Workhouse, and where situate.	Date of Visit.	Visiting Commissioner.	LOCAL GVT. BOARD	No. of Inmates of unsound mind.
				145344	F.
Hartford.	Royston at Royston.	9 November 1899.	Dr E. Marriott Cooke.	18 NOV 1899	11
					M 3
				TOTAL No.	14.

observa-⎫
tion Report⎬

When I visited this Workhouse to-day, there were
3 men and 11 women classed as of unsound mind. Proper authority
was produced to me for the detention of the two fresh cases.

I found them all comfortable, neat in dress and, excepting some feeble from old age, in good health. The rooms
which they occupy were very clean, and the beds and bedding
were in excellent order.

I regret I am unable to report any improvement
in the bathing arrangements by the provision of a better hot
water supply. The consequence is the imbeciles have as a rule
a bath only once a month, instead of weekly as they should,
and the uncleanly practice still prevails of bathing 2 and 3
at least in the same water.

I am informed that the Guardians investigated
the case of Alice Docwra referred to by Mr Bagot in his last
report and came to the conclusion there was not sufficient
evidence to prosecute John Woods.

I think there is need for greater precautions
being taken to prevent the young imbecile women in this Workhouse being taken advantage of by the male inmates. I noticed
to-day two were of the women working in the Kitchen were in
dangerous proximity to some men in the dining room and that they
had, at the time I speak of, no supervision whatever from a paid
official.

There has been no record of the use of mechanical
restraint.

The Union Workhouse c. 1900
(Royston Museum Collection - From a photograph by R. H. Clark)

The Cottage Hospital c. 1900 - Barkway Road. This was replaced in 1924 by the present hospital. It is
now a private residence.*(Royston Museum Collection)*

HEALTH

Early pioneers in medicine realised that insanitary conditions had a direct effect on health in the community and a great deal of pauperism was as much to do with sickness as idleness and improvidence. Could the drain on funds available for poor relief be diminished by reducing certain illnesses? It began to be realised that " the noxious exhalations" given off by rotting animal or vegetable matter in ditches, stagnant drains, cesspools, middens, and in houses themselves, caused illness. The subsequent recommendations were that the accumulations of refuse should be removed compulsorily. Night soil should be flushed into the drains and hence top sewers and cesspools should be abolished. The reformers, at first, came into conflict with vested interests such as private water companies, but some large authorities began to appoint medical officers of health and collect statistics. They learned of the infection carried by drinking water and eventually, the culmination of all the efforts of the early pioneers was the publication of the *Public Health Act (1875),* which remained the charter of English Public Health for sixty years.

One of the great achievements in the field of Public Health was the vaccination against smallpox. Although from 1854 every infant was supposed to be compulsorily vaccinated, it was not until 1871 that the legislation began to be effectively implemented, following a severe outbreak of the disease. It was possible after 1898 for parents who objected to vaccination on grounds of conscience to apply to a local magistrate for exemption, but by then the vaccination campaign had done its work and smallpox as a major killer had been eliminated.

During the rest of the nineteenth century, great advances in environmental conditions and in the combating of infectious diseases were made. A bureaucracy developed and in 1900 it was well established, with sanitary inspectors and medical officers. The end of the nineteenth century also saw the completion of large storage reservoirs and efficient slow and rapid methods of purification by filtration and other processes.

It was recognised towards the end of the nineteenth century that ill-health in adult life was often determined by poor childhood circumstances and some examinations of children had begun to take place. Also, when official statistics for infant mortality were published, the highest figure was reported in 1899 (about 155 deaths under one year per 1000 live births), and it was realised that there had been no improvement on the previous 60 years. In addition to these facts, the poor state of health of some recruits to the Boer War had caused great concern.

In consequence of this 1900 marked a move towards the health of the individual. Such things as the School Medical Service and action in the area of childbirth were to be gradually introduced early in the twentieth century.

The Cottage Hospitals

Cranley village, near present day Crawley, was the birthplace of the Cottage Hospital. In 1859, a Mr. Albert Napper opened the hospital because of the lack of local beds for his patients. The nearest voluntary hospital in Southwark, was 35 miles away on largely unmade roads. This was the situation in most of rural Britain.

For those patients who could not be taken to hospital or be nursed at home, the only alternative was to suffer the indignity of accepting shelter in the nearest workhouse infirmary where they faced not only wards with totally untrained staff but what was considered to be the ultimate degradation in the eyes of their neighbours, becoming a pauper. By being labelled a pauper they were on a par with criminals, although in their case the only 'crime' was being trapped by poverty and sickness together.

Treatment at home would appear, on the face of it, to be a good thing but it had its drawbacks. Most cottages were small, consisting of a kitchen, back shed and perhaps two bedrooms. The windows were small and frequently not made to open and there was very little in the way of bedding and general comforts. For a sick person or a badly injured labourer, there was very little comfort as the family was ever present and of course if he were absent from work too long he stood a good chance of losing his position; not an ideal environment for a quick recovery.

In complete contrast the rich man, when sick, had the benefit of a warm house, plenty of good food, drink, a good supply of opiates, and servants to attend to his every need.

It was to combat the situation described in the former paragraph that the Cottage Hospital movement was established. It was designed to provide residential care for village people who had no other hospital available. As the name suggests, the hospitals were set up in converted cottages and catered for about six to ten patients at any one time. Medical treatment was provided by a resident nurse and by regular visits from a general practitioner.

The number of serious accidents was increasing with the work involved with more sophisticated agricultural machinery, so it was absolutely necessary for the doctor to be a capable surgeon; an added bonus was that working in these hospitals enabled doctors to keep their surgical skills up to date.

Patients were usually expected to pay something towards the cost of the scheme, even if that were as little as 2s. 6d. a week. The remainder of the funds came from charity.

In 1869 **Royston Cottage Hospital** was built in the Barkway Road at a cost of about £1,000, raised by subscription. In 1900 it had two storeys, containing four wards with eight beds. It was supported by donations and annual subscriptions from the public, together with small weekly payments from those patients who could afford it. There were no paid officers except a matron and a nurse. H. R. Archer M.D. was the surgeon, H. S. Tuke the Secretary and Mrs Phoebe Baker the Nurse-in-charge. She retired in 1900 after 30 years service and was provided with a pension from money raised from a public appeal. Her replacement was a Mrs Ellen Collins, whose daughter was also employed as a qualified assistant nurse.

Each month the Royston Crow gave details on the previous month's patients; typical examples below:-

January 5th	
Patients - in Hospital on 1st December	4
admitted during December	2
discharged in December	5
in Hospital, 1st January	1

March 2nd	
Patients - in Hospital on 1st February	1
admitted during February	3
discharged during February	1
in Hospital, 1st March	2

There also flourished in the town the **Royston Nursing Association,** which in November 1900 was able to publish its fifth annual report explaining the details and costs of work carried out during the year and at the same time reminding the townspeople that more money was required. This was a voluntary organisation formed to provide nursing in the home. It was run by public subscription, and contributions were raised by the various organisations and churches. Actual gifts of equipment and food were also donated as necessary. Miss Trowsdale was the nurse during 1900 but she intended to resign her post in January 1901.

Each week there appeared in the Crow a return from the Herts. Convalescent Home, St. Leonards, as follows: Week ending January 3rd - Patients in the Home, 14 ; Discharged, 11; Admitted, 3. It is to be assumed that the residents could avail themselves of this facility.

During 1900 there was discussion about the eventual construction of an Isolation Hospital. Estimates were received from Architects MacAlister & Tench. A hospital was eventually constructed much later in Garden Walk.

Architects' Estimate

1	Administration Block	£974 0 0
2	Small Wards Block	£698 0 0
3	Small Wards Block	£1099 0 0
4	Laundry & Mortuary Block	£390 0 0
5	Entrance Lodge	£339 0 0
6	Gas House	£45 0 0
7	Acetylene Installation	£125 0 0
8	Water Supply (including piping in Garden Walk)	£165 0 0
9	Drainage	£230 0 0
10	Gravelling Paths and Fences	£287 0 0
	Total including Surveyor's Fees	£4382 0 0
	Architect's Estimate	£4500 0 0

Source - Public Record Office MH12 /4657

THE ESSENTIAL SERVICES

The network of utilities that we all take in our stride - gas, water and sewage disposal, electricity, and telecommunications - originated in the nineteenth century cities. Networks of national integrated systems were not always the case. In the nineteenth century, utilities first emerged as small specialised networks geared towards many uses, using a wide range of organisations and technologies and their coverage was haphazard. These sprang out of the forward-looking attitude of entrepreneurs. Industries organised their own electricity and water requirements; town gasworks were built by ambitious municipalities for lighting their streets; and the first phone and telegraph systems were used mainly by large organisations and emergency services. The utilities have long since merged to be operated with standard technology, administration and wealth, with the ability to keep pace in a rapidly changing scientific environment. What then was available to the people of Royston in 1900?

The Water Company
Royston's New Reservoir

1900 saw what was probably the largest and most expensive single building operation ever to have taken place in Royston until then, namely the construction of the reservoir that can be seen today to the south-west of the town.

This was undertaken by the Royston Water Company, which was founded in 1859, to supply piped water to Royston and the surrounding area. By 1896 the then existing system, based around the well and pumping station in Queen's Road, was inadequate to meet the demands of the growing town so the directors of the Company decided to build what became known as the 'New Works'. This was to be a well and pumping station on the west side of London Road, which can still be seen today in the valley below Royston Hospital, and also a new reservoir. There were no major problems with the construction of the pumping station but there were with the building of the reservoir to the extent that at one stage the company was being taken to court over the question of trespass.

Originally the Company wanted to purchase land between 'the Barkway and London Roads' for the reservoir and so proceeded to negotiate with Lord Hampden, the owner of the land. In the end they made an offer of £150 for an area of just over 6 acres and an agreement about the purchase of the land appears to have been reached by early 1899. The first signs of the trouble ahead appear in the minutes of the directors' meeting held on 4th March 1899 when, after deciding to accept the tender of Jacklin and Co. for £995 to build the reservoir, they were informed that there was a question regarding the Company's right of access to the land they had just bought from Lord Hampden. The directors believed that they did have a right of access to their land via the track off the London Road that leads to Flint Hall Farm, but they decided to investigate an offer by a Richard Goodman of Ampthill who was willing to sell them " a portion of his land adjoining the North Side of the old road to Therfield".

The dispute about the Company's right of access appears to have been unresolved because on the 27th September 1899 Jacklin and Co. were "instructed to remove the fastening to Gate (if necessary) across the Right of Way with as little damage as possible and proceed to put up the fence to the Company's land". This appears to have happened because on the 10th November 1899 they were informed that the owner of the track, a Mr. Titchmarsh, was applying to the High Court to restrain them "from entering upon or making case of a private road leading to Flint Hall Farm and for damage and costs". Though the directors maintained they had a right of access to their land, and were prepared to fight the action against them, they decided to ask Jacklin and Co. to quote for the cost of building the reservoir on the site offered by Richard Goodman.

The legal dispute appears to have dragged on for a couple of months until eventually, at a meeting held on the 20th December 1899, the directors agreed to abandon the original site, buy the land on offer from Richard Goodman and instruct Jacklin and Co. to begin building the new reservoir. Construction then appears to have proceeded throughout 1900 without any major problems, if the lack of evidence in minutes of the directors' meetings is anything to go by. However, there were two problems that had to be resolved. Firstly, that of disposing of the land that they had purchased from

Lord Hampden. The Company finally sold this back to Lord Hampden after a meeting with him in London. The second problem was that the cost of the whole building project appears to have been a lot more than was originally expected. The company's legal costs over the disputed right of way had come to £129 2s. 5d. and by November 1900 the total cost of building the new reservoir and pumping station had reached £5,887 8s. 7d. When this is compared with Jacklin's original tender, which for both the reservoir and the pumping station, was for £2,325 it is clear that the company needed to raise more money. They did this by issuing £1,850 of 4% debentures which were eagerly bought, the majority by the people of Royston. By way of comparison the secretary to the Water Company at this time was paid £50 a year.

Construction of the reservoir appears to have been largely completed by September 1901 when the directors discussed the fencing and gates that were to be put up and Jacklin was instructed "to put up a Lightning Conductor near the Reservoir". The last discussion of the cost of the project occurred on 24th November 1901 when the directors were told that the total was £7,073 4s. 6d. The last specific discussion on the whole project by the directors was on the 29th January 1902 when they concluded the "New Works are now practically complete and the supply of water sufficient for the present consumption."

D Plowman - Source Hertfordshire Record Office PUW 6 1/2.

Working on the New Works on the London Road *(Royston Museum Collection)*

25

The Gas Company

In 1900 Royston had its own gasworks, which was situated on a large site where Mill Road and Stamford Avenue now converge. This was first opened in 1836 and continued for very many years. An inspection report in the Hertfordshire Record Office gives us this description: " The retort house is yellow brick, probably 40ft by 25ft with a slate roof with ridge ventilation. There is a new manager's house adjoining; flint with brick quoins, 2 floors and slate roof built about 1890. The original manager's house was stucco on brick, 2 floors, with a slate roof and built about 1872. There is a column guided 2 lift gas holder".

To return to 1836, a few days before Christmas the talking point was a white leaflet, which contained the following information:

> ### Royston Gas, Coal, and Coke Company
> *The company propose to supply gas by meter only at the rate of 12s. 6d. per thousand feet, the amount to be collected quarterly. The Service Pipes will, in all cases where lights are ordered before the completion of the Works be laid to the front walls of the house at the expense of the Consumer. All meters will be furnished by the Company and may be purchased or hired, at the following prices:*
>
> *Three light meter, price £2 4s. 6d.; Rent per quarter, 25s.;*
> *Five light meter, £2 12s. 6d.; 25s. 6d.;*
> *Ten light meter, £3 8s. 6d.; 35s. 6d.;*
> *Twenty light meter, £4 11s. 6d.; 45s. 6d.*
>
> *The company having made these arrangments and calculations on plan of securing to the consumer an efficient supply of gas, with fittings and apparatus of the most economical rate possible, will feel themselves bound to withhold the supply of gas in case of non-compliance with the above regulations.*
> *Persons wishing to take gas will be furnished with the necessary information on application to the Secretary - By order of the Board of Directors; H. W. Nash, (Secretary), Royston. December 14th 1836.*

Although the above information is well before 1900, it is interesting to see how the initial steps into what became an essential part of life were taken and how Royston, a small rural town, could provide its own pioneers. Those who saw through these initial steps were men of vision, acting for the public good without thought of personal gain. The company made gradual progress and eventually became incorporated in 1860 with a capital of £3,500 and in that year, ten million cubic feet of gas were made. This had increased to 15 million by 1910 when coal cost 19s. a ton, and coke sold locally for 16s. 6d. a ton. The earnings of the Company allowed a 10 percent dividend to be paid and income tax was deducted at the rate of 1s. in the pound. It was only at this stage that the directors received renumeration for the first time, a fee of 10s. 6d. for each occasion when the Board met.

The Fire Service

The Fire Station was located in Fish Hill adjacent to St John's Congregational Church. It had been previously situated since 1785 on Market Hill in the old Parish Room and had moved to Fish Hill in 1897, paid for from the Diamond Jubilee Fund. The cost was under £200. It was run on a voluntary basis, the Superintendent being in 1900 E. Matthews and the Foreman J. Course. The firemen were alerted by maroons; one bang meant a fire in town two meant one out of town. Their appliances were of course horse-drawn.

A basic plan had been set up of the town's fire hydrants and the main areas covered were Baldock Street, Market Hill and Fish Hill. Three fires were recorded for 1900 - on the London Road, at the home of E. Titchmarsh and at Wicker Hall. The newspaper reports appear in the second section.

Payment to Firemen

After the setting up of District Councils the costs of the Fire Brigade came under the wing of Royston Urban District Council and in the December meeting of the RUDC, the question of payment for the firemen and the duties they performed were considered as follows:

Your Committee have under consideration the question of charges to be made by the Council for services of the Fire Brigade rendered outside the Urban District and have drawn up a Schedule of Charges which your Committee recommend should be adopted by the Council and if adopted be printed and published.

PAYMENT FOR FIREMEN (December 1900)

The Firemen for the first hour, each	4s.
To Firemen for every subsequent hour, each	1s.
To Firemen when called to a fire but not required, each	4s.
To Pumpers and other men employed by the Brigade, for the first hour each	4s.
To Pumpers for each subsequent hour, each	4s.
To Call Boys, each	2s.

Your Committee have also considered the question of payments to be made to the Firemen and others for their loss of time and trouble in attending at fires whether within or without the limits of the Urban District, and beg to recommend that the following payments be made, viz.:

Use of Manual Fire Engine (including cleaning the same, cleaning and oiling hose, etc., and oil), for 24 hours work (not exceeding)	£2 2s. 0d.
Services of the Brigade for the first hour	£2 0s. 0d.
Services of the Brigade for every subsequent hour	10s. 0d
Services of the Brigade when called to a fire and not required	£2 2s. 0d.
Services of Brigade members left on duty, per hour each	1s. 0d
Pumpers and other men employed by the Brigade, for the first hour, each	1s. 0d
Every subsequent hour, each	6d.
Call Boys, not exceeding, each	2s 0d.
Refreshments, Damages to appliances or to any person's property used by the Brigade Horse Hire, &c.	As per Vouchers

The above payments to be exclusive of allowances for cleaning, &c., of the apparatus.

The Brigade were called out to attend a fire at Wicker Hall, Royston, a few months ago, and your Committee recommend that the men be paid for their services on that occasion in accordance with the above scale.

Charges for services rendered by the Brigade beyond the limits of the Urban District to be paid to the Council by the person or persons on whose behalf the Brigade may be sent for.

Dr. Archer moved the adoption of the report, and said the recommendations were similar to the scale which had been in successful operation at Baldock for many years. The Council having taken over the Fire Brigade, the Insurance Offices objected to pay for a fire to a public body, and the Council could not pay without doing this. As part of the arrangement the Fire Brigade Officials would present an annual report as to the work and efficiency of the Fire Brigade.

Tax and the Fire Station.

During 1899 there was correspondence from the Inland Revenue that suggests that Royston Urban District Council had queried the Taxes due from them relating to the Fire Station. The following letter is the response from the Inland Revenue and in January they duly received the demand for the tax year 1899-1900 to be paid by March 6th of 6s. 8d. (Schedule A at 8d. in the £, the amount on which duty was payable being £10.)

The Reply from the Inland Revenue *(Royston Museum Collection)*

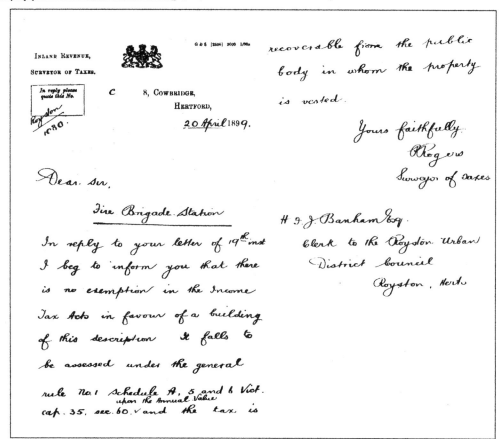

INLAND REVENUE,
SURVEYOR OF TAXES.

In reply please quote this No.

Royston 1080.

C   8, COWBRIDGE,
HERTFORD,
20 April 1899.

Dear Sir,

__Fire Brigade Station__

In reply to your letter of 19th inst I beg to inform you that there is no exemption in the Income Tax Acts in favour of a building of this description It falls to be assessed under the general rule No 1 Schedule A, 5 and 6 Vict. cap. 35. sec. 60. and the tax is

recoverable from the public body in whom the property is vested.

Yours faithfully,
R Rogers
Surveyor of Taxes

H J J Banham Esq.
Clerk to the Royston Urban District Council
Royston, Herts

Royston Fire Brigade c. 1900 *Photograph R. H. Clark (Royston Museum Collection)*

Front Row - 3rd left - J. Course; 4th left - W. G. Bedwell. Back Row (man with whip) - E. Logsdon.

The Police and the Courts

In 1900 the Police Station and Magistrates' Court was situated in Priory Lane on the east side of the Market Place. The building was opened in 1883 and consisted of magistrates' room, lock-up accommodation and police residences. The police station was built on the site of an old pig market at a price of £3,340. It replaced an old lock-up in a High Street house which was rented by the police. The house on the corner of the complex was used as an Inspector's House. A report in the *Crow* at the time of the opening of the Police Court, indicated that it was well received: "The substantial character of the building in all its parts and the excellence of the appointments creates a very favourable impression. The furniture, tables, chairs etc. in the Court are exceptionally well-made and to these a suitable complement has been added in a pair of handsome inkstands. The Court is a commodious and well-lighted building and apparently well suited to the purposes for which it is intended". Before 1883 the magistrates in Royston had sat in the Bull Hotel. The new courthouse was opened by the Chairman of the Bench, Mr. H. Fordham, and on its first day there were three cases for the first sitting, typically parents prosecuted for children's non-attendance at school - fine 6d. with 2s. 6d. costs. The doors to the three cells within the complex were actually older than the buildings themselves, having been taken from the Old Hertford Gaol which was demolished at the same time as the building of the new Station.

By 1900 the Hertfordshire Police Force was well established. In 1900, Inspector James Hart was the senior officer and there was a mounted policeman, Police Sergeant Reed, and Police Constables Knight, Gray (until November when replaced by Constable Robbins) and Compton. There were also constables stationed at the following places - Ashwell, Barkway, Sandon, Therfield and Hinxworth.

Police Constable George Knight was later to make a name for himself in the Hertfordshire Police Force. He was an ex-baker who joined the force in 1896 and was stationed in Royston. He was brought to the notice of the superintendent at Hitchin, a John Reynolds, when he came to court; he was noticed for his acuteness and encyclopaedic knowledge of police procedure. After his first promotion to clerk sergeant at Hitchin, he later rose to be Chief Constable in 1928.

The Special and Petty Sessions were held regularly in the Police Station on alternate Wednesdays in every month at 11a.m. and reported in the *Crow* and judging by the reports in the newspaper of wrong doing, the Police in 1900 had not much to fear as the main offences seemed to be in connection with drink, brawling and non-compliance with lighting regulations on the highway, prosecutions for children absent from school, some naughty behaviour on the part of the youngsters and some rowdiness at election time.

The County Magistrates for the Petty Sessional Division of Odsey

Hale Rev. J. Godwin M.A. Therfield (Chairman)	Fordham Herbert G. Odsey House, Ashwell
Balding Daniel Barley, The Beeches, Royston	Fordham Ernest Oswald, Odsey House, Ashwell
Crossman Alexander, Cokenach, Barkway	Phillips Joseph E. Melbourn Street, Royston
Fordham Edward Snow, Elbrook House, Ashwell	Phillips John, Earls Hill House, Royston
Fordham Frederick J., Yew Tree House, Royston	Clerk - Wortham Hale 1899: Banham H F.J. 1902

The members of the Royston Urban District Council were also ex-officio magistrates. The following places were included in the petty sessional division: Ashwell, Barkway, Barley, Bygrave, Caldecote, Clothall, Hinxworth, Kelshall, Reed, Royston, Sandon, Nuthampstead, Therfield, Wallington and Newnham.

On Fish Hill was to be found the County Court. This was held bi-monthly and the following parishes were under its jurisdiction:- Abington Piggots, Anstey, Ardeley, Ashwell, Aspenden, Barkway, Barley, Barrington, Bassingbourn, Buckland, Buntingford, Great and Little Chishill, Cottered, Croydon, Fowlmere, Foxton, Heydon, Hinxworth, Great and Little Hormead, Kelshall, Kneesworth, Layston, Litlington, Meesden, Melbourn, Guilden Morden, Steeple Morden, Nuthampstead, Reed, Royston, Rushden, Sandon, Shepreth, Shingay, Therfield, Thriplow, Throcking, Wakeley, Wallington, Wendy, Westmill, Whaddon and Wydial. For bankruptcy purposes this court was included in that of Cambridge.

Its purpose was "for the more easy recovery of Small Debts and Demands, and for the Trial of other Causes of Action when the Claim or Damage does not exceed £50. Compensation for Assaults and Batteries can also be obtained at this Court. Actions can also be brought for any larger amount of Debt and Damage, provided both parties consent thereto." Quote from *Warren's Companion. - Royston Museum*

Judge	His Honor W. H Gunning Bagshawe QC 1899: His Honor John Shortt 1902
Registrar and High Bailiff	H. D. Nash
Clerk	Frank Humphries
Bailiff	Sidney Betts 1899: R.S. Trudgett 1902

The Post Office

When the building, now an estate agent's premises and until recently known as the Royston Old Post Office, was erected in Melbourn Street in 1888 it was expected that the building would meet the requirements of the district for 100 years. It turned out, however, that it was soon found to be inadequate for the volume of business being transacted and had to be replaced in less than half that time by the imposing new building in Baldock Street (now in its redevelopment as a Public House to be called the Old Post Office!). The Postmaster, with his increased responsibilities, was paid £114 p.a. and there were 24 subpostmasters in the district sharing £223 p.a. There were 9 stampers, messengers and postmen on the establishment, who earned a total of £939 p.a. The postmaster earned a further £115 for assistance.

The Postmaster in 1900 was a J. W. Carter who was appointed in 1896 after a year of drama in 1895 when the previous Postmaster, Charles Lucas, absconded to Columbia with some £200 of the PMGs takings. J. W. Carter was to leave at the end of 1900 to take up a new post in Lincolnshire and was succeeded by Henry Beer.

Letters from London arrived at 8 a.m., 11 a.m. and 6 p.m. The office was open from 7 a.m. till 9 p.m. for the sale of stamps and for telegrams on weekdays from 8 a.m. till 8 p.m. On Sundays the office closed at 10 a.m. (*The following information from Kelly's Directory*)

Dispatch of Mails

Collection	Letters to:-	Last posting time
First	London and all places.	9. 30 a.m.
Second	London, Hitchin, Baldock, Bedford, Hatfield, Stevenage, Welwyn, St.Neots, Biggleswade, Sandy, Peterborough, most towns on the G.N. railway, Yorkshire &c. For evening deliveries.	11. 55 a.m.
Third	Cambridge, Norwich, King's Lynn, Ely, Wisbech, March, Bury St.Edmunds, Huntingdon, Thetford, Downham, Soham, Chatteris, St.Ives, for evening deliveries.	1. 25 p.m.
Fifth	London and delivery in country by first post the following morning.	4. 10 p.m.
Sixth	Cambridge (for evening delivery).	6 p.m.
Late day	London and all places, for first delivery in London and those places places having a midnight dispatch from G.P.O., Peterborough, York, the North generally,and Scotland.	7. 30 p.m.

Places having second deliveries

Time	Places
9. 50 a.m	Litlington, The Mordens, Kneesworth, Whaddon, Arrington, Orwell, Fowlmere, Thriplow, Melbourn, Meldreth, Shepreth, Therfield, Sandon, Croydon, Tadlow.
11. 55a.m.	Barley, Barkway, Great Chishill, Heydon, Chrishall.

Second post letters in some cases are only delivered in a direct route from one post office to another.
Sunday dispatches - London and Eastern counties, 7. 30p.m. London and all places, 10 p.m.
On Sundays there is only one delivery at Royston, which commences at 7 a.m.; at 8 a.m. and until 10 a.m. callers can obtain their letters.

Mail Cart Arrivals

From:-	Arrives at:-	Returns to:-	Departs at:-
Arrington	9. 15 p.m.	Arrington	5 a.m.
Cambridge	3. 05 a.m.	Cambridge	11 p.m.
Hitchin and Baldock	11 p.m.		
Buntingford	10. 15 p.m.	Buntingford	4 a.m.

Wall Letter Boxes

Position	Cleared Weekdays	Sundays
Near Railway Station	9. 10 & 11. 40 a.m., 1.10, 3.45, 6. 55, and 9. 10 p.m.	6. 55 p.m.
Melbourn Road	9. 20 & 11. 30a.m., 3. 40, 6. 45 p.m.	8. 40 p.m.
Barkway Street.	9. 15 & 11. 50 a.m. 1. 20, 3. 55, 6. 55 and 9.45 p.m.	12. 25 p.m.

Parcel Mails

Destination	Dispatched at	Parcels can be posted until
For all parts	12. 05 p.m.	11. 55 a.m.
Cambridge and Eastern Counties	1. 30 p.m.	1. 25 p.m.
All parts	1. 50 p.m.	1. 45 p.m.
All parts except Eastern Counties	7. 50 p.m. 10. 00 p.m.	7. 30 p.m.
All parts	10. 30 p.m.	9. 00 p.m.

The Post Office
Melbourn Street (1888 - 1936)

The post box below was the one available in 1900 in Barkway Street and details of collections are shown in the chart opposite.

The handcart below was used for many years by the Post Office. The wicker basket was made by an early society for the blind.

Manufacturing wicker baskets for the Post Office was one of the earliest contracts carried out by organisations for the blind.

These items are housed in Royston Museum.

Stamps printed courtesy of Stanley Gibbons.

31

Telephone

Where would we be to-day without the telephone? How would we communicate with family, friends, business associates etc. Yet 100 years ago the telephone was barely in existence. In Royston, as in most British towns, the telephone hadn't appeared as yet; no local business advertisement in the *Royston Crow* quotes a telephone number.

The first telephone exchange in Britain was opened in London in 1879. In 1890 and 1891 London was linked with Birmingham and Paris respectively.

During the 1890s major developments in the beginnings of the telephone industry took place in America. A quarter of a million telephones were in use and the main areas of growth were beginning to be not urban but rural, with the telephone becoming a major instrument of social transformation.

The number of people in Britain prepared to use the telephone increased only slowly from 45,000 in 1890 to 210,000 in 1900, but the Bank of England still had no telephone till after 1900. In fact at the end of Victoria's reign it was almost as cheap for a domestic servant to take messages etc. as it was to pay for a telephone.

There was not much optimism that the telephone would become a popular means of communication One newspaper claimed in 1900 that an overwhelming majority of the population was most unlikely ever to use the telephone at all.

In 1898 the following advice was given by a member of the Association for the Protection of Telephone Subscribers: "the telephone should be primarily answered by a servant and there should be further internal connection with other rooms". It was obvious that the prevailing social system was much stronger than the infant telephone system.

However unlikely it seemed to some people at the time, the telephone was destined to make an impact and eventually in June 1900, the Secretary of the G.P.O. asked for consent for the National Telephone Company to erect works in respect of Royston District but it was only in December 1903 that the town eventually got its first telephone exchange.

The first G. P. O. Telephone Directory, Royston (1903)
(Not 1900 but interesting nevertheless - Source BT Archives)

	ROYSTON, HERTS	
	Postmaster - H. BEER.	
	Superintending Engineer - J. JENKIN, 100 Hills Road, Cambridge	
1	CALL OFFICE	Post Office
2	Abbott, W. J., Upholsterer	High Street.
3	Banham, H.F. J., Solicitor	Kneesworth Street.
4	Barclay & Co., Ltd., Bankers	High Street.
5	Bevan, D. A.	The Priory.
6	Gimson & Co., Builders	Baldock Street.
7	Goodman, T., Grocer	High Street.
8	Grundy, A.F.	The Sycamores.
9	Holland, Hon., S., Dock Director	Kneesworth.
10	Jacklin & Co., Builder and Contractor	North Works
11	Layton G. M. R.	Icknield Bury
12	Nash, Son and Rowley, Auctioneers, &c.	Baldock Street.
13	Nash W. T., Merchant	Station Yard
14	Phillips, G. F.	High Street.
15	Pigg, J., Nurseryman, &c.	Old North Road.
16	Sanders, R E., Coach Builder.	Kneesworth Road
17	Stamford, J., Jobmaster	Station Road.
18	Whitaker, C. G., & Co., Drapers, &c.	The Cross
19	Wilkerson, S., and Son, Limited, Corn Merchants.	Kneesworth Road.
20	Windsor, Dr. C. W.	Surgery.
21	Wortham, Nash, and King, Solicitors.	High Street.

EDUCATION

Until the Industrial Revolution the state played no role in education. It was believed that any form of education for the lower classes would give them ideas above their station. However by the 1830s education was seen as a means of taming the rough and rowdy working class people who had gathered in the slums of the new industrial towns. It was thought it would ensure that they fully realised their place in society and thus avert any potential for revolution.

The Church was seen as an ideal vehicle for these ideas and in 1833 the government gave, for the first time, a grant of £20,000 on a pound-for-pound basis to religious bodies who would build schools. This rose in 1840 to £30,000.

Every decision about education worked on the basis of class division to ensure that everyone kept to their place in the scheme of things. Schools, at this time, were listed according to their social status. At the top came the great public schools such as Eton, which in turn were copied by a series of new public schools which arose so that the middle classes could copy their 'betters'.

Until 1870 the education of the lower orders had been the only concern of the state and this was in a confused state due to the divide between Anglicans and Dissenters. Slowly, because of reports from inspectors, the position changed and in the 1850s teacher training colleges emerged and the funding of elementary education rose rapidly, as did the standard of literacy.

In 1870, *Forster's Education Act* stated that the state had a duty to provide schools in enough locations so that no child should be denied an education. In 1880 school attendance was made compulsory; in 1891 elementary education became free, and by 1900 education had become the largest item on the national budget. The law as regards attendance had also been made more stringent. In 1899 no child could go to work under the age of twelve, and between twelve and thirteen only after passing, and not merely getting into, the fifth standard, and even between thirteen and fourteen children could not go to work unless Standard IV had been passed or 250 attendances had been made for the previous five years.

In 1900 we find the main schools in Royston to be the British School (Mixed) in Fish Hill, (enlarged in 1888 for 170 children and where the average attendance was 139) and the National School (Boys and Girls), Market Hill, (built in 1835 and enlarged in 1886 for 300 children - average attendance 125 boys and 114 girls). There was also a Parochial Infants' School (built about 1827 and enlarged in 1888 for 145 children, where the average attendance was 136), and two private establishments - Bridge House School (Kneesworth Street) and Victoria House School (Old North Road).

Future developments in the provision of schools was not to be until the construction of a new school in Queen's Road, opened in 1910.

The British School and National Schools (Some notes on their origins)
British Schools

Joseph Lancaster, a Quaker, founded the Lancasterian Society in 1808 to allow him to put his own educational ideas into practice. (The society changed its name in 1810 to the British and Foreign Schools' Society.) Lancaster used a system of teaching which allowed one teacher to control up to a hundred children. Schools were established in many towns and mostly attracted pupils from nonconformist families. The teacher had a number of 'monitors' who each had to look after the work of a group of other pupils - a division. These monitors were the older scholars but they could be as young as twelve years. The advantage of this system was its low cost. After the school day was over the monitors received lessons from the teacher to prepare for the next day. Most of the schoolwork was presented in small sections; such as a set of spellings or a multiplication table which the children had to learn by heart. However, in spite of meeting an urgent need for basic education, its main drawback was the sterile rote learning and the inevitable noise in the schoolroom.

National Schools

The "National Society for the Education of the Poor in the Principles of the Established Church" was founded in 1811. It helped the development of Church of England schools by giving grants to assist building projects and to pay for teaching staff. The schools it supported became known as 'National Schools'. In most of the National Schools the monitorial system, similar to the one used in the British Schools, was used at their inception.

In the Church.of England Schools, the vicar usually visited each week, rehearsed children in the Catechism and conducted prayers. Once a year the children were examined in Religious Knowledge by the Diocesan Inspector. On some Saints' Days children went to church in the morning and perhaps enjoyed a holiday afterwards.

As can be seen from the entries in the logbook of the British School which appear later in the monthly reports, the monitorial system of the early British and National Schools no longer existed and we find certificated and probationer teachers allocated to different standards. Monitors were still in the schools but it was usually a prelude to becoming a pupil teacher.

The Heads of the schools were required to keep logbooks which were to be a 'bare record' of events in the school, and 'no expressions of opinion' were to be entered. Into these logs were entered the results of the annual inspections, financial information, staff details, information on attendance and reasons for poor attendance, unusual occurrences and comments on monthly tests etc. These are to be found in the County and Public Record Offices. The logbooks survive in Hertfordshire Record Office for Royston British School and the National School (Girls' Section) for 1900. Unfortunately, the logbook for the National School (Boys' Section) before 1905 has disintegrated.

Every school had to provide essential 'offices' for its pupils. In the nineteenth century earth closets were used and the change to water closets came about gradually with the development of mains water supplies.

Before 1890, a system called 'payment by results' was in place. A school inspector called once a year to examine the children. The examination tested reading, writing and arithmetic. If the results were poor the amount of grant was reduced and so was the salary of the teacher. As it was seen to have failed in its objective to raise standards, this system was replaced in 1890 by grants for attendance, discipline and organisation and group achievement. Details of these grants were kept in the logs and evidence is seen in the logs of a striving for a higher grant.

As part of the annual grant was given for regular attendance by the pupils, there are frequent references to attendance, and to encourage good attendance, medals and certificates of merit were awarded each year at the prize-giving and a great deal of praise was heaped upon the recipients and their parents.

The syllabus offered in the schools was no longer the sterile rote learning of Reading, Writing and Arithmetic. Cookery, Needlework and Drawing were also on the curriculum. The 'object lesson' was an important addition. These lessons made it possible for more informality and gave pupils an opportunity to experience and hear about things beyond their own experiences and environment; such randomly chosen topics as Elephant, Lion, Tiger, and Chocolate might be covered.

Information from the Department of Education regarding the levels of the different standards

	Standard 1	Standard 2	Standard 3	Standard 4	Standard 5	Standard 6
Reading *	To read a short paragraph from a book, not confined to words of one syllable.	To read with intelligence a short paragraph from an elementary reading book.	To read with intelligence a short paragraph from a more advanced reading book.	To read with intelligence a few lines of prose or poetry selected by the inspector.	Improved Reading.	Reading with fluency and expression.
Writing	Copy in manuscript character a line of print, on slates or in copy books, at choice of managers; and write from dictation a few common words.	A sentence from the same book, slowly read once, and then dictated. Copy books (large or half text) to be shown.	A sentence slowly dictated from the same book. Copy books to be shown (small hand, capital letters and figures,)	Eight lines slowly dictated once from a reading book. Copy books to be shown (improved small hand).	Writing from memory the substance of a short story read out twice; spelling grammar and handwriting to be considered.	A short theme or letter; the composition, spelling, grammar, and handwriting to be considered.
Arithmetic **	Notation and numeration up to 1,000. Simple addition and subtraction of numbers of not more than four figures, and the multiplication table to 6 times 12.	Notation and numeration up to 100,000. The four simple rules to short division (inclusive).	Notation and numeration up to 1,000,000. Long division and compound addition and subtraction (money).	Compound rules (money) and reduction (common weights and measures).+	Practice, bills of parcels, and simple proportion.	Proportion, vulgar and decimal fractions.

Notes   * 'Reading will be tested in the ordinary class books, if approved by the Inspector; but these books must be of reasonable length and difficulty and unmarked....'

    ** 'The work of girls must be judged more leniently than that of boys...'

    + ' The 'weights and measures' taught in public elementary schools should be only such as are really useful:- such as Avoirdupois Weight, Long Measure, Liquid Measure, Times Table, Square and Cubical Measure, and any measure which is connected with the industrial occupation of the district.'

The Victorian Schoolroom - Trevor May

This Revised Code was dated 1879 and by 1900 the individual examination of children, 'payment by results', had already ceased, but it is interesting to see the expectation at different ages. Standards roughly corresponded with age. Standard 1 - age 6 to 7, Standard 6 - age 11 to 12. In 1882, a Standard 7 was introduced into the code to cater for children who wished to stay on at School beyond the minimum leaving age. This included the study of Shakespeare, Milton and other eminent writers, instruction on how to write a theme or letter and in arithmetic, the working of averages, percentages, discount and stock.

In April 1900, the schools received a circular entitled *"The Curriculum of the Rural School."* Some excerpts follow.

The staff were told of "the importance of making the education more consonant with the environment of the scholars....................
teachers should lose no opportunity of giving their scholars an intelligent knowledge of the ordinary rural life and showing them how
to observe the processes of nature for themselves....................and to develop in every boy and girl that habit of inquiry and research so
natural to children....................in this way they will gain much more real knowledge of common implements, fruits, leaves and insects
than if they had been described by the teacher and read about in a lesson book...............The Board also attaches considerable
importance to work being done by elder pupils outside the school walls .... elementary mensuration, making sketch plans of
the playground and surrounding area................. or cultivation of a school garden.................... the teacher should take the children on
school walks and give simple lessons on the spot about animals etc................The lessons thus learned can be carried forward into the
classroom by Reading, Composition, Pictures and Drawing.............It is to be confidently expected that the child's intelligence will be
so quickened by the kind of training suggested that he will be able to master with far greater ease than before, the ordinary subjects of
the school curriculum ."

Original in Hertfordshire Record Office H/Ed.1/47/5.

A circular from the Department of Art and Science laid out the rules for Drawing in Elementary Day Schools.

Standard   I   Drawing, freehand and with the ruler, of lines, angles, parallels, and   the simplest right-lined
                         forms. (To be drawn on slates or on paper, at the option of the Manager,)
Standard   II   Similar work to that of Standard I, to be drawn on paper only.
Standard   III   *(a)* Freehand drawing of regular forms and of curved and right lined figures from the flat.
                         (b) Simple geometrical and right lined figures to be drawn with a ruler.
Standard   IV   *(a)* Freehand drawing from the flat.
                         (b) Simple scales and drawing to scale.
Standard   V   *(a)* Freehand drawing from the flat.
                         (b) Drawing from rectangular and circular models, and from easy common objects.
                         (c) Geometrical figures with instruments and to scale.
Standard   VI   *(a)* Freehand drawing from the flat.
                         (b) Drawing from models of regular form and from very easy common object.
                         (c) Geometrical drawing more advanced than in Standard V;* or
                         (d) Plans and elevations of plane figures and rectangular solids in simple positions with sections.*
Standard   VII   *(a)* Freehand drawing from the flat.
                         (b) Drawing from models of regular form and from easy common objects, more advanced than
                           Standard VI.; or
                         (c) Drawing any common objects and casts of ornament in light and shade.
                         (d) Geometrical drawing more advanced than in Standard VI*; or
                         (e) Plans and elevations of plane figures and rectangular solids in simple positions, with sections.*
*Girls are not required to take the subjects specified.

Original in Hertfordshire Record Office H/ Ed 1/47/5

VICTORIA HOUSE
SCHOOL
ROYSTON,

Principal - **Mr. STEVENSON, M.C.P.**
And under same management over 30 years.

Boys are prepared for the *Business* or *Professions* and when desired for *Civil Service, College of Preceptors* and other Examinations.   *Backward* boys receive careful and individual attention.

A few little boys from seven years of age, to work with two or three others, are desired, References to parents and others.

Next term commences Tuesday, January 23rd.

BRIDGE HOUSE SCHOOL
ROYSTON,

Principal - MISS F. ASHTON
Next Term commences on
MONDAY, JANUARY 22nd

RULES OF A BRITISH SCHOOL

1. TO ATTEND SCHOOL CONSTANTLY AT NINE IN THE MORNING AND TWO IN THE AFTERNOON.
2. TO ATTEND SCHOOL WITH HANDS AND FACE CLEAN, HAIR COMBED AND SHOES BRUSHED.
3. ON ALL OCCASIONS TO SPEAK THE TRUTH.
4. TO BEHAVE WITH PARTICULAR AND SOLEMN REVERENT QUIETNESS WHEN READING HOLY SCRIPTURES.
5. TO BEHAVE WITH SOLEMNITY IN ALL PLACES OF PUBLIC WORSHIP.
6. TO AVOID ALL BAD COMPANY.
7. NEVER USE BAD WORDS OR ILL NAMES.
8. TO AVOID ALL QUARRELLING AND CONTENTION.
9. NEVER TO MOCK LAME OR DEFORMED PERSONS AND TO BE KIND TO All MEN.
10. TO AVOID CRUELTY, AND NEVER TEAZE OR IN ANY WAY HARM BRUTE CREATURES.
11. TO BE SILENT IN SCHOOL.
12. TO ENTER AND LEAVE SCHOOL ORDERLY.
13. TO OBEY THE RULES AND ORDER OF THE SCHOOL.

Whenever a boy is about to leave School, it is expected he will inform the master

The British School c. 1900
(Royston Museum Collection)

The National School (Girls' Section) c. 1900
(Royston Museum Collection)

After Elementary School

Although most children left elementary school and proceeded into employment at the statutory leaving age, it was beginning to be realised at the end of the century that education ought to continue beyond elementary school and indeed it was possible to continue education full-time. Details of examinations for the award of scholarships appeared in the local press, both for Hertfordshire and Cambridgeshire which opened a new school in 1900 and the William Lee Charity set a scholarship examination annually.(See next page)

For those who did not wish to, or could not, continue in education full-time, there were in Royston several opportunities for advancement. The Evening Continuation School was organised in the schoolrooms under the superintendence of the local Headmasters. For the more sophisticated it was possible to attend different series of University Extension Lectures and for those of a practical inclination, there were Technical Classes in Drawing, Joinery, and Wood Carving, as well as a series of lectures on First Aid.

THE "WILLIAM LEE" CHARITY

Examination for Scholarships
June 1901

Directions

(1) On the first line of each paper given you, write your name in full.

(2) Do not write the question, but put the number of each question before your answer.

(3) Show all the working in Arithmetic.

(4) Three hours will be allowed for the examination.

COMPOSITION.

(Your answer should not take up more than a page of your examination paper.)

Write an account of the happiest day you have ever spent,

or

Write an essay on "The Sky".

SPELLING

Write in two columns the twenty words dictated to you.

(It is useless to make alterations, as alterations count as mistakes)

ARITHMETIC

(You may work any three of these sums)

(1) A draper had two pieces of cloth of the same quality, but of different lengths. One piece cost £27-0-1½ , and the other piece £19-11-1½ . The larger piece contained 29 yards. How many yards were there in the smaller piece?

(2) A is 27 years older than B, and 15 years younger than C who is 54 years of age; D is as old as A and B together. Is C older or younger than D, and by how much?

(3) A man having given 5/9 of his money for a sheep, and .375 of the remainder for a pig, had £1.6875 still left. What sum had he at first?

(4) A boy in flying his kite lost 3/5 of the string. He added 65 feet, and then found that it was just 5/6 as long as it was at first. What was its length at first?

GEOGRAPHY

(You may answer three questions only)

(1) (a) How is it there has been so much about Australia, in the newspapers lately?

    (b) Briefly describe one route from England to Australia , and say, as nearly as you can, how long the journey would take.

    (c) Which is the hottest part of Australia, and why?

(2) (a) Where is British Columbia?

    (b) How would you get from Liverpool to British Columbia, and about how long would the journey take?

    (c) Mention anything that is sent from British Columbia to England.

(3) (a) Which is the "Dark Continent", and why is it so called?

    (b) Which parts of that Continent are occupied by the English?

    (c) Name three long rivers and three important towns in that Continent.

(4) Say what and where the following are, and mention anything of interest you know about any of them - Delagoa Bay, Sierra Leone, Colenso, Paardeberg, Pekin, Port Jackson, Singapore, Rhodesia.

GENERAL KNOWLEDGE.

(You may answer not more than three questions)

(1) What do you know about the following days - May 24th, June 21st, November 5th, December 25th?

(2) Give the names of three common trees, and say how you could tell them.

(3) What is meant by the Census, and what did the last Census show with regard to the population of England?

(4) What do you know about the following - Lord Milner, Shamrock 11, Hector Macdonald, The Ophir, Lord Hawke, De Wet, Lord Hopetoun?

Originals of examination paper, letter and certificate in Royston Museum Collection.

Nothing Changes

An excerpt from a letter received by the correspondents of schools from the Education Department (1898)

"The serious mischief that results from the practice of stone-throwing has again been brought forcibly under the notice of the Department by the recent death, under the most painful circumstancs, of an experienced engine driver, who died in consequence of injuries caused by a stone thrown from a railway bridge under which his train was passing. It was not proved that the stone was thrown by a child, but my Lords, after enquiry, have ascertained that there is no doubt that school children are the offenders in many similar cases, where life or property is endangered.

I am to request that the Managers of your school will be so good as to caution the children seriously against the practice of mischievous or reckless stone-throwing, and to point out to them the disastrous consequences which may ensue."

My Lords have endeavoured on previous occasions to check the practice of stone-throwing at telegraph wires and insulators............." The letter went on to remind schools of previous communications in 1875 and 1885.

Hertfordshire Record Office HE1/47/5

SCHEDULE III.

School District of _____ Royston Union _____

LABOUR CERTIFICATE.

AGE AND EMPLOYMENT.

I certify that _Harry Nottage_ ,

residing at _Reed_ ,

was, on the _22_ day of _Nov 1900_ 18 , not

less than ~~eleven~~ 12 years of age, as appears by the registrar's certificate [or the statutory declaration] now produced to me, (¹) and has been shown to the satisfaction of the local authority for this district to be beneficially and necessarily employed.

(Signed) _A Sharpe_

(²) Clerk to the (³) _School Attendance Committee_

for the above district.

'(¹) Strike out what follows if the child is qualified for full time employment.

(²) or other officer.
(³) School Board or School Attendance Committee.

W D & L (135cs)—384r.—50000-3-98

PROFICIENCY.

I certify that _Henry Nottage_

residing at _Reed_

has received a certificate from _F. W. H. Myers Esq_ one of Her Majesty's Inspectors of Schools, that he (or she) has

(⁴) reached the _3rd_ Standard

(Signed) _W Pryce_

Principal Teacher of the _Barkway School_

School.

or (²) Clerk to the (³)

for the above district.

Dated the _____ day of _____ 18__

To reach a standard a child must be individually examined in reading, writing, and arithmetic in that or a higher standard and must pass in each of these subjects.

Early Educational Documentation. A sign of things to come???

Bridge House School - 1898

Photographer R. H. Clark (Royston Museum Collection)

GETTING ABOUT

The Railway

The building of the railway in the early part of the nineteenth century had an enormous impact on the life of ordinary people. In 1825 the Stockton and Darlington Railway opened and by 1850, more than 6,000 miles of track had been laid and by 1870, 13,000 along with the necessary tunnels, bridges, viaducts and stations. In addition to its impact as an engineering undertaking the coming of the railways had great economic effects. The cost of coal for instance fell by three quarters. The railways meant that raw materials and finished goods manufactured in the factories of the Industrial Revolution could be transported quickly across country to different towns and to the ports for export.

The railways improved communications by post and telegraph. As telegraph poles were placed alongside the railway tracks, this helped to increase the speed of the dissemination of news. During the latter half of the nineteenth century a large part of society had more money to spend on things other than those necessary for mere existence, as had been the case in earlier centuries, and advertising became a part of everyday life with familiar brand names setting the trend. Where in earlier days a town might have a few small shops now it had drapers, milliners, hardware stores, chemists etc. selling goods from an ever- increasing variety of sources. Such was the situation in Royston in 1900.

Another way in which the railways improved life for the everyday population was the increased mobility made possible. Before the railway, a visit beyond a neighbouring village could be an undertaking. The railways meant that travel to other places could develop, and the turning point came with cheap excursions to London in 1851 to see the Great Exhibition. After this, cheap journeys to London, the seaside or some other place of interest led millions of people to move around in what previously had been the prerogative of the middle classes and stays at seaside resorts became common. By 1900 a pattern of leisure had become established as a distinction from work and Bank Holidays were in place. Royston was favoured by people using Royston and the Heath as their destination on excursions and holidays. People also rented houses in the town for the summer months. The clubs and societies in the town regularly used the railways for their annual outings, the Volunteers for their trips to camps, and local cricket and football teams to "play away" and accompanied by their supporters.

In 1900 Royston station, part of the Great Northern Railway, played a much more important part in the life of the town than it does today, when road transport has taken over many of its functions.

The station consisted of a grey brick building on two floors with two platforms, each with wooden canopies on iron pillars. There were two tracks with a brick-based water tower at the far end of the 'up' platform. The buildings on this platform included booking office and a general waiting room, ladies' waiting room and lavatories. On the 'down' platform was another waiting room and the station master's office. The stationmaster for 1900 was Mr. William Ainger employed at £100 per annum.

On each side of the track were industrial buildings, extensive goods yards, sidings and a brick built goods shed of four bays. The following firms had their own sidings, situated where the modern car parks are to be found, giving access to the main line:

Farmers' Manure Company. *Fordham and Howard, Coal Merchants.*
Nash and Company. *Phillips' Brewery.*
T. H. Smith and Son. *Wilkerson and Son.*

There was a crane capable of lifting five tons and the goods depot, which was essential to the prosperity of the town and surrounding villages, had a capacity to deal with Parcels, Furniture Vans, Carriages, Horse Boxes, Prize Cattle and other Livestock, for which holding pens were available. Flocks of sheep could be seen being driven through the town and supplies of barley were sent to the breweries in the Midlands. All this activity provided work for many people. Several clerks were at work over and above the porters and other manual workers.

As well as being essential to the economic health of the town, it is obvious that the railway company was mindful of customer requirements in their leisure time as details of special fares and arrangements for stopping at nearby stations were usually to be found in the advertisements for local activities and entertainments.

Below is a sample of the type of advertisement which appeared weekly in the Royston Crow during 1900 giving details of the times and places to visit.

Cheap Trips to London
Thursday January 11th and January 25th
Saturday, January 13th
Saturday, February 10th (**Football Match Cambridge University
  v. Blackheath**)
Saturday, February 17th (**Football Match Oxford v. Cambridge**)
Thursday, February 15th
Thursday, March 8th and 15th (**Horse Shows**)
Saturday, May 12th (**Kempton Park Races**)
Saturday, April 14th (**Alexandra Park Races**)
Saturday, May 26th (**Harpenden Races**)
Saturdays, June 16th and June 23rd
Wednesday, July 11th (**Temperance Fete**)
Saturday, July 14th (**Tonic Sol-fa Fete**)
Saturday, August 18th (**National Co-operative Festival**)
September 13th, 15th, 24th, 27th (**Holiday Trips**)
Thursday, October 11th (**Dairy Show**)
Thursday, October 25th
Friday, November 9th (**Lord Mayor's Show**)
Tuesday, November 13th
Thursday, November 29th (**Cycle Shows &c.**)
Wednesday, December 12th (**Football Oxford v Cambridge,
  Smithfield Club Cattle Show, &c.**)
Boxing Day, Wednesday, December 26th (**Pantomimes &c.**)

**GREAT NORTHERN
RAILWAY**
CHEAP HOLIDAY EXCURSIONS
WEDNESDAY, JULY 4TH, for 1 day,
to LOWESTOFT, from Royston at
7.20a.m., Meldreth 7.27, Shepreth 7.30,
Foxton 7.35, Harston 7.37.
TO LONDON, THURSDAY, JULY
5TH, (**Cricket, Oxford v Cambridge**)
from Harston at 7.49a.m., Foxton 7.52,
Shepreth 7.55, Meldreth 8.00, Royston
8.10, Ashwell 8.19, Baldock 8.29,
Hitchin 9.15.
ALSO Saturday, JULY 7TH,
(**ALEXANDRA PARK RACES**) from
Harston at 7.49, and 9.34a.m., Foxton
7.52 and 9.37, Shepreth 7.55 and 9.40,
Meldreth 8.00 and 9.45, Royston 8.10
and 9.55, Ashwell 8.19 and 10.05,
Baldock 8.28 and 10.14.
Tickets, Bills,&c., at Stations.
CHARLES STEEL, *General Manager,*
LONDON, KINGS CROSS *June, 1900.*

Fares to and from London.
1st Class - 6s. 11d. 2nd Class.- 5s. 3d.
3rd Class- 3s. 8½ d.
Returns - 13s. 10d.; 10. 6d.; 7s. 5d.

LONDON, HITCHIN, ROYSTON AND CAMBRIDGE.

B Stops at Foxton on Saturdays to leave passengers from Cambridge.   C Stops at Royston on Wednesdays.
D Stops when required to take up London passengers.

The Horse.

Although by 1900 the long journeys by stage coach had been superseded by the railway network, horse drawn transport was still the principal method of travelling any distance locally. Many exotic sounding names had entered the language at this time: gig, dog cart, brake, phaeton, brougham, hansom, landau, curricle, coupe, tilbury etc and towards the end of the century all these had become simpler and lighter; this development being helped by the invention of the steel spring.

This type of transport had its own infrastructure, albeit in decline after the demise of the stage coach, providing work for livery stables, coach builders, blacksmiths, harness makers, waggoners and carriers. A carrier's cart called regularly at the local pubs and villages for people who did not own their own outfits and in December 1900 J. Stamford set up his own horse bus to ferry people to and from the station for 6d (2½p). The local fire brigade used horses to propel their apparatus and there was a mounted policeman stationed at Royston Police Station.

It is common nowadays to criticise the motor vehicle's role in terms of atmospheric pollution of the environment. However, can the polluting effect of the two million horses in London at the turn of the century ever be imagined now? Crossing sweepers were even employed to ensure that ladies could get across the street without getting their gowns horribly fouled. This fact may be irrelevant as far as Royston is concerned, but in 1900, pollution must have been considerable both to the eye and the nose. Even today after the passing of a couple of horses the evidence of their journey is obvious.

The stage coaches had been instrumental in building up a network of roads in Britain and the progress in road building had reduced the length of time between the larger cities a very great deal. The stage coach companies had fought against the advent of the railways by constructing cuttings to reduce the time taken on journeys (such as those on the Newmarket and London Roads) but to no avail and many roads were nothing more than dusty tracks. There was no central administration for roads and responsibility was divided amongst many bodies. Only in 1902 did the Roads Improvement Association bring about an inquiry into the administration of roads. It was considered that bad roads were bad for efficiency and many towns had inadequate thoroughfares, but it was to be 1909 before a Roads Board was established to give money to councils for road improvements. One of the items on the agenda of Royston Council in December 1900 was the watering of the roads in the town. They were of the opinion that this consolidated them and reduced wear and tear.

The Bicycle

In 1900 one of the alternatives to walking in getting around the town would have been the bicycle and by 1900 the bicycle had achieved a form that we would recognise today.

The first bicycles, known as *velocipedes,* appeared in France in 1861. These had a pair of pedals attached to the front wheel. Further French progress was halted by the Franco-Prussian war and that marked the start of a fruitful trade in Britain. From the *velocipede or boneshaker* as we know it, evolved the extraordinary high wheeled vehicle the *penny-farthing.* Many improvements were gradually introduced but they did not solve the problem of many a bicycle trip ending in disaster. As the rider sat almost directly above the big front wheel, equilibrium was disturbed and a pothole could result in the cyclist being thrown off head-first. It was realised that the rider's weight needed to be further back.

Different designs were tried and the idea of chain driven wheels eventually emerged; soon the rear wheel driven cycle as we know it evolved. A model was finally introduced in 1885 and by 1887 the resultant design seems very familiar. The invention of the pneumatic tyre in 1887 was to be another refinement.

At first, there had been much opposition to the bicycle from other road users and many unjust and restrictive bye-laws appeared. However, in 1888, Parliament finally gave cycles the same legal status as horse-drawn carriages and cycling was able to flourish. Advertisements show the range available in 1900 and by then adaptations had even been introduced to accommodate ladies' fashions.

Each week the lighting up times for bicycles were published in the *Royston Crow.*

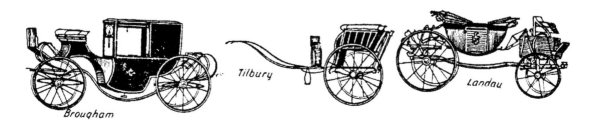

Brougham

Tilbury

Landau

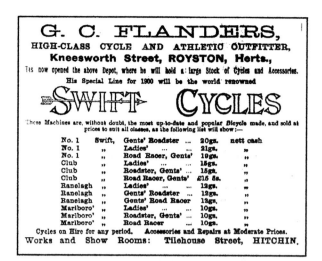

Carriers Operating in the District

DESTINATION	PICK UP POINT	CARRIER	DEPARTURE DAY
Abington, Whaddon	Hoops		Wednesday
Anstey	Sun	Smith	Wednesday
Arrington	Falcon	Pett	Thursday
Ashwell	Angel	Holloway	Friday
Aspenden, Buckland, Buntingford, Braughing, Puckeridge, Standon, Great Hadham.	Angel	Walpole	Saturday
Barkway	Chequers	Tofts, Bentley, Whyman.	Wednesday
Barkway, Reed	Chequers	Tofts	Wednesday
	Sun	Tofts	Daily
Barley	White Lion	Machon	Daily
Bassingbourn	Stamford's Yard	Wednesday, Saturday	Daily
	Hoops		
Bassingbourn & Kneesworth, Litlington, Morden	White Horse	Ingrey	Daily
Buntingford, Chipping, Buckland.	Chequers	Aylott	Wednesday.
Croydon	Falcon	Cooper	Wednesday
Elmdon	Chequers	Jeffrey	Wednesday
Heydon, Chrishall, Barley	Chequers	Waters	Wednesday
Kneesworth	Stamford's Yard	Howe	Daily
Langley, Rickland Green, Stansted, Clavering, Quendon, Newport	Red Lion	Flack	Wednesday, Friday
Litlington	Hoops	Smith	Wednesday
London	White Horse to the Catherine Wheel, Bishopsgate St.	Wedd	Thursday returning Saturday
Melbourn, Meldreth	Falcon	Guilver	Daily
Melbourn	White Horse	Wedd	
Morden, Great & Little, Litlington, Whaddon	Hoops		Wednesday
Morden, Great	Hoops	Oakley	Wednesday
Morden, Little	Angel	Saunders	Wednesday
Orwell	White Horse	Scott	Wednesday
Shepreth, Cambridge	White Horse	Chamberlain	Wednesday
Therfield, Reed	Sun	Nathan Pratt	Tuesday, Wednesday, Thursday, Saturday
Wendy	Hoops	Wenham	Wednesday

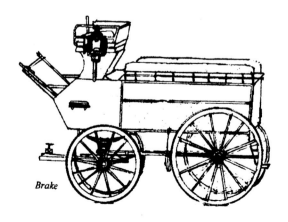

Brake

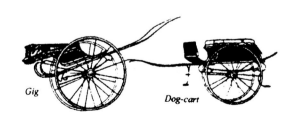

Gig   *Dog-cart*

Pleasures in Store - The Coming of the Motor Car

The motor car is so much part of our lives that it is not possible to think of a time when it was not with us. However, it was only 1986 that marked one hundred years of its existence. In 1900, therefore, there was none of the basic infrastructure required to sustain a motoring public - there were no petrol stations or garages, nor any of the accompanying businesses built upon the sale of tyres, spark plugs and exhaust pipes for cars.

In 1886 the world took its first tentative steps towards the age of the car as we know it. If we look back into the years of the nineteenth century, Britain was at the peak of her industrial strength, yet it was through Daimler and Benz in Germany that the motor car became established in 1886, after the development of the internal combustion engine. Even so it was to be a decade later before it progressed in Britain. There were two main reasons for this. One was the success of the railways and the second legislation.

Just before the advent of the railways in Britain, there had been a brief appearance of steam-powered road-going vehicles. However, these depended on huge clumsy and dangerous steam engines and consequently various Acts of Parliament held back the beginning of the motorisation of Britain by driving all such traffic off the roads. For example the *'Men with the Red Flag' Act* of 1865 stated that each vehicle had to be preceded sixty yards ahead by a man with a red flag. This enforced a walking pace and was intended to warn horse-riders and horse drawn traffic of the approach of a 'self-propelled machine.' The restrictive effect of such legislation had a great effect on engineers. Although working on the internal combustion engine at the same time as Daimler and Benz, their efforts amounted to nothing.

Early engineers worked to try to remove the obstacles in the way of the motorisation of Britain and eventually in 1895 a systematic campaign was organised to explain to the public the advantages of the car. The first copy of *Autocar*, a magazine still in existence today, was published, and an exhibition of available Daimler cars was organised to which influential people were invited. It was thanks to these campaigning efforts that Parliament finally enacted a new law in 1896, *The Light Road Locomotive Act* which opened the door to the motorcar in Britain, by raising the speed limit to 12 mph (where it was to remain until 1903) and removing the preceding pedestrian rule - the man with the red flag.

As the century drew to its close, the motor trade gradually became established. *The Automobile Club*, which had been formed in 1897 held its famous Thousand Mile Trial in 1900. At this time there were still tens of thousands of people in Britain who had never seen a motor car and this trial was to show them what a motor car was like and what it could be expected to do. It would also severely test designers' products over distance and hill climbing. In June of that year some of these vehicles were seen in Royston.

The word 'petrol' was added to the English language in 1893 after the association of Simms & Company and Carless, Capel & Leonard, two pioneer firms concerned with 'spirit for the use in the internal combustion engine.' 'Petroleum' did exist but as the trade name for paraffin oil. They were almost certainly the first refiners in Europe to make a petroleum product, fully deodorised and doubly-distilled of such a light specific gravity, on a commercial scale.

There was a great deal of prejudice and ignorance about the new fuel. Regulations introduced in 1896 stipulated the need for extreme caution when dealing with it. It had to be stored or conveyed in unbreakable metal tanks. These tanks had to be labelled with the words 'mineral spirit, highly inflammable, for use with light locomotives'. The amount of spirit was limited and the tanks had to be filled away from artificial light. In those pre-electric light days, illumination of storage places posed quite a problem. Clearly gas and ordinary oil lamps were dangerous if leakages occurred. Once again Carless, Capel and Leonard came up with an answer, the Benzine safety lamp 'especially suitable for lighting coach houses where cars driven by petrol motors are kept'.

The firm was also instrumental in persuading the railways to introduce reasonable rates for the carriage of petrol. This was an important breakthrough in the establishment of an infrastructure for the distribution of petrol in Britain since it enabled Carless, Capel & Leonard to make deliveries to a network of suppliers around the country.

Until an infrastructure of petrol stations had been created, motorists making long journeys with their cars had to lay careful plans to ensure that they would be able to obtain fuel. Sometimes they even had to wait until it arrived by train and, ironically in the dawning motor age, petrol was sometimes being delivered by horse drawn vehicles. A list published in 1901 gave the places where petrol might be obtained and this included ironmongers, chemist shops, and even private houses.

In 1900, several local people were involving themselves in the sale of petrol and in October the Council renewed licences to the following traders in Royston, W. H. Hinkins, F. Gimson, G.H. Innes, A. Humphrey, and R.Walker, thereby placing themselves firmly on the threshold of the motor age. In fact legend has it that the Hon. C.S. Rolls, of Rolls Royce fame, when he was a student at Trinity College, Cambridge at the turn of the century, called at W.H. Hinkins' shop in the High Street for petrol. Rolls was in fact reputed to be the first person to own a car in Cambridge. Gradually other businesses in the town became involved in their own way in the growing industry. For example, N. Varty, engineer, Mill Rd. began manufacturing motor engines in 1902.

At this time also a whole new industry arose based on motoring wear, as cars were of an open design and motorists were exposed to the weather. The roads were simply compacted material and dust was thrown up onto the motorist. Therefore if a driver wished to keep warm, dry and clean, he had to dress appropriately in protective clothing.

The time was yet to come in 1900 when cars would have to be registered with the County Councils (1903) and a formalised system of vehicle tax and tax on petrol would be introduced (1909). Although a little later than the chosen date of this book, the following details are for those interested in the history of the motor car. The first written evidence of a car from Royston officially registered was in February 1904. It was of a car owned by Edmund Brook Nunn of Brooklands, Royston. This was a 12HP Aster, with petrol engine, and a stone coloured dog cart body, weighing 12cwt, registration number AR 331.

The motor cycle was also at this time at a very simple stage of development and the first motor cycle was registered to Walter Gregory of Gower Road in December 1903. This had a 2¼ HP engine with a rear drive weighing about 110 lbs, registration number AR41.
(*The registers are to be found in Hertfordshire Record Office*)

The close of the nineteenth century and the beginning of the twentieth was a time of change and the impact of the car was instrumental in helping to accelerate the speed of changes to come.

The following is an extract from details of the flotation for shares in the Horseless Carriage Company. It was found in a frame in the office of Wilson, Carriage Builder, Kneesworth Street. (*Full document - Royston Museum*)

AFTER WORK

In 1900, many of the leisure activities that we take for granted could not even have been imagined. However, Royston was certainly not a town with "nothing to do" and an extensive network of clubs and societies and other functions existed and it would be a very retiring individual who did not find himself involved in one activity or another, either as an organiser or merely a supporter of arranged events. (Nevertheless, one soldier writing home from South Africa did express surprise that Royston should be lively when celebrating successes in the war !).

In addition to the actual societies there were the public houses for those with a desire for a liquid leisure time. Although these had decreased in number by 1900, there were still many to be found.

The Churches

At this time the Churches had a considerable hold on the leisure time of the populace. Besides the Sunday Services, which most people attended, there were other peripheral activities which would have had a great influence on the moral tone of the times. As we can see later from the monthly reports, these church-based organisations were very active.

The main places of worship in the town was the Church of England Parish Church of St John the Baptist in Melbourn Street, the early origins of which can be traced back to before 1200. During Victoria's reign, this was enlarged considerably. The living was a vicarage, with residence in the gift of the Bishop of St Albans and held from 1877 by the Rev. Joseph Harrison M.A. of Clare College, Cambridge, and Rural Dean of Baldock, who remained until 1925. The Curate in 1900 was the Rev A.T. Boodle. The organist was Charles Attridge, Headmaster of the National Boys' School. The St John the Baptist Mission Room was to be found in Kneesworth Street under the leadership of Captain Clegg. This was to be replaced later by a Mission Room in Queen's Road in 1904.

The Congregational Chapel in John Street was first founded in 1690 and from 1706 used premises in Kneesworth Street. About the year 1790 a division arose within the dissenting church and in spite of efforts to resolve differences an influential part of the church membership left and formed a new church. The Chapel in John Street (known as the Old Meeting) was erected in 1843, reseated and restored in 1884, and remained in use until 1922. The building eventually became derelict and it was demolished in the 1960s to make way for a supermarket, now the site of a restaurant. The school room still remains as the Masonic Hall. The Rev W. Trevor Lewis was the Minister in 1900.

The Congregational Chapel in Kneesworth Street, built in 1795, was the new church and became known as the New Meeting. This was restored in 1887 and had a small attached burial ground. This chapel is now business premises. In 1879 on nearby ground, a Sunday School (now the home of Royston Museum) was erected. The Minister in 1900 was the Rev George Packer. The two congregational churches reunited in 1922.

In 1887, the Weslyan Chapel was built in Queen's Road. In 1900 it was part of the Cambridge Circuit and various pastors attended to its needs.

The Market Hill Mission met in the British School under the chairmanship of Mr. Goodman and in 1896 a small chapel was erected near Barkway Street by the Particular Baptists.

Each Church had its own Sunday School. These had been introduced initially in the latter part of the eighteenth century when children were in demand by manufacturers and their free day was Sunday. One newspaper owner in Gloucestershire used his own resources to open schools for the many ill-disciplined and illiterate children employed all week in the pin factories and let loose on Sunday. When the idea became known it captured the popular imagination and in 1785 the Society for the Establishment and Support of Sunday Schools was founded. It formed local committees and the aims of the Sunday Schools were religious and social rather than intellectual. The rules of the Society required the teaching of reading but not writing or arithmetic and reading obviously refers to the Bible or religious manuals. The movement grew and it was estimated that there were about one and a half million children attending Sunday School in the mid-nineteenth century. The number of voluntary teachers increased and the interest of the upper classes and philanthropists was secured by making them 'visitors' of the Sunday Schools. It is said that the Sunday Schools initiated the idea in this country of universal education applied to children of all ages, free of cost. At the same time they gave to our educational system a religious and denominational flavour which lasts to this day. In Royston there was a District Society of Sunday School Teachers made up of the parishes in the Union, which met regularly for the interchange of ideas.

The Temperance movement was closely associated with the Churches. Throughout the nineteenth century movements of one kind or the other had grown up espousing views which extolled total abstinence from liquor to adopting temperance in drinking habits. Whatever the denomination, they had their own temperance activities and from reports of their activities, temperance seems to have been a major concern in 1900 and a bill was being guided through Parliament with a view to tightening up the licensing laws, closing Public Houses on Sunday, and restricting the sale of alcohol to children. It is difficult to assess the results of this movement but there was eventually in the new century, a reduction in Public Houses, a fall in consumption of all kinds of alcohol, and much more legislation.

It was not all moral teachings however. There were treats and outings for the children and anniversaries to celebrate.

Associations connected with the Churches in Royston

Young Mens' Church Association
Nonconformists Young Men's Society
Church of England Temperance Society
United Teetotal Society
Band of Hope (Juvenile Temperance Movement)
Parish Church Choir
Kneesworth St. Church Choir.
Church Army
Church Missionary Society

Sower's Band (Juvenile workers of the Church
Missionary Society)
British and Foreign Bible Society
Bible Class
International Bible Reading Association
Society of Christian Endeavour
Children's Guild of Courtesy
Boys' Brigade.
Lay Preachers' Association
Royston and District Society of Sunday School
Teachers
Wesleyan Society

Typical Programmes for the Young Mens' Associations

ROYSTON
Young Men's Church Association
PRESIDENT - THE VICAR

The 17th Session will commence on **Monday next, October 8th,** in the **New Rooms** at the **Church House**, with a **Promenade Concert** at 8 p.m. **Mr. E. E. Hayward**, of Cambridge, will sing. **Refreshments** at moderate charges.

Members allowed to introduce a friend.

The Opening Annual Soiree will be held in the Institute, on Tuesday, October 25th.

Mr. Douglas Beaufort. Special engagement of this popular entertainer at the Institute, Monday, November 19th.

The Rooms at the **Church House** are open every week-day evening, from 7.30p.m. to 10p.m.

Elocution, Debates, Lectures, Musical Evenings, &c., will be held each week alternately.

The Lectures will include a series by **Dr. H. R. Archer, on** "First Aid" to the Injured.

The Library will be open on Wednesday, October 10th, at 8.30p.m.

Ladies are Invited to use this Library, at 1s. each the Session. Upwards of **60 New Volumes** have just been added.

Two Bagatelle Boards, Chess Draughts, Dominoes, and other Games.

£2 will be given in **Prizes for Elocution, Chess Draughts, Bagatelle, Essays, &c.**

Morning, Evening, and Weekly **Newspapers Regularly Supplied.**

Permission is given to members over 18 years of age to smoke in the Reading Room only.

Subscriptions - Members over 18 years of age, 5d. per month or 2s. 6d. the Session; under18, 4d. per month or 2s. the session, payable in advance.

The first election of **New Members** will take place on Monday, October 15th.

All those who wish to become members are requested to give in their names as early as possible to

REV. A. T. BOODLE or MR A. WILKERSON
Hon. Secs. & Treas.

Nonconformist Young Men's Society, Royston.
JOHN STREET SCHOOL-ROOMS
THE WINTER SESSION commences MONDAY NEXT, OCTOBER 1st, 1900.

The Rooms will be opened each week-night from 7 to 10, except Saturday, when the Rooms will be closed at 9.45.

Elocution Class, 2nd and 4th Monday in each month at 8.15 p.m.

Horizontal and Parallel Bars.

Debates, Lectures, Musical Evenings, &c., on Friday evenings.

Bagatelle Board, Draughts, Chess, Dominoes, and other games.

Member's Subscription, 4d. per four weeks, or 2/- the Session, payable in advance.

Young Men wishing to join are requested to give in their names at once to either of the Hon. Secs.,

Walter C. Titchmarsh

Gerald K. Kelly

THE LIBRARY
In connection with the above the Library will re-open on Tuesday, October 2nd., from 9 till 10p.m. Ladies are invited to use this Library of over 1,100 Vols.

TERMS - Members of above Society Free; Ladies 1s. per Session (from October 2nd till end of April). Names should be given and ladies' Subscriptions paid in advance to E.W. Stone or Jas.Course, - Librarians.

Young Men's Church Association (1898) *Photograph R. H. Clark (Royston Museum Collection)*

Royston Military Band

This photograph is one taken in the 1890s by Frank Hinkins. However many people are present who were still in the town in 1900. *(Royston Museum Collection)*

Left to right
W. Wilson - Cymbals; Arthur King - Bass Drum; Albert Freeman - Side Drum; Abbis Collins - Eb Circular Bass; H. Blows - Trumpet; Mark Beale - Tenor Saxhorn; Chandler - Euphonium Bb Bass; James Course - Bass Clarinet; George Sharpe - Euphonium in C; Albert Wilkins Eb Tenor Saxophone; E. Wilken - Bass Valve Trombone; Crew Attridge - Cornet; George Robinson - Tenor Valve Trombone; John Beale - Cornet; Thompson - Clarinet; Herbert Hinkins - Cornet; Barnard Bullard - Clarinet; Frank Sheldrick - Piccolo; Harry Greenhill - Clarinet; William Howard Hinkins - Conductor, Clarinet.
Another member of the Band was absent through illness; Charles Hinkins - Clarinet or Bb Soprano Saxophone.

Royston Military Band

In 1900 there had been a band in Royston, of one sort or another, for over 100 years. Under the auspices of the Hinkins' family they had played an important and beneficial part in the social life of the town. People of all beliefs and classes were associated and intermingled in these musical activities.

Towards the end of the nineteenth century the Temperance Movement (a forerunner of the Salvation Army) was gaining momentum with support from employers who wished to keep their young apprentices from the evil clutches of drink. It was not uncommon for an apprentice to have to pledge abstinence for the duration of his apprenticeship. A brass band could put across the message in a way that could not be ignored if only by sheer volume of sound!

William Howard Hinkins (1845-1924), founded the 'Royston Teetotal Band', a prime example of the 'wind and water' bands. In its early days this band had a uniform said to be a 'kind of Buffalo Bill' affair. From 1891 to 1903, when slight alterations were made, the band wore a neat military-looking uniform of blue-black cloth, with close fitting tunics having black corded facings, gold piped collar, gold cord shoulder straps, pill box caps with gold lace band and black chin straps, and gold braid stripe on the trousers.

By 1887 woodwind and string had been added and in 1891 it became the Royston Military Band, with its own constitution, which had the distinction of playing for the Queen Victoria's Diamond Jubilee Celebration on Therfield Heath in 1897.

Funding for these bands was always a problem; money for tuition, instruments, music and uniforms had to be raised by subscription and donations from bandsmen and their friends. Throughout 1900 on many occasions, they could be found playing an integral part in many of the activities of the town and such was its success that it is still in existence in 1999 as Royston Town Band.

Borrowing Books

Although there were no public libraries as we know them, it was possible to have access to books. The associations had their own libraries for the use of members and friends and the adjacent advertisement indicates what was available from Warren Bros. A Book Club was also in existence which discussed, bought and circulated books amongst its members.

Political Groups

Three groups with political associations met in the town. They were: The Conservative Club (President and Chairman, Mr. J. E. Phillips, Secretary Arthur Gamble); The Royston and District Liberal Association (President, H. G. Fordham JP, Secretary, Charles Freston); and The Royston and District Women's Liberal Association (Secretary, Miss E. Titchmarsh). That this last association existed, gives us a hint of things to come. Life was beginning to improve for women. In the 1880s they could go to university, become doctors and take part in competitive sports such as tennis and golf and 1897 had seen the formation of the National Union of Women's Suffrage and the appearance of women's magazines showed how women's affairs were gaining in importance.

The Institute

By 1900 the Royston Institute, first founded as a Mechanics' Institute in 1831 and later developed in 1855 as a Literary Institute in the building now housing the Town Hall, was no longer required. It opened in 1855 with an Exhibition of items illustrating science and art, natural history and archeology &c., which was attended by 7000 people and for the latter half of the century the Institute continued to provide intellectual activities for the town and housed the first town museum and a library. However, with the growth of the many other associations and societies, activities and educational opportunities, both in full-time education and during the evening, the Institute had outlived its usefulness, although the actual building was used for the many fund raising concerts and entertainments. It was taken over by the Town Council, negotiations and decisions concerning financial details taking place during 1900. The contents of the museum were auctioned by Nash, Son and Rowley in 1901.

Sport

The sports' clubs were very active and during their season had regular fixtures on the Heath and away, travelling as far as Cambridge, Finchley, Ashwell, Haverhill and Hitchin to name a few. Rail travel had made it relatively easy for teams and spectators to move around. The weekly reports in *The Crow* give us an indication of their activities. Remembering that the population of the town was apporoximately 3,500, it is quite an extensive programme.

The Heath has a long history of military use, racing and use by the townspeople for "healthful sports and recreation". In 1888 a Board of Conservators was appointed to manage the Common. They could make bye-laws and regulations for keeping order on the Common, and ensue right of free access. The first Conservators were Rivers Richard Smith, George Walter Howard and Walter Charles Titchmarsh. There were as many as 80 race-horses in training on the Heath, payment for which was made to the Conservators.

Cricket

Cricket was first established on the Heath in 1790 and started life as an upper class sport, but by 1900 there were two Cricket Clubs in Royston; the Royston Cricket Club and the Victoria Cricket Club, catering for all levels of society and playing both home and away games. A pavilion was erected in 1895. Information on matches played and their results are in the second section of the book.

Golf

Until the invention of the gutta percha golf ball in the 1850s, golf was a game played only by the wealthy. Clubs and balls were expensive with a ball costing three times as much as a golf club. With the new ball there was a lowering of costs which resulted in golf becoming a popular game, leading to a demand for more courses, although at first people did not think it could ever rival cricket as a spectator sport. The Royston Club started on May 1st 1892. In the local press it was stated "....the new links are the green of Royston Golf Club, and the Secretary is Mr. Rowley of Royston....". It was further stated that any resident could now join the new club without paying an entrance fee, providing their names were sent to the Secretary by May 24th 1892. In 1894 a new clubhouse was built at a cost of about £300.

By 1900 Royston Golf Club had an excellent golf links, their own comfortable clubhouse, both needing staff to service them, thus providing employment for the local townspeople. *Kelly's Directory* quotes: "the links are considered as among the best inland courses in the Kingdom." Membership had reached 220 and caddies were an essential part of a day's golf. In 1899 the Golf Club Committee fixed a scale of wages for the caddies as follows:

> *First round of the day or any part of a round exceeding nine holes ninepence (approximately 4p). For subsequent rounds also exceeding nine holes ninepence. For 9 holes or less sixpence(2½ p). On match days payments as above to be one shilling(5p) instead of ninepence, and ninepence instead of sixpence.*

The spread of the railways meant golfers could travel out from overcrowded London courses and from Cambridge to join the new club at Royston. There was an excellent train service and reduced fares were allowed from Cambridge or King's Cross on showing a member's ticket. Carriages met all trains and during 1900 James Stamford introduced his horse-drawn bus which could carry six passengers and their luggage from the station to the Golf Club. In the town there were several good inns and hotels for refreshments.

Some of the activities reported in *The Crow* in 1900 were competitions for the Captain's Prize, the Monthly Medal, the "Hill" Gold Challenge Cup played over three days at Whitsun, and competitions with other clubs. In 1900 the officers were:- President Viscount Hampden; Club Captain W. P. Harrison; Secretary and Treasurer G. F. Phillips; Professional R. Hepburn. There was no ladies' club until 1911.
Source - History of Royston Golf Club, Cortney Publications, 1992

Football, Hockey and Tennis

Football Clubs were active in 1900, the game having gained popularity in the 1850s. In 1900 there were first and second XI football teams. Hockey was played both by the gentlemen and the ladies of the town. As with the other sports both clubs played home games on the Heath and away fixtures. Details of matches played and the results are to be found later in the book. It is a little difficult to know the exact status of tennis in the town. In the newspaper there were advertisements for tennis equipment but there are no reports of a club having existed.

19th Century Drinking Tankards

Above Pewter Mug from William the Fourth.
Below This engraved glass tankard was used in the 'Bushel & Strike'. Many of Royston's Inns, as befits a market town, had agricultural names. The bushel was a circular wooden drum used to measure one bushel of corn, the strike was the wooden stick used to level off the corn when the bushel was filled.

The labels show three different types of beer bottled at Phillips' Brewery. The bottling section of the brewery was opened in 1899.

(Royston Museum Collection)

52

Public Houses

In addition to the public houses still remaining in Royston today, there were others in existence. They catered for those who preferred a more relaxing leisure activity.

SUN - an eighteenth century building which survives as the first private house at the foot of Sun Hill at the junction of Back Street (Upper King Street).

BUSHEL & STRIKE - in Back Street (Upper King Street).

ANGEL - on the east side of the High Street, running through to Market Hill. It gave its name to Angel Pavement - the shopping precinct built in 1965.

FALCON - a pre-reformation inn on the south side of Melbourn Street, west of the corner of Church Lane and opposite the later site of the Manor House Social Club.

THREE HORSE SHOES - the thatched house on the west side of London Road opposite the Warren, the only thatched house remaining in Royston.

PLOUGH or **OLD PLOUGH** - an alehouse on the west side of the Market Hill, on the corner of George Lane extending into the Market Hill footpath. J. L. Ward ran a common lodging house here charging 1s a night or 6d. if help was given with the chores. It was cleared in 1939.

EAGLE TAVERN - a small country public house situated on the road between Royston and Barkway. This was supposed to be the only place in Royston where a very old game called Ringing the Bull was played until its closure in 1960. It remained in same family from 1872 to 1906.

CROWN AND DOLPHIN - originally called the Dolphin and was situated just north of the corner of Melbourn Street and Kneesworth Street.

CROWN or **OLD CROWN** (known in the 1870s as the Crown and Commercial Hotel). This was situated on the north side of Melbourn Street at the Cross between Kneesworth Street and Lower King Street. It jutted out from Middle Row into the North side of Baldock and Melbourn Street and was demolished in 1929 when it had become a serious obstruction to traffic.

HOOPS - to be found on the west side of the High Street on the site of Dewhursts the Butcher.

PRINCE OF WALES - on the corner of Barkway Street and Barkway Road opposite Prince Andrew's Close.

RAILWAY TAVERN - existed as a beer house, from about 1878. In spite of applications, a spirit licence was refused until 1938. It was on the site of the North Road Garage opposite Queen's Road.

RED LION - a famous posting inn situated on Market Hill with a frontage onto the High Street south of the Angel. During its early life it had been the centre for various social activities.

WHITE HART - at the foot of Market Hill near the corner of John Street.

RED COW - a beerhouse on the North side of Baldock Street; now The Jockey.

WHITE HORSE - some conjecture that this inn occupied the site of an earlier hostlery The Swan. The number of coaches operating from here in the eighteenth and nineteenth century would seem to indicate a long history and reasonable size. Around 1900 it was noted for its dances at the time of the Royston Fair.

WILLIAM IV - a very small licensed house on the north side of Baldock Street and on the west side of the Fleet.

WOOLPACK - in Kneesworth Street opposite the Coach and Horses.

DEVIL'S HEAD - beer house at Wicker Hall, more accurately, The Saracen's Head.

Other Associations which met regularly

Chess Club
Royston & District Teachers' Association
Royston Foal & Colt Society
Royston Horticultural Society
Association for the Prosecution of Felons
Royston Coffee Tavern Company
Royston Independent Foresters' Friendly Society
Ancient Order of Foresters' Friendly Society

Ancient Order of Odd Fellows (Hand of Friendship Lodge)
Royston Tradesman Friendly Society
Amateur Music Society
Royston Minstrels

Dancing and Music Lessons
were also available in the town.

The Volunteers

Another source of activity available to the men of the town was to join the Volunteer Corps. In 1887 the 1st Hertfordshire Rifle Volunteer Corps elected to become one of three volunteer battalions of the Bedfordshire Regiment; thus in 1900 the Volunteers in Royston were correctly known as 1st (Hertfordshire) Volunteer Battalion Bedfordshire Regiment (E Company). In 1897 the battalion changed its uniform from grey, facings scarlet, to scarlet, facings white. However, they continued to wear brown leather accoutrements rather than white and trained as rifles rather than infantry of the line.

This Company was made up of men from Royston and the surrounding district and the Armoury was to be found in Melbourn Street. They regularly practised drill and rifle-shooting on the Heath and had opportunities to fraternise with people outside the town. They attended camps and field days both locally and away from home and in 1900 there are reports of their attendance at a field day in Hitchin, a camp at Shorncliffe in Kent and at a shooting competition at Runnymede Ranges at Staines. The Battalion had a cyclists' section and it was possible to play in a band. E Company held an annual shooting competition in September and prizes of money and cups for this event were awarded in the following March at the Prizegiving Dinner.

In 1900 the Government grant for Volunteers was 38s. per man, per year, which was barely two thirds of that required and they had to look for outside help for finance particularly for prizes for drill and shooting to encourage the volunteers.

Volunteer Companies had not been called upon before 1900 to serve abroad. However, a company of three officers and 113 men, from the three volunteer battalions of the Bedfordshire Regiment assembled in Bedford in January, set sail for service in South Africa in February and landed at Cape Town in March 1900 and after duty on the lines of communication joined the 2nd Battalion, Bedfordshire Regiment, near Bloemfontein in May. The volunteer company remained a separate sub-unit within the Battalion and although the greater part of the Company's service was taken up in routine convoy escorts and outpost duties they did see some action during July and August around Naauwpoort and Winberg. The company returned to Bedford in April 1901. The worth of the volunteers had been proved and their service was marked by the award of the Queen's South Africa Medal with appropriate clasps.

Local Views *Extracts from comments by Col. Longmore of the Battalion*
(Volunteers Prizegiving March 6th 1900.)

".........the Company of Volunteers gone out from this county would before long have an opportunity of sharing in the triumphs which would undoubtedly be reached by their line Battalion, the 2nd Beds, for there was not the slightest prospects of their being employed merely on lines of communication but that they would be sent up to the front to General Clements..............."

"............the country might look forward to many important changes in the Volunteer force. It was essential that there should be more artillery and cavalry provided for them. But there were other changes which must be made. It was only reasonable and right that if they gave up their time at drill, at the range or in camp, their wives and families should be in as good position as if they were at work while they were doing so for in doing that they would be doing work far exceeding in importance to their country any work done by a civilian. While the Volunteer was working to preserve his country he should certainly not be a financial loser."

" ....Volunteers should raise themselves to a standard of efficiency much greater than in the past. He need not remind them to attend every drill and use their splendid range on every possible occasion and to give a little more time in camp. He did not know what the financial offers of the Government might be in this respect..........He felt sure he should not appeal in vain to employers. In allowing their employees to go to camp, they would be carrying out a form of national insurance. If employers let it be known that amongst men who served as volunteers were the men they regarded as worthy of promotion, there would be no difficulty in getting the men to undertake the service. But there were others who were not young enough to come forward as recruits. All he could say to them was *pay! pay! pay!* "

Volunteers and Camp

News of payments to be made for attending camp were received at the end of March 1900

Under the new regulations by which the Government is encouraging a more general and a longer camp training for Volunteers, notices have been issued to the members of E Company setting forth the allowances to be made for different periods of attendance in camp and asking for answers as to which period the Volunteers will attend. The advantages to be allowed are:- for 1 week an allowance of 10s. and 1s. per day pay, for a fortnight 30s. and 1s. per day pay, for three weeks 50s. and 1s. per day pay, for a month 70s. and 1s. per day pay. Married men attending camp for 2,3 or 4 weeks will also in addition to the above pay, receive a separation allowance of 8d. per day for wife, and 2d. for each child under 16. Sergeants will receive the pay of their rank, viz., 2s.4d. per day and separation allowance.

Members in 1900 (not a complete list)

Captain & Hon. Major George Cautherley.

Sergeant Alfred Clarke - Drill Instructor; Surgeon - Captain Bindloss.

Lieutenant J. H. J. Phillips; Lieutenant J. E. Jarvis.

Chaplain - Rev. J. Harrison.

Prize List (for shooting competition held in September 1899). Prizes presented at the Prize Giving held in March 1900.

CHALLENGE CUP COMPETITION

1. Pte. A. W. Stamford Challenge Cup & £2
2. Corp. A. King (£1 15s.)
3. Pte. R. King (£1 10s.)
4. Pte. H. J. Thurnall (£1 5s.)
5. Sergt. Paterson (£1 2s. 6d.)
6. Col. Sergt. A. Pedley (£1)
7. Pte. French (17/6)
8. L. Corp. Woodcock (15/-)
9. Sergt. C. Bullard (12/6)
10. Pte. Beadle (10/-)
11. L. Corp. T. Pack (10/-)
12. L. Sergt. Buckingham (7/6)
13. Pte. Edwards (7/6)
14. Sergt. H. R. Smith (7/6)
15. Pte. Turner (5/-)
16. L. Sergt. C. Hinkins (5/-)
17. Pte. H. Chapman (5/-)
18. Pte. Meadows (5/-)

RECRUITS' COMPETITION

1. Pte. C. Duce (£10)
2. Pte. H. Lindop (17/6)
3. Pte. D. Reed (15/-)
4. Pte. J. Hamshaw (10/-)
5. Pte. A. Harwood (7/6)
6. Pte. G. Mowberry(5/-)
7. Pte. G. Dear (5/-)

DRILL PRIZES

Total Drills for which prizes count are 5 Battalion and 32 Company. Total 37

1. Sergt. Paterson & Pte. W. Beadle (equal) £1 each (37 attendances)
3. Pte. W. Sell 10/- (35)
4. Pte. A. W. Stamford 8/- (34)
5. Pte. H. Meadows 8/-, Col-Sergt. Pedley 8/-
7. Sergt. H. R. Smith 6/-, Pte. F. Clements 6/-
9. Sergt. Buckingham 5/-, Pte. J. Badcock 5/-, Pte. A. Stacey 5/-, Sergt.C.Hinkins, 5/-, Pte. J. Beale 5/-
14. Pte. M. Harper 4/-, Pte. J. James 4/-, Pte. R. Thompson 4/-, Pte. W. Whitehead 4/-, Pte. J. Allam 4/-

SQUAD COMPETITION

1. *Sergt. Paterson's Squad* - Corp. Woodcock, Pte. G. Edwards, Pte. French, Pte. J. James, Pte. Meadows, Corp. King, - 40 points - Prizes 5/- per man.

----

2. *Col-Sergt. Pedley's Squad*. - Corp. T. L. Pack, Pte. A. W. Stamford, Pte. W. Beadle, Pte. Stacey, Pte. R. King, L. Sergt. Buckingham. - 36 points - Prizes 4/- per man.

----

3. *Sergt. H. R. Smith's Squad* - Pte. Chapman, Pte. Turner, Pte. Thurnall, Sergt. Bullard, Lance-Sergt. Hinkins, Pte. Sell. - 31 points - Prizes 3/- per man.

Other names appearing in the report of the 1900 competition. Pte. C. Phillips; Pte. Cocks; Pte. Carter; Pte. Scoot; Pte. H. J. Thurnall.

There also seem to have been some promotions. - Corporal A.W. Stamford (not Private); Corporal Woodcock (not Lance Corporal); Corporal Meadows (not Private); Corporal T. Pack (not Lance Corporal).

1st (Hertfordshire) Volunteer Battalion Bedfordshire Regiment (E Company)

Pictures of Officers in 1900 (Extracted from an earlier group picture. By 1900 uniforms had been changed from grey, facings scarlet, to scarlet, facings white). *(Royston Museum Collection)*

Captain & Hon Major
George Cautherley.

Chaplain Rev. J. Harrison.

Col-Sergeant Pedley.

The Volunteers at Camp *(Royston Museum Collection)*

This photograph shows the members of E Company at camp most probably in 1900/01. They are wearing the scarlet undress tunic which had been introduced in 1897. This was distinguished from full dress by the pockets at the waist and the absence of white piping down the front.

To help in pinpointing when this photograph was taken there are some clues. Two people have been identified - Charles Hinkins (Front - 2nd. left) whom we see from the Prize Lists was indeed a Sergeant in 1900 and Charlie Duce (Back row - 3rd. left) who was a recruit in 1900. Also, in a later photograph (1903) taken of E Company the gentleman (4th left) had become a Sergeant by 1903.

(Charlie Duce had failed the medical examination because of defective vision after volunteering for the Boer War.) This appears later in the monthly news reports.

An esteemed member of the regiment retires.

"Throughout the lengthy period of 37 years, during which Dr. Balding served with the 1st VB Beds. as its Surgeon, the regiment was remarkable for its general all round smartness and efficiency, and to this its Surgeon contributed in no small degree. After 20 years' service he was awarded the Volunteer Decoration, than which there is no higher honour bestowed upon an officer of the Auxiliary forces. On retiring in 1899/1900 with the rank of Lt. Colonel, he was granted the right to retain his rank and to wear the uniform of the Corps."

A quote from *Hertfordshire Leaders, Social and Political, 1907.*

Dr. Balding

Volunteer Medals

The photograph below shows the obverse and reverse sides of the medal which was presented to members of the Volunteers after long service. The ribbon was dark green.

A Volunteer Trophy

(Royston Museum Collection)

The silver cup was awarded in shooting competitions. It consists of a cup supported by three rifles surrounded by a laurel wreath.

Entertainments

Travelling shows and circuses visited the town and in addition to these, the societies often provided public entertainments, either for general amusement or for fund-raising purposes, such as amateur dramatics, recitals or variety entertainments. Many of these activities employed the use of the *magic lantern, phonograph* and *cinematograph.*

During Victoria's reign, the *magic lantern* grew from a novelty into one of the most popular entertainments of the time. Details of its origins are vague and initially it was seen in shows provided by wandering entertainers who travelled through towns and villages with their equipment strapped to their backs. The growing popularity of this form of entertainment was closely linked with a series of inventions which made the lantern much more sophisticated.

Until the early nineteenth century, illumination was by oil lamps which were too weak to cast images onto large screens. This situation was transformed by the invention of limelight which provided an intense, bright light. This light was generated by burning oxygen and hydrogen and training the resulting flame onto a cylinder of lime which, when hot, produced the intense light. Many accidents occurred due to mishandling of the apparatus and the problem of safety was only fully solved with the coming of electricity. The use of photographic glass slides which replaced the earlier hand painted slides and the arrival of mechanical slides which enabled the lanternist to recreate moving scenes, such as a train travelling, helped to ensure its growing popularity.

At the close of the century the magic lantern was at its most popular and it seemed to have a guaranteed future. Toy lanterns were available and there was a growing market for slides of classic children's stories. Some alarm was felt at the growing competition from the advent of moving pictures and the cinema, (the first public demonstration of the 'cinematographe' took place in Paris, on December 8th, 1895), but during the 1890s this invention was plagued by technical problems and was not able to achieve the professionalism of a magic lantern show. The early cinematographs were extra additions to the magic lantern and as the spool for winding on film was yet to be invented the film was often scratched.

Thus in 1900 there was not much concern about the cinema taking over. A much more important discussion was how to lengthen the lantern season from its traditional high point around Christmas and the winter months to the spring and summer. The magic lantern had become so much a part of Victorian life they could not imagine how they could manage without it.

Always keen to extend their influence, lanternists led the demands for the introduction of the magic lantern into the classroom. Their argument was that it was something more than a toy and that it could transform the teaching of subjects like history, geography, science and geology. However, this idea met with strong resistance from teachers and educationalists who considered that it was only suitable for entertainment at Christmas or as a special reward for regular attendance and good behaviour.

On the religious and moral front the magic lantern had much more impact. It was taken up enthusiastically by the temperance societies. The Band of Hope, with 3 million children in 1900, used the magic lantern for promoting its temperance message. Constant reminders of the evils of drink were illustrated in which there was a clear moral message - that drink led to poverty, violence and ill-treatment of children and the downfall of adults. The business of the original R. H. Clark painted lantern slides and sold lanterns and he himself visited many East Anglian villages with his lantern, where he was an entertaining speaker.

The *phonograph* was the precursor of the gramophone. In 1877 Thomas Edison realised that it would be possible to indent in wax vibrations of his speech using a stylus attached to the centre of a diaphragm. He decided a cylinder was mechanically better than a flat disc and using a cover of tinfoil the stylus made an indentation in the foil. However, this device had various shortcomings - the foil was easily damaged, was not easy to listen to, and the recording was impossible to copy. In 1888 Edison produced a phonograph which used an all wax cylinder on which a recording lasted approximately two minutes. The power for driving these machines was either by treadle, or electric motor using cumbersome wet-cell batteries. In America, these machines were marketed initially for dictation but during the 1890s a more profitable line was discovered in the reproduction of music. In Royston, in 1900, Edgar W. Stone, of the High Street advertised "Popular Phonograph Concerts" using "Edison's largest and best Electric Phonographs."

The Magic Lantern

This lantern was previously owned by the Hinkins' family. Below are two of the title slides of the many sets of slides for use in the Magic Lantern. (*Royston Museum Collection*)

One of Edison's Phonographs

The Standard manufactured 1898 - 1900.
Photograph © The British Library Board.

Memories of Royston Fair about 1900

Fairs were held regularly in Royston and the following account of the Royston Fair deals with the one held in October. It was written, in the 1950s, in the *Royston Crow*, by a contributor who wrote under the pseudonym of *Jimmy* and whose articles appeared regularly in the paper.

"I've often wondered how the date of Royston Fair (first Wednesday after October 11th) came to be arranged and fixed. Probably there is as much logic in it as there is in the fact that five and a half yards make one rod, pole or perch. Maybe that the same idiot arranged it - but there it is, there it has been and there it will be. In the past it was no doubt a "red letter" day in the year, both for Royston and also for all the district round. To me as a boy of 12 to 15 years, it was of great importance and a time of excitement that I have never forgotten.

Of course there are two days of the fair, the Thursday always known as Little Fair Day. These are both pleasure fairs, but on Wednesday there was always a Horse Fair held on the Warren, when horses and ponies appeared from nowhere in quite large numbers. I can so well remember seeing them run up and down the Warren and even in London Road just to show off their good points to prospective buyers. I remember (pardon me if I frequently use the words "I remember") hearing of one old fellow who was dissatisfied with a purchase saying "Now look you here. You said how he hadn't got any fault. Blarm - he's blind in one eye and you knowed it," to which the owner replied, "Now sir, you can't call that a fault - that's only a little failing he's got".

For weeks I used to save up my Wednesday penny for the fair. My old grandmother, by whom I was brought up, used to say to me, "Here you are, here's a penny and don't make a beast of yourself with it," and I took her advice, for with other odd pennies, I had managed to collect perhaps a shilling or so by Fair Day. The National Schools, where I attended, were given a day's holiday. Mr. Attridge, the schoolmaster, knew very well that half the boys would play truant if he didn't.

The morning I usually spent seeing the flying horses, the swing boats, the stalls being erected, sometimes offering to lend a hand and having done so to the best of my ability, was told, "Take your hook home. Your mother'll wonder where you've got to".

On Fair Day the town seethed with people from the country. They came on foot, in carriers' carts and often in farm carts and waggons and bicycles. This was the great day when the farmworkers came down to Phillips's to pay for the beer consumed during the harvest. The beer was as essential as the harvest itself. Master Phillips used to give them two or three pints each free gratis and for nothing. Teetotallers were not much encouraged on fair days.

The carriers' carts came packed and the traps had to be carefully balanced as too much weight behind might lift the horse up. Old Mr. Silk of Barkway, Mr. Scott of Orwell and Mr. Meachen of Barley and many others whose names I forget had a bumper day and bumper loads.

The fair itself started in the afternoon and by three to four o'clock was in full swing, with the roundabouts and swingboats at full go and the shows really beginning to wake up.

Shows! My goodness, what wonderful shows they were to me! - wild beast shows (Woomwell's collection), fat women shows, boxing booths, where anyone could get a good hiding for 2d., by having the privilege of a round or two with the proprietor, and the public could see it all for a penny or two.

By the way, outside the fat woman show, the public used to be shown a discarded dress, yards and yards round, which she had just left off.

There were performing fleas which were harnessed to midget coaches which were seen to be pulled along and many other suitable performances.

The flying horses were the great attraction, and to me as a boy with a mechanical mind, the steam engine which drove them was really a wonder. I remember it had on it the maker's name - Savage, King's Lynn. All the brasswork was polished. But better still, how I loved to watch the tiny engine which drove the organ, and how I wished I could make one like it. (As a matter of fact I made a smaller edition of it in later life, and for many years it used to feature on Harris's roundabouts. Harris was the owner of the gallopers.)

ROYSTON 1900

S & J Ralls

A Year in the Life of a Small Market Town

LADDS (stationery section), 21 High Street, ROYSTON
ROYSTON CAVE ART & BOOKSHOP, 8 Melbourn St, ROYSTON
ROYSTON PUBLIC LIBRARY, Market Hill, ROYSTON
*ROYSTON & DISTRICT MUSEUM, Kneesworth Street, ROYSTON

Reviewers write:

What a treat this is for local historians! No stone (including the famous 'Royse Stone') is left unturned as Stan and Jean Ralls piece together a year in the life of a small market town at the turn of the century. It was a year in which Royston enjoyed a heatwave that called for sunbonnets on the workhorses; also it was a bad year for Mrs Coxall who had lost her husband in an accident and was then told that her eldest son had died at the front in the Boer War. Add to this the meetings of the Band of Hope, a farm tragedy and the retirement of a popular local postman - and you have at least some idea of the rich detail that makes this such an intriguing trip down memory lane.

- **Alan Kersey** *(Cambridge Evening News)*

Most of England's market towns act as a focus to their own surrounding area and maintain a somewhat insular view of the world beyond. Usually, this has led to continuity of purpose and of action by successive generations - as is splendidly illustrated by *Royston 1900*. Fact is delivered seriously, but interspersed with much that is in humorous vein. (Just read the saga about the fixing of the salaries of the Master and of the Matron of Royston's Workhouse.) I raise my hat - everyone wore one in 1900! - to Stan and Jean Ralls, who have so brilliantly caught the spirit of the late Victorian age. This book deserves a national audience in addition to the very substantial local one that it will undoubtedly attract.

- **F John Smith**

This is a fascinating book that can be enjoyed by young and old. I would suggest that there is something of interest on every page; it need not be read in strict order, just open it anywhere and a snippet or statistic will seize you, e.g. count the baptisms and deaths during the 12 months and see how similar they are; then read about a serious accident to a stable lad, and how eight inches of snow closed the schools for two days. These absorbing facts make good social history - so do keep on reading!

- **Ann Smith**

It is with great satisfaction that I have previewed Stan and Jean Ralls' millennium publication "Royston 1900". This most entertaining book brings vividly to life the pure Royston (a fairly typical market town) - in reports frequently studded with the old familiar family names and streets. Those who have long been interested in Royston past and present will surely discover much that is new to them, whereas folk who have become curious to know more of ancient Royston's recent history and way of life will find no more satisfying publication.

- **Peter Ketteringham**

The authors have wisely given close attention to the everyday, very human aspects of community life in Royston 1900 - public notices, advertisements, church activities, the hospital and the workhouse, magistrate court proceedings and the like. These certainly bring out the authentic flavour of 'A Year in the Life of a Small Market Town'. The detailed subject headings and the photographic illustrations (by Les Smith) combine with intensely readable text to make this a handsomely unique *fin de siecle* presentation, which can become, for its readers, a most entertaining 'armchair companion'.

- **Fred Sillence**

There were other names associated with Harris. There were the Shaws - Larry Shaw and Sons, and the Nightingales, who used to have sweet stalls. Larry Shaw and two others used to go the round of the dancing rooms with really good music. Larry played the harp, while the other two played the violin and cornet. The cornet man used to collect the money from the dancers as they polka'd past them. You see, he was the only one of the three who could hold his hand out and still keep playing.

Several dancing rooms were available. The large room at the Green Man was of course very popular and on the spot but the large club room at the White Horse in Melbourn Street ran it very close.

There were one or two other musicians. One was a real expert with the English concertina, but I can't remember his name. This extraordinary influx of outsiders needed to be fed and many of the pubs provided a Fair Day Dinner consisting of roast beef, Yorkshire and Christmas plum pudding. Eaten together, they were generally excellent fare for the occasion.

In the fair itself one could buy really good sausages, perfectly cooked over coke stoves. You could have a hot dog and bread for 2d. Milk stalls were there and sometimes little saucers of boiled peas with vinegar and pepper for 1d. a saucer. No fruit such as bananas and tomatoes were heard of at that time. Walnuts were offered at 16 to 20 a penny.

One of the great attractions at the fair was Twiner's crockery stall, where plates and dishes, tea and dinner sets went at ridiculous prices. He had a great way of attracting clients. He'd put up a piece and offer it at a price and if no one wanted it he just smashed it on the ground.

One of the greatest thrills of my boyhood was at the Royston Fair. I had come to my last penny when to my astonishment I came to a kind of platform stall bearing six wonderful microscopes, which were being demonstrated by a kindly looking man of altogether different type to all the others. I sidled up to them rather curious to have a look down at whatever there was to see.

"Look young lad, you'll like to have a look here. It's only one penny for all six views. This one shows you the circulation of the blood as it is in the human body. You can see it perfectly through a frog's foot." And so I did. To me it was one of the most wonderful things I had ever seen. The movement of both red and white corpuscles was really wonderful. He was extremely kind to me and encouraged me to stay as long as I wished.

It was indeed an unforgettable sight. One of the other microscopes showed the eggs of the oyster with all the magnificent colours. Another was a slide showing that human hair is tube-like, and another was to show the scales of a butterfly's wing.

It was truly a thrill I have never forgotten and perhaps may have started my love of nature on the right track.

In the evening the tricksters usually turned up and with "thimble rigging" and "find the lady" tricks, emptied the pockets of the credulous. There used to be one man particularly clever at the game. He usually held an open purse in his left hand and deliberately seemed to put three two-shilling pieces in it and offer it to the public standing around for 2s. When it was undone it was found to contain three pennies only. If no one bought it he simply handed it to one of the crowd to open, and sure enough there were the three florins to show them. What an honest man he was !

It was considered great fun to use the water squirts sold at a halfpenny each, and many of the girls caught colds through having their hair and clothes being wet through.

Another frightening thing was some of the men getting too much to drink. Instead of making them merry it was just the opposite and unpleasant fights were quite frequent.

The fair was kept up to past closing time (11p.m.) and many of the country people had to drive home. No doubt many of them didn't arrive home until next day.

These notes are just an expression of how I saw Royston Fair in my young days."

Employees of C. G. Whitaker & Co., Drapers and Outfitters (1899)

Photographer R. H. Clark. (Royston Museum Collection)

<u>Back Row:</u> Miss Drage, Mrs. F. Fardell, Mrs. Sillence, Mrs. F. Simons, Miss Pickett, Mrs Higgs, Miss Rayner.
<u>Centre Row:</u> Miss H. Humphrey, Miss Richman, Miss L. Humphrey, Miss Fardell, Mrs. Craft, Mrs. C. Smith.
<u>Front Row:</u> Miss N. Renaut, Mrs F. Greenhill, Mrs. Foster, Mrs. Amer.

These members of the dressmaking department worked from 8.30a.m. to 8p.m. and on three days from 8.30a.m. to 9.30p.m. An apprentice would have served her time for two years with no pay and then received 5s. in her first year. An experienced dressmaker received 12/6d. to £1 per week. The story is told that this photograph caused controversy. As they were dressed in their Sunday best it was thought that the photograph had been taken on a Sunday. This was not socially acceptable. However, the photograph had actually been taken on a Thursday afternoon.

WORKING IN ROYSTON 1900

The lists in the following section have been compiled mainly with the help of the 5th edition (1899) and the 6th edition (1902) of *Kelly's Directories*. For the most part, there is continuity between the two dates so 1900 would be covered. Where there is any difference, the date when the entry appeared in Kelly's has been shown. These lists are not fully comprehensive as the majority of workers shown would have been in charge of the establishment either by ownership or in a managerial capacity. However, during researches, several names of employees in some of the concerns in 1900 have been discovered. These have been included in the list. In addition to these, there would have been a vast cohort of workers for whom no accurate records of employment have survived, eg shop assistants and labourers. Even the census for 1901, full details which are to be published in 2001, will only tell us what people did for a living and not necessarily where they were employed.

It can be seen from the lists that the possibilities for employment within the town itself were considerable in concerns both large and small, and from the various advertisements throughout this book it can be seen that all the providers of employment were nothing if not versatile, making the town almost self-sufficient. Most people, therefore, had the opportunity for suitable employment, from simple labouring in the trades and farming, working as assistants in the shops, taking up an apprenticeship or gaining work in the professions. In addition to this we find advertisements every week in *The Crow* for jobs further afield (albeit usually in domestic service) which the more adventurous could try for. Joining the army was another way for the young men to work away from the town. From letters written home from the Boer War, we discover that several men joined different regiments in both commissioned and non-commissioned ranks.

One particular form of employment is worthy of special mention, that of domestic service. It was at the turn of the century that domestic service reached its peak. By 1901 it was not only the major employer of women in the country, but with a total labour force of nearly one and a half million persons it formed the largest occupational grouping of any kind - bigger than mining, engineering or agriculture.

In the Victorian era the number of those able to afford resident domestic staff rose sharply. The view developed that the employment of domestic staff was in itself a sign of respectability and an indicator of social status, rather than a mere aid to the smooth running of the household. As small shopkeepers, tradesmen and clerks moved in growing numbers into the servant-keeping classes, so the distinctions between employer and maid were more firmly drawn. The annual wages paid to servants indicated a very finely-graded heirarchy and ranged from £70 for a butler, £65 for a housekeeper, £36 for coachman, £30 for a cook down to a mere £10 to £12 for a laundry or scullery maid.

Only one business *Robert H. Clark & Son* has remained in the same family since before 1900. Robert H. Clark opened his business in the High Street on May 1st, 1877. He had been apprenticed to the watch and clock and photographic trades at Forest Gate, London. He became a lantern slide expert and a maker of commercial and religious sets of slides then in great demand. Eleven ladies were employed to paint and pack slides and many types of lanterns were sold. Also during his career he left an excellent photographic record of the town at the turn of the century. His son R. H. C. Clark was also a photographer, who trained in Birmingham, and a photographic studio was made from the slides studio, which had been built with north-facing windows. He continued in the shop daily until 1970 and died in 1971, aged 84 years. His son Robert H. Clark continued the business as a photographer until his death, aged 50, in 1981. The founder's great grandson C.R.H. Clark transferred the business into larger premises further up the High Street, with a newly built studio and offices, in June 1990.

Robert H. Clark who opened the original business in 1877

The Market in 1900, as it had been for many years previously, was still an integral part of the life of the town as a place of agricultural trading and livestock buying and selling and the Corn Exchange, erected in 1836, was the focal point of trading at the market held every Wednesday.

The main auctioneer for the town was Nash, Son and Rowley who placed an advertisement each week in the *Royston Crow* for these markets. The firm also auctioned other items beside the purely agricultural. Details of some of these can be seen later in the monthly accounts. Another auctioneer, George Jackson, is mentioned in the list of traders in Royston but the main place of work appears to have been Hitchin.

Local farmers had access to other markets further afield such as Hitchin, and Cambridge and Ely. Again they were kept fully informed about them in the newspaper where full details were to be found each week.

ROYSTON MARKET.
SALE OF FAT & STORE STOCK.
Messrs. NASH, SON & ROWLEY
Will sell by Auction
EVERY WEDNESDAY,
on the Market Hill, at **Two o'clock precisely**
FAT AND STORE BULLOCKS
COWS AND CALVES
SHEEP, LAMBS, AND PIGS
HORSES, CARRIAGES, IMPLEMENTS
HAY STRAW, &c.
Owners may have Neat Stock Advertised Free of Charge, if desired, and they are particularly requested to send in their Stock by 1.30 o'clock on the Morning of the Sale.

Messrs. NASH SON & ROWLEY, Estate Agents and Valuers, Royston, Herts.

Other Markets advertised in *The Crow*

For Week Ending July 13th
SATURDAY:-
Sale of Small Farm at Great Munden, at the Dimsdale Arms Hotel, Hertford, by George Jackson & Son.
MONDAY:-
Grain, Moyes & Wisbey's Stock Sale at Cambridge Cattle Market.
Messrs. Chalk's Stock Sale at Cambridge Cattle Market
TUESDAY:-
J..R. Eve & Son's Stock Sale at Hitchin Market.
George Jackson & Son's Stock Sale at Hitchin Market.
WEDNESDAY:-
Nash, Son & Rowley Stock Sale at Royston Market.
THURSDAY:-
Grain, Moyes, & Wisbey's Stock Sale at Ely.
Sale of plant and Machinery, &c., at Hitchin, By E. A. Andrews

---

HITCHIN CATTLE MART.
In consequence of the Foot and Mouth Disease Order
Messrs. J. R. EVE & SON
Will not hold their Weekly Sales until further notice.
Estate Offices: Hitchin, Bedford and Luton, 21st February, 1900

William T. Nash - Farmer

Deposited at County Record Office, Cambridge. (ref 296/ SP304)

ROYSTON,
Within 1 hour of King's Cross, on the Hitchin and Cambridge Branch of the Great Northern Railway.

————

Particulars and Conditions of Sale
OF THE SUBSTANTIALLY BRICK-BUILT
Freehold Residence,

Situate on an elevated position, on a Chalk subsoil, adjoining the Cambridge Main Road, commanding extensive views of Cambridgeshire including Ely Cathedral, within 10 minutes' walk of Postal and Telegraph Office and Royston Heath, with one of the finest inland Golf Courses of 18 holes, known as

" QUIES COTTAGE "

Containing Entrance Hall, Dining and Drawing Room, Lavatory, Kitchen, Wash House, 3 Principal Bedrooms, Housemaid's Closet, Bath room with H. & C. Water; There is a

Flower & Vegetable Garden,

Adjoining, having an extensive frontage to the Cambridge Main Road, which could be utilised for Building Purposes if desired,
WHICH MESSRS.

NASH, SON & ROWLEY

Have been instructed by the Rev. T. H. Lonus, to Sell by Auction, at
THE CROWN HOTEL, ROYSTON, Herts.,
On FRIDAY, SEPTEMBER 21st, 1900,
At 5 p.m. precisely.

MESSRS. WORTHAM, NASH & KING,
Solicitors,
Royston.

People at Work

HIGH STREET

Abbott & Sons	Cabinet makers and upholsterers
Archer Joseph	Saddler and harness maker
Baker James	Confectioner and baker 1899
Baker William Robert	Grocer 1899: baker, confectioner, grocer 1902
Barclay & Co Ltd	Bankers. Head Office 54 Lombard St. London
Bateson Elias	Cabinet maker 1899
Bedwell William (Mrs)	Plumber and decorator 1899
Bedwell William George	Plumber and decorator 1902
Bishop John B	Cabinet maker 1902
Bowskill William	Refreshment rooms
Brown Harry	Tobacconist
Bullard Charles Henry	Basket maker
Bullard Oswald	Cycle maker
Camps Simms	Boot and shoe maker; Camps & Co 1902
Cash Grocery Stores	Manager - David Mellor
Clark Robert Henry	Watchmaker and jeweller; Slide Manufacturer. 11 employees
Coe Charles	Butcher
Course James	Watchmaker
Ebbut David	Painter and plumber
Fawcett Harold	Solicitor 1899
Gimson Frederick Harley	Ironmonger
Goodman Thomas	Royston & District Supply Stores
Greenhill John	Licensee Chequers Public House, bricklayer
Harradine Henry	Shop keeper
Haywood Edwin	Collector of Land, Assessed and Income Taxes; Assistant Overseer 1902 Deputy Superintendent Registrar 1902.
Hillary Arthur	Clothier and draper 1902
Hinkins William Howard	Plumber & painter (and builder 1902)
Hood Arthur	Watchmaker & jeweller
Hoy William	Butcher
Jerrard Louisa (Mrs)	Ladies outfitter
King John Pearmain	Linen draper
Kingston Alfred	Journalist
Logsdon Edwin	Licensee Bull Hotel 1902
Matthews Ernest	Chemist, dentist, wine & spirit merchant: Superintendent - Fire Engine
Miller Martha (Mrs)	Toy dealer
Moore Edmund Walter	Licensee Angel Public House
Morgan Edwin A	Chemist, druggist, ophthalmic optician, insurance agent
Morley Arthur Edgar	Butcher
Newsome Kate (Mrs)	Milliner 1902
Norman Sarah A (Mrs)	Tobacconist
Porter Alfred	Toy dealer (and hairdresser 1899)
Putt M (Mrs)	Licensee The Bull Hotel 1899
Robinson Joseph	Licensee Hoops Public House
Shell Thomas	Clerk to the Guardians, Rural District Councils of Ashwell & Melbourn: Assessment & School Attendance Committees. Clerk to School Boards of Bassingbourn & Kneesworth UD, Foxton & Therfield: Superintendent Registrar 1899
Sharpe Arthur	Clerk to the Guardians; Assessment & School Attendance Committees of Royston Union, School Boards of Bassingbourn & Kneesworth UD, Ashwell, Foxton, Therfield : also to Ashwell and Melbourn Rural District Councils Superintendent Registrar Royston District 1902
Smith G.J. & Co	Boot and shoe makers
Stone Edgar William	Draper
Thair Ernest	Hairdresser
Titchmarsh Edward	Draper and grocer; Agent for W. A. Gilbey Ltd Wine and Spirit Merchants
Thurnall John Edward	Land surveyor and valuer; agent to County Fire Office
Victoria Temperance Hotel & Restaurant	Manager D. Dellar 1899: Proprietress Mrs G. B. Foreman 1902
Walker Robert	Chemist and druggist
Warren Brothers (Robert & Charles)	Printers, publishers, book & music sellers, stationers, bookbinders, engravers, newsagents, stamp distributors & circulating library Herts and Cambs Reporter and Royston Crow (published Friday) Editors - Robert Warren, Alfred Kingston Other employees - Alfred Carter, Edgar Rawlings, (Composing Room) Albert Reeve, Irad Webster, John Dellar

Wortham & Dalton Nash 1899	Solicitors
Wortham, Nash & King 1902	
Wortham Hale	Solicitor & Commissioner for Oaths; Clerk to magistrates for Odsey & Arrington & Melbourn divisions; Clerk of the Peace & County Council for Cambridge 1899
Nash H. Dalton	Solicitor & Clerk to Commissioners of Taxes; Registrar & High Bailiff of County Court; Clerk to the Conservators of the Royston Heath.; Clerk to Commissoners of Taxes 1899 Solicitor for the Herts, Cambs & Essex Association for the Prosecution of Felons
King William Byatt	Solicitor and Commissioner for Oaths; Clerk to the Commissioners of Taxes & Board of Conservators of Royston Heath 1902 Solicitor to N Herts., Cambs & Essex Association for the Prosecution of Felons

THE CROSS

Beale John	Baker and Confectioner
Henderson & Co.	Printers, stationers and agents for the Herts & Cambs Reporter: Jeweller 1902
Whitaker & Co.	Drapers and tailors: G.H. Jacob (Manager) Staff - Miss Drage; Mrs F. Fardell; Mrs Sillence; Mrs F. Simons; Miss Pickett; Mrs Higgs; Miss Rayner; Miss H. Humphrey; Miss Richman; Miss L. Humphrey; Miss Fardell; Mrs Craft; Mrs C. Smith; Miss N. Renaut; Mrs F. Greenhill; Mrs Foster; Mrs Amer
Porter John George	Licensee Old Crown & Commercial Hotel

KNEESWORTH STREET

Ashton Fanny (Miss)	Bridge House School
Banham Harold F. J.	Solicitor and Clerk to Urban District Council 1899 Commissioner for Oaths; 1902 Clerk to Justice Odsey Petty Sessional Division Herts & Arrington: Melbourn Petty Sesional Division of Cambs:& Royston, Ashwell & Melbourn Joint Hospital Board 1902
Biller John	Insurance Agent 1899
Clark Leonard E.	Butcher
Clark Robert Henry	Photographer and Lantern Slide Manufacturer
Congregational Church	Rev. George Packer A. T. S; William Oliver - Caretaker
Conservative Club	Secretary Alfred Anthony Gamble: Caretakers - Mr & Mrs Stockbridge
Coote Joseph	Licensee - Coach & Horses and fishmonger
Dennis Thomas J.	Grocer and draper
Farrow James Richard	Sanitary plumber, building contractor
Flanders George C.	Cycle agent 1899
French Rufus Augustus	Tailor
Greenhill Dennis	Licensee - White Bear P H
Higgins Thomas Simms	Watchmaker and jeweller
Howard George Walters (Britannia House)	Machinist & carting contractor
Humphrey George Frederick	Harness maker
Jacklin & Co.	Building contractors
Jenkins Henry James	Licensee Crown and Dolphin Public House Mineral water manufacturer 1902
Lilley John Edward	Baker and confectioner
London Central Meat Co.	Manager - William George Fletcher 1899 Charles F. Warwick 1902
Mason Michael	Coal merchant
Mason Josiah	Printer & stationer & agent for Royston Weekly News 1902 Market Hill 1899
Nash William T.	Farmer 1902
Norman Emmanuel	Blacksmith 1899
Norman Herbert	Blacksmith 1902
Pickett George	Beer retailer Railway Tavern
Sanders Ralph Erskine	Coach builder
Smith T. H. & Sons	Flour millers (steam)
Spink Edward William	Florist 1899
Stamford James	Cab Proprietor Agent for Great Northern Railways
Stearns Frederick	Shoemaker 1902
Stone E. F. (Miss)	Organist and teacher of music
Wand & Co	Ironmongers
Wiffen John	Beer retailer
Wilkerson Samuel & Son Ltd.	Corn, cake and seed merchants
Wilson Charles Cook	Blacksmith
Wilson Robert	Tailor
Wilson William	Carriage builder
Woollard John George	Grocer
Young Daniel	Cycle agent and repairer 1902

RAILWAY STATION

Ainger William — Stationmaster:

Other employees:- F. W. Chapman (Clerk 30/- per week); Assistant Clerks - A. E.. Wallis 28/-; O.W. Kemp 24/-; E. P. Easter 24/-; G. L. Baker 24/-; A. B. Drury 28/-: J.Pidwell 24/-; P.M. C.Hayman (Probationary Clerk) 10/-; E. M.Keeping 10/-; Richard Samuel Thompson - Porter

Baker George S. — Coal agent 1899
Nash W.T. & Co — Coal merchants
Fordham & Howard — Coal merchants 1899
Fordham S.H. &Co — Coal merchants 1902
Farmers' Manure Company — Manager W. T. Nash

OLD NORTH ROAD (Kneesworth Road)

Dellar Benjamin — Confectioner
Henderson Alfred — Music depot 1899
Jacklin Leonard — Apartments
Pigg John Chappel — Nurseries
Stevenson Charles — Boarding school - Victoria House

MELBOURN STREET

Amer Henry — Tinplate Worker
Balding, Archer 1899 — Surgeons
Balding,Archer & Windsor1902

Archer Herbert Ray MD — Surgeon and Medical Officer No 1 District Royston Union
LRCP London. MRCS Eng. — Deputy Coroner Royston Div., County of Herts. Medical Officer for Post Office & G.N. Railway1902; Surgeon to the Cottage Hospital 1902

Balding Daniel Barley — Surgeon,
FRCS Eng, VD — Public Vaccinator No 1 District Royston Union 1899: Coroner Royston Div. of County of Herts.

Windsor Charles William — Certifying Factory Surgeon & Medical Officer to Workhouse
MA,MD,BC. Camb
MRCS Eng., LRCP London
Law J. H. — Licensee - Falcon Public House
Lee Mary (Mrs) — Umbrella Maker
Motts Rose (Miss) — Dressmaker
Norman Ernest — Cycle manufacturer & repairer
Percy Thomas — Licensee - White Horse Public House
Pool George — Boot and shoe Maker
— Curator Royston Cave
Post Office — Postmaster J. W. Carter (1896-1900). H. Beer 1901
— Clerk - J. T. Freeman; M. Beale, J. A. Bonnett
Sanders Ralph E. & Son — Coach builders, cycle manufacturers & agents and motor engineers
Shell Frederick — Nurseryman
— Deputy Supt Registrar
Sherrard Richard G. — Trainer of race horses
Smith James — Surveyor and Collector to the Urban District Council: Assistant Overseer and Collector of Taxes: Deputy Registrar of Births and Deaths Royston Sub-District and Deputy Registrar of Marriages Royston District County of Hertfordshire.
Stockbridge and Sons — Seed and Corn Merchants
St. John The Baptist Church — Vicar - Rev. Joseph Harrison; Curate - Rev. Boodle.1900
Thurnall Harry Joseph — Artist (Baldock St 1899)
Town Hall — Clerk - H.F.J. Banham
— Caretaker- G. Robinson
Armourey — Volunteer Battalion (1st (Hertfordshire) Bedfordshire Regiment (E Co.)
Witts Thomas — Surveyor & Collector of Taxes to the UDC; Assistant Overseer.1902
Woollard M. A(Mrs) — Baby Linen Warehouse

MELBOURN ROAD

Additional Churchyard — Caretaker - John Beale
Betts Sidney — Bailiff to County Court 1899
Chapman Henry James — Inland Revenue officer
Dellar James (Mrs) — Apartments
Hayward Frederick Willian — Dairy man
Hewson Fred MRCVS (The Roystons) — Veterinary surgeon; Inspector for the Odsey & Buntingford Division, under the Contagious Diseases (Animals) Act
Nonconformist Cemetery — Secretary - Walter Beale22
Trudgett Richard S. — County Court Bailiff 1902
Streather George Edwin — Stone and marble mason
Webb William James — Sanitary Inspector to Royston Urban & Melbourn Rural District Councils; School Attendance and Vaccination Officer, Royston Union

MARKET HILL

Ashby George	Licensee - Boar's Head Public House 1899
Barron Alonza	Bill poster & town crier 1902
Barron and Son	Basket makers and wire workers 1899
Bateson John	Blacksmith
Foster EB; GE; CFC; CF.	Bankers (Branch of Cambridge)
	Manager W. B. Cross
	Drawn on Prescott, Dimsdale & Co. London EC
Hagger Ann (Miss)	Greengrocer
Police Station	Inspector - James Hart
	Police Sergeant - George Reed (mounted); Police Constables George Knight,
	(Richard Gray to November), Arthur Robbins (from November) and Compton
Innes G. H. & Co	Ironmongers
James Eliza (Miss)	Shopkeeper
Jackson George	Auctioneers, estate agents,valuers - Also at Hitchin
King Arthur	Saddler and harness maker
Martin Frederick	Shoemaker
Mason Josiah	Agent *Royston Weekly News* 1899
Osborne Thomas	Licensee - Red Lion Public House
Pickett Thomas	Licensee - Green Man Public House
Potter Thomas	Licensee - White Hart Public House 1899
Rainbow Albert	Licensee - White Hart Public House 1902
Robinson George	Shopkeeper 1902
Royston Weekly News	Published Friday; agent J. Mason
Smith Rivers R.	Agricultural seed and wine and spirit merchant
Soundy and Powell	Drapers
Stockbridge William	Hairdresser
Townsend John James	Licensee Boars Head Public House
Ward James Lloyd	Beer retailer
Ward James	Tailor
Williamson Edward	Shoemaker 1899
Woods Edward	Greengrocer
National School	Girls - Head - Mary Constance Greenstreet
	Teachers - L M. Higgins; E. Bedwell; F. Ainger
	Boys - Head - Charles Attridge. Assistant Master - Mr. A. F. Rudling
Infant School	Head - C. Walbey

FISH HILL

British School	Head - Charles A. Freston
	Teachers - J. Clarke; D. Norman; E. Bement
	Correspondent - Thomas Gimson
County Court	Judge - His Honour W. H.G Bagshawe QC 1899
	H. Dalton Nash - Registrar and High Bailiff
	Judge His Honour John Shortt QC 1902
Craft Thomas	China dealer and baker
Fire Station	Superintendent - Ernest Matthews
	Foreman J. Course

JOHN STREET

Hagger Lawrence	Butcher
Congregational Church	Rev. W. Trevor Lewis

BALDOCK STREET

Bush Alfred R.	Beer retailer 1902 (The Red Cow)
Gimson & Co	Builders and Contractors and Undertakers: Charles Whyatt - Manager
Hepburn Robert Gray	Professional golfer (Barkway Rd 1899)
Jones James	Beer retailer (King William 1V Beerhouse) 1899 - 1900 : John Evans 1900 - 1902
Marsh Guy D'Este	Racehorse trainer 1899
Nash, Son and Rowley	Auctioneers, surveyors, land agents, valuers
Nash Charles	Farmer
Phillips J & J.E. Ltd	Brewers Managing Director - James Edward Jarvis

A. Stanford - foreman	J. Bass - bottling foreman	J. Hale - labourer
H. Oliver - mashroom	G. Carr - malster	J. Ellis - labourer
A. Stacey - drayman	W. Ingrey - driver	E. Blows - painter
F. Rayment - blacksmith	W. H. Quarrie - traveller	F. G. Parrott - clerk
C. Palmer - cellarman	J. Wedd - carpenter	T. Garner - nightwatchman
C.S. Bass - cellarman	C. Bentley - cooper	
D. Ingrey - drayman	H. Wilkerson - bricklayer	

Spink Edward William	Beer retailer 1899
Thurnall Harry Joseph	Artist 1899 (Melbourn St. 1902)

Royston Golf Club	Secretary - George F. Phillips
	Professional golfer (Barkway Rd 1899)
Royston Water Co Ltd	Manager & secretary - William T Rowley; Chairman & Director John Phillips
	Directors F. J. Fordham C. Whyatt; Auditor W. Beale.
	Secretary and Manager - W. T. Rowley
Waller Benjamin W.	Racehorse owner 1902

BACK STREET

Carrington Bros	Carpenters & undertakers 1899
Clarke Henry	Dairyman 1902
Edwards George	Licensee - Bushel & Strike Public House
Horn William	Shoemaker 1902
Marshall Thomas	Shoemaker 1899
Pryor George P	Corn & hay dealer
Shepherd Ellis	Tinplate worker
Turton Eliel	Carpenter
Wilson Elizabeth	Dressmaker 1902

SUN HILL

Stamford William	Town Crier 1899

NEWMARKET ROAD

Bevill Charles	Stud stables

MILL ROAD

Biffen Thomas T.	Grocer and beer retailer
Cane Francis	Deputy Registrar of Births Melbourn Sub-district
	Deputy Registrar Melbourn District, Royston Union
Driscoll Richard	Trainer of horses 1902
Howard Arthur	Grocer
Lees Mary Elizabeth (Mrs)	Apartments
Pearce Charles	Butcher (formerly Gas House Rd 1899)
Pearce Abraham	Butcher 1902
Pigg John Chappel	Nurseries
Reynolds Frederick	Baker 1902 (formerly Gas House Rd 1899)
Royston Gas Co Ltd	Managing Director E. Matthews, Secretary Walter Beale
Thurley Richard	Beer retailer & builder (formerly Gas House Rd 1899)
Varty N. & Sons (Royston Ironworks)	Hydraulic, mechanical & brewers engineers, iron founders ;
	Manufacturers of trefoil & clover seed mill machinery & Coopers patent compressed brick cutting table & patent of Northern furnace bar: Also cycle agents 1899
	Motor car engineers; cycle repairers 1902: Manager - Mr Onions

MORTON STREET

Birne Samuel	Race Reporter
Folan Willam	Insurance agent
King Sarah Ann	Apartments 1902
Sergeant John	Trainer of horses 1902

GOWER ROAD

Davies John	Registrar Births, Deaths and Marriages & Relieving Officer for the Melbourn District, Royston Union & Collector to the Guardians
Gregory Walter	County Council main road surveyor for Buntingford
Jacob George Henry	Tailor's cutter
Pigg John Chappel	Seedsman and florist 1899
Stimpson Richard	Prudential superintendent

LONDON ROAD

Howes Ernest	Beer retailer - Three Horse Shoes
Hudsons	Cambridge & Pampisford Breweries Ltd; stores
Marshal Thomas	Shoemaker 1902

QUEENS ROAD

Humphrey Abraham	Grocer
Pryor John	Shoemaker
Wesleyan Chapel	Cambridge Circuit Rev. C.H. Hocken, 1899; Rev. Wm Bradfield. & Rev. Wm Moulton 1902

ROCK ROAD

Tuck Cambridge	Market gardener

THE WARREN

Marriott Ernest	Cycle maker & dealer 1902
Whitehead Brothers	Stone, marble, granite & monumental masons & general contractors, Est. 1840

BARKWAY STREET

Asplen John	Licensee Black Horse Public House
Miller Nathan	Cowkeeper & cabinet maker

BARKWAY ROAD

Lime Kiln

Nelson Thomas	Beer retailer - Prince of Wales
Wilson Luther	Wheelwright
Davies Edwin	Collector to the Guardians, Relieving Officer & Registrar of Births, Marriages and Deaths,
(Radnor House)	Royston district, Royston Union
Cottage Hospital	1899 - Matron Mrs Phoebe Baker, Secretary H. S. Tuke
	Surgeon D. B. Balding;.
	1902 - Matron Mrs Ellen Collins (appointed 1900); Secretary W.B. King
	Surgeon H R Archer;. Nurse Miss Collins (appointed 1900)
Woodward Henry N.	Sanitary Inspector, School Attendance and Vaccination Officer Royston 1899

HEATH

Pratt Edward	Beer retailer 1899

BALDOCK ROAD

The Workhouse	Master - John William Wesson
	Matron - Mrs Wesson
	Industrial Trainer (1898 - 1900) - Miss Hart
	Nurse - Miss Jones - to July
	Miss Broughton - August to October
	Miss S. J. Roberts (appointed November 1900)
	William Cleak - Porter

Miscellaneous

Anderson William	Labourer	Harradence William	Labourer	Rayment Thomas	Employee W. H.
Badcock Joseph	Carter	Hoy Alfred	Drayman		Hinkins.
Bancock George	Employee Mr.	Humphrey William	Labourer	Reynolds Ernest	Baker
	Haywood.	Johnson Edward	Gentleman	Reynolds L.	Brewery Workman
Banham James	Stableman	King Alfred	Labourer	Roberts Ernest	Painter
Barnard William	Labourer	Kingston Robert	Shepherd	Roberts Frederick C.	Painter
Barnes David	Coachman	Lavercombe John	Clerk	Ross Hugh	Artist
Bateson John	Blacksmith	Mason Frederick	Groom	Sewell George	Bank Cashier
Bowen George	Gardener	Miles John	Engineer	Tansley George	Gardener
Darlow Samuel	Stableman	Miller Harold Warren	Furniture Maker	Thompson Richard	Railway Porter
Deller Albert	Painter	Muncey Albert	Coachman	Trowsdale, Miss	Nurse (Royston
Dellar Wilfred	Painter	Muncey Henry	Shepherd		Nursing Ass.)
Goldie Barre	Stockbroker	Munns James	Drayman	Tuck James	Farmer
Giffen Charles	Labourer	Newman Frank	Labourer	Webb Edward	Engine Driver
Hagger Alfred	Labourer	Noades John	Labourer	Woods Henry	Stableman
Harman Harry	Stoker	Perry Noah	Soldier	Wright George	Butler

GIMSON & Cº
(CHAS WHYATT.)
Builders, Contractors & Undertakers
BALDOCK STREET
ROYSTON, HERTS.

Situations Vacant

WANTED, trustworthy person as COOK, wages £20, two in family, housemaid kept, small dairy. Apply, to "House," *Reporter* Office, Royston.

ROYSTON WORKHOUSE - COOK (male or female) wanted at once - temporarily; salary 10/- per week with rations.
For particulars apply to the Master.

WANTED, a suitable MAN, to go with Coal Cart, &c.; wages 16/- per week; a cottage will soon be available. Apply with reference to Mr. A. P. Onions, The Factory, Royston.

WANTED, a coal-yard MAN, wages 18/-. Apply, by letter in own hand writing, with reference, to W. T. Nash & Co., Royston, Herts.

WANTED, about the middle of January, a good GENERAL SERVANT for a private house, two in family. Apply Mrs. Putt, Bull Hotel, Royston.

WANTED, a good PLAIN COOK, small family. Apply to Mrs. G. F. Phillips, Archway House, Royston.

Two or three good BRICKLAYERS and a CARPENTER wanted at once. Apply to Carrington Bros., Builders and Contractors, Back Street, Royston.

Lad wanted at once. Apply C. H. Coe, Butcher, High Street, Royston.

WANTED at once, strong active LAD, not under 18. N. Varty & Sons, Engineers, Royston.

DRESSMAKING Wanted - Assistants to the Dressmaking. Apply, J. P. King, Royston.

WANTED, GENERAL SERVANT, at once, 18 to 20, good character, £10 to £12. Craft, Royston.

WANTED, a young MAN, about 20 with a knowledge of glass preferred. Fredk. Shell, The Nurseries, Royston.

HOUSEMAID in small family of two persons where three other servants are kept. Apply in first instance to P.M., Messrs. Warren, High Street, Royston.

WANTED, at once, Horse-keeper and Stockman, middle-aged, married preferred, good cottages and gardens found close to work, constant employment. Apply A.B., *Reporter* office, Royston.

WANTED, BOYS, for bottle-washing shed, not under 14. Apply, the Brewery, Royston.

GOOD PLAIN COOK wanted. Apply, Mrs. W.B. King, Mount Lodge, Royston.

W. R. BAKER, requires a respectable LAD for house work and for delivering goods. The Pioneer Stores, Royston.

WANTED, an APPRENTICE for the Upholstery. Apply to, Abbott & Son, Royston.

WANTED, MAN, as Gardener and General Servant; good wages to quick man. Apply, Mr. Joseph Nunn, Royston, Herts.

WANTED, a handy Man who understands gardening. Churchman. Cottage rent free. Apply, Vicar, Royston.

WANTED GIRL, to take charge of two children. Apply to Mrs. Godfrey Faussett, Melrose, Mill Road, Royston.

WANTED, some respectable employment for a strong Lad, 16 next birthday. Write for particulars to R. M.., *Reporter* Office, Royston.

DRESSMAKING - Good Bodice hand wanted. Apply, J. P. King, Royston.

WANTED, a GENERAL SERVANT, Housemaid kept. Apply, Mrs. E. Titchmarsh, High Street. Royston.

WANTED, a LAD, to look after pony. Apply, W. Bedwell, High Street, Royston.

PAINTERS.-Two good Brush Hands at once. Apply, W. Bedwell, High Street, Royston.

WANTED, Out-door Apprentice or improver. Apply, J. Archer, Saddler, Royston, Herts.

TAILORS.- A good Coat or General Hand wanted. Apply, W. Ward, Tailor, Market Hill, Royston.

BAKERS--Wanted, a respectable young MAN, able to mould, serve rounds, attend to horses, &c., or one willing to learn the business. Apply, D Baker, Heydon, Royston.

••

Away From Home

WANTED, a STOCKMAN, one who can milk; good house and gardens and 15/- per week. Apply Almshoe Bury, Hitchin, Herts..

WANTED, 40 experienced BRICKLAYERS AT ONCE, 8d. per hour. Saxon Cement Co., Ltd., Cambridge.

WHEELWRIGHTS.- wanted, a good, steady Man for a constant place. Apply, Geo. Huddlestone & Sons, Haslingfield, Cambs.

THOROUGHLY respectable GIRL wanted, about 16, for general house-work; another servant and boy kept; good opening for capable girl. 10, Princess Road, Finsbury Park.

WANTED at once, steady man as HORSE KEEPER, wages 15/- a week with extras; 6 horses; good character indispensable. Apply, A. Farr, Walkern, Stevenage, Herts.

WANTED, a steady MAN to occupy farm-house, near high road and feed stock and take charge of a team, wages 15/- a week, good character. Apply to Arthur Pickett, Duck Lane Farm, Ashwell, Herts.

WANTED, COOK-GENERAL, for a family, wages £18 to £20 according to experience, also NURSE, WAGES £18 to £20, housemaid kept. Write to Mrs Davey, 32 Russell Road, Kensington, London.

WANTED, capable Man in Yard and Stables, Wife required to clean Offices, free house and 25/- weekly. Apply, Young Bros., King's Cross, Hay Market, London, N.

WANTED, active, healthy women, to train as Sick and Monthly Nurses for country cottagers; regular wages and uniform. Address, stating age, present employment to:- Mrs Briscoe, Bourn Hall, Bourn, Cambridge.

W. STAMFORD,

6, Sun Hill, ROYSTON,

PERFORMS THE DUTIES OF

TOWN CRIER & BILL POSTER

He solicits the patronage of the Public, which he hopes
to merit by a proper discharge of his duties.

W.S. also attends Parties at the Residences of the Gentry as usual.

William Stamford *(Royston Museum Collection)*
The Town Crier's bell is also housed in the Museum.

William Stanford had at one time been licensee of the White Horse. An old resident paints a delightful picture of him. " It was the custom at that time to take a list of names of all members who attended the Institute and it was one of the duties of the custodian, who at that time was Mr. William Stamford, who kept the White Horse Public House, and as he was sometimes inclined to indulge in having a little drop too much to drink, he was not always to be relied on for correct names and numbers, so it was his custom if he was not quite fit, to get one of us lads to keep accounts for him, and I might say that a few pranks were sometimes played on him on his return to shut up at ten o' clock. He will be well remembered as the Town Crier, and in this capacity caused some amusement as some of the announcements got a little mixed." *Reminiscences of Royston by E. W. Bicker - 1931 (Royston Museum)*

Men at Work c. 1900 - at the beginning of the communication revolution which was to change the world in the twentieth century. *(Royston Museum Collection)*

72

Wм. H. HINKINS,
High Street,
ROYSTON.

W. H. Hinkins was a very versatile trader who obviously believed in the dictum "It pays to advertise". Every week in the *Royston Crow* there was a different detailed advertisement for his goods and services.

HOUSE PAINTING, DISTEMPERING, PAPERHANGING.

Special Designs, &c., prepared for high-class Decorations.
Gilding of every Description.
Glass Embossing.   Graining.
Sign Painting & Writing
Ornamental Lead-Light and other Glazing.
GENERAL HOUSE RENOVATIONS AND REPAIRS

P A I N T S
GENUINE LIQUID PAINTS,
In Tins ready for use.

These are very superior to the Tinned Paints generally sold, and differ from them in the following respects. viz:

1. The Tins *contain* the weight of the Color specified; in most of those sold by Dealers the tin is included in the weight.
2. Our paints are carefully prepared, they contain only the best Baltic Linseed oil, American Turps, pure Dryers, *Genuine English* White Lead, and pure Colors, and are finely strained.
3. We are enabled to give the *fullest guarantee* with these Paints, as crushing, grinding, manufacturing and tinning are done on the Premises under our personal superintendence.
4. Their superiority in covering power, brilliancy and durability, is so well-known as to need no comment.
5. We give our guarantee on every tin.
6. They contain no Barytes, Paris White, or other adulterating materials: the adulteration of Paints is a general practice.
7. They are simply good old-fashioned Paints precisely the same in every respect as those we use, and *though* slightly higher in price than the Paints sold by Dealers, are in reality far cheaper.
Prices, 6d. per lb. for Tins of 10lb. and upwards; Small tins 3d. each. 5d. per lb. for 28lbs. and upwards, or 4½d. per lb .for 112lbs. and upwards of one colour in largest tins.
50 Colors and Shades are kept in stock, and we have pleasure in making (at slightly higher prices) any other colors, even in small quantities, to customers' patterns at short notice.
N.B. - in ordering special colours*[sic]* it is better to state their purpose.
The tins are also of our own make, with Patent Self-opening Tops.

PAPERHANGINGS
Wholesale and Retail

The Trade in buying of us receive the same discount allowed by the London Houses, and thus save the Railway Carriage.

All other customers will find that in our READY-MONEY prices we are as low as any Co-operative Stores.

All our books are at the "low rates" agreed by the leading makers, *not* at the high prices adopted by some Dealers for the purpose of allowing greater discounts.

Bath, Range and Stove Work
Repairs of Roasting Jacks, Locks
Moderator and other Lamps, and of General Tin, Copper and Brass Ware,&c.
Re-tinning.   Speaking Tubes.
Re-lacquering, Bronzing, and Electro-Brassing and Coppering.
Scales and Weights repaired and adjusted.
Cutlery ground.
Electric, Pneumatic and Crank Bell Fitting.
Ventilating and Sanitary Work.

A Large Stock of Tin, Copper, Enamelled and Galvanised Ware.

We rectify any unsound article returned within 24 hours

Our General Stock comprises a great variety of Goods to meet the every-day requirements of the Household, at very low prices.

LAMPS, BATHS, FILTERS, PUMPS, &c., LET ON HIRE

SPECIFICATIONS AND ESTIMATES FREE

We do not fear competition when all the Tenders are based on the same specifications, but when they differ in the least there can be no just comparison. If favoured with your enquiries, our Ready-Money Quotations for Painters', Plumbers', and other work, will in fair competition, probably secure your orders

ACETYLENE GAS LIGHTING.
(Apparatus may be seen in Action).

Every Householder his own Gas Maker!!

Suitable everywhere, but especially useful where Coal Gas is not obtainable. The cost of Acetylene is equal to Coal Gas at 2/6 per 1,000 cubic feet; it gives a pure and brilliant light, free from smoke, dirt or smell, is portable, **easily managed,** less trouble than oil lamps, **safer** than Coal Gas, (as the smell being more pungent gives immediate notice of escape) and is not injurious to the eyes. With our improved Automatic Generators there is **No Danger.**
Existing Gas Pipes & Fittings can be used.
Specifications and Estimates for lighting Private Houses, Churches, Chapels, Schools, Factories, Workshops, Street Lamps, &c., on application.

HEATING OR WARMING BY HOT WATER.

Attention is respectfully asked to the fact that the above is considerably **cheaper** and **more effective** than by Coal or Gas Fires, as **one** Fire does the work of many, and the **great saving** thereby effected soon covers the cost of fitting up &c.

The absence of dust, dirt, and other products of combustion is also a **great ecomonical feature** affecting the Housemaid's work and injury of Furniture, Decorations &c.

Under the system we adopt, and with the most ordinary attention, there is **absolute safety,** and explosion is practically impossible.

Plans and Estimates prepared and executed in accordance with the most approved modern principles, for Private Houses, Shops, Greenhouses, Churches, Chapels, and other Public Buildings, &c.

Herts & Cambs Reporter

AND ROYSTON CROW.

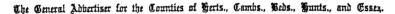

The General Advertiser for the Counties of Herts., Cambs., Beds., Hunts., and Essex.

The *Herts and Cambs Reporter* and *Royston Crow* or *The Crow,* as it was popularly known, was founded by a native of Royston, John Warren Jnr (1818-1884). It was his father who had first moved into the town in 1812 and who in 1847 bought the established printing business of Mr Stamford, who had been the first printer in the town. *The Crow* remained in the family until 1930 when the business was sold to Joseph Cooke.

The first edition of the *Royston Crow* newspaper was printed in January 1855. Initially 1,000 copies a month were printed to be sold for 1d. each (2d. if sent by post). Sales do not appear to have been very good since the paper became little more than an advertising sheet and copies were given away free of charge. In September 1876, *The Crow* became a weekly newspaper, being produced in an eight-page broadsheet format. Two years later the paper had *Herts & Cambs Reporter* added to its title to indicate the extended coverage the paper was envisaging.

The eight-page format was in operation throughout 1900. Advertisements appeared on page 1. Page two carried an instalment of the regular piece of fiction, railway timetables and more advertisements. On January 19th, 1900 a new story began, entitled *By Decree of the Seven* by Edmund Mitchell. National news and articles of general interest filled page three with more advertisements and public notices on page four. Pages five and six carried the editorial and local news; page seven mainly national news including parliamentary affairs, and page eight town and district news. During 1900 the war in South Africa was reported extensively and included the publication of letters from soldiers serving in South Africa.

In 1900, the newspaper maintained that it was "the only paper printed at or within 13 miles of Royston". A brief statement of its aims and charges appeared weekly in the newspaper. The editorial comments were written under the name **Corvus Cornix**.

The *Columbian Printing Press* on which the paper was printed at the turn of the century in its original premises, still exists in Royston Museum. The press was housed on the first floor, where the low ceiling caused some difficulty, and a hole had to be made in the ceiling to accommodate the counter weight.

This type of press was the most common form of printing press used by provincial printers during the nineteenth century. It was designed in 1813 in the USA, and first introduced into Europe in 1817 and produced high quality work. It was operated with a simple system of levers and counterweights and required less exertion to use than many rival machines.

Printing was a slow and laborious process and fifteen men were employed in the composing room alone and the press itself was handled by two men, one to ink the type with a two handed roller, and the other to place the sheet and operate the press.

This OLD FAMILY NEWSPAPER has now been established over 40 Years and during that lengthened period, it has enjoyed the confidence of the public and the patronage of ADVERTISERS. It assiduously maintains the privilege of independent criticism in all local matters, and as no pains are spared to ensure the full and impartial reporting of all local events, therefore enjoys the support of ALL CLASSES. Its large circulation and the wide area over which it extends, recommends it as the

BEST PAPER for ADVERTISEMENTS

For all Auctioneers, Professional and Business men, and others having property to dispose of or any want to make known, &c. &c. *Proprietors and Publishers*-------WARREN BROS, ROYSTON, to whom all communications and Advertisements may be sent.

ADVERTISEMENTS

Terms for Official, Auctioneers', Tradesmen's and General Advertisements may be obtained on application. A series of thirteen or more insertions on special and moderate Terms.

NO ALTERATIONS of Contract Advertisements can be attended to UNLESS SENT BEFORE THURSDAY

PRE-PAID ADVERTISEMENTS

Advertisements from PERSONS WANTING SERVANTS, SERVANTS WANTING SITUATIONS, and all similar Miscellaneous Announcements, will be inserted as follows:-
Not exceeding 16 words, 1 insertion 9d., 3 insertions 1s. 6d.
24 words, 1 insertion 1s. 0d., 3 insertions 2s. 0d.
32 words, 1 insertion 1s. 3d., 3 insertions 2s. 6d.

The second weekly local paper available in Royston through its agent Josiah Mason was the *Royston Weekly News*, published on Fridays.

Corvus Cornix

Alfred Kingston was a co-editor with Robert Warren and chief reporter for *The Crow* and wrote under the pseudonym **Corvus Cornix**. Many of his observations on life in 1900 are recorded in section two of this book.

He was born in Dunstable, Bedfordshire and before arriving in Royston had worked for the Midland Railway Company and began a career in journalism in 1873 working both in Luton and Chesterfield. He eventually came to Royston in 1876 and contributed a great deal to the building up of the newspaper. He took an active part in the life of the town, being elected onto the first Council on the formation of the Royston Urban District Council. He continued to work in the town until 1903 when he found it necessary for reasons of health to give up the night work, that working on a newspaper frequently brought, and to remove to London to carry on his literary work.

He wrote several books, concerning the Civil War, *Phonography in the Office* (at the request of Sir Isaac Pitman) and the books most familiar to Roystonians, namely *Fragments of Two Centuries* (a series of descriptions of country life in the time of George III, drawn from the district around Royston), *The Heath and Its Wild Flowers,* and *History of Royston,* which is still the standard work relating to the history of the town before 1900.

After his departure from Royston he continued to write the editorial note for *The Crow* until July 1917.

This photograph appeared in the supplement issued by *The Crow* on the occasion of its centenary in 1955.

Warren Bros.

Throughout this book many advertisements appear illustrating what was available from Warren Bros. and from these we see yet again the versatility of another Royston business. Besides printing *The Crow* and dealing with associated processes such as general printing and book binding, they were involved in the sale of greeting cards and stationery of all kinds and the selling of local and national daily papers and magazines. They sold sports equipment - hockey sticks, tennis racquets, croquet sets and footballs; they hired out and sold pianos and organised piano-tuning and sold music; they advertised photographic services; they organised a circulating library and they sold books, their waste paper and such items as fire-screens.

Robert Warren (1863 - 1947)

Upon Robert Warren (the second son of the founder), in conjunction with Alfred Kingston, devolved the responsibility of continuing and extending the scope of the newspaper when his father died in 1884. For 27 years these two were co-editors and to this partnership the paper owed much of its success. He had a sound knowledge of what was news and how to present it. In order to equip himself completely for the business of printer and newspaper proprietor, he had spent many hours in the composing room and became in every way a practical printer, and as such he was the guiding light in the extensive business for many years until his retirement in 1930.

Charles Warren (1864 - 1949)

Although Charles Warren was not directly concerned with the production of the newspaper, he was responsible for the retail side of Warren Bros., and the despatch and so forth of the paper to the numerous agents. He was, however, interested in local affairs and participated in most activities in the town helping to fill the paper's columns wth news.

John Warren (1862 - 1910)

The eldest son of the founder of the newspaper was John Warren. He did not take an active part in the paper's development because of ill-health. He died aged 48 in 1910. During his life, however, he was a member of E Company and won several prizes for shooting.

J. JACKLIN,
5, *North Terrace,*
ROYSTON.

This print, probably taken from a letter-heading of the nineteenth century, shows Jacklin's yard on the east side of Kneesworth Street, opposite the railway station. Only the three-storey residence now remains. The buildings on the corner of Queen's Road occupy what was the frontage of the yard, and the houses around Clark Road are on the site of the workshop area.

Sights, Sounds and Smells of 1900
A Roystonian Conveys the Atmosphere

The Royston of yesteryear, just like other towns, was lively with fully-occupied people, most engaged in lengthy manual labour, throughout each working day. The labour had its own sounds too for the town's main streets and market place echoed to many horse-drawn carts of the butchers, the bakers, and the grocers. There would be the lumbering handcarts of men - each one known and greeted as a personality - delivering bread. There would be many, many whistling errand-boys, on their heavy trade cycles.

Royston had a splendid variety of smells, too, at the turn of the century. In the central area alone, you would sniff a heavy, though not unpleasant scent from the brewery, in Baldock Street, and the delightfully fresh odour of baking from Lilley's (subsequently Monty's Radio), Beale's, at the bottom of the High Street by the Cross, and long-established Craft's (now Day's) at the lower end of Fish Hill.

To these odours were added many more, from goods openly displayed at fishmongers, greengrocers, and butchers, so you will realise - though it is hard to do so in these days of sanitised foodstuffs - how directly the senses of Royston people were stirred in the town of long ago: and that is without taking into account the all-pervading presence and smell of horse manure.

20th Century Royston, The First Fifty Years. Fred. Sillence

76

THIS AND THAT

Charities in 1900

In 1900 various charities were in operation in Royston providing services to the poor and needy of the town. The following is a brief description of these charities.

Sir Robert Chester, in his will dated 3rd. May 1638, directed his executers to give a rent charge of £5 4s. per annum for bread to the poor. This sum was paid out of the manor of Royston and was distributed in bread by the vicar and the churchwardens.

In 1609 *Robert Warden* left a yearly sum of £2 12s. out of a tenement in St. Peter Cornhill, London, to be distributed in bread every Sunday to the poor. The property charged with this payment belonged to the Merchant Taylors' Company, and the annuity was regularly received from them and distributed in bread.

In 1687 *Sir Thomas Foot* gave an assignment of £42 of Exchequer annuities for the benefit of the poor of certain parishes, including the parish of Royston. The endowment of the charity for Royston came to be represented by £56 4s. 6d., £2 10s. per cent. annuities, producing £1 8s. yearly, which was distributed in bread to the poor every week.

Joseph Wortham, by his will in 1689, gave 30s. yearly out of his messuage in Royston to the poor, 20s. thereof to be distributed in bread at candlemas to poor widowers and widows of Barley. The sum of 26s. out of the Falcon Inn, Royston, was received yearly in respect of this gift and distributed in bread.

Lester Brand by his will in 1851 gave a sum of money represented by £434 15s. 9d. consols with the official trustees, producing £10 17s. 4d. yearly, which was applied in the purchase of coal and blankets for the poor.

A charity, for the general purposes of Royston Cottage Hospital was founded by will proved at London 13 June 1899, of *Mrs Sarah Ellen Pyne.* The endowment consisted of a sum of £542 consols with the official trustees, producing £13 11s. yearly, which was applied towards the salary of a district nurse. The same scheme also directed that a sum of consols equivalent at the price of the day to £1,000 sterling should out of the residuary estate of Mrs. Sarah Ellen Pyne be applied in providing a site for, and building of, a mission room for the parish of Royston, eventually erected in Queen's Road..

The *William Lee* charity was founded by will dated 8 October1527, and was regulated by a scheme of the Charity Commission dated 30 June 1893. The property consisted of two shops, (owned by Messrs. Whitaker & Co., and Mr. George Pool), and dwelling-houses in Royston, (commonly called the Cave Estate owing to the opening from one of these houses to the Royston Cave). The rents from these properties together with interest from investments produced an income of £242 10s. 3d. in 1900. The net income was applied in accordance with the scheme in subscriptions to Herts. Convalescent Home, Royston Nursing Association, Addenbrooke's Hospital and Royston Cottage Hospital; in assistance to invalids in hospitals, and in exhibitions to children from public elementary schools. In 1900 the Trustees of this estate were:- Thomas L. Gimson (Builder);Thomas Goodman (Provision Merchant); Charles Whyatt (Builder); D.V. Balding (Surgeon); T. S. Higgins (Jeweller); W. J. Abbott (Upholsterer); W. T. Nash (Coal Merchant); G. W. Howard (Coal Merchant); H. Smith (Miller).

There were almshouses belonging to the parish, in Kneesworth Street, endowed by deed in 1833 by *Mrs. Barfield,* widow of a dissenting minister, at one time resident in Royston, for eight widows of good moral character and not under 60 years of age: the allowance to each widow was five shillings weekly and a ton of coal each year. The income was £120 a year, obtained from money in Indian stocks. In 1846 an almshouse was built by the late *Charles Beldam* and in 1885 four almshouses were built in Queen's Road and formed a private charity (as distinguished from trusts which were subject to the control of the Charity Commissioners); these houses were intended for spinsters, chiefly of, but not limited to, Royston; each inmate received 30 shillings a month, the income being derived from the rental of a house built at a cost of £1,000.

Source: Victorian History of England, Hertfordshire Record Office.

Cemeteries

In 1900, there were two cemeteries available. The Nonconformist cemetery of one acre in the Melbourn Road was formed in 1865, at a cost of £800 and had one mortuary chapel; it was the property of the Royston Cemetery Co. Limited, the secretary of which was Walter Beale, Sun Hill House. The second was the Church Cemetery (Additional), of nearly two acres, also in Melbourn Road. This also had a mortuary chapel and was formed and consecrated in 1878 at a cost of about £600.

The Population of Royston in 1901

From the 1901 Census Returns

Censuses were held in 1891 and 1901 but it was thought better to use the information from the latter census as it was nearer the year under consideration. Because of the rule which doesn't allow access to the complete records for 100 years the following information was obtained from the report published giving just the statistics of the census but no details of the inhabitants. Anyone who is interested will be able to see them in the year 2001. The following table shows the distribution of the population :-

AGE	MALE	FEMALE	TOTAL
0 to under 5	176	170	346
5 to under 10	183	169	352
10 to under 15	169	197	366
15 to under 20	146	186	332
20 to under 25	121	158	279
25 to under 30	103	172	275
30 to under 35	111	129	240
35 to under 40	97	111	208
40 to under 45	94	104	198
45 to under 50	81	107	188
50 to under 55	83	90	173
55 to under 60	65	71	136
60 to under 65	66	70	136
65 to under 70	54	51	105
70 to under 75	44	37	81
75 to under 80	15	37	52
80 to under 85	11	23	34
85 to under 90	3	10	13
90 to under 95	1	2	3
95 and over	0	0	0
Totals	1,623	1,894	3,517

Housing Statistics

The census report gives details of the number of tenements occupied and the distribution of the population within them. It must be remembered that the correct meaning of the word tenement is a 'building where people live, usually rented'.

The census tells us that there were 814 of which 271 had less than 5 rooms.

Number of rooms	Number of tenements
1	13
2	22
3	34
4	202
Total	271

Distribution of People in the Tenements.

Persons per Tenement

Rooms per Tenement		1	2	3	4	5	6	7	8	9	10	11	12
	1	13	-	-	-	-	-	-	-	-	-	-	-
	2	9	7	4	-	1	1	-	-	-	-	-	-
	3	7	3	5	4	5	4	2	1	1	1	-	1
	4	21	43	37	30	34	16	14	4	2	1	-	-

Example:- There were 34 situations where 5 people lived in a 4 room tenement.

The Haunting of the Old Post Office

In 1949, after hearing of the alleged ghostly happenings in the Old Post Office in Royston, a gentleman by the name of Mr. Paul Underwood, visited the town and later wrote an article for the *Physic Researcher.* He described a meeting with Mr. J. T. Freeman, an employee of the Post Office for some considerable time. He was a mere clerk in 1900 and the last postmaster of the building - a position he held for 25 years.

Mr Freeman told how new members of the staff who would have to perform night-duty there, were invariably warned that during the night they would probably hear "the woodchopper". This was the name given to one noise, which was heard very frequently from 1894 onwards and which resembled the noise of wood chopping. This noise was heard at different times throughout the night and for varying periods, occasionally several times in one night. At least one person refused to continue night duty there. No satisfactory explanation was ever found.

At the time Mr. Freeman had suggested the noise might originate in the stable of Mr Joseph Phillips just across the road. He felt the noise might be horses kicking their stable floor. However, Mr Underwood thought that had the horses been the correct answer, the noise would have been regarded as normal and not been described as a wood chopping noise.

Another mysterious noise for which no explanation was ever found occurred in either 1898 or 1899. At 3 o'clock one morning Mr. Freeman heard a loud noise of smashing glass. He immediately examined all the windows, but found them intact. At 3.15 the incident was related to the mail driver who thought Mr. Freeman had been imagining things; he was doubtless very surprised to hear for himself a few minutes later the sound of smashing glass and on making immediate investigation was no more fortunate than Mr. Freeman in discovering the cause. The backs of some of the High Street shops led into the Post Office yard and early next morning Mr. Freeman made a point of noting that there were no broken windows in the vicinity.

On one occasion Mr. Freeman, who was living over the Post Office at the time, heard doors banging downstairs. Taking a poker to protect himself against any intruder he descended to find all the doors open and stationary. Moreover, when he came downstairs, footsteps appeared to follow him about as he searched unsuccessfully for any one who could be responsible for the noises. On another occasion Mr. Freeman also saw a key turning in a door leading to the cellar and was unable to discover the cause.

One of the things that is most convincing concerning the possibility of supernormal happenings at the Old Post Office is the fact that identical noises to those related were remarked upon by workmen when the building was converted into a Community Centre many years later. The foreman, a Mr. Ashton, related that two very practical and hard-headed men stated that they heard doors banging below; descending to surprise any unauthorised person who had entered the building, they were astonished to discover all the doors precisely as they had left them and to hear footsteps following them about. They communicated these experiences to Mr. Ashton, who discovered that they knew nothing of the reputed haunting or of the noises periodically heard many years before. He himself was of the opinion that there was definitely something strange about the building during the evening and at night. On one occasion when in the cellar he definitely felt that someone or something was down there too.

Mr. Underwood considered that the cellar was the most interesting part of the Old Post Office and that it was significant that the cellar adjoined Royston Cave (reached from the boot shop of Mr Pool opposite). It was possible that some kind of echo originating in the vicinity of the cave, perhaps transmitted with alarming clarity through the medium of the chalk sub-soil, might account for some of the many peculiar noises heard throughout the years in the Old Post Office. As the wall between this cellar and Royston Cave was only three feet in thickness, he felt that this proximity may have had some connection with the many apparently inexplicable noises heard in the building. Alternatively, he also thought that as certain hauntings appear to deteriorate gradually, almost like a battery running down, these noises may be the remnants of a genuine haunting.

Some Residential Addresses

KNEESWORTH STREET/ROAD & OLD NORTH ROAD

Abbott Mrs   Hesman House
Andrews Miss   Britannia Terrace
Ashton Miss   Britannia Terrace
Banham Harold FJ   Old Palace
Beer Henry   The Manse 1902
Bird James
Cheshire Alfred   Park Cottage
Cambridge Mrs   Clifton House
Crossley Richard   Forman
Dewsett Miss   Ivy Lodge 1899
Farrow James Richard
Fawsley Mrs   The Laurels
Fordham Frederick George
Fordham Miss 1902
Fordham Francis John   Yew Tree House
Fordham Mrs   The Rookery
Garrett Mrs 1902
Gimson Frederick Harley
Gimson Thomas Luke   The Acacias
Grundy Mrs   The Sycamores
Howard GeorgeWalters   Britannia House
Humphries Frank 1902
Jacklin Arnold   North House
Jacklin The Misses   North House
Jarvis James Edward 1902
Jennings The Misses
Kelly Mrs
Lea Mrs 1899
Lees Markham 1902
Lilley Mrs 1902
Mason Michael   North Villas
Nash William Thomas   North Lodge
Nunn Edward 1902
Nunn Miss 1902
Perrie.Mrs North Villas
Rowley William T St Leonards Villa
Rudgard Edward William 1899
Rudgard George R 1902
Sanders Ralph Erskine
Sharpe Arthur   Ivy Lodge 1902
Shell Thomas   Heath View 1899
Slee Henry   Hawthorn Villas 1899
Smith Harry   The Pightle
Stevenson Charles   Victoria House
Stockbridge Frank Pearce
Stone Miss
Stone Mrs
Sward The Misses   The Green
Titchmarsh Alfred (Flint Hall Fm 1902)
Titchmarsh Miss
Titchmarsh Mrs   Britannia Terr 1899
Trudgett John 1899 (Barkway St 1902)
Varty Frank 1902
Wade George 1899 (Melbourn Rd 1902)
Wand Edward 1899
Weston Thomas   Northfield House
Whitfield William 1902
Whitfield Miss 1902
Wilkerson George 1902
Wyman Miss   North Hall

MILL ROAD

Cory Mrs 1899 (North Rd 1902)
Driscoll Richard 1902
Jacklin Mrs Melrose
Onions Alfred Factory House
Pimm Rev Michael H. Curate 1899
Putt Mrs   Huntingdon Place 1902
Shell Mrs 1902
Varty Thomas 1902
Varty Mrs 1899
Walbey Albert 1902
Ward Miss 1902

GOWER ROAD

Brown Henry
Smoothy Mrs

MORTON ST

Harber Rev Stephen
Hughes Mrs 1902
Bird, The Misses

ROCK ROAD

Witts Thomas W 1902
Bentley Charles

BALDOCK STREET/ROAD

Abbott William John

Barnes Frances   Heathside
Beale Leonard Lilly
Clarke Robert Henry 1902
Nash Charles
Nunn Joseph Phillips
Nunn Miss
Phillips George F 1899 High St 1902
Phillips Mrs 1899
Phillips John JP   Earls Hill House
Phillips John 1902
Quarrie William 1902
Sandys George 1899
Stredder William 1899   The Grove
Thurnall Harry J 1899 (Melbourn St 1902)
Thurnall John E 1899 (Melbourn St 1902)
Thurnall Mrs 1899 (Melbourn St 1902)
Warren Charles 1902 (London Rd 1899)
Watts Miss West Cottage 1902
Whyatt Charles

HIGH STREET

Archer Herbert Ray MD
Cautherley George
Daintry William
Fordham Frederick Nash Bank House
Fordham Percy Frederick Bank House
Gamble Alfred 1899 (London Rd 1902)
Phillips George F Archway House 1902
Squire Mrs 1899 London Rd 1902
Titchmarsh Walter

SUN HILL

Beale Walter Sun Hill House
Nash Henry Dalton Mount Lodge 1899
King William B   Mount Lodge 1902

BACK STREET

Vaughan Edward
Vaughan Joseph

MARKET HILL/PLACE

Lewis Rev WT (Cong)
Smith Rivers R

CHURCH LANE

Noades John

THE WARREN

Beale Mrs 1902
Farnham William 1899
Leete Miss 1902
Smith The Misses 1899

MELBOURN STREET

Bevan David Augustus The Priory
Frost Alfred George
Hewson Fred The Roystons
Marshall Miss 1902
Nash Miss
Phillips Joseph Edward Jun
Phillips The Misses 1902
Pyne Mrs 1899
Sherrard Richard
Smith James
Smith Mrs 1902
Stockbridge Horatio
Thurnall H J 1902 (Baldock St 1899)
Thurnall John E 1902 (Baldock St 1899)
Thurnall Mrs 1902 (Baldock St 1899)
Tuke Henry S
Windsor Charles 1902

MELBOURN ROAD

Balding Daniel Barley   The Beeches
Lomas Rev Thomas Henry (Wesleyan) 1899
Wade George 1902 (Kneesworth Rd 1899)
Fordham Emily Selwyn

LONDON ROAD

Besant William LW 1902
Bullard Mrs   South Bank
Cautherley Miss
Davies Miss 1902
Farnham William 1902 (The Warren 1899)
Godber Miss 1902
Goodland Gilmore 1902
Harrison Rev J   The Vicarage
Mitchell Walter Rose Cottage
Saunderson Mrs 1902
Smith Rev John Frederick 1899
Squire Mrs 1902 (High St 1899)
Stockbridge William Pearce
Titchmarsh Alfred   Flint Hall Farm 1902

Kneesworth Rd 1899
Warren C Hill View1899 (Baldock Rd 1902)
Wortham Hale DL 1899

NEWMARKET ROAD

Bailey Mrs Elmwood House
Goodman Thomas   The Plantation

BARKWAY ST

Trudgett John 1902 (Kneesworth St 1899)

GEORGE LANE

Barron Benjamin

GREEN STREET

Rand William

Kingston M Whitehall
Packer Rev George Hillside
Sanderson Rev Ernest H   York House

Houses & Accommodation Wanted and To Let.

TO LET, in Royston, a small convenient HOUSE with Garden. Apply to T. Goodman, Royston.

TO LET BEDROOM and SITTING-ROOM Furnished to Let, suitable for invalid lady (trained nurse). Terms according to requirements. Address, "F.N" *Reporter* Office, Royston.

TO LET on London Road, Royston, eight-roomed HOUSE, with nice garden; high and healthy situation. Apply, Bullard, South Bank, Royston

---

WANTED, small house, Royston or neighbourhood, £10 to £12. Apply, by letter, to "House", Office of this Paper.

TO BE LET, 2 SEMI-DETACHED HOUSES With gardens, immediate possession. Apply ABBOTT & SON, UPHOLSTERERS, ROYSTON.

WANTED, for August and September, Furnished House, in or near Royston; two to three sitting rooms, six or seven bedrooms. Write with particulars, Z.Z. Office of this Paper.

WANTED, small HOUSE,of about eight rooms, with good garden, in detached position. Kelly, The Elms, Ashwell.

TO LET FURNISHED APARTMENTS, Bath (h & c), Board if required. Apply, Mrs. L. Jacklin, Melrose, Mill Road, Royston, Herts.

WANTED, for month of August, 1 sitting and double-bedded room, in or near Royston, preference given to a farm; lady, gentleman and 1 child. Reply, W. F., 3 Wilson Road, Southend-on-Sea.

WANTED, a detached country COTTAGE, 4 or 5 bedrooms, 2 or 3 sitting rooms, with good garden with flower garden, trees, &c., and small kitchen garden, small orchard and meadow desirable rent £40 to £50. Herts or borders of Cambridgeshire, about 3 miles from station on G.N.R. Stable and coach-house. Good water supply and drainage.
Address, H. M. *Reporter* Office, Royston, Herts..

TO BE LET, detached Residence, containing 8 rooms, pleasantly situated in well-timbered grounds, 1½ miles of Royston Station, on main road, inclusive rent £30.
Auctioneers' Offices; Royston, Herts.

WANTED, small House, Royston or neighbourhood, £10 to £12. Apply by letter, to 'House', Office of this paper.

A Typical Wedding Scene

The back of this photograph was inscribed 'Nip Reynolds' Wedding'. It is by no means certain but it may have been the wedding of Ernest William Reynolds to Kate Draper which took place in the Parish Church on July 5th, 1900. *(Royston Museum Collection)*

A Prize Winning Dog

This is a photograph of one of the prize winning Smooth Fox Terriers owned by Mr. G. W. Howard. They sported such names as Royston Remus, and Royston Recorder.*(Royston Museum Collection*)

A selection of the money in circulation in 1900.

Some of this was still in circulation for many years after this date and will be remembered, probably with affection, by people who grew up during pre-decimal days. The date stamp gives some indication of the life of the notes.

Although there were notes of higher denominations, the five pound note would have been the most familiar to ordinary people. It was printed in black and white and was quite large by today's standards, measuring 8 inches by 5 inches.
Printed courtesy of the Bank of England.

Pictured above:-

crown - worth 5/- (25p)
half-crown - worth 2/6d (12½p)
florin - worth 2/- (10p)
shilling - worth 1/- (5p)
sixpence - 6d (2½p)

*threepence - 3d
*one penny - 1d
*halfpenny - ½d
*one farthing - ¼d

*no realistic comparison
 with decimal currency.

In addition to these the gold sovereign (about the size of a £1 coin) and the smaller gold half-sovereign were in circulation.

It was possible to obtain a five pound and two pound gold coin but they were not in common usage.

Illustrations courtesy of Spink and Son, London.

A Cause for Sadness

Original in Royston Museum

Although this memorial card is dated 1901, it is very relevant as this records the death of the baby baptised in the Parish Church on May 13th, 1900. The name Baden Powell would have been chosen as he was a popular figure of the Boer War. He was the commander of the forces at the relieving of Mafeking. The same Baden Powell later went on to form the Scout movement.

The Absent-Minded Beggar

This song was written by Rudyard Kipling during the Boer War and was intended for public performance. It was set to music by Sir Arthur Sullivan and featured regularly in social occasions in the town during 1900, for example, it was sung at the annual meeting of the Conservative Club in February and at their celebrations for the Queen's Birthday in May.

When you've shouted "Rule Britannia," when you've sung "God Save the Queen",
When you've finished killing Kruger with your mouth,
Will you kindly drop a shilling in my little tambourine
For a gentleman in khaki ordered South?
He's an absent-minded beggar, and his weaknesses are great,
But we and Paul must take him as we find him.
He is out of active service, wiping something off a slate,
And he's left a lot of little things behind him!
Duke's son - cook's son - son of a hundred kings -
(Fifty thousand horse and foot going to Table Bay!)
Each of them doing his country's work (and who's to look after their things?)
Pass the hat for your credit's sake, and pay! pay! pay!

There are girls he married secret, asking no permission to,
For he knew he wouldn't get it if he did.
There is gas and coal and vittles, and the house rent falling due,
And it's more than rather likely there's a kid.
There are girls he walked with casual, they'll be sorry now he's gone,
For an absent-minded beggar they will find him
But it ain't the time for sermons with the winter coming on.
We must help the girl that Tommy's left behind him!
Cook's son - Duke's son - son of a belted Earl -
Son of a Lambeth publican - its all the same to-day!
Each of them doing his country's work (and who's to look after the girl?)
Pass the hat for your credit's sake, and pay! pay! pay!

There are families by thousands, far too proud to beg or speak,
And they'll put their sticks and bedding up the spout,
And they'll live on half o' nothing paid 'em punctual once a week,
'Cause the man that earns the wage is ordered out.
He's an absent-minded beggar, but he heard his country call,
And his reg'ment didn't need to send to find him.
He chucked his job and joined it - so the job before us all
Is to help the home that Tommy's left behind him!
Duke's job - cook's job - gardener, baronet, groom -
Mews or palace or paper-shop - there's someone gone away!
Each of them doing his country's work (and who's to look after the room?)
Pass the hat for your credit's sake, and pay! pay! pay!

Let us manage so as, later, we can look him in the face,
And tell him - what he'd very much prefer -
That, while he saved the Empire his employer saved his place,
And his mates (that's you and me) looked out for *her*.
He's an absent-minded beggar and he may forget it all,
But we do not want his kiddies to remind him,
That we sent 'em to the workhouse while their daddy hammered Paul,
So we'll help the homes that Tommy left behind him.
Cook's home - Duke's home - home of a millionaire -
(Fifty thousand horse and foot going to Table Bay!)
Each of 'em doing his country's work (and what have you got to spare?)
Pass the hat for your credit's sake, and pay! pay! pay1

THE NEWS IN BRIEF
Royston
1900

This section is compiled on a monthly basis using articles appearing in the *Herts and Cambs Reporter (Royston Crow)* for the year 1900. In addition there are details of school life from the Heads' logbooks of the British School and the National Schools Girls' Section, (the logbook of the Boys' Section before 1905 has disintegrated) and details from the Parish Registers.

The *Herts and Cambs Reporter* at that time was a 'broad sheet' newspaper, much larger than the present day newspaper. The size of the print was extremely small and there were few illustrations. Consequently an enormous amount of information could be presented. To provide as extensive coverage of events as possible, it has been necessary to edit some of the articles a great deal. A book of twice the size of this publication would have been needed to reproduce them in their entirety.

In the interpretation, which has been adopted in transcribing the articles, some adaptation has been necessary. At that time sentences tended to be very long and complex in construction, there was greater use of capital letters for emphasis and differences in the use of vocabulary and punctuation. Also many of the articles were very long-winded and filled with details of the minutiae of the occasion. Where possible the original language has been used but if complexity and verbosity has hidden the essential detail, alterations have been made, hopefully not spoiling the effects that the writers were trying to convey.

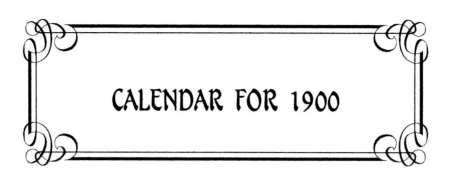

CALENDAR FOR 1900

	JANUARY					
S	M	T	W	T	F	S
	1	2	3	4	5	6
7	8	9	10	11	12	13
14	15	16	17	18	19	20
21	22	23	24	25	26	27
28	29	30	31			

	MAY					
S	M	T	W	T	F	S
		1	2	3	4	5
6	7	8	9	10	11	12
13	14	15	16	17	18	19
20	21	22	23	24	25	26
27	28	29	30	31		

	SEPTEMBER					
S	M	T	W	T	F	S
						1
2	3	4	5	6	7	8
9	10	11	12	13	14	15
16	17	18	19	20	21	22
23	24	25	26	27	28	29
30						

	FEBRUARY					
S	M	T	W	T	F	S
				1	2	3
4	5	6	7	8	9	10
11	12	13	14	15	16	17
18	19	20	21	22	23	24
25	26	27	28			

	JUNE					
S	M	T	W	T	F	S
					1	2
3	4	5	6	7	8	9
10	11	12	13	14	15	16
17	18	19	20	21	22	23
24	25	26	27	28	29	30

	OCTOBER					
S	M	T	W	T	F	S
	1	2	3	4	5	6
7	8	9	10	11	12	13
14	15	16	17	18	19	20
21	22	23	24	25	26	27
28	29	30	31			

	MARCH					
S	M	T	W	T	F	S
				1	2	3
4	5	6	7	8	9	10
11	12	13	14	15	16	17
18	19	20	21	22	23	24
25	26	27	28	29	30	31

	JULY					
S	M	T	W	T	F	S
1	2	3	4	5	6	7
8	9	10	11	12	13	14
15	16	17	18	19	20	21
22	23	24	25	26	27	28
29	30	31				

	NOVEMBER					
S	M	T	W	T	F	S
				1	2	3
4	5	6	7	8	9	10
11	12	13	14	15	16	17
18	19	20	21	22	23	24
25	26	27	28	29	30	

	APRIL					
S	M	T	W	T	F	S
1	2	3	4	5	6	7
8	9	10	11	12	13	14
15	16	17	18	19	20	21
22	23	24	25	26	27	28
29	30					

	AUGUST					
S	M	T	W	T	F	S
			1	2	3	4
5	6	7	8	9	10	11
12	13	14	15	16	17	18
19	20	21	22	23	24	25
26	27	28	29	30	31	

	DECEMBER					
S	M	T	W	T	F	S
						1
2	3	4	5	6	7	8
9	10	11	12	13	14	15
16	17	18	19	20	21	22
23	24	25	26	27	28	29
30	31					

JANUARY

New Year Services

At the Parish Church, in consequence of New Year's Eve falling on Sunday, the usual midnight service was not held, but the ordinary evening service at 6.30 was of a special character. The full choral service commenced with the well-known hymn, "O God our help in ages past," and the other hymns were appropriate to the occasion. The Vicar, Rev. J. Harrison, read the lessons and the service was intoned by the curate, Rev. A. T. Boodle. The sermon was preached by the Vicar, who took for his text Genesis iii, 9, "Where art thou?" upon which the congregation were reminded of the personal application of this question to each individual life.

On Sunday a midnight service was held in the John Street Church Schoolroom. This was the only midnight service held in the town and in consequence there was a good number present, representatives from the other Nonconformist churches taking part.

The departure of the old year and the advent of the new was signalized by the ringers at the Parish Church who rang a peal of bells shortly before midnight, and during the next hour the music of the handbells was heard in the streets which were perambulated by the ringers in accordance with their annual custom.

[No mention was made in the report of moving into the next century. Remember 1901 had been officially designated as the start of the new century]

SCHOOL NEWS

British Mixed School

On January 8th school was reopened with an attendance of 158 out of 172 on the books. The staff for 1900 were Mr. Charles Freston (Headmaster), J. Clarke, D. Norman and E. Bement. On January 12th the Head reported that attendance had been poor owing to the great amount of sickness in the town.

On Friday evening, January 26th at 7 o'clock, the prize distribution took place. A good number of parents and friends were present. The prizes consisted of books, 11 of which were 'specials' given to children who had not missed a single attendance or been late once during the year. Prizes for good writing and good conduct were given by friends to Anne Mobbies, Nelson Fardwell, George Hinkins and Edward Cane and a workbox by Miss Clarke to May Gaylor for improvement in Needlework.

The Prize Giving

The subsequent account in the *Royston Crow* reported as follows, "....specimens of the scholars' work in the form of drawing, writing and some tempting cookery by the girls, were arranged round the room and on the master's desk were piled up volumes of books to be given as prizes. The children carried out a programme of music and drill under the direction of Mr. Freston, and acquitted themselves so well - especially in the dumb-bell exercises and musical drill - that all present must have been delighted with the young people's part in the performance." Mr. Freston continued the proceedings by outlining the general administration of the school and its attendance and reminded parents of the requirements of the law on school attendance. Mr. Beale and Mr. Titchmarsh also addressed the parents, praising the good work and speaking about the value of education for their children.

The Inspector's Report

The tone, discipline, and attainment of this school alike bear high testament of the zeal and skill of the teachers. The attendance continues to be extremely good.

Amount of Grant Awarded after Inspection (British School)

Principal Grant	14.	0.	On average attendance	148 @ 20/6	£154. 14.	0.
Discipline and organisation	1.	6.	Needlework girls	76 @ 1/-	3. 16.	0.
Singing by note	2.	0.	Drawing boys	71 @ 1/9	6. 4.	3.
Object Lesson (Geography)	2.	0.	Cookery girls	20 @ 4/-	8. 0.	0.
English	2.	0.			£165. 14.	3.
	20.	6.				

National School (Girls' Section).

School Returns.

On January 8th, school re-assembled and the Headmistress, Miss M.C. Greenstreet, reported that only 113 were present. A great deal of influenza in the town accounted for the poor attendance. Staff for 1900 were L.M. Higgins, E. Bedwell, Florence Ainger (probationer), and G. E. Greenhill (monitress). Cookery classes were re-opened.

H.M.I. Report for 1899

The tone of this school is excellent; discipline maintains the improvement previously noted. The teachers show conscientious care although they do not quite reach the level required for the higher grant. The fourth standard arithmetic, the fifth standard spelling and mental work are the points requiring attention. If a good staff is maintained there seems to be a probability that the higher grant may be deserved next year. The re-flooring of the room is a great improvement

Bridge House School

At the examinations in the third class of the College of Preceptors, held in December, five pupils of the Bridge House School (Miss F. Ashton) were examined and all of them passed.

COUNCIL AFFAIRS

Cowsheds

The Drainage Committee presented a report as to the Cowsheds in the District, showing that in five cases the Cowsheds were not in accordance with the New Regulations, either as to lighting, ventilation and drainage, and recommended that notices be served upon the occupiers requiring the defects complained of be remedied.

Milk and Tuberculosis

The clerk of Royston Urban District Council has received a long letter from the London County Council on the subject of milk and tuberculosis in respect of milk sent up from the country to London, but he did not think it applied to this District as it was not thought that milk was sent up to London from the Royston Urban District.

Access

Mr. James Smith applied for a licence to stage plays in the Royston Institute until May. However, discussion took place about the fact that at an earlier performance, a late arrival was unable to gain access and there was concern that in the event of a panic there might be difficulty in getting out. It was decided that a man should be placed at the door at all times during performances.

Slaughter House

An application to register premises on Fish Hill as a slaughter house was rejected as it was not considered a good thing to have any slaughter houses in the middle of town.

Footpaths

The Highways Committee presented a report at the January meeting of the Council on the subject of paving and footpaths. The state of various footpaths had been studied and certain works were deemed necessary to put all the footways in a satisfactory condition. Several recommendations were made. Examples - *Kneesworth Street*, east side - from Queen's Road to the Old Palace - York kerb, path of Victoria Stone with granite setts in gateways: *Barkway Street, north side* - from corner of Boar's Head to corner of road to Police Station, York kerb, gravel path with granite setts in gateway: *Church Lane* - From cesspool in front of Mr. J. Noades' house to north end of Church Room - drain for storm water with path of Victoria stone over. From Melbourn Street to Lady Dacre's Room, tar path.

The Surveyor's total estimated cost was £971. 3s. 0d.

THE BOER WAR
LOCAL VOLUNTEERS FOR SOUTH AFRICA

Enthusiastic Send-Off for E Company Men

As part of the 8,000 Volunteers for service at the Front, drawn from the Volunteer Battalions throughout the country, one company of 110 men were called from the Volunteer Battalions of the Bedford Regimental District. Three men from E (Royston) Company, from 18 who had volunteered, were selected to represent the Company after passing a medical examination: Privates Sell, Harper and Bidnell.

On Tuesday, January 23rd, the departure of the E Company men from Royston aroused a good deal of interest, not only among the E Company, but among the townspeople. Assembling at the Armoury in Melbourn Street at 1.30 p.m., the members of the Company appeared in uniform and were attended by the Band. The Rev. J. Harrison, the Chaplain of the Company, was present to see the men off, headed by the Band playing "Soldiers of the Queen", and accompanied by some hundreds of people, the men marched to join the 2.30 p.m. train for Hitchin and Hertford. At the Railway Station the crowd of well wishers was largely increased.

The E Company men were drawn up in the station yard facing their three comrades about to depart for the Front, and in this position they were addressed by Captain Cautherley in a few suitable cheering words. He said, ".... the three men were in an enviable position on being selected to represent their Company.... He could assure the three men that their comrades at home and the people of the town and neighbourhood would be all interested in their fortunes at the Front and would anxiously follow the papers to see what the Hertfordshire men were doing..." On behalf of the Company he wished them, "God speed, good luck and a speedy and safe return."

The three men were provided with a generous outfit thanks to local gifts added to the Government allowance. The following items in the outfit were provided officially, but in several cases increased: 2 pairs of boots, 1 pair of canvas shoes, 1 pair of braces (increased to 2), 1 cloth brush, 1 razor and shaving brush, 2 pairs of socks (increased to 4), 1 towel (increased to 2), 1 tin of dubbin (increased to 4). To the above the following were added 1 small enamelled plate and mug, 1 large knife and cord, 1 small knife, fork and spoon, 1lb. of soap, 2 wooden pipes, 1lb. of tobacco, 2 shirts and 1 housewife.

Letters from South Africa

Extracts from letter to Mrs Ilett of Garden Walk, from her husband, *Lance-Corporal Ilett* of the Suffolk Regiment from Green Point, South Africa. First he describes his journey out to Africa via Madeira, then goes on to say, "......my work is to escort the Boer prisoners. They are a big raw-boned lot of men with plenty of pluck in them; so I expect we have not got an easy job with them........I don't look forward to a pleasant Christmas. I expect to go to the front which they say is at a distance of 20 days march................ It is very hot here, and what with the black kind of dust, I am more like a sweep than a soldier..... Things are very dear here, whiskey 20s. a bottle, tobacco 8s. lb. and beer 1s. a quart...........I must close now as it is getting dark and we are not allowed any lights."

Trooper W. Hart, of the 1st Life Guards, son of Inspector Hart of Royston Police Station, wrote home from Cape Town, telling of the work other than fighting, which the soldiers in South Africa had to do. Whilst in Cape Town he describes, "breaking mules for our men in case our horses get killed or lost". He was also "anxious to get up country to try my luck. We see plenty of white people here (Cape Town). They are very kind and gave us a good tea on Christmas Day, only the worst of it is the weather is so very hot".

Corvus Cornix Comments

It is a gratifying feature about the present struggle in South Africa, that with every new branch of our forces raised for service at the front a special effort accompanies it in the direction of nursing and hospital accommodation.   Probably in no War ever entered into has a more comprehensive organisation been provided for those who have the misfortune to be wounded..........The calling out of a force of the Imperial Yeomanry has suggested scope for this force to have a Field Hospital of its own. An appeal has been made to this end. That this particular Yeomanry Hospital has peculiar claims upon the generosity needs no enforcing.The Royston District has, in proportion to the population, a very large number of men at the Front, and hitherto has been exceedingly fortunate in regard to casualties. However, losses of the Suffolks, which include Cambridgeshire, have brought home to this district what war means. Immediate neighbours Shingay, Melbourn and Bassingbourn have losses to record.

Wounded from South Africa

The Committee of Royston Hospital decided to place two of their beds at the disposal of the War Office in connection with the wounded arriving from South Africa.   They asked, if their offer was accepted, for men from Herts and Cambs.

Purchase of Horses

A buyer of horses for the Army was in the town on Thursday and it is understood that he obtained some suitable purchases from the district.

Amount Raised from War Fund Entertainments

Collected during the performance and sent to the *Daily Mail Fund* £12 16s. 0d.
Other receipts (less expenditure of £6 16s. 9d.) - £28 4s. 9d. sent to *Mansion House Fund.*

Rare Bird

Mr. Joseph Nunn wrote to the newspaper concerning a bird, rarely if ever, seen in this country: "A fine example of the rare bird the tawny pipit - Anthus Campestris - was feeding on the lawn, within a few yards of my house, on Sunday morning".

Two Accidents

On Thursday an accident occurred to a man named Henry King in the employ of Mr. L. E. Clark. While he was riding a horse he was thrown, fell upon his head and was badly cut. He was taken to the surgery and received medical attention.

Mr. A Porter, High Street, met with an unfortunate accident when in the street near his shop. He came into conflict with a cyclist and had a bad fall, and is, we learn, suffering from shock.

Death on the Way Home

An inquest was held early in the month on the death of Solomon Christmas aged 62. He was found dead on the way home from work. Various people gave information. J. L. Ward of the Plough said that he had resided at the Plough for three years. He was a tailor by trade but had generally worked as a labourer. During the previous month he had often complained of feeling unwell. His brother, Abraham, who had not seen him for 15 years, thought he had a wife and child. On the day of his death he was working at cutting chaff with Edward Webb who related that the deceased had been unwell. On his way home, he found Christmas unable to continue and went to fetch a trap for the deceased but he was dead when he returned. The coroner had found the deceased well nourished and there had been no sign of injury. His heart and lungs, however, had been found to be diseased and that in his opinion was the cause of death.

PETTY SESSIONS
Asleep without lights

Joseph Racher, of Royston, was charged with being the driver of a wagon without a light in the Melbourn Road. He was fined 10s with costs. He was further charged with being asleep whilst in charge of the same wagon at the same time and place. As he had already been fined, the Bench dismissed the case.

Also, *Herbert Jones*, a boy, was fined 5s. for having a cart without lights in the Baldock Road.

Drunk to Drown Sorrows

Daniel Rosendale, was charged with being drunk and disorderly on January 8th at Royston. The defendant said that he was excited for his wife lay dead at the time. He supposed he was guilty. He was incapable. P.c. Gray said he saw the defendant holding on to a fence, drunk and incapable, surrounded by children. He was a man who never did any work. The chairman said that he didn't have to work if he was a man of independent means but he would have to pay 6s. The defendant agreed to do this and said he was obliged to the Bench and to the policeman who took him home.

Slippery Customers

Seven Royston boys were each fined 6d, after being charged with sliding on the highway in Royston in December. They were warned not to do it again. They were *Archibald Barron, William Pigg, George Coote, Herbert King, Thomas Ward, Victor Pratt and Harry Garner.*

Sad Death of Elias Bateson

By the death of Mr. Elias Bateson, which took place on Tuesday, January 9th, after a long illness, the town has lost one of the oldest tradesmen, he having been in business in the High Street as a cabinet maker and upholsterer for nearly fifty years. He was of a quiet and retiring disposition, and devoted the whole of his time and energies to the carrying on of his business. During his career he was called upon to sustain very severe trials in the loss of his three children, his eldest son at an early age, and the other son and daughter after a promising career opening before them, one in a prominent part of his father's business, and the other as headmistress of Gamlingay Board School. About six years ago he lost his wife, a severe blow, from which he never recovered. He had been confined to his bed for nearly two and a half years and he bore his heavy affliction with great patience and resignation, and passed away peacefully. The deceased was 71 years of age. The funeral will take place in the Kneesworth Street Congregational Chapel Burial Ground.

THE BOARD OF GUARDIANS

Water and the Workhouse

An estimate for the cost of a water supply to the workhouse had been received for 1s per 1000 gallons. The Water Company was prepared to carry the 2 inch pipe on the Baldock Road to the workhouse gate free. The requirements of the workhouse are for 500-1000 gallons. It was recommended that 1inch service pipe be laid from the company 2 inch main to the cistern in the roof and a stop-cock on the ground floor and a ball-cock in the cistern.

The editor of the *Herts & Cambs Reporter* made the point that it was not very clear from the minutes if the committee recommended the entire substitution of the water supply for that now taken from a well on the workhouse property or merely a connection with the Company's mains to enable them to supplement the supply when pumping labour is insufficient. The editor thought that, considering the reasonable terms offered, the Guardians should convert to a full mains supply.

A Treat

A letter was read from the owner of Hilda's Performing Dogs offering to present a free show for the inmates. This offer was accepted with thanks and it was left to the master to arrange a time.

Boarding Out

Mr. A P. Humphry, on behalf of the Children's Boarding-Out Committee, reported that there are now 15 children boarded out under their supervision. During the past year one girl has gone to service and supports herself, while two children have been returned to the Workhouse; in one case at the request of the foster parent, and in the other at the request of the lady visitor who considered the home unsatisfactory. Three other children have been boarded out in new homes during the year. The reports of the visitors, medical officers and schoolmasters, continue to be satisfactory. The Committee will be glad to hear of suitable homes and persons willing to take charge of children. There are now two children in the Workhouse waiting for homes.

Observations of the Editor on the New Century and the Elections

There will be no Parish Council Elections in 1900. That is a very significant fact because it is one which will interest the largest number of places in the country. The reason why, is not at all a sentimental one. It is not because there will be no leap year when in the ordinary way a leap year would have been due; and it is nothing to do with the dispute about when the Twentieth Century begins, or the incapacity of some people to take the trouble to see the absurdity in which the counting of 1900 as the first year of a new century would land you. No, it is simply due to Parliament and the local Government Board, acting perhaps on intuition that the parochial life of England might be spoiled by too much of a good thing, and the ambitious Parish Councillor be tempted to drift away to the Towns for the greater dignity of a Town Councillor. So it has come about the Parish Councils are to be triennial. The Councillors now in office are to remain until April, 1901, and after that the elections will be for three years to bring them into line in this district with the District Councils.

The Urban District Council and the Institute

A public inquiry before the Local Government Board Inspector was held on the subject of an application by the Royston Urban District Council to borrow £340 for the purchase and adaptation of the Institute for public offices and £150 for a contribution towards the cost of paving certain main road footpaths.

The formal transfer of the Institute only awaits the settlement of the question of how money should be raised. The terms of the resolution agreeing to the transfer of the building were that the Council was to take over all existing liabilities. These included a sum of about £90, due to the bankers, arising out of the renovation scheme carried out 15 years previously and never cleared off.

In consequence of no repairs having been carried out upon the building, it had got into a condition requiring a thorough renovation . The necessary adaptation of parts of the building for the purpose of Council meetings and a proposed new exit staircase for the safety of the public using the building were estimated to cost £340 and, as it was considered unfair to tax the ratepayers, the loan was required. The same thoughts governed the application for £150 for paving certain footpaths.

Mr. Banham produced plans of the proposed alterations and the inspector went over the building and appeared well pleased with the substantial character of the building and with the proposals for improving the building to the uses required by the Council and for the safety and convenience of the public using it.

Death of Orris Beale

The deceased, aged 65 years, was born in Royston in 1835. On leaving school he entered service and acquired a knowledge of the drapery trade. At the age of 19 he found himself surrounded by companions who, like many throughout the kingdom, were induced by the reports of gold discoveries in Australia to leave their native home and cross the sea. The deceased left England in 1854 and became engaged in the same class of business in Sydney. After a period of 17 years he paid a visit to his old home and later that year he was married to Miss E. Leete. They subsequently removed to Newbury where he was in business for 27 years. In the early part of 1899, he retired from business and returned to Royston where it was hoped he would be able to enjoy a few years of well-earned rest and leisure. Unhappily these hopes have not been realised, for it was found after he returned to Royston that he was suffering from a disease of the heart. Despite the skill and assiduous attentions of the doctors, and of professional nursing he succumbed to the painful malady. His death will be deeply regretted by a large circle of relatives and friends, by whom he was greatly esteemed for his cheerful disposition and generous warm-hearted conduct towards those with whom he was associated.

THE DISSOLUTION OF A PARTNERSHIP

ASHWELL STATION, BALDOCK, HERTS
January 15th, 1900
We beg to give you notice that the firm of
FORDHAM & HOWARD
Coal merchants of Royston, Ashwell, Baldock, and elsewhere, has dissolved partnership by mutual agreement from January 15th, 1900. The entire business is now transferred, and will be carried on by Mr Sydney H. Fordham under the name of
S.H. FORDHAM & Co.
Mr. G.W. HOWARD who is retiring from the business takes no part in the management from this date.
Messrs. S.H. FORDHAM & Co., will retain the services of Mr. G.S. BAKER, at Royston, and Mr. G.H. KIDD, at Baldock, who will continue to give every attention to your esteemed orders. The address of the firm will be as above.

BRITANNIA HOUSE,
ROYSTON , HERTS
January 15th, 1900

MR. GEORGE W. HOWARD, while thanking his friends and the public for the kind support and patronage, for so many years past conferred upon him whilst a partner in the firm of FORDHAM AND HOWARD, Coal Merchants, begs to inform them that the partnership hitherto existing between him and Mr. Sydney H. Fordham has been dissolved by mutual agreement, and that, not having disposed of his share in the goodwill of the said business, it is his intention to continue to carry on the Coal Trade as usual in Royston and the Neighbourhood under the name and style of
G.W. HOWARD & Co.
Mr. Howard trusts that his long connection with the Business will assure to him a continuance of support and be a sufficient guarantee to the Public that their requirements will always receive careful, personal attention.
Quotations of all descriptions of Coal and Coke in small or large quantities will be forwarded on application.
All orders for the present will be received at the above address.

Volunteers for the Front
To Serve with the Yeomanry
J. Pickett, son of Mr and Mrs Pickett, of the Green Man.
W. Mumford, son of the late Mr John Mumford, formerly trainer at Heath House.
C. Hollebone, also trainer at Royston, a few years ago.
To Serve with the London Imperial Volunteers
Fred Greenhill, son of Mr and Mrs Greenhill, of the White Bear.

Bagatelle Match

The friendly contests between members of the Young Men's Church Association and the Nonconformist Young Men's Society, were resumed on Wednesday evening at the rooms of the last named society.

ROYSTON PARISH CHURCH
BAPTISMS

January
14th   James Guy, son of James Edward Jarvis (Brewer) and Rosa Emily Jarvis.
Gertrude Osborne daughter of George Bowen (Gardener) and Ellen Adora Bowen.

MARRIAGES

6th   Arthur John Lavercombe (Clerk) to Olive Laura Stonebridge.

BURIALS

January
3rd   Habika Maclay Nunn, of Marylebone, aged 76 years.
13th   Emma Groom, of Stroud Green, aged 54 yeaars.
Solomon Christmas, aged 62 years.
15th   Mary Ann Rosendale, aged 66 years.
Mary Reynolds, aged 79 years.
George Pearman, of Barkway, aged 63 years.
30th   Elizabeth Grace Banham, aged 28 years.

Two burial services were conducted by the Congregational Church.
Mr Orris Beale, on January 2nd, aged 65 years.
Mr Elias Bateson, on January 12th, aged 71 years.

Other deaths reported:
William Fortune on January 11th at Royston Workhouse, aged 60 years.

SPORT
An Unusual Match on the Heath

A hockey match of an unusual character was played on the Heath, between Royston Football Club and the Hockey Club. The footballers seemed to have the advantage because one or two of the usual hockey players also play football, but as the rest seemed almost equally at home with the sticks, even though they had not played before, a good game was witnessed. Result: Hockey Club 4 - Football Club 3

Golf
January
6th   Monthly Medal Competition.
18th   Captain's Prize Competition.

Football
January
13th   Royston v Camb. Rovers (away). Score 1- 4.
Royston 2nd XI v Melbourn 2nd XI (on Heath). Score 10 - 1.
20th   Royston v Baldock (on Heath). Score 7 - 1
27th   YMCA v NYMS. Score 2 - 1.

Hockey
January
25th   Royston v Pembroke College (on Heath). Score 1- 4.
30th   Royston v Emmanuel College (on Heath). Result - a draw.

NEWS FROM THE SOCIETIES

**ROYSTON AND DISTRICT
WOMEN'S LIBERAL ASSOCIATION
THE ANNUAL
PUBLIC MEETING**
Will be held in the
KNEESWORTH STREET SCHOOLROOM
On Wednesday, JANUARY 17TH
When the address will be delivered by
MRS GWYNETH VAUGHAN
AND OTHERS
CHAIR TO BE TAKEN AT 7 30 P.M.

Royston Women's Liberal Association

The advertised meeting was duly held in the Kneesworth Street Congregational Schoolroom. Mrs. E. O. Fordham had been unable to preside and her place was taken by W. C. Titchmarsh. In a short introductory speech, he spoke of the public life during the four-and-a-half years of Conservative Government as a period of constant alarms, culminating in the crisis which had involved them in the War in the Transvaal.

Mrs Gwyneth Vaughan then addressed the meeting, especially on the Labour Market for Women.

She knew that the Liberal Camp was divided over the War in South Africa and that this should "stir them up to further activity to secure votes for women, so that they might have a voice in the administation of the laws of Empire...................."

She was sorry about the stringent restrictions which ruled the labour market for women. So long as women had no voice in the Government who made the laws of the country, they ought not to restrict women from earning their own living. Since the restrictions came into force women were being driven out of the market.. As an instance of these regulations she stated that one large employer now employed 30% less women......... It was true that domestic service was paid much better but all women could not turn their hand in this direction and in other branches of labour women's wages were getting lower. She urged the members to "put their shoulders to the wheel thus to get women placed on a more equal footing in the labour market and it behoved them to make it easier for those who came after them."

ROYSTON UNITED TEETOTAL SOCIETY
On THURSDAY NEXT, JAN. 18TH
At 8.0 p.m.
IN JOHN STREET SCHOOL-ROOM.
ADDRESS BY
Mr. J. R. WETHERILL.
(Of Oxford)

Royston Town Cricket Club

The annual meeting of the club was held in the Victoria Restaurant on Tuesday, January 30th, 1900 There were present-Messrs. S. Camps, T.S. Higgins, T. Percy, W.C. Titchmarsh, A. T. Titchmarsh, C. H. Titchmarsh. Charles Warren and E. Williamson. Mr T.S. Higgins was voted to the Chair.

The report for 1899 was read. The season was on the whole a satisfactory one. Ten matches were played of which four were won, three lost and three drawn.

The matches won were against, Grove Athletic, Hitchin, Mr. Wilkinson's X1, and Lord Robarts X1. Those matches lost were against The Tom Tits, The Nihilists, and the Three Counties Asylum.. The drawn matches were against The Leys School, Stamford Hill and Hitchin. The match which had been especially enjoyable had been the one at Wimpole Hall, the team being generously entertained by Lord Robarts.

The performance of the members batting and bowling averages were discussed.

Thanks of the club were extended to the Hon. Subscribers, the Conservators, and to members who had lent their horses to roll the ground.

Mr. Charles Warren, Hon. Treasurer, presented the 1899 balance sheet. The season had commenced with an adverse balance of £1 11s., but the income was increased during 1899. The receipts amounted to £26 5s., and the expenditure £25 15s. 2d. leaving a balance in hand of 9s 10d.

The officers for the coming season were elected as follows:-
President - Mr . F. J. Fordham.
Vice-Presidents - Viscount Clifden, Mr John Phillips, Mr Joseph E. J. Phillips, and Mr D. A. Bevan.
Captain - Mr. Simms Camps.
Vice-Captain - Mr. W. C. Titchmarsh.
Joint Hon. Secs.- Messrs. W. C. Titchmarsh and Charles Warren.
Committee - Rev. A. T. Boodle, Messrs. J. Bailey, Harry Fordham, T. S. Higgins, A. J. Jacklin, T. Percy, Harry Stamford, A.T. Titchmarsh, and A. Walbey.
It was decided to arrange 10 matches against the following clubs: Cambridge "Tom Tits",Cambridge "Nihilists", Camden (Cambridge), Ley's School, Mr. G.S. Wilkinson's X1, Arlesey Asylum, Hitchin (2) and 2 London Clubs on Whit Monday and August Bank Holiday.

Nonconformist Young Men's Society

The second half of the winter session opened on the evening of Friday, January 5th, in the John Street Congregational Schoolroom, with a lecture, with lantern views, on the Boer War.

The lecture was given by Mr. W. C. Titchmarsh, who gave a brief history of the position of the Boers in South Africa, and of the circumstances which led up to the present war, as well as of some of the most interesting places and incidents which had figured very much in the papers. The lantern views shown by Mr. E. W. Stone included a good number of scenes from the earliest stages of the war and of the country, and of conditions of life therein. The lecture, both in description and illustration, proved of a very interesting character. There was a very good attendance of members and others.

JANUARY 19th
A LECTURE
G.E. GREEN, Esq., M.A.., (Cambridge)
Subject--- "PHILIP VAN ARTEVELDE" or "They never fail who die in a great cause."
Collection at the close on behalf of the funds of the society.

Joint Concerns

The Church Army and the Mission Room

On the evening of January 16th, there was an interesting gathering at the National Schools, the larger room being chosen both for convenience, and also as a means of bringing before Church people generally the very excellent work which is being carried on at the Mission Room, at the north end of town, which, under Capt. Pegg, and his predecessor, Capt. Richardson, has more than justified the special effort in coupling with the Mission Room the services of a Church Army representative.

After a few words the Vicar, the Rev J. Harrison, introduced the speaker. This was Captain Thorne from the Church Army Labour Home at Cambridge who spoke about the work of that organisation. There were 70 or 80 Labour Homes throughout the Country and their purpose was to lift those who were down to their lowest depth. There were at the present time over a hundred thousand men, women and children tramping the roads and other poor outcasts vastly outnumbering the Army that was fighting in South Africa. He described the kind of men who were taken into their homes and how they were treated until they had regained their self respect and once again became repectable members of society.

The Vicar then described the work of Captain Pegg, who was doing admirable work at the Mission. He had a constant and systematic way of visiting people and getting at them which the clergy were not always able to do. The Mission Room was a nucleus around which a grand work was growing up for that part of the town and he hoped extending to all parts. The cost of the work was £79 19s. per annum. There was a guarantee of two-thirds of the expenses from two gentlemen and the Mission Room offertories &c. supplied the other third. The Vicar finally expressed his deep gratitude for Capt. Pegg's work, to which he would continue to give his support and prayer.

A WEDDING

On Tuesday, January 16th, the marriage took place at the Kneesworth Street Congregational Church, of Miss Hilda Gertrude Howard, daughter of Mr. James Howard, of Royston, and Mr. George Edward Bull, of Landbeach, in the presence of a number of friends and well wishers. The bride who was given away by her father, was dressed in blue grey and white, and carried a shower bouquet, and wore a gold kerb bracelet and brooch, the gift of the bridegroom. The three bridesmaids (sisters of the bride and groom,) wore pale heliotrope and cream hats, and also carried bouquets. The service was conducted by the Rev. Packer. Miss Jacklin and Miss Butler presided at the organ and the Wedding March was played as the newly married pair left. The three bridesmaids were presented with gold brooches, gifts of the bridegroom. They left by the 5 p.m. express for London for the honeymoon.

Successful Birds

At the Liverpool Poultry and Pigeon Show held this month, Mr. P. F. Fordham, with four exhibits, took 1st, 3rd, and 4th, with Carriers, and a Trumpeter. The entries of pigeons numbered 2,430.

Nursing Association

The offertories at the Parish Church on January 14th were on behalf of the Royston Nursing Association and amounted to £6 9s. 11d.

The Book Club

The Annual meeting of the above Club took place on, Tuesday, January 9th with Mr. W. Beale in the Chair. Various titles of new books were proposed and voted to be purchased for circulation and certain publications were to be discontinued - Lady's Realm, Sunday Strand and English Illustrated.

FEBRUARY

BAD WEATHER

A Great Snowstorm

One of the most severe snowstorms ever remembered in the month of February set in on Tuesday evening, February 13th, at about six o' clock and increased in violence during the evening, until quite a hurricane and a blizzard raged through the night. By daylight on Wednesday morning, it was seen that there had been added to the snow already on the ground from the previous falls, an average fall of about eight inches.

In the streets of Royston by the time the footways were cleared, there were huge walls of snow along each side of the street, the like of which have not been seen for a long time, but it was in its effects upon communication with the surrounding district that the storm did its worst.

The first passenger train reached Royston at ten instead of an hour earlier. The Mail Van which was timed to come through from Hitchin to Royston about 4 a.m. did not start from Hitchin owing to the non-appearance of the connecting London coach, and could not have got through to Royston even if it had started.

The road to Barley was so completely blocked with deep drifts, near the "Eagle Tavern" that it became impossible to get horses and carts through.

Many people who habitually attend Royston Market were unable to travel for the same reason, and some of those who attended the Royston Board of Guardians, finding the road blocked in places, had to drive across the open field. Altogether it was the worst day we have had for many years.

Tobogganing and Skating

The exhiliarating recreation of tobogganing down the hills of the Heath was enjoyed to perfection at the end of last week. Runs were made from the top of Lankester Hill to the Baldock Road. Skating early in the week was indulged in on every available piece of ice in the neighbourhood.

Lack of Snow Clearing (Editor's remarks)

One thing that has been forgotten by many persons in Royston is that the local Bye-laws require occupiers of premises adjoining the pavements and footpaths to move snow from them. Many inhabitants of the town had recognised their duty but there were a good many exceptions, some of which were notable for the extent of snow the unfortunate pedestrians had to trudge through.

The Heath Flooded

On February 16th the Heath was flooded - a rare occurrence. Under ordinary circumstances rainfall on the Heath is lost sight of by speedy absorption. However, the sudden melting of a heavy snowstorm with the ground frozen beneath has the effect of carrying water off before it can soak in. By the end of the day, the water had filled the pond, overflowed into the road and for hours continued down towards Mackerel Hall cottages where it flooded the ground floors. A channel was cut to divert the water into a deep well, no longer used, which was very soon filled to overflowing. Nearby meadows were awash with lakes. During the night, however, the accumulation on the road disappeared. A similar experience had occurred twelve years previously.

THE BOER WAR

The Queen's War Present

Of the chocolate boxes sent out by Her Majesty the Queen, containing chocolate as a present for each of the soldiers serving in South Africa, on New Year's Day, the first to reach Royston has been that sent home by Private G. Wiffen of the Scots Guards, who has sent his box home to Mrs. Wiffen, his mother. The box is a very elegant one both in design and execution, and forming a specially interesting memento of such an occasion.

More E Company Volunteers for the Front

In consequence of some members of the other companies selected being rejected in medical examination, the company was called upon for a further draft. Four additional members were called up for examination, Privates Whitehead and Duce (Royston) and Privates Gayler and Clements (Baldock). Private Clements did not pass the local examination and the other three went to headquarters for examination.

There, Whitehead and Gayler were passed, but Private Duce, in every other respect an eligible man, and the winner of the recruits' prize at the Royston range in 1899, had the disappointment of being rejected through a defect of sight in one of his eyes. As on a previous occasion these two men were given a cheering send off. Captain Cautherley addressing the members of E Company said they could consider themselves to be in the proud position of having sent five men to the front. This gave the company the distinction of sending out a larger number than any other Company in the Battalion. Private Whitehead was presented with £3 6s. by the Conservative Club of which he was a member.

A Disappointing Sequel

Much disappointment was caused when the Volunteers, after proceeding to Headquarters and being sworn in, were rejected, on the slight ground of being a fraction below the usual standard of chest measurement. It seems that when earlier volunteers were rejected, more than were required were called up to fill their places and some had to be stood down. Privates Whitehead and Gayler were not discharged but it was not known if they would eventually be needed. These events caused a good deal of irritation locally, especially as it had happened after the men had passed their medical examination and got their equipment ready.

Letter from the Front

Excerpts from a letter from *Private W. Thair*, of the King's Royal Rifles, to his brother Mr E. Thair, of Royston.

" ....I should like to receive a letter or papers as we never get any news out here. How is the war going on? We only know what we are engaged in ourselves................I expect that before this letter has hardly left the Camp we shall be on our way to Ladysmith to help to support Sir Charles Warren. He has done some splendid work....... but it is such a hard job to get the Boers out of the hills or kopjes as we call them. .... I hope the War will soon finish. It is a job to get anything, as everything is getting so expensive. We can go days and are never able to buy anything, not even tobacco or matches, which is about our only comfort............ We have only the suit we stand up in and when we go on some of these marches we get drowned with rain or else through walking through rivers up to our waist, and after we get in we find we have no blankets, no tents, no towels, and have to walk about all night to get dry and warm, which is no easy matter as the nights are so cold. If the day is very hot, we know it too, as it makes us feel very queer."

The Receipts from the Concert

£12 17s. 6d. from which expenses will have to be deducted.

TRAGEDY AT FARM
Woman Found in a Well
At Flint Hall Farm

A very distressing fatality occurred at Flint Hall Farm, situated on the hill just off the London Road, and in the occupation of Mr. A.T. Titchmarsh. The farm has a house attached occupied by John Hagger, his wife and family, the father and some of the sons being employed on the farm. The family discovered on Monday morning that Mrs Hagger was missing, and when at breakfast time she was not at her usual post attending to her household duties, they naturally became alarmed. The father was ill in bed, and Mrs Hagger had, it seems, suffered from influenza recently, and was noticed to have been at times somewhat strange in manner, and had complained of pains in her head. The house was searched and having failed to find the lady, the search was continued outside. Near the house is an old well-house over a very deep well which goes down through the chalk a distance of nearly 400 feet. Failing everywhere else in their search, the police with the assistance of the blacksmith Mr. J. Bateson and some grappling irons tried the deep well for some time without result, but at last caught on something which proved to be the dress of the deceased and in this way the body was drawn up by the exercise of much patience and care, for the task was a very difficult one. It was seen at once from the severe injuries to the head and face that the poor woman had probably been killed by falling such a tremendous depth before she reached the water.

The jury decided that the deceased had died from the injuries received by falling down the well, but how she got into the well there was no evidence to show. The Coroner asked a question about the age of the deceased and the elder daughter said she believed her mother would have been 51 years of age next month. The deceased had brought up a large family of children, 6 of whom were still at home and naturally very much sympathy was felt for the husband and children.

Fire in Mill Road

A fire broke out at Mr. J.H. Norman's cowsheds near the Gas Works in Mill Road. It appears that the fire broke out in a building adjoining the cowshed. In this building were a cow and two calves. Between nine and ten o'clock, flames were seen rising from the building by Mr. Pearce, Mr. Jackson, of the Gas House, and others. Mr. Norman was sent for, and other assistance was soon on the spot but it was too late to save the building or to save the cow and calves which were burned to death. The poor animals were found lying in a heap in the middle of the ashes of the ruined building where they had been overcome by the flames from which there was no escape. Mr. Norman's losses, it is understood, are covered by insurance.

Skaters were allowed the use of Priory Pond upon the very reasonable condition of a charge of 3d. per head. The sum realized was 9s. 9d. which has been devoted to the Royston Nursing Association.

AT THE WORKHOUSE

Refusing to Work

George Bennett, a stranger in the neighbourhood giving an address in London, was brought up before F. J. Fordham Esq., at the Police Station, on February 1st, charged with neglecting and refusing to perform his task of work, breaking 6 cwt. of granite, while an inmate of the Casual Ward of the Royston Union. The case was proved by E. W. Cleak, the porter, and the prisoner was sent to prison for fourteen days.

Clerk's Offices

At the meeting of the Board of Guardians, the clerk, Mr. Sharpe, mentioned that his offices would cease to be in the High Street and would be removed to premises in Back Street in the rear of the offices of the solicitor Mr. W. B. King.

Medicine for the Paupers

A letter was read from the Local Government Board expressing regret that the Guardians had not seen their way to fall in with the board's suggestion in regard to providing medicines for the poor in the Workhouse.

The Clerk's reply was as follows:- "I am directed by the Guardians of the Royston Union to acknowledge the receipt of your letter of the 27th ult......... and to inform you that as the Workhouse is so small, the Guardians do not consider it desirable to make any change in the arrangements whereby the Medical Officer is required to provide medicines for use in the Workhouse.........."

Letter- Public Record Office MH12/4657

NEWS FROM THE SOCIETIES

The Conservative Club

The annual meeting of this club was held at the Club House on Tuesday evening. Mr. J. E. J. Phillips (president) was in the chair. The Committee's report for the year was presented and stated that 28 new members had been elected, and 9 had left the town, giving an increase of 19 members. There was also a slight improvement financially. Parcels of books had been received from the Association of Conservative Clubs, and 131 volumes had been issued to members. The Chairman moved the adoption of the report. He also referred to the fact that Mr. Raymond Greene, M.P for West Cambs, was going out to South Africa with the Yeomanry and would be away for some time. They would, he was sure, wish him a speedy and safe return. (Applause).

After the election of officers, the remainder of the evening was spent in a smoking concert, in which songs of a patriotic character were sung. "The Absent-Minded Beggar" was sung by Mr. Abraham Wilkerson, after which a collection for the *Daily Mail* War Fund was made, and 15s. was collected. The other songs were sung by Messrs. J. H. J. Phillips, H. R. Smith and L. Darlow, Mr. C. Attridge accompanying the songs. A topical recitation was given by Mr. S. Camps, introducing at the end a verse of the National Anthem, which the company joined in singing.

The Royston Tradesmen's Friendly Society

The 81st annual report of this old established Friendly Society, which dates back to 1818, has just been issued to members. The society has paid the large sum of £427 for sick pay. The society has made provision "for increased sick pay up to £1 per week and an annuity to all incoming members at the age of 65 when their contributions cease".

Its total funds now stand at £6,137 0s. 9½d., and its membership is made up of 183 full members, and 10 junior members. The secretary is Mr. A. Gosling.

Church Of England Temperance Society

A meeting of this Society was held in the Boys' National Schoolroom, on Friday evening, February 16th, Mr. E. W. S. Royds, of the Herts. Band of Hope Union, who has frequently visited Royston, was met with a cordial welcome once more, and held the attention of all present by his racy entertaining way of contrasting the foibles and follies of drinking customs and habits with the advantages of abstinence and sobriety. As usual his chatty style of address was supported by a series of magic lantern views. The Vicar, Rev. J. Harrison, presided.

Victoria Cricket Club

The annual meeting of the Victoria Cricket Club was held on Monday evening, February 26th, at the Victoria Restaurant. There was a large attendance, nineteen being present. Mr. Charles Warren was in the chair.

The annual report for 1899 was presented.

During the season fourteen matches were played resulting as follows: Won 7, lost 6, drawn 1. The matches won were against Cambridge "Leda", Mr Higgins University X1, Cambridge "Pelicans", Cambridge Liberal Club, Fowlmere, Cambridge Rodney, and Buntingford. Matches lost- Mr Bailey's X1., Mr S. Rivers Smith X1., Fowlmere, Ashwell, (twice), Cambridge Rodney. The Drawn match was with the Cambridge Liberal Club.

Details of the performance of the players in batting and bowling were discussed The balance sheet showed a deficit of 19s. 2½ d. carried from 1898. The 1899 expenditure was £4 6s. 0d.and receipts £4 11s. 6d., leaving an adverse balance of 13s. 8½ d.

The officers for 1900 were elected as follows:-President, Mr. Charles Warren: Captain, Mr Harry Stamford: Sub-Captain, Mr A. Walbe.y: Hon. Secretary and Treasurer, Mr I. Humphreys: Committee members, Messrs. J. Dellar, E. Hagger, G. Kelly, G Pickett, C. H.. Titchmarsh, R. S. Trudgett and P Wilkin.

The subscription remains as usual at 2s.6d.

Daily practice would commence on Monday, April 30th.

It was decided to arrange half-day Saturday matches against Cambridge "Pelicans", Cambridge "IOU's," and other Cambridge University X1s., Fowlmere (2), Ashwell (2), Barrington (2), Cambridge Rodney(2), Cambridge Liberal (2), and probably a London Club.

Retirement of Rural Postman

Mr. T. Baker, who for 36 years has acted as rural postmaster between Royston, Barkway, Barley, Great Chishill, Heydon, and Chrishall, has this week retired on a pension, well earned. Mr. Baker was a familiar figure in the above villages, through which he has passed, and repasssed uninterruptedly for so many years, leaving Royston at 6a.m. and returning from Chrishall in the evening, and reaching Royston at 7p.m. At first he commenced as a foot messenger, when the post office was conducted by the postmaster Mr. Daintry, in a small room at the Falcon. In later years the letters not only grew in number, but the Parcels' Post was added, with the result that a horse and cart became necessary. The hilly district was a hard one to work in inclement weather, and many a rough journey, now stuck in the snow, now lost in the darkness and the fog, is remembered by Mr Baker. Curiously enough his duties terminated on Tuesday the 13th and the first journey of the postman, who went out on his beat on Wednesday morning, had to be made in the heavy snowstorm, with the result that the cart could not get through the drifts and the letters had to be taken on foot.

PETTY SESSIONS

Obscene Language

At the Petty Sessions, before Herbert George Fordham Esq., in the chair and Frederick John Fordham, Esq., *William Bowskill,* High Street, Royston, was charged with using obscene language in the Back Street, Royston, on 31st January and pleaded guilty under great provocation. P.c. Knight said on the night in question at 3.30 p.m. he received instructions from Inspector Hart to accompany Mr. Postle to the defendant's house. They went together and saw the defendant. The witness asked if he had a dog there, and the defendant said, "Yes I have but I will talk to Mr. Postle and not a .... like you." The defendant came out into the street and used other bad language, and said he would not be seen in the same street with a ...... like the witness. The witness then went away, and some time afterwards he saw the defendant driving a cart, when he shouted out, "summons you...... if you like." The defendant said he did not dispute the words he said but he thought they had been added to a little. He bought a dog from a man on the London Road, and when he found out it belonged to Mr. Postle he offered to give it up. He was very annoyed at Mr. Postle behaving in the way he had. The Bench said whatever provocation had been given such language was very disgusting, and they could not pass it over lightly. The defendant would have to pay 4s. fine and 16s. costs.

Charge of Permitting Drunkeness

Dennis Greenhill, landlord of the White Bear, was charged with unlawfully permitting drunkenness on his premises. The case arose out of a conviction previously of two persons.. After much discussion of all the circumstances, the case was dismissed but the Bench thought it was a proper case to bring before them for investigation.

At the previous session *William Howard* and *Lawrence Hagger* had been found guilty of being drunk on licensed premises. P.s. Reed described how he found them on the premises of the White Bear. Howard, being a first offender, was fined 2s. 3d. and 7s. 9d. costs, Hagger had to pay 10s. and 7s. 9d. costs.

SCHOOL NEWS

British School

As Miss Bements' doctor had forbidden her attendance at school for a few days on account of sickness, the timetable had to be departed from on Monday, February 12th.

On Wednesday, February 14th school closed on account of the very severe snowstorm.

Thursday, February 15th brought another snowstorm and school closed at noon for the rest of the day.

Miss Bement resumed duties on Monday, February 19th. Attendance was much better.

On Tuesday, February 27th information was received from the Department of a Supplementary Grant of £14. 0s. 0d. towards the construction of W. C.s.

National School (Girls)

February 2nd was a Prize Giving half-holiday. 16 medals had been given for perfect attendance through the year; 36 Certificates for Regularity and Punctuality; 40 Prizes for Good Conduct and a few extra prizes for Examination results. Special Medal for the best girl in the school was given to Sissie Biffin who has now left school.

On February 12th and 13th Cookery Classes were held on account of a small exhibition of Cookery to be held for parents.

On February 13th. a meeting of the National School Branches of the Guild of Courtesy was held in the evening. The girls afterwards showed some specimens of Cookery and Needlework.

Such heavy snow occurred on February 14th that not quite half the children came to school, so they were sent home for the day. On the 15th, 91 were present in the morning, but the snow became so heavy again that school was closed for the afternoon.

The Rev. J. Harrison declared the registers correct and the school in good order on February 20th and on February 28th the children attended Ash Wednesday Service in the Church at 9.15.

It was decided that for the rest of Lent the Children's Service would be on Thursday instead of Wednesday February 28th.

Prizegiving

The scholars attending the National Schools (Boys and Girls) assembled in the Boys' School for the annual prizegiving at the hands of the Vicar, Rev.J. Harrison. The Vicar spoke before giving the prizes and said that it was the 23rd time he had come to the school and his first was therefore long before they were born. The Boys' Schoolroom did not then exist and the Girls' room was not as nice as it was at present. He was pleased to report that the attendance was very good and that the Government grant had increased since 1894 until it was, in 1899, £250 18s. 6d He hoped that the school would eventually receive the highest grant.

Medals were presented for regular attendance. There were more medals for boys than girls but two girls from the same family had won medals in five consecutive years. This meant not missing a single day even for sickness. They had also to be punctual. The number of boys receiving medals had doubled and the Vicar hoped the girls would try their best to do the same but he always considered that in many respects boys could be more regular than girls, because weather and such things did very often signify more for a girl.

Guild of Courtesy

The Annual meeting of the Children's Guild of Courtesy connected with the National Schools was held in the Boys' School, on Tuesday evening, February 13th. Notwithstanding the snowstorm, a large number of children, parents and friends were present. They had started the branch three years previously and membership had increased and was now 80 girls and 66 boys.

The Vicar reminded the boys and girls of the little things which marked the boy or girl of good manners and consideration from others and urged the remembrance of their duty to others, and doing unto others as they would be done by

The speaker, Rev. Clement Bryer from Hitchin, explained that the aim of the Guild of Courtesy was to inculcate in the children habits of kindness, attentiveness and thoughtfulness in little things. It was a pleasing thing that there were so many teachers willing to make an extra effort to instruct children along these lines, and if parents would second the efforts of teachers they would be doing something to make these rules not only a part of school life but a part of home life.

The speaker then addressed the children on the duty of good manners, not only for special occasions, but in their home life not only observing rules of courtesy because they were told to but cheerfully carrying out their spirit.

SOME COUNCIL MATTERS

Water There was much discussion at the monthly meeting of Royston Urban District Council about the laying of a new water main. The Water Company intended laying 3 inch main from the junction of Mill Road and Melbourn Road to Garden Walk. The positioning of fire hydrants was also discussed.

A Question of Sewage

Extensions to the sewage system were discussed this month. Some estimates had been prepared - one for the London Road - £110, and one for part of Melbourn Road - £240. The clerk said that if sewers were necessary for public health the authority had a duty to provide them even though the expense would be great. There was some doubt as to the necessity of carrying out work on the Melbourn Road but because of the proximity of cesspools to the Water Works, a sewer should be laid in the London Road without delay.

Also, in this connection, smells from the Sewage Farm were considered. These smells were thought to have arisen because chemical refuse from the Gas Works, turned into the sewers from time to time, caused not only a nuisance but occasioned damage to crops on the land. Such action was liable to a penalty under the Public Health Act 1890. The Gas Works would be informed.

Approval and Disapproval.

Approval was given for a Caretaker's cottage in Back Street for the Trustees of Kneesworth Street Church.

Two other applications from Mr. Warren and Mr. Innes were returned to the architects for amendment, as they did not in certain respects conform to the Bye Laws.

Cost of the Cottage

At the Annual meeting of the Kneesworth St. Church, Mr. T. Gimson explained proposals for the erection of a caretaker's cottage. The subscriptions for the work at present amounted to about £120. It was decided to accept Mr Carrington's tender of £255 for clearing the site and erecting the building.

A fresh appeal to the congregation for further subscriptions would be made.

Private Footpath

A letter from Mr. T. Cooper to the Urban District Council called attention to the condition of the path in Gower Road, hitherto kept up by the owners there, and asking the Council, now that the rateable value was increasing down there, to help to put the path into a better condition. The Clerk was directed to reply that as it was a private road the Council could do nothing in the matter.

AT THE COUNTY COURT
JOHN PIGG v H. B. TRUEFITT

In this case the plaintiff, John Pigg, nursery man, of Royston sued the defendant, H.B. Truefitt Limited of Old Bond Street, London for £19 13s. 4d. for goods supplied and delivered, and for work done in the garden of The Cottage, Royston, occupied by the defendant's daughter and her husband, Mr. and Mrs. Johnson, who it turns out had not had the means to pay the bill. It was alleged that the work had been ordered by the defendant, the father of Mrs Johnson, who was a visitor at the time of the order. There had been a misunderstanding about who had ordered the work After hearing the evidence, the Judge decided that it was the business of the person for whom the work was done to pay the bill and not a visitor. Therefore, there was a judgement for the defendant for consent without costs.

ROYSTON PARISH CHURCH

BAPTISMS

February

4th. Edward Paul Morlock, son of Edward Johnson (Gentleman) and Nora Johnson.

Emily and Maud, daughters of Frederick William Humphrey (Labourer) and Agnes Humphrey.

11th Winifred Agnes Giddows, daughter of Ernest William Thair (Hairdresser) and Ada Mary Thair.

25th Harold Frank, son of Frank Newman (Labourer) and Sarah Ann Newman.

Frank, son of John Bateson (Blacksmith) and Mary Ellis Bateson.

MARRIAGES

February   None

BURIALS

February

9th Elizabeth Hagger, aged 50 years.

Mary Ann Plumb, aged 67 years.

24th Albert Pymont, of Flamstead, aged 37 years.

Other deaths reported in February

26th (ult) Emma Sward, aged 64 years member of John St. Congregational Church.

24th (ult) James Cubis, of Bassingbourn, Royston Workhouse,aged 93 years.

27th (ult) George Driver, of Barrington, aged 62, Royston Workhouse.

31st (ult) Sarah Seymour, Royston Cottage Hospital, aged 51 years.

2nd   Robert Wilkerson, Wrexham Terrace, aged 4 days.

8th   Thomas Barker, of Bassingbourn, aged 79 years.

20th   James Day, Queen's Road, late of Meldreth, aged 89 years.

A Letter from the Conservative M. P. to his Royston Constituents.

TO THE
ELECTORS OF
WEST CAMBRIDGESHIRE.

Headquarters ImperialYeomanry,
Norwich,
30th January, 1900

GENTLEMEN,

It is due to you that I should make you acquainted with the course I have felt it my duty to take at this anxious time in our Country's history. Directly it became necessary to establish the Imperial Yeomanry I volunteered for active service, and have had the honour of being appointed to serve in South Africa with the Loyal Suffolk Hussars, in which Regiment I have long held a commission.

I am convinced that the Electors of West Cambridgeshire will not deem my response to the Country's call to arms as a dereliction of my duties as their representative in Parliament, or even as indicating that I lightly regard the trust reposed in me, but, on the contrary, I hope and believe that my Constituents will account any services I may be able to render in South Africa as services rendered to themselves.

I am glad to be able to inform you that I have made arrangements for the performance of my routine duties as your representative in Parliament by one whom I can thoroughly trust, and any letters addressed to me at the House of Commons, and marked on the envelope "West Cambridgeshire,"will receive prompt attention.

I much regret having to cancel my engagements to attend those meetings in the Constituency to which I had looked forward o with so much pleasure. Still more deeply do I regret that necessary preparations for a long and possibly eventful journey, will prevent me taking a personal farewell of very many friends and supporters in West Cambs., and that I am compelled thus formally to say "Good-bye." If, in the chances of War, it is given to me to return, one of my earliest pleasures will be to revisit you, It will be a matter of great pride if I am then allowed to feel that, in your estimation, I have not unworthily borne a part in furthering the resolute determination of the whole Empire to repulse an unrighteous invasion, to establish a lasting peace based upon good government, liberty and justice, and at the same time to permanently secure the integrity of Her Majesty's Possessions in South Africa.

I remain, Gentlemen,
Yours very faithfully,
W. RAYMOND GREENE.

Local Men for the War

Lieutenant Larking of the E(Royston) Company 1st Herts V.B. Beds Regiment, has offered his services and has been accepted in the Imperial Yeomanry Corps of Gentlemen, which is at present drilling daily at Chelsea, in readiness for saling from Liverpool a few days hence for the Front.

2nd Lieutenant. Ian Phillips (son of Mr. John Phillips, Earl's Hill House), will go out to the front with the Herts Militia, now at Dublin. The Battalion, having volunteered for active service, leaves Dublin on Sunday and sails for the Cape.

Mr. Audley Blyth, owner of the steeple chaser Elliman, who is well known in Royston, has joined the 13th Company of the Imperial Yeomanry, the Duke of Cambridge's Own which left Southampton for the Cape in the Dunvegan Castle. The members of this Company go out at their own expense, provide their own outfit, and give their pay to the Widows' and Orphans' Fund.

The promotions of the Militia Infantry Battalion in the *London Gazette* contained the following: "3rd Princess of Wales Own (Yorkshire Regiment), *2nd Lieut. B.C.D. Nash* to be Lieutenant." He sailed for the front when the whole Battalion 1,200 strong, left from Southampton.

Trooper J. W. Pickett, second son of Mr. and Mrs. Pickett, of the "Green Man," the first Roystonian to volunteer for the front, who has been accepted for the Imperial Yeomanry, has been home during the week in the smart khaki uniform of the Imperial Yeomanry, and will sail in the "Cymric," from Liverpool next week.

Trooper Bertram M. Andrews, youngest son of Mr. H. M. Andrews of Royston, has also been accepted for the Imperial Yeomanry.

Private A. H. Cunningham, late of Royston, was one of the list of wounded in Buller's advance across the Tugela at Potgieter's Drift. Private Cunningham, lately employed at the Royston Brewery, is in the 2nd Battalion Devonshire regiment, which had 32 wounded in the above action.

The Royston Water Company Limited

The ordinary yearly meeting of the Share holders of the Company, was held on Saturday, February 24th, at the Offices of the Company, Mr. John Phillips in the chair.

The following report on the position of the Company was presented by the Directors.

The Report

The Directors have the pleasure of handing you herewith a statement of accounts for the year ending 31st December, 1899, and owing to the exceptional expenditure they can only recommend that a dividend of 4½ per cent be paid upon the Preference Shares, 2½ per cent upon the original Ordinary Shares, and at the rates of 1¾ per cent upon the Additional Ordinary Shares, which would absorb £127 15s.; that the preliminary expenses re New Property be written off amounting to £47 14s. 4d.; that £200 be written off as depreciation of Freehold Buildings and Plant; that the Balance of £32 7s. 7d. be carried forward to next year's account.

Owing to the opposition of the tenant of Flint Hall Farm, who obtained an injunction restraining the Company from passing over the portion of road granted by Viscount Hampden for access to the land purchased of him for the site of Reservoir, the Company have been compelled to abandon that site, and have now purchased another suitable site upon which the reservoir will shortly be built. (The fresh site is on the west side of the London Road towards Wicker Hall on an equally elevated site).

The New Pumping Station and Main are now nearly completed, and the Directors hope to supply the Town from the new Well in a short time.

The Directors retiring are Messrs. J.Phillips, F. J. Fordham, and C. Whyatt, all of whom are eligible for re-election. Mr. W. Beale is re-eligible as Auditor..

Secretary and Manager, Mr. W. T. Rowley.

Report

Gentlemen, in accordance with the duties of my office I beg to submit the following report. The Water and meter Rents have this year risen from £767 3s. 6d. to £842 2s. 5d., which shows the largest increase in any one year since the fomation of the Company. The Balance on Profit and Loss Account also shows an increase of £342 0s. 9d., after again writing off one fifth of the cost of obtaining Provisional Order.

From the balance sheet it appears that the Company's Capital now consists of £2,300 in 230 shares of £10 each fully paid, £200 in 20 4½ per cent Preference Shares, and £5,000 in 500 fully paid £10 shares (new issue). On the credit side of the account there is the sum of £2,411 5s. 5d. for the new property, while the cash in the bank and on Deposit, not yet appropriated, amounts to £2,780 19s. 10d.. The result of the year's trading appears in the Manager's Report given above.

The report and balance sheet were adopted, and the retiring Directors, and Auditor were re elected.

Corvus Cornix on the Volunteers

A great deal has been made of the readiness of our Volunteers to offer their services for the front, and the country is entitled to take all credit for such a splendid testimony to the principle of voluntary service. But if voluntary service is to be a real factor in the situation, more consideration will have to be given by the War Office to men who are prepared to give up situations and part with friends than has been shown of those who were bandied from pillar to post ....and then sent back. It seems that the War Office tape was not made for an emergency, and it is just the kind of thing which will do harm to a popular movement.

Another lesson of the times is the growing importance of the defensive force of our Volunteers who are left behind. In the commercial world we have heard about things that are "made in Germany" and the competition of Continental nations and there has grown up, out of this agitation, the movement for technical instruction. The victories of peace are of course much higher ends to train for than those of war, but so long as war is to be the scourge of mankind.........it is better to secure for the country a defensive force at home, by training of its citizens which shall interfere as little as possible with their daily life.

The Royston district has probably more men at the front in proportion to population than any similar district in England; hence the almost personal interest which is everywhere felt in this War is accentuated in this locality. If all parts of the United Kingdom had contributed the same proportion of men, the total British forces in South Africa would be about 350,000, instead of 150,000.

No Sport was reported in February. There was bad weather so this probably indicates that no fixtures took place.

MARCH

NEWS FROM SOUTH AFRICA

Death Of A Royston Man

We regret to learn of the death of a Royston man at the Front. *Driver Charles William Styles* (eldest son of Mrs. Coxall of Royston), of the Steam Transport, Royal Engineers, who was with Buller's forces.

A letter has this week been sent home to his sister from his chum, giving an account of his death from enteric fever, which must have happened about a month ago. In the letter home it is stated that "the officers and captain told him (his chum) that they were sorry to lose such a comrade."

Much sympathy will be felt with Mrs. Coxall and family in this bereavement, following so soon after the death of Mrs. Coxall's husband by a fatal accident.

***

Earlier in the month his mother had received a letter, mentioning the narrow escape he had in the big Battle of Colenso, which makes the death even more poignant.

"It seems hard to see soldiers getting shot beside us. I had a narrow escape up at the big fight at Colenso, but we were not in action We were dropped on by surprise, so we had to run for it, but we are still quite safe and hoping to return to England once again without getting disabled, as some of them are getting their arms and legs shot off.....

Ask Harry to come and have a look at the Boers. They are such a lot, rough, with long beards and all in plain clothes and they even put their wives and children in front of themselves, so that we should not fire at them, but we fire at them just the same. I got nothing but bully-beef and dog's biscuits for Christmas Dinner."

Narrow Escape

Private J. Hayes, cook at the Royston Union, who went out as a reservist attached to the Suffolks, has written home from De Aar, under date January 10th, a letter to Mrs. C. Marshall, Godfrey's Terrace (his sister).

"I have had dysentery once or twice, but thank God I am all right now. I have had a touch of fever before we went to Colesberg, but I went and am glad I did as I know a little what war is like. But of course this war is not like others the English have had. The others were child's play to this one. The country seems all hills, of course there is a little flat ground but it doesn't go far. There are hills that it takes us some time to climb and when we reach the top we want to have a sit down, but we don't get the chance to......I am pleased to say that I went to Colesberg. I had shots fall a foot off me. To speak the truth they fell all round me, and in fact I was not the only one that had narrow escapes. But thank God I did not feel the weight of one of them, and I can assure you I was not in want of any of old Kruger's pills. I have laid under heavy fire, both rifle and shell fire for five hours one afternoon, and pieces of shell bursting close to us but they were all right so long as they did not hurt me."

The Costs of War

Trooper W. Hart of the 1st Life Guards writing from the Modder River:

"It is an awful sight out here. You can see the Boers lying dead in all directions They only lie them on the level ground, and then they cover them over with dirt, and when the wind blows it shifts all the dirt from them, and the stink is something awful. We pulled over 100 Boers from the Modder River the other day, and we have to drink the water from the River! It isn't good but we have to drink it.......They have given us £4 each so we buy lime juice out here at 3s. a bottle, and condensed milk and bread, but we have to make it last a long time, because we are not getting any more pay until we get back to England........Have you received my box of chocolates? They are fetching £10 each out here, so don't eat any of it till I get home."

Policemen Volunteering for Army

In response to the invitation of old soldiers to return to the Army for one year to meet the present emergency, a number of the Hertfordshire Constabulary have volunteered to return to the service. The first to offer his services in this Division in Sergeant Reed, the mounted officer stationed at Royston, who has seen service in the Soudan.

Parcels for the Front

The parcels of comforts for the men at the Front which Miss Cautherley arranged to receive, have come in liberally and a substantial lot of useful gifts have been dispatched by Miss Cautherley. These include 20 well-made shirts, 94 pairs of socks, (which are specially useful and welcome), 18 belts and scarves, 30 helmets and "tams", 66 pocket handkerchiefs, pillows, notepaper, envelopes, and pencils. Miss Cautherley desires to thank all donors for so liberally responding, and to state that she will be arranging to send another parcel next month.

"Why we are at War"

At the Nonconformist Young Men's Society Rooms, at the end of last month, the Rev. T. H. Lomas presided over an interesting debate on the question "Why we are at War" which was very ably opened by Mr. A.T. Titchmarsh. A large number of members, including several junior members, took part in the debate, and the views expressed plainly indicated that the question is not so easily answered as at first sight it may seem to be, or at any rate, that there is sufficient variety of points of view to furnish material for an interesting debate.

A Jaw Breaker

At the Police Station, before D. B. Balding Esq., on March 26th, a ferocious looking individual, giving the name of *Thomas Loader* (45), was brought up charged with wandering abroad and begging alms in the Kneesworth Street.

P.s. Reed said, about 11. 30 a. m. on Monday morning, his attention was called to the defendant by a person living in Kneesworth Street, to whom the defendant had applied for alms, and used insulting language. A witness heard him ask for something to eat, and he then went up to him and said he would take him in charge. The defendant said, "You let me alone or I'll kick you in the...........guts." When the defendant was asked if he had any questions to ask the witness, he replied, "No, but I would like to break his jaw for bringing me here!"

The sergeant was asked if the person who had complained was to be called. P.s. Reed said he had endeavoured to get him to come but had been refused. Mr Balding remarked that in future such cases had better be met by a summons to appear. The defendant was sent to prison for seven days.

Draughts Match

On Thursday evening March 8th, a friendly match of draughts between the Nonconformist Young Men's Society and the Young Men's Church Association was practically brought to a finish at the N. Y. M. S. rooms. The match was concluded later in the week and resulted in the Young Men's Church Association winning by 21 games to 15.

CONCERNING CHILDREN

Boys' Brigade

The proposal to form a Boys' Brigade for Royston has taken practical shape. On the evening of Monday, March 5th the Armoury in Melbourn Street was fairly besieged by the young "Soldiers of the Queen", who had been singing through the streets over the relief of Ladysmith. About 70 boys, mostly between 12 and 15, gave in their names. Sergeant Paterson, of the E Company VB, who has undertaken the drill and instruction of the Brigade, will therefore have his hands pretty full, and the first need will be a sufficiently spacious building in which to drill, until the long evenings come when this can be done in the open air.

Death of Miss Titchmarsh

We regret to announce the death of Miss E. A. Titchmarsh, which took place at her residence in Kneesworth Street, after a very short illness. The deceased lady was in her eightieth year, and during the whole of her life had been a devoted friend and cheerful worker at the Kneesworth Street Chapel. She had taken a special interest in the Sunday School, of which she was for many years a teacher, and at one time was the superintendent, and in the school treats for which she collected subscriptions, with Miss Simons, who lived with her, and always took an active part in arranging public teas &c, at the chapel. She also collected for the British and Foreign Sailors' Society, and in these and many ways her loss will be greatly felt.

The funeral took place in the Chapel Burial Ground, in the grave in which the late Mrs. George Titchmarsh (sister-in-law) was buried.

The funeral service was conducted by the pastor, Rev G Packer, in the presence of a large number of friends, the deacons, teachers, &c, not withstanding very inclement weather.

The old associations severed by the death of the deceased are shown by the fact that she and Miss Simons had lived together for nearly forty years, and their faithful servant had been with them thirty-six years.

British Mixed School

The Head reported that Rose Pulley had left and gone to Littlington. Florry Carter had left to attend the Girls' National School. Two children (Annie and George Lewin from Baldock) were admitted, making 169 on roll.

On the 29th of the month, the usual bi-monthly examination was given. The work throughout was satisfactory with exception of the Arithmetic in Standard 3 and a fag end of Standard 1 in reading. The writing of Standard 1 showed a marked improvement under Miss Norman and the handwriting throughout was generally neat and of a very good style. Considering that this was only the 4th month of the School Year, the Head considered the work well done.

Kneesworth Street School Prize-Giving

The annual prize-giving to the scholars took place in the Schoolroom at the beginning of the month. The Rev. G. Packer, the pastor, presided and the attendance included a number of parents and friends and teachers. The prizes were distributed by Mrs. Clarkson, wife of the Pastor of Bassingbourne Congregational Church, and in doing so she spoke a few words of a cheering and encouraging character to parents, teachers, and children.

The prizes included several special volumes awarded to the scholars who had collected for the London Missionary Society.

The children's part in the proceedings did not end, however, in the receipt of the numerous prizes, but also embraced a programme of singing and recitations &c.

A Problem of Age!

Edward Titchmarsh, farmer of Royston, was summoned for employing a boy called Cornelius George Wood, of Royston, under school age, he being 10 years of age, and contrary to the provision of the Elementary Act, on 12th February 1900. Defendant said he employed the boy but was not aware but that he was under the age of thirteen, or he should not have employed him. As soon as he found out he was doing wrong he discharged him at once.

Mr. Webb, School Attendance Officer, said he was told by Mr. Titchmarsh's son that he understood the boy was over 15. The Chairman said the defendant would have to pay 10s. including costs.

At a later Petty Sessions Cornelius' father, Walter Woods of Black Horse Lane, Royston, was summoned for not sending his child to school according to the Bye-Laws. The defendant did not answer when the case was called, and P.c. Knight proved service of summons. Mr. W. J. Webb proved the absence of the boy from school on the date mentioned in the infomation, and there was a further certificate from Mr. Attridge, the Master of the National Boys' School, showing that between March last year and March this year the School was open 419 times and the boy in question was absent 419 times.

It was stated by the police that the defendant was fined 6d. a short time ago. He was fined 2s. 6d.

THE BOARD OF GUARDIANS AND THE WORKHOUSE

Bathing of Vagrants

The Clerk to the Board of Guardians (Mr. A. Sharpe) read a letter received from the Local Government Board enclosing an extract from a report from Col. Preston, Local Government Board Inspector, and asking for the observations of the Guardians thereupon:

"I consider it most unsatisfactory and dangerous that the Nurse should attend the female vagrants. I fear that the imbeciles are not bathed according to instructions."

The Chairman said that they had already answered the Local Government Board that the bathing of imbeciles was being carried out. As regards the Nurse and female vagrants, the Local Government Board knew perfectly well what the duties of the Nurse had been. There might be something in what Col. Preston said as to the risk of the Nurse coming in contact with the vagrants in the case of infectious disease, but as long as vagrants were sent there he did not see how this could be altogether avoided.

At a later stage the Visiting Committee recommended that the bathing of female vagrants by the Nurse be discontinued, and that the wife of the Porter be asked to undertake the duty of bathing the female vagrants. As the Porter's wife as laundress received £15 a year, the Committee recommended that £5 be added to her salary for the additional duties.

The Nurse's Salary

The Nurse (Miss Jones), having applied for an increase of salary, the board proceeded to consider the application.

In answer to a question it was stated that the salary was £25 and Miss Jones in her letter stated that this was below the amount paid in most Unions.

The master (Mr. Wesson), was called in and answered various questions as to the nature and extent of the duties which the Nurse has to discharge.

The Nurse was called in and answered questions as to her duties and said she had heavy calls upon her time when a number of the female vagrants required bathing. *[It looks as if the recommendation above was not yet in practice].*

Mr. Jackson proposed an increase to £30 a year, Mr. Stockbridge seconded. Mr. W. W. Clear proposed that the salary be increased to £28, which was seconded by Mr.T.W. Russell.

For the amedment 12 voted and 7 against and it was therefore carried that the salary be increased to £28.

ROYSTON UNION
THE BOARD OF GUARDIANS of the above Union will at their Meeting to be held on WEDNESDAY, the 14th day of March,1900 receive TENDERS for the supply of OUT-DOOR PAUPERS in the undermentioned Districts with best SECONDS BREAD ,one day old, at per 4lb loaf,for 13 weeks , from the 28th day of March, to the 26th day of June, 1900

DISTRICTS

No.1 Royston No.2 Ashwell, Hinxworth,Guilden Morden, Steeple Morden:No.3 Barkway, Barley, Chishall, Great, Chishill Little, Heydon, Nuthampstead: No.4 Reed, Therfield, Kelshall; No 5. Barrington, Fowlmere, Foxton, Melbourn, Meldreth, Shepreth, Thriplow; No 6 Abington Pigotts, Bassingbourn, Kneesworth, Litlington, Shingay, Wendy, Whaddon.

The bread must be delivered to the Paupers in every parish, twice in every week, and at such times and places, and in such quantities as the Guardians and the Relieving Officers shall direct.

The Board will, at the same time, receive Tenders for the supply of the Workhouse, for the same period, with the following articles:

BEST SECONDS BREAD(one day old), at per 4lb loaf
BEST SECONDS FLOUR, at per sack
GOOD OX BEEF(without bone or shins in pieces of not less than 4lbs. weight) at per stone of 14lbs
Fore quarters MUTTON, (whole), at per stone of 14lbs.
Beef and Mutton for the Officers' table, at per stone of 14lbs
GOOD BEEF SUET, at per lb.

The contractor will be required to convey the Meat to the Workhouse, in flats, to be provided by and at his expense.

The Board will also receive Tenders for the supply of the Workhouse, for 27 weeks , *from the 28th day of March to the 2nd day of October, 1900*, with the following articles:-

SPLIT PEAS, at per bushel.
NEW MILK,at per gallon.
GROCERY, DRAPERY, SHOES and LEATHER.
COALS, at per ton, delivered at the Workhouse.
BEER, at per gallon
GOOD WHEAT STRAW, in trusses, at per load, delivered

Specimens of the Drapery may be seen at the Workhouse, and tenders must be made with reference to such specimens

The Board will also receive Tenders for strong ELM COFFINS for the above Districts and the Workhouse for the same period of 27 weeks

The Tenders must be sent to the Clerk in his office in Back Street, Royston or to the Board Room at Royston and marked "Tender"*before Eleven o'clock on Wednesday, the 14th day of March 1900*, at which time the samples (which must be sent free of expense), of the Bread, Flour, Grocery, Peas, Drapery, Shoes, and Beer, must be exhibited in the Board Room

Forms of Tender may be had gratis at the Clerk's office, Royston, Herts.

Each Contractor must deliver the articles contracted for free of expenses, and at the times, places, and in the quantities ordered, and if required, enter into a bond, with approved security, for the due performance of the Contract.

Payment for the bread supplied to the out-door Paupers will be made in the middle or at the end of the Quarter, but payment for all other Articles, whether contracted for quarterly or half-yearly, will be made at the end of the quarter.

Guardians do not bind themseves to accept the lowest or any of th Tenders. By order of the Board.

A SHARPE Clerk to the Guardians *1st March, 1990.*

CHURCH MATTERS

The Church House
Opening by the Bishop

The opening of the Church House, the substantial building erected on the site of the old Church Room, for the use of the Young Men's Church Association, and for other Church purposes, took place on Saturday evening, March 17th. The presence of the Bishop of St. Albans in the town for the Confirmation Service on Sunday was taken advantage of in a request to his Lordship to open the place. The building, which has a frontage to the pavement leading into Church Lane and Melbourn Street and rear to the west entrance to the Churchyard, is well adapted by situation and arrangement for the purposes intended, and the site available has been made the most of by the architect.

Confirmation at the Parish Church

The Bishop of St. Albans was in the town this month to hold a Confirmation Service. The Confirmation took place in the presence of a large congregation and nearly 40 candidates presented themselves - 25 girls and 12 boys.

Heath Conservators

This month a meeting of the Conservators took place to elect new members. Finances were also considered and the balance in hand was £28 14s. 9d. There were discussions about how improvements to the Heath might be made. One suggestion, which had been made three or four years previously, concerned Heath Pond and the desirability of providing a larger sheet of water there for skating purposes. As the Water Company had a pipe laid on beyond the pond, in times of frost it could be possible to flood the pond. It had been fully thrashed out at the time. One objection was that it would be a white elephant only in use once in four or five years. If there was money to spend it should be for the benefit of the majority of towns people regularly using the Heath. Trees and seats should also be considered. There was one matter which needed to receive publicity, concerning young people. It was pleasing to see young people enjoying themselves but at the same time there was a lot of thoughtlessness in running about all over the pavilion seats and dirtying them so as to make them scarcely fit to sit down upon.

Sunday School Union

The annual meeting of the Sunday School Union took place in Kneesworth Congregational Schoolroom on Thursday, March 1st, and was attended by a number of teachers and friends from Royston and other parishes in the Union.

The chairman pointed out that Royston was a young society and hoped eventually that all the fifteen schools in the district would belong to it. Village schools had in the past been isolated and such meetings helped people to encourage each other.

As to the importance of religious education, if parents trained their children properly in this matter the work of the Sunday School would be much easier than it was. There was some difficulty in finding enough teachers and he wondered if rather than having one large room with 150 children and teachers attempting to teach 12 or 15, there was a case for three sections: one for infants, one for juniors and one for seniors.

Death of Mr. J. Baker

The death was announced of Mr J. Baker, a well known tradesman in the High Street, who had for some years carried on the business of baker and confectioner and eating house keeper, and was thus well known to townspeople and visitors. The deceased, who had been for many months a great sufferer from a painful malady which left little hopes of a recovery, leaves a widow and a large family, for whom much sympathy is felt. The funeral took place on Thursday, March 22nd at the Cemetery at 3.30, at which time many of the shops in the High Street had shutters up as a mark of respect. The funeral service was conducted by the Rev W. T. Lewis.

111

A GOVERNMENT IDEA

(and a local grocer's Mathematics)

WAR TAXES.

In raising the necessary Funds
for the
SOUTH AFRICAN WAR
The Chancellor of the Exchequer
has had to raise the
DUTY ON TEA
by
2d. PER LB.

This takes effect immediately,
and all Teas taken from the Bond
since Monday last have paid the
increased Duty.

The Grocers of Royston have
however agreed not to raise their
Prices until Monday next, March
12th, on which date all Teas will be
advanced **2d**. per lb.

The Increased Duty
Makes Common Tea Very Dear

On a pound of Tea, retailed at 1/- or
1/2 per lb., there is a duty of 6d. paid
by the consumers to the Government,
which is a tax of 50 per cent. (or one
half) on the nett value of the leaves.
Contrasted with this, Goodman's
Celebrated Tea, now at 1/8 per pound,
which is charged with the same duty of
6d., is 70 per cent Tea and only 30 per
cent tax. These hard-facts are worthy
of consideration, as Common Teas,
which are deficient in quality and
wasteful in brewing, are taxed at the
same rate per lb. by the Customs,
making Common Teas at least 20 per
cent more costly than Good Teas.

Good Teas are represented by

GOODMAN'S TEAS

At 1/8, 2/-, and 2/6 per lb.
Which go far in brewing and are
economical in use.
**THE ROYSTON & DISTRICT
SUPPLY STORES,
High Street, ROYSTON**

A Tea Distributor's Response - This advertisement appeared in the
local paper in the same month that the tax was announced

LOCAL MILITARY ACTIVITY

Field Day at Royston

The Cambridge University Volunteers, en route for their annual Camp training at Aldershot, followed the practice of previous years by some of them marching part of the way and joining the rest of the Battalion by rail later. The marching portion made Royston their chief halting place after being billeted in the Town Hall in Saffron Walden on Friday night.

On Saturday morning, March 17th, the march was resumed for Royston where a military greeting awaited them in the form of a Field day with Companies of the 1st (Herts) Battalion of Volunteers of the Beds. Regiment. From Hertford and Hitchin there came by special train the Haileybury Cadets and the Hitchin Company including the Cyclists' Detachment. These companies were met at the station by the Royston Military Band which played them through the town to the rendez-vous.

As the University Volunteers were outnumbered by the Hertfordshire Volunteers, it was decided that E (Royston) Company should join the 'Varsity Men', and thus make two evenly balanced forces for the ensuing " Battle of Barkway Hill."

The Battle of Barkway Hill

The general idea of the movements on Barkway Hill was that the rearguard of a Western force, the Haileybury boys and the Hitchin men, forming a force of 190 men, were to hold Barkway Hill until 4.30 and then retire on Kneesworth, while the Eastern force, consisting of the C. U. V. and the E Company, numbering about 150, was acting under orders to discover the rear-guard force holding the hills and drive them in. There were two official umpires. The spectators, who did the amateur part of the umpiring, were many hundreds strong, notwithstanding the keen east wind blowing across the hills.

Many military manoeuvres were carried out in the vicinity of Barley Hill beyond the Eagle Tavern, in the direction of Seven Rides and Flint Hall Farm and Green Walk plantation. Eventually, the front attack reached the crown of Barkway Hill where the Hitchin men lined a sheltering bank, and the Haileybury men, from inside the plantation, were able to blaze away with their Martinis with their tell-tale smoke. Against such fire the C.U.V. had no cover and it was decided by the umpires that Barkway Hill was impregnable, and the "retreat on Kneesworth," according to the programme, was partially executed by the Company falling in, the University men first, then the Band followed by the red coats behind, and marching into the town for refreshments.

The scene both in the field and as the Companies defiled down the steep hill into the town, was a picturesque one and both spectators and men appeared very well satisfied with the afternoon's work and play. On Saturday night the University men were billeted in the Institute where a plentiful supply of straw and rugs helped to keep out the rigours of a cold night.

Church Parade

The Church Parade took place on Sunday at the Parish Church, to which the Volunteers marched headed by the band. There was a large congregation at the Church, in which the whole of the North aisle and some of the front pews were reserved for the Volunteers.

On leaving the Church the men marched up the High Street, headed by the band, under the direction of the Bandmaster Mr. W. H. Hinkins. On Market Hill they were dismissed, and assembling shortly afterwards at the Institute, they fell in and commenced the march to the next halting place at Baldock, taking their lunch to have by the way. The Band played them out of town.

A Celebration

The members of the E Company 1st (Herts) V. B. Beds Regiment had their annual gathering for the presentation of prizes at the Royston Institute on Tuesday, March 6th, when a public dinner took place attended by a large number of Volunteers and guests from the town and neighbourhood. The company present numbered 100.

A hot dinner was provided by Mr. J. G. Porter, of the Crown Hotel, and despite the cold night and the distance the hot joints had to be taken, did his part admirably.

After dinner Capt. Cautherley proposed in felicitious terms the health of Her Majesty the Queen, of all sovereigns that had ever reigned the most beloved and reverenced, of all women, the most womanly. (Applause). The toast was received with the singing of God Save the Queen.

Capt. Cautherley in his address to E Company expressed himself dissatisfied with the shooting as the Company had fallen back to second place in the Battalion. There was no excuse for the want of good shooting for they had the best range in the whole Battalion. He was glad to say that numbers had risen. In the previous October they were 80 strong and since that time he had sworn in 45 recruits. After a few more remarks concerning the War, discipline and long-service, prizes were presented for shooting and drill and the long service of some members was acknowledged. A toast was proposed for the "Honorary Subscribers" without whose help the Company would be in a sorry plight The government grant for Vounteers was only 38s. per man per year, barely two thirds of the amount required.

Stack Fire on the London Road
Prompt Arrest and Curious Confession

Messrs. W. T. Mottram of Buntingford, on their way to Royston Market on Wednesday March 21st, saw a man leaving a field, about one mile and a half from Royston on the London Rd., where one stack of a group of eight or nine was burning. They at once turned back and secured the man and took him to Royston Police Station. People working in the neighbourhood managed to contain the fire to the original stack which could not be saved. Foreman Course of the Royston Fire Brigade arrived at the scene on his bicycle and it was apparent that no good could be done with a fire engine. The stack was valued at £15.

Later a man, from Greenwich, was charged with setting fire to a stack worth £15. His account of events was as follows, "I came from Cambridge about six this morning. I laid down by the side of the stack, and I felt cold and set fire to the straw to keep warm......."

Left Behind

On Monday last, March 12th, Private Harry Webb, a Reservist, living at Mackerel Hall, had been home on leave since being called up for service with the 2nd Beds., and on that day left to return to headquarters at Bedford in readiness for leaving for Southampton, whence he was to sail on Wednesday. At Hitchin he appears to have spent the rest of the day, and getting a little refreshment, returned to Royston instead of going to Bedford. The authorities at Bedford, finding he had not turned up, communicated with the Police at Royston, who found Webb at home on Tuesday night. He was bundled off with all speed to Hitchin and thence to Bedford, but only reached headquarters on Wednesday morning, when his comrades were about sailing from Southampton. The result has been that he is left behind to be dealt with by the Authorities at the Regimental headquarters.

After the Show

Following the Parade of Stallions which was less than usual because of the inclement weather, the annual meeting of the *Foal and Colt Society* was held in the Bull Hotel, Mr. J. E Phillips presiding.

The results of the Show were discussed. There had been an increase of entries in all classes and the quality of some classes had been excellent especially the 2-year old class. *Mountjoy* would be available for members during the ensuing season at the usual Two Guinea Fee. The Stallion Fund is well maintained, and is the most important branch of the Society's work. The Committee hoped that all tenant farmers who were subscribers would avail themselves of the opportunity of trying to improve their breed of horses which is the object of the Society.

A honorarium of £10 was agreed to for Harold Smith for the large amount of work he had done for the Society in the previous two years whilst his father had held the Secretaryship.

The new officers for the coming year were elected. These were Mr. Francis John Fordham (President), Mr. Rivers Smith (Hon. Secretary), Mr .F. J. Fordham (Hon. Treasurer).

A Curiosity

A curiosity in the form of a pig with two tails has been on view at Mr. Hoy's in the High Street during the week commencing March 19th.

ROYSTON PARISH CHURCH.

BAPTISMS

March
4th   Herbert John, son of Albert John Muncey (Coachman)
       and Martha Georgina Muncey

MARRIAGES

March
1st   Ernest Cecil Glenie (Publican) to Helen Wilkerson.

BURIALS

March
6th   Henry Holloway, aged 77 years.
24th Mary Miller, aged 57 years.
27th Arthur Sharp, Mount Terrace, aged 6 months.

Other births, marriages and deaths reported in March
24th (ult)   Rebecca Chamberlain, of Shepreth,
             Royston Workhouse, aged 78 years.
26th (ult)   David Judd, of Whaddon, Royston
             Workhouse, aged 87 years.
24th(ult)   Eliza Ann Titchmarsh, Kneesworth Street,
             aged 80 years, buried Chapel Burial Ground.
2nd   Henry Holloway, Norman's Hill, Royston,
             aged 77 years.
2nd   Cooper Wilkinson, Royston, aged 81 years.
7th   Sarah Cane, of Melbourn, at Royston
             Union Workhouse, aged 68 years.
14th   Ann Williams, of Steeple Morden, at
             Royston Workhouse, aged 82 years.
17th   Elizabeth Clements, of Ashwell, at Royston
             Union Workhouse, aged 75 years.
19th   James Baker, Royston, aged 40 years.

Births
26th   At the Falcon, Royston, to the wife of John
             Howe Law, a son.

Marriages
22nd   William Joseph Wilkerson to Alice Mary
             Layton, at the Kneesworth Street Church,
             Royston, by the Rev. G. Packer, Pastor.

SPORT

Hockey

March
6th   Royston v Caius College (on Heath). Score 1- 6.
9th   Royston v Emmanuel College (on Heath). Score 1 - 6.
15th   Royston v Trinity College (on Heath). Score 1 - 3.

Ladies' Hockey

3rd   Royston v Hitchin (away). Score no goal draw.
7th   Royston v Hitchin (away). Score 2 - 1.

Football

March
3rd   Royston v Old Radleians (on Heath). Score 1- 3.
15th   Royston v St Catherines (on Heath). Score not given
17th   Royston v Camb. St Marys(on Heath). Score 3 - 0.
24th   Royston v Ashwell (away). Score 4 - 2.

Golf

March
15th   Captains' Prize Competition
       Monthly Medal.
13th   Royston G. C. v. Cambridge G. C. (played at Royston)
       Cambridge won.

Success

Miss Mabel Cooper, late pupil teacher in the Royston National (Girls') School, has obtained a first class in the Queen's Scholarship Examination held in December last, and has been accepted as a student at the Norwich College.

Royston Chess Club

The winding up meeting of the above club for the present season, was held this month when the secretary, Mr. E. Haywood, presented his accounts and balance sheet which showed that the club was flourishing and would begin the next season with a clear balance sheet. The Club had 23 members and expected to increase that number in the following season. The club had played and won its first match on March 20th the previous year against Cambridge Conservative Chess Club.

Corvus Cornix on Private Roads

The Royston District Council had before them for the first time the question of the relationship of the Council to the making up and taking over of private streets. This came up in the form of an application from the owners of the largest part of the land fronting on the new roads of Morton Street and Green Street, the Royston Tradesmen's Benefit Society. Too often the condition of such roads is allowed to stagnate between the local authority shielding itself behind the fact that "it is a private road" and a large number of owners who cannot be induced to bear the brunt. Happily now, most authorities see that where a street is laid out for building purposes, houses are built on it and rated for the district rate, the occupants are entitled to the advantages given to other streets in the district. In a general way a person buying land upon such a street gets it at a lower rate and knows that there is an implied responsibility of some day making a road. If he does not carry out the implied obligation, the law empowers the authority to do it for him and charge upon him his portion of the cost.

COUNCIL MATTERS

A Letter to the Council about the Fleet

Gentlemen,

I beg to inform you that I have called the attention of your Sanitary Inspector to the filthy and most insanitary state of the lane, commonly known as The Fleet, running north from the Baldock Road, in the Urban District of Royston. The whole place is a disgrace to any civilized community; some of the cottages are scarcely fit for human habitation.

I am, gentlemen,

Yours faithfully,

Joseph P. Nunn.

A Response

The Medical Officer of Health and the Sanitary Inspector had visited the site and felt the remarks in the letter were unjustified. The only thing they saw was one house where there was a larger quantity of house refuse than there should have been and another where they considered a privy pit should be converted into a pail closet. The chairman proposed the Sanitary Inspector should keep his eye on the place and endeavour to get the Medical Officer's recommendations carried out.

(Inspector of Nuisances Report for Year 1899)

Animals removed, being improperly kept	10
Complaints received.	10
Cottages repaired	5
Cesspools abolished.	1
Drains cleared out and repaired.	10
Dung heaps removed	5
Houses inspected	200
Houses newly erected	12
New Closets erected	12
New Drains made	12
Notice to abate nuisances	5
Nuisances abated	26
Travellers vans visited	35
Visits to slaughter-houses, bake-houses, dairies and cow-sheds	30

Vaccination

Royston Petty Sessions

The bench granted a certificate of exemption under the Vaccination Act to Frank Drayton, of Barley, in respect to the vaccination of his child.

Extracts from the Report of the Medical Officer of Health

The death rate for the previous year for all ages and all causes worked out at 16.0 per 1000. The rate for the preceding year had been 14.5 per 1000. The death rate for the whole of England and Wales for the same period was given at 18.3. The total number of births is 88 equal to a birth rate of 22.8 per 1000. The birth rate in England and Wales is 29.3. There had been one death from Whooping Cough, two from Infantile Diarrhoea and one death from Influenza. Infant mortality, as represented by the ratio of deaths of children under one year to 1000 registered births is 113, which indicates a decrease of nearly one third over the previous year.

The deaths from Phthisis (any disease which causes wasting of the body, e.g. pulmonary tuberculosis) are more than double those of the previous year, and the death-rate is 2.3.

There has been a decrease of deaths from Cancer, and an increase of deaths from diseases of the respiratory organs.

He had to make the unusual statement that not a single case of infectious disease scheduled has been reported. The only other infectious diseases which have been present are a few cases of Mumps, Whooping Cough or Chicken Pox and Infantile Diarrhoea which had necessitated the closure of the Infant School for three weeks.

Another Letter to the Council

Extension of Sewers

Gentlemen,

At your last meeting I believe you had under your consideration the question of extending the sewerage down the Melbourn Road, and no great hopes were held forth that the extension would take place.

As a ratepayer may I be allowed to ask that you will speedily and favourably reconsider the matter and endeavour to extend the benefit to this portion of the town. Houses have recently, and are still in the course of, being erected in this road, and others are contemplating building, and the district bids fair to be a well-populated one.

The system of earth closets, which I believe is generally adopted, is to say the least of it, most disagreeable. Surely as ratepayers we have the right to participate in as far as practicable, the benefits which the sewerage undoubtedly bestows.

I am, gentlemen,

Yours very faithfully,

Chas. A. Freston

APRIL

Easter in Royston 1900

The traffic to and from Royston Station was fairly heavy and the Company favoured their patrons with excursions both up and down. On Saturday 20 persons were booked by excursion to London and nearly 200 by the Bank Holiday excursion to Royston.

There was as usual a large number of visitors to the town and neighbourhood for the Easter Holidays. Cycling, which would otherwise have been a delightful exercise on the present good hard roads, was sadly interfered with by the gales of wind which prevailed more or less during the whole of the holidays. On the Bank Holiday the weather was not so bad as on Good Friday, but it was very boisterous and, with occasional showers, interfered somewhat with the outdoor amusements. The excursion from London brought down 200 on Monday and during the afternoon a large number resorted to the Heath to witness the football match between Royston and Mount Lodge. Swing Boats and stalls were also present, and were fairly well patronised by young people.

Corvus Cornix on the Joys of the Bicycle

The exceptional gales of wind during the Easter Holidays played great havoc with the cycling prospects over the land. What a very remarkable part the cycle now plays in our periodical holiday making was shown by the rush of bicycles to the great railway termini in London towards the end of last week. At each of these great starting points for the country thousands of bicycles were dispatched, and this part of the traffic formed quite a special business requiring special vans. "But there's many a slip 'twixt the cup and lip", and it is to be feared that the great majority of those bicycles never got used this Easter, or, if used, the discomfort and risk of riding in a high wind proved a small return for the trouble, even when it was not attended with danger. Some of those whose destination was from West to East, I am told, had a "high old time," and with the modern contrivances of free wheels were driven by the wind without exertion, like a ship at sea. Which reminds me that it seems about time that somebody invented a bicycle sail, as a complement to the free wheel, and then the cyclist, starting with the wind at his back, would go merrily along with no concern except that of the old woman who prayed for a change of wind before her return. Fifty years may suggest that we have not reached the limits of the bicycle yet, and that it may be quite safe to prophesy a time when the cyclist will look back with pity upon the ancient wheelman of to-day who has to depend upon his legs for nearly all the progress he can make.

A Mishap in the Gas Lighting

Considerable surprise and inconvenience was occasioned one Saturday night by the sudden failure of the gas lighting, both in the streets and in the houses and business premises in the centre of town. Several of the street lamps went out entirely and the same thing happened to lights in some of the shops, while in other cases the light was nearly extinguished but soon recovered. It was believed that the cause of the mishap was the gas holder at the works being temporarily wedged against the side by the force of the gale. With this movement, the inflow of gas was suddenly checked and pressure was relaxed.

An Interesting Visit

Mission work in The Arctic Region

On Friday, April 6th, an interesting meeting took place in the National Schoolroom in aid of the Church Missionary Society, when a visit was paid by the Rev. E. J. Peck, missionary to the Eskimo. He referred to his early life and travels, first for ten years in the Navy, and then going out on one of the Hudson Bay Company's ships as the first missionary ever sent to the Eskimo.

After various descriptions of difficulties he went on to describe the building of a "Church", with a sealskin covering, which the dogs ate; efforts to spend Christmas in conventional English fashion, only to find that for the lack of trees, the children's Christmas tree had to be rigged up by means of a pole and hoops covered with fancy paper and loaded with toys; and the voyage out among the seal hunters, to carry on missionary work among the little colonies of snow huts in which the Eskimo lived.

The missionary was also able to describe the lasting successes of his work, and to testify that during the whole of his life spent in the Arctic regions he had met with nothing but kindness from the Eskimo.

SCHOOL NEWS

British School

During the month Beatrice Davis left to go in business and two boys, Reg Pegram and Edgar Webb, left to go to work. Rose Pulley who left the school earlier was readmitted. Since leaving she had attended no school whatever. School was closed at noon on the 12th to reopen on Monday, April 23rd, 1900.

National School

School closed on April 12th and reopened on April 23rd.

ROYSTON NATIONAL BOYS' SCHOOL

Wanted at Easter, Male Probationer for Pupil Teacher age 14-16; or an ASSISTANT MISTRESS (Article 68) under Headmaster; Lower Standards.
Liberal Terms. Particulars, &c.,
Vicar, Royston, Herts

The Choir Supper

The adult members of the Church Choir were entertained to their annual supper at the Chequers on Friday, April 27th, the Vicar Rev. J. Harrison presiding. After an excellent repast, served by the host Greenhill, a pleasant social evening was spent. The health of the Vicar was proposed by the organist (Mr. Attridge), who referred to old associations and to the wrench it would be if ever the Vicar should leave them. The toast was received with musical honours. The Vicar responded, and acknowledged the good feeling which had always existed between them. He was especially pleased with the fact that there had been so few changes in the Choir for so many years, and that they had always been so ready to respond to any calls upon them for extra services at Church. The health of the oldest member of the Choir, Mr. W. Hood, was next proposed and cordially received. During the evening a pleasing incident occurred in a visit from the Rev. M. H. Pimm (late curate of Royston), whose health was proposed and drunk with musical honours. Songs were sung at intervals, the Vicar accompanying the songs on the piano and a recitation was given by R. Wilkerson.

THE EVILS OF DRINK

Temperance
United Teetotal Society

The Rev. W. Mottram, of London, a cousin of George Eliot, the novelist and a well-known lecturer and temperance advocate, delivered a lecture in the Kneesworth Street Congregational Schoolroom on Wednesday evening, April 4th, on the subject of "Wrecks of genius, or life-lessons for young men of the Twentieth Century".

Mr. Goodman presided and referred with pleasure to the fact that two Bills had been read a second time in Parliament, bearing on temperance reform - one to prohibit the serving of intoxicating drink to children under sixteen years of age and the other for Sunday closing in Monmouthshire.

The Rev. Mottram delivered his lecture, remarking that the greatest change in the drinking customs of society had been attributed to public opinion and that drunkenness was thought now to be only an indulgence for the vulgar and uneducated....... He urged that lessons of the past had shown that neither education nor social position nor genius, was a safeguard against the ravages of drink.............Referring to "wrecks of genius", he quoted Alexander the Great, William the Conqueror finding Harold's warriors in drunken revelry, King John, James I, Charles II, George IV, Pitt, Fox, Byron, Burns, Charles Lamb and Landseer, as examples of the highest gifts ever bestowed upon men being wrecked by heavy drinking and slavery to intemperance.

More on Temperance
Free Church Council

A meeting took place on April 5th in the Kneesworth Street Schoolroom. The chairman thought that the organisation ought to use their influence "to help on the day when public houses should be closed on Sunday". He would like to see Sunday trading done away with and in this matter, he appealed to the ladies especially to use their influence in this work.

The speaker Rev. G. P. Chapple, of Melbourn, gave a talk about his journey in New England, Massachusetts. It struck him that there the temperance sentiment was more advanced and the organisation more effective. The electors were able to vote on a town by town basis on, "Shall licences for the sale of intoxicating liquor be granted in this town?". The results differed from town to town but in some small towns not a single elector voted in favour of the drink saloon.

Also, the minority report of our Royal Commission recommended one public house for 700 people; whereas in Massachusetts, even where licences were granted, one was only allowed to 1,000 people.

Temperance Again
Church of England Temperance Society

The speaker at this meeting, Mr. Titterington, while recognising the support of the non-abstaining section of the Society, said that he preferred the safer standpoint of a total abstainer, and drew from the ordinary experiences of life, a justification of this position.

He referred to the incident of the editor of *The Globe*, learning from a "sandwich man" in the street that he was a man with a university education and could bring ten others from the street in half an hour, who had held university degrees, all reduced by drink, as an illustration that neither education nor social position was any guarantee against falling. As in other aspects of life, it was not merely the single glass but the hidden danger and the unexpected moment of temptation that had to be guarded against. A father with a family found his boys imitating him in everything he did as they grew up from childhood; hence the vital importance of "leading them straight".

And Again!!
Church of England Temperance Society

Another meeting of the Society was held in the National Schoolroom on Monday evening, April 23rd and was very well attended. The Vicar, Rev J. Harrison, presided. The meeting was addressed by ex-Sergeant Deeks, who has a cheery practical way of presenting aspects of temperance work, and an earnest manner of enforcing its needs as it presents itself to one engaged in rescue work in connection with Police Courts, &c. The first part of his speech was addressed to the young on the importance of beginning early in life to take the right stand and to take the right turn for life and going straight. In the second half, he spoke to the older people on the power of example. At the close the Vicar called attention to the Bill before Parliament, which had passed its first and second reading, for prohibiting children under 16 years of age being served at a public house. At present the youngest child that could walk and carry a jug could be sent to a public house and a child of 13 could sit and drink on the premises. He thought that whether he was a total abstainer or not, every right-thinking man must desire to see this Bill, for preventing children being served at public houses, become law.

MORE NEWS FROM SOUTH AFRICA

Private J. Blows, of the 8th (King's Royal Irish) Hussars, son of Mrs. John Blows, Norman's Hill, Royston, has written home to his father and mother:

"I must tell you that we are on our way to Bloemfontein......... two days and two nights in the train, and then we will be in the field, which I am longing for; but I think the worst is all over now, but I thought we would be in the firing. You should see the hill they have to drive the Boers out of. You know the cutting in the London Road, that is nothing to this out here. They are quite as steep and about six times as tall, and when you get half-way up you might get knocked down again.........We have left Cape Town now for two days, and we will be another ten days before we get out of the train, and I may tell you that it is hard for us. We get 1lb. of tinned beef and six hard biscuits a day."

Private Frank Beale, of the 1st Lincolns, son of Mr. John Beale (caretaker of the Additional Burial Ground), has written home from Orange River, under date March 11th.

"I am very sorry to tell you that it is my luck to be in hospital again with enteric fever, but I am very glad to say that I am getting on all right again. I have seen something since I have been out here. Tell Bill I nearly got my neck broke. I do not want to do any more riding. That is what I think drove me sick."

Trooper Hines, servant to Captain Bell-Smyth, on Lord Methuen's staff, son of Mr.G. Hines of Royston, has written a letter from Kimberly in which he says:-

" I have been in two expeditions since I have been here. It was a Boer village and we went to see if it was occupied by Boers or not. When we got close to the place our troops opened out for fighting order but finding no opposition we marched straight into the place, which was a very nice place and no end of fruit which we helped ourselves to. The women told us the place had been held by about 500 Boers, but when they saw us coming they sloped, leaving everything behind, which we burnt and a lot of ammunition. After that the Union Jack was hoisted and the Dutch flag pulled down. The majority of the people seemed pleased to see us, but they told when they heard we were coming they were all afraid, as they thought we should do as the Boers do, loot everything we could get hold of, but of course we did not as it is not allowed.

We retired to Kimberly, leaving a few troops to guard the place. Kimberly is getting a little more near the mark now, shops have plenty of good things, although you want bags of money. You cannot buy anything under a tickey, which means 3d. For instance a newspaper, a box of matches, a pair of boot laces, or any little thing. You see they do not use coppers at all, as the lowest paid men get about £4 a week, and some get £8, so this is the place for money."

[This was when a general servant's post was advertised in Royston at an *Annual Salary* of £10.]

A. Siggins, of HMS Tartar, Ladysmith to his sister Mrs. Beale, wife of Mr J. Beale (caretaker at Additional Burial Ground), dated March 10th:

"We do not get much time for writing. We have a lot to do on the field to look out for the Boers. They are a sly lot of rats. We have been out here for three months and there has been a lot of fighting and we have lost a lot of men. We got to Ladysmith after 12 days' fighting, and when we shelled the Boers they flew for their lives........... The poor men who had been shut up in Ladysmith are looking bad. They were living on horseflesh and 1¼ biscuits a day.....They have lost a lot of men with fever. I don't think the war will last much longer..........I daresay you heard about the fight we had at the Tugela........We were with them and how we got out of it I don't know.......I had a bullet hit the top off my little finger,and it took a piece of skin off , but it did not hurt much."

A Sad Sequel
Death at the Front

At Estcourt, Able Seamen Siggins of HMS Tartar, April 15th. The deceased sailor was well known in Royston, where this intimation will be received with regret.

A Runaway

In the middle of the afternoon of Saturday, March 31st, a great deal of excitement was caused in the centre of town by a horse and cart. It appears that the horse, belonging to Mr. L. E. Clark, butcher of Kneesworth Street, was standing attached to a cart in his yard. Suddenly the horse took it into its head to make a dash for the street. A man who was in Mr. Clark's employ was knocked down and one of the wheels passed over him, but without any serious injury. Getting into Kneesworth Street the horse turned for the Cross, and as at that time there were a number of conveyances, cyclists, and pedestrians, in the street, there seemed every chance of serious consequences.

The critical point at the Cross was fortunately cleared, and the runaway dashed up the High Street. Outside Mr. Goodman's shop was a heavy tumbril cart and another conveyance standing and the runaway swerved clear of these, but only to go rattling on to the kerb on the opposite side of the road. Up the street it ran, with its owner after it. Cyclists made for the nearest turning, but cycles left unguarded were not so fortunate. Outside Dr. Archer's house two were left standing in the ordinary way against the kerb. The wheel of the runaway trap caught the handles of these and whirled the machines round, but without doing much damage. Higher up the street, near the Angel, a brewer's dray was standing and to clear this the runaway would have to go to the other side of the road which it just failed to do. The wheel caught in and interlocked with the dray and the speed was suddenly checked with the result that the horse broke from the harness and ran on leaving the trap behind. It was stopped a little further up the street. That such a comparatively small amount of damage should have been done was very remarkable.

An Interesting Will

An important case before the Chancery Division involves the legal interpretation of the will of the late Mrs. Sarah Ellen Pyne who died at her home in Melbourn Street in May 1899. She had in many ways shown a generous regard for all charitable and public objects needing support. It was not therefore surprising to learn that charitable purposes should have a prominent place in her thoughts in the disposal of her wealth.

Leaving a fortune of over £76,000, the deceased lady bequeathed more than half of this to relations and friends, and as to the residue, amounting it is understood, to about £35,000, her will made this provision, that it should be used for "charitable purposes, and in such shares and proportions as may be hereafter set forth in any codicils". In the the event, however, no codicil could be found.

The application of the funds to any particular charitable purposes will have to be dealt with under the direction of the Court of Chancery at a later stage, should the Judges decide in favour of the intention expressed in the will. It is understood that the case will come before the Court of Appeal and the result will be of great interest locally.

SPORT

Golf

April
5th   Monthly Medal.
28th   Royston v Finchley. Royston won by 19.

Football

April
7th   Royston v Hitchin Town Reserves (away). Score 1- 1.
16th   Royston 1st X1 v Mount View (on Heath). Score 1- 1.
16th   Royston v Haverhill Rovers (away). Score 2 - 6.

ROYSTON CRICKET CLUB

PRACTICE commences on Monday, April 30th.
Those wishing to join the Club are requested to give in their names as early as possible to the Hon. Secs. W. C. Titchmarsh, Charles Warren.

SEASON, 1900
ROYSTON VICTORIA CRICKET CLUB.

The above Club has commenced practice on Royston Heath, and will continue daily, starting at 6.30 p.m., throughout the Season. Subscription, 2/6 the Season, payable on or before May 31st. No practice will take place this season on wet evenings. Anyone wishing to join are requested to give in their names without delay to I.H. HUMPHREYS, *Hon. Secretary. & Treasurer.*

Drink Driver

At the Police Court a man from Cambridge was fined 10s. with costs after being charged with being drunk and disorderly in charge of a horse and trap. P.s. Reed who was on duty in the High Street with P.c. Knight saw the defendant driving down the High Street with a pony and cart in which were a women and child. He was whipping the pony all the way down the street and was very drunk and had no control of the reins whatsoever. The pony turned sharply down into John Street and nearly overturned the cart, and went by the Fire Station into Church Lane.The women were shouting apparently frightened of being overturned.

Child Maintenance

*Henry Jenkins,*of Royston, was summoned by Adelaide Pryor, a single woman, of the same place, to show cause why he should not contribute to the support of her illegitimate child. It appeared in the course of the evidence that the defendant, who is a married man, had previously adopted a child of the complainant's as his own, and the case occupied the Court for a considerable time. There was an absolute denial by the defendant, and after hearing the complainant's evidence the bench dismissed the case.

A Case of Artificial Manure

Alfred King, of Royston, was brought before D. B. Balding Esq., at the Police Station charged with stealing a quantity of artificial manure to the value of 8s., the property of Mr. G.P. Pryor, his employer, for whom he had worked as a labourer twelve months. David Barnes, coach man to Mrs Henry Fordham, saw King working on land in Garden Walk. When King had finished work he saw King leave on a horse and cart. Just outside the gateway he saw him take a sack which was half full of something out of the cart, walk about ten yards and return to the cart without the sack . The witness informed the police of what he had seen and on further investigation it was found to be artificial manure. King was bound over in the sum of £5 to appear at the next Petty Sessions and need not be kept in custody.

A Rate Defaulter

Edward Johnson, trainer, of Royston, was summoned for refusing to pay a poor rate of £2 13s. 1½d and an Urban District rate for Royston of £2 2s. 6d. The defendant did not appear and said he did not consider himself liable. It appeared however, that the defendant had paid the first instalment of the Urban District Rate and the Chairmen said that clearly admitted liability. An order for payment forthwith, for the amount claimed and costs, or distress in default was made.

Housing Dispute

Clark v Oyston

The plaintiff, Henry Oyston, sued the defendant for the rent of a house which had been let to him for £3 a year. The defendant left after 14 days notice on December 15th, 1898 but the plaintiff claimed that a yearly tenancy required half a years notice and he now claimed half a year's rent in lieu of notice.

The defendant declared that the house was not fit to live in but the judge told him he should not have gone in.

The law bound a landlord in the case of a working man to make a house fit to live in at the time he went in or he could not claim rent, but the defendant could not after a year and a half in the house refuse to pay his rent because the house was not fit.

There would be a judgement for the plaintiff for the half-year's rent and costs, payment 2s. a month.

Doubtful Liability

Wilson v Woods

The plaintiff, Robert Wilson, tailor, of Royston sued the defendant for 12s. 6d. for a pair of trousers supplied in 1895. The trousers were ordered by the defendant's son, about 17 years of age, and were supplied for him.

The defendant said he did not owe the money. His son was an apprentice at the time earning only a small sum and he had not authorised his son to order clothes from Mr. Wilson. His son was now in the Militia.

His Honour said there was no evidence that the father had given any authority to the defendant or had ever dealt with him. He should advise him in future, if anyone came to him whose parents had not dealt with him that he would do well to inquire into it or he ran some risk. He must give judgement for the defendant with costs. The defendant applied for costs for his attendance and was allowed 2s. 6d.

JOHN STREET CONGREGATIONAL CHURCH, ROYSTON.

A SALE OF WORK

Will be held in **THE INSTITUTE**

On THURSDAY, APRIL 26th, 1900

Commencing at 3 pm. In addition to the

PLAIN AND FANCY NEEDLEWORK STALL

THERE WILL BE

A WORK COMPETITION STALL

Articles for competition, the Materials of which must not cost more tthan sevenpence, must be sent to Miss E S Titchmarsh, not later than Monday, April 23rd.
Entrance Fee 2d.

A FLOWER AND FRUIT STALL   A SWEET STALL

VOCAL AND INSTRUMENTAL MUSIC

During the Afternoon and Evening

The following Ladies and Gentlemen have kindly promised to assist:-

Mrs HELEN COLEMAN, A.R.A.M.

Misses BAKER, CRAIG(Medallist, L.R.A.M), HYLLESTED, HINKINS, M. HINKINS, STOCKBRIDGE and STONE.

Messrs. J. COURSE. C. HINKINS, H. HINKINS and SPENCE

At 5.45 there will be a

LADIES' MONKEY BRAND POLISHING COMPETITION

(For polishing Dirty Pennies).

The following handsome prizes have been given by Messrs Lever Bros. Ltd of Port Sunlight, Cheshire - Soap Makers to Her Majesty the Queen:

FIRST PRIZE- A handsome case of best Electro-plated Teaspoons and Tongs, value £1.1s 0d

SECOND PRIZE 18 Tablets Sunlight Soap

9 Tablets Lifebuoy Disinfectant Soap

A Case   8 Tablets of Swan White Floating Soap

Containing   9 Starlight Toilet Soap

6 Monkey Brand Soap

6 Dozen Sunlight Clothes Pins

With a beautifully illustrated certificate for each prize winner.

Entrance Fee, 6d. each, to be paid in pennies, on or before Wednesday, April 25th, to Mrs. E.W. Stone or Miss Stone.

--.

In the Lower Hall there will be POPULAR CHILDREN'S CONCERTS, at 6.15 and 8.15. Admission, 2d
PHONOGRAPH CONCERTS, at 7.15 and 9.15
Admission, 2d.
Air Gun Shooting Gallery, Bran Tubs, Post Office, & Various other Attractions.

REFRESHMENTS at very Moderate Charges.

Admission - From 3 to 5.30, 6d. ; after 5.30, 3d.

ROYSTON AND DISTRICT WOMEN'S LIBERAL ASSOCIATION

A PUBLIC MEETING

WILL BE HELD IN THE

KNEESWORTH STREET SCHOOL-ROOM,

on WEDNESDAY, APRIL 11TH,

WHEN ADDRESSES WILL BE DELIVERED BY

MRS SHELDON AMOS,

and

JAMES JACKSON, Esq.,

(Eighty Club)

Chair to be taken at 7.30pm.

Sale of Work

The object of the Sale of Work and Concerts was to raise funds to meet the special expenditure incurred in painting and renovating the Chapel.

The whole event was extremely well patronised both in the afternoon and in the evening that the success of the undertaking was assured. The total receipts amounted to the sum of £86.

WEDNESDAY NEXT
ROYSTON MARKET, HERTS.
SPECIAL SALE

Messrs. NASH, SON & ROWLEY

Will Sell by Auction on the Market Hill, Royston, WEDNESDAY NEXT, APRIL 11th, 1900
at 2 o'clock. pm,

USEFUL WORKING HORSES
3-year-old CART COLT and a PONY,
AGRICULTURAL IMPLEMENTS,

Including 2 Road Waggons, 3 Spring Carts, 3 Wagonettes, a 14-coulter Compost and Seed Drill by Smyth, an 8-coulter Drill, Clod crusher, Single and Double Furrow Ploughs, 8 Sets of Harrows, Turnip Hoes, 2 Grass Mowers, 2 Reapers by Samuelson, Cake Breakers, Root Pulpers, Weighing Machines, Iron Pig Troughs, &c., &c., several Sets of Harness.

Entries can be made up to 1 pm. on day of Sale. Catalogues may be obtained of Messrs. Nash, Son & Rowley, Auctioneers and Valuers, Royston, Herts.

Parcels For The Front

Miss Cautherley desires to thank the contributors of parcels of comforts for the men at the Front, who have enabled her to forward in her second despatch some fifty parcels. That the neighbouring villages, from which so many men have gone to the War, have an interest in this very praiseworthy effort, is shown by the fact that a large number of the parcels sent on this occasion came from Miss Hale of Therfield Rectory.

ROYSTON PARISH CHURCH
BAPTISMS

April

22nd   William and Florence, children of Harry Harman (Stoker) and Florence Ada Harman.

29th   Elizabeth Mary, daughter of James Baker (Baker) and Emma Baker.

29th   Ivy Alice, daughter of Ernest William Cleak (Porter) and Alice Emily Cleak (Union House).

MARRIAGES

April

1st   Joseph Badcock (Carter) to Alice Woolston.

7th   James Frederick Banham (Stableman) to Alice Elizabeth Richardson.

16th   Richard Samuel Thompson (Railway Porter) to Agatha Leah Pond.

BURIALS

April

28th   William Kingston, aged 84 years.

THE BOARD OF GUARDIANS

Praise and Helpful Suggestions

Col. Preston, Local Government Inspector, was at the Workhouse this month. He said that some time ago he had visited the Workhouse and found it in good order and the inmates contented. He thanked the Board for carrying out the various suggestions he had made about the bathing of vagrants and the purchasing of new bedsteads for the House.

He now suggested that the House Committee at present appointed to act by rota, should be replaced by a Standing Committee which would be a permanent authority between the Master, the Officials and the House.

He also referred to the out-relief and noticed that it was still rather high while the indoor relief was going down. Another matter he wished to mention was the question of children's teeth. Dentists had been appointed in several Unions, and it was known that there had been thousands of young fellows refused for the Army and Navy owing to faulty teeth, simply for want of care and attention. If they had a dentist who could come in once a quarter and look over the teeth of the children, it would not be very costly.

He was very glad to say that the number of vagrants relieved at the Vagrant's Ward had been greatly reduced during the year which he thought was the result of good administration and the working cells provided. He ended by saying that the Workhouse had been remarkably improved during the three or four years he had known it.

The New Assessments

A special meeting of the Royston Union Assessment Committee was held on April 20th for the purpose of hearing appeals against the new assessment of the Urban District and civil parish of Royston. Owing to the fact that since the Urban District was formed, the whole of the parishes and parts of the parishes previously forming the township of Royston were made into one parish and that a great many inequalities from the different bases of parochial assessment were found to exist, the Urban District Council brought the matter forward, and the Overseers for Royston, falling in with the proposal for a revised assessment, obtained the consent of the Assessment Committee to carry it out. For certain special properties such as the Railway Company, Gas and Water Companies, Brewery Company, Manure Company, Messrs. Smith's Mill, and the licensed houses of the town, a professional valuer was obtained in Mr. Castle, of the firm of Castle and Sons.

Rise in Salary Rescinded

At a meeting of the Board of Guardians, Mr. E. O. Fordham moved that a resolution passed at a previous meeting, increasing the nurse's salary, be rescinded. He reminded the Board that at a previous meeting they had increased the salary of the nurse from £25 to £28 a year. However, at the last meeting it had been decided that the duty of bathing the vagrants should be transferred to the porter's wife, the laundress. It was therefore thought by the committee that it would be desirable to rescind the resolution increasing the nurse's salary, and make it £25 as before, and add £5 to the salary of the laundress for taking the duties of bathing the female vagrants.

Renewals

At the monthly meeting of the Council, the Clerk read a letter from the Local Government Board sanctioning the re-appointment of Dr. Anningson as Medical Officer of Health and Mr. W. J. Webb as Inspector of Nuisances.

========

The Council agreed to the renewal of a licence to store calcium carbide to Mr. W. H. Hinkins.

MAY

Close Shaves

A Narrow Escape

A very narrow escape from collision at the Cross occurred on Wednesday, May 2nd, when a motor car, a carriage, and a lady cyclist travelling along three of the four cross roads seemed likely to come into a dangerous conflict. The motor car was coming out of Baldock Street into Melbourn Street, the carriage from Kneesworth Street into the High Street and the lady cyclist was coming down the High Street; all met within a few inches at the Cross, but the carriage and the cyclist pulled up, and the motor car, which was not travelling so fast as one sometimes sees them at this dangerous spot, just cleared without a conflict, though the horse in the carriage swung round with the shafts of the carriage upon the body of the vehicle.

A Midnight Alarm

Shortly after midnight on Monday, May 21st, a narrow escape from a serious fire occurred on the premises of Mr. E. Titchmarsh, grocer and draper, in the High Street. It appears that the inmates of the house woke and discovered a smell of fire, and on looking into the yard saw fire proceeding from the window of the kitchen, on the south side of the yard next to Mr. Matthews' premises. Mr. Titchmarsh and his sons and assistants and Mr. E. Matthews very promptly set to work and fortunately soon got the fire under control and extinguished without the necessity for calling upon the Fire Brigade. Had the discovery been made any later a serious fire might have ensued. It is supposed the fire was caused by a flue.

NEWS FROM THE FRONT

Trooper H. Pickett of the 12th Lancers, has written home to his parents at the Green Man, Royston, a letter from Bloemfontein, in which he says:

"We got up to the Front very quick on the 29th of March. We had a very hard fight 12 miles out of Bloemfontein. We went out about 3.30 in the morning and got in action at 8 o'clock....
You talk about humming birds - the bullets were whizzing round our heads. I was a bit frightened at first, but not so much now...............We don't get much to eat. All we had these three days was a biscuit-and-a-quarter a man and water bottle of dirty water to drink. We had seven killed and fifteen wounded and I thought my last time had come to a finish................They give as much as 2s. 6d. for a pipe of tobacco or a cigarette and 2s. for a biscuit to who will sell it. When we got to camp at night I was for guard, and about one o'clock in the night the sentry-go thought he saw a mounted man on horseback and he challenged three times, and no answer came so he fired at it and then woke up the guard and we all fired at it. The alarm went out and the whole regiment was turned out, and what do you think it was in the morning.? Why, a dead horse riddled with bullets! It had run astray out of the lines which the sentry thought was one of the enemy's scouts. We thought the enemy was attacking us that night......................Did you get the photo of the draft I sent? You might send us a few papers *(Crows)* and a few cigarettes but pack it so that it cannot get wet, as most of the parcels sent out here are wet................... We are advancing to-morrow at 3 o'clock. The people in England think it is very nearly over, but they are mistaken. You cannot see the Boers until you get right on top of them. When they see a Lancer they scoot like the........, they don't like our lances."

A Royston Man
Home From Ladysmith

Private Joseph Turtlebury, of the 5th Dragoon Guards, son of Mr. and Mrs. Turtlebury, of Queen's Road, Royston, was, we believe, the only soldier from Royston who went through the siege of Ladysmith. After the hardships of the siege, Private Turlebury was invalided home for a two months' leave. He gave a short interview on his experiences.

Facts First Hand

A Narrow Escape

On one occasion I had a close shave. We were on ammunition escort duty and were resting lying in a circle when a Boer shell burst in our midst and took off the front part of my saddle on which my head was resting; besides knocking over a few ammunition boxes on to my mate no further damage was done.

What we had to eat

Some part of the time we were only allowed one biscuit a day and horse flesh, also mealies, which had been condemned as unfit for the horses; we were glad to eat! We did not get half the things that were sent out for us. I got Lady White's present of pipe, tobacco and underclothing. All the plum pudding we had we made ourselves in which we put for suet the grease supplied for greasing our boots.

Cheers that frightened the Boers

I was in six different fights. On one occasion the Boers came out of cover and were proceeding across the open plain to make an attempt to capture Ladysmith. It was so unusual to see them thus that the officer in charge of us said, "Give them a cheer boys" which we did, whereupon they all took to their heels!

Down with fever

On January 8th I went into Hospital suffering from enteric fever and remained there until the town was relieved on February 28th. After this we had almost anything we liked to ask for. They were very kind to us. I came home in the S. S. Assaye arriving at the Royal Albert Docks on Monday, April 30th. I was a few days in Hospital at Woolwich and thence to Shorncliffe for clothes, arriving home in Royston on Wednesday evening.

Drink Again

William Howard, carpenter, of Royston, was charged with being drunk in the High Street, Royston.

The defendant admitted having a little too much to drink.

Inspector Hart described finding the defendant helplessly drunk in the High Street, Royston, and had to take him home.

The Chairman said defendant would have to pay 6s.

SCHOOL NEWS

National School(Girls)

On the 16th the Annual May Entertainment was given by the children and a half holiday was granted in consequence and on the 21st another half holiday was given in honour of the Relief of Mafeking.

On Ascension Day, the 24th, the children went to Church at 9.15 and had a holiday for the rest of the day.

Georgina Greenhill gave up her work in the school and her place was taken by Isabella Gaylor.

On the 30th, Mr. Bartlett visited the Boys' School, and came in to the Girls' Department for 5 minutes.

A Good Report.

The annual May-day Entertainment by the scholars in the National Schools was this year given a little later than the proper date owing to other fixtures near the beginning of the month. It came off in the Institute on Wednesday evening and as usual afforded a great amount of pleasure to a large audience of parents, friends and the general public. The building had been smartly decorated above the platform with groups of flags, drapery, &c., and when the 80 or more performers took their places on the platform, the girls dressed in white, the scene was a bright and cheery one. The Vicar, Rev. J. Harrison, presided, and the entertainment was under the direction of the teachers in the Boys' and Girls' Schools.

The programme contained fewer individual items and very little sameness about it; in fact, from the beginning to end it was more or less combined movement and action. Where individual parts were given the result was excellent, and so well rendered were the items of the programme that encores would have been as thick as blackberries but for an intimation from the Vicar that time would not allow.

The Vicar, in the interval, between first and second parts, said a few words, especially to parents of scholars.........The reports of the Government Inspector were of a satisfactory character, and the attendance had averaged 93 in the Girls' School and 92 in the Boys', while a number of them had received medals in succession for not having missed a single attendance during the year. He reminded parents that, not by order of the managers, but by the Government, the age of leaving school had been raised to 13, when they could leave if the 5th standard had been passed, otherwise they must remain until 14, although if 250 attendances had been made during the past five years they would be excused the standard at 13. If, however, they kept up the 250 attendances for the five years there would be no doubt about them passing the Standard. He reminded parents, therefore, that it was for the best interest of the children that a little sacrifice should, if necessary, be made.

After the second part of the programme had been completed, buns were given to all the children in the Schools by Mrs. J. E. Phillips.

British Mixed School

On May 4th A. Bartlett Esq. paid a visit without notice and stayed the whole morning.

During the week beginning May 7th, Miss Bement was absent from school owing to the illness of her grandmother and because of this, the timetable had been departed from on several occasions and cookery classes were held instead of usual lessons. Three boys left school on the Friday to go to work viz. Rowland Baker St.VII, Stanley Fisher St. VI and Reg Carrington St .V.

Cizzie Hales was readmitted on the 14th making 161 on roll and Miss Bement resumed duties. Miss Clarke superintended an extra cookery class in the afternoon to enable the girls to make their full attendance.

There was a half-holiday in the afternoon of the 21st in commemoration of the 'Relief of Mafeking'.

On the 31st the usual bi-monthly examinations were given. Work on whole was not up to the usual standard, carelessness in working being very apparent. The Head thought this might have been partly due to the intense excitement manifested amongst the children on the news of the 'Surrender of Pretoria'. Standard III work was exceptionally neat and well done but the Arithmetic and Reading of Standard 1 were poor and not what they should have been.

The class subjects throughout were very well done, especially Standards II and III, who answered readily and with intelligence. Standard I was not up to the standard of the others.

The Head thought it was due mainly to the laxity of discipline and he had spoken to the teacher concerned repeatedly on this point. The Upper Standard work continued good on the whole.

A CAUSE FOR CELEBRATION

Thanksgiving for the Relief of Mafeking

The relief to the public mind over the relief of Mafeking, found expression in the Parish Church on the morning of Sunday, May 20th, when the Vicar, Rev. J. Harrison, expressed at the opening of the service in a few words, the sentiment of thanksgiving in the public mind that the heroic defence had ended in victory for the brave defenders and welcome relief to the sufferers. "Praise God from whom all Blessings flow" was sung by the choir and congregation, and at the close of the service a verse of God Save the Queen was sung.

Corvus Cornix on Mafeking

The flood-gates of popular sentiment were fairly opened on Saturday and the demonstrations which followed were the measure of a deep reserve of pent-up feeling which has been accumulating around that heroic little drama in the Veldt, where British valour and endurance have written one more brilliant page in history, which can be read with admiration. If Mafeking is remembered as one of the most memorable sieges in history, there will be something equally remarkable for the young to carry in their memories during the coming century-- the great wave of popular enthusiasm with which the relief of Mafeking was received from the largest city to the smallest village. Even London, the huge elephantine city, burst all the swaddling bands of custom and went almost wild with delight until the banks of the Thames might almost have been mistaken for the banks of the Seine. For once the Britisher must have puzzled the foreigner by his tendency to explode and shout himself hoarse in the fullness of his joy.

The Relief Of Mafeking
A BONFIRE

The good tidings of the relief of Mafeking reached Royston late on the evening of Friday, May 18th and on Saturday the first bunting appeared in the streets and soon flags appeared throughout the town and the Church bells rang later in the day. At first it seemed that Royston would not do anything unusual to celebrate the event. However, there was a proposal to have a Bonfire on the Heath and during the afternoon cart-loads of all kinds of combustible materials from empty packing cases to solid timber were making their way up to the top of the hill above the Rifle Butts, to the site of the bonfire on the occasion of the Duke of York's marriage.

By six o' clock 25 loads had been hauled to the top along with 150 faggots. At 7 o'clock Mr Hinkins' band played in the streets and a lively time was occasioned by the carrying round the town of a respectable effigy in frock coat and tall hat of the redoubtable Kruger.

The lighting of the Bonfire was timed for 9.30 and at ten past nine the band started from the top of the High Street towards the Heath. Around the fire about two or three thousand people were assembled. As soon as the fire was well alight the band played the National Anthem and fireworks were set off. For nearly an hour the fire burned but in time the crowd returned to the town singing patriotic songs which went on until 11 or 12. The demonstrations were orderly and gave the police no unpleasant duties to perform. The shops closed early to give the assistants the opportunity to join the celebrations.

District Teachers' Association

A meeting of this association was held on Saturday afternoon in the National Schools; Mr. T. H. Quarry (Fowlmere) in the Chair.

The Chairman made a suggestion that as the Association had decided to abandon their annual soiree this year, the teachers in the various schools in the district should be asked to open in their schools subscription lists for the Indian Famine Fund, inviting scholars and others to subscribe. Mrs. Walbey (Royston) consented to act in the interests of the Fund, and it was decided to send notices to the teachers.

A resolution was passed on the subject of tenure for teachers, urging the Government now that the Superannuation Scheme is in force, to make provisions for securing the teachers against capricious and unjust dismissal.

Reporting the Show

The Annual entertainments organized by the Vicar, with the assistance of ladies and gentlemen of the town and neighbourhood, in aid of the Royston Church Choir Fund, which have been such attractive fixtures in previous years, came off at the Institute on Tuesday and Wednesday evening last. Again the programme took a dramatic form, and with three short pieces, and an excellent orchestra, there was a variety of attractions offered. Mr. A. C. Veasey, who had been assigned prominent parts in two of the pieces, found the calls of his country interposed, and a substitute had to be obtained. On the other hand, several other ladies and gentlemen in the locality found a place in a full programme. There was a large attendance at the opening night on Tuesday, and the audience were well repaid for their presence by a performance of a uniformly high standard of merit........The entertainment was repeated with success on Wednesday evening, and on this occasion while the Vicar was apologising for the absence of Lieut. Veasey, a telegram came from that gentleman, wishing them every success with the entertainment.

Mr. Thair as usual assisted in the costumier's department, and Mr. W. H. Hinkins supplied scenery.

The Queen's Birthday.

The Queen's birthday was inaugurated on Thursday, May 24th, by a joyous peal on the Church bells from five to six in the morning. At 9.15 there was a children's service at the Church, at which the National Anthem was sung. At the British School during the morning the children attending the school sang the National Anthem, and flags were floating in various parts of the town. In the evening Mr. Hinkins' Military Band played the National Anthem and patriotic selections in various parts of the town, and later a number of young men and boys made things lively by processions with flags flying, and horns blowing until a late hour.

Queen's Birthday At The Conservative Club

On Thursday evening, May 24th, the members of the Conservative Club celebrated the occasion of Her Majesty's Birthday with a supper and convivial evening. The room had been decorated by Mr. E. W. Thair with patriotic colours, &c., and Mrs. Stockbridge (caretaker) had brought into the room pictures of our military heroes surrounded with wreaths of evergreen, so that the otherwise bare room presented a very pleasing appearance. A substantial supper was placed upon the tables at eight o' clock, and soon everyone was doing justice to the same.

After various toasts had been drunk to the Royal Family and the Imperial Forces, and to the Club itself and to its success, Mr. H. R. Smith sang the 'Absent-Minded Beggar' and other members contributed to the evening with other musical items and a recitation. A collection was made for the A.M.B. Fund, realising 11s. 6½d. The singing of the National Anthem brought the meeting to a close.

THE INSTITUTE, ROYSTON, HERTS.
MESSRS. NASH, SON & ROWLEY
Have been instructed by the Executor of the late Miss Thomson, deceased, to Sell by Auction, at the Institute, Royston, on Friday, May 18th, 1900, at 12.30 p.m., the whole of the well-made

FURNITURE, and Effects (as removed from the Residence, Morton Street, Royston, for convenience of Sale), comprising a 5ft Mahogany Secretaire Book-Case, Mahogany Extending Dining Table, 6 Mahogany-framed Chairs and Couch in horse-hair, Mahogany Easy Chairs, Chiffoniers, 6 Rosewood-framed Chairs and Couch in red plush, Rosewood Music Waggon, 3-tier Whatnot, Oil Paintings, Engravings and other Pictures, Bagatelle Board, 2 Copper Tea Urns, Window Curtains, Brussels and other Carpeting, Fenders and Fireirons, Overmantels, 2 Oak Hall Chairs, about 300 VOLS. OF BOOKS, and Various Publications with Lithograph Sketches and Illustrations, Iron Brass-Mounted Bedsteads, Feather Beds and Bedding, 7ft. Mahogany Wardrobe, Mahogany and Painted Chests of Drawers, Mahogany Washstands, Bedroom Ware, Dressing Tables and Glasses, Cane-seat Chairs, &c., Tea, Dessert and Dinner Services, Quantity of Glass, Knives and Forks, Kitchen and Scullery Utensils, Treadle Sewing Machine, Microscope, etc., etc. Catalogues may be obtained of the Auctioneers, Baldock Street, Royston, Herts.

JOHN STREET CONGREGATIONAL CHURCH
A JUMBLE SALE
Will be held in the
SCHOOL-ROOM,
On FRIDAY, MAY 18th.
Left-off Clothing or any article that the owner has no further use for will be accepted and may be sent to either Mrs. E. W. Stone or W. C. Titchmarsh, or goods will be sent for if the owner will communicate with either of the above.
****
At the actual sale £9 was raised.

SPECIAL FEATURES FOR 1900
Stouter Boards and New Style of Mounting Stove Screens
WARREN BROTHERS'
NEW FIRE SCREENS
PRICE ONE SHILLING EACH
2/- SCREENS IN NEW SHAPES AND ENLARGED SIZE
NEW PHOTO FRAMES
PENNY FLOWER POT COVERS,
The most marvellous Penny Line ever offered
Fine White Manilla Shavings 1d., 2d.,& 3d. per bundle.
GOLD AND SILVER SHAVINGS 1d. PER PACKET.
WARREN BROS.,
HIGH STREET, ROYSTON

Proposed Joint Infectious Hospital

The Joint Hospital Board, consisting of representatives from the three authorities of the Royston Urban District Council, and the Melbourn and Ashwell Rural District Councils, formed for the purpose of providing hospital accommodation for infectious diseases, has come to a deadlock. The Board had purchased land in the Garden Walk outside Royston, and employed an architect for preparing plans for a Hospital to be erected thereon.

These plans have been submitted to the Local Government Board, who have sent them back with requirements which would add very much to the already heavy estimate for the building. In fact if carried out as the local Government Board suggests, it is understood that the cost of the building would be nearly £5,000 and about double what was originally contemplated. At a meeting of the Hospital Board it was decided that they could not carry out the plans as required by the Local Government Board.

NOTICE

J.B.BISHOP,
(Late E. BATESON)
CABINET MAKER, UPHOLSTERER AND GENERAL HOUSE FURNISHER,
HIGH STREET, ROYSTON

J. B. B. having been in Business with his Uncle (the late Mr. Elias Bateson) for the past ten years, begs to inform the Gentry and public generally of Royston and District that he is now carrying on the above business.

J. B. B. while thanking them for their kind support in the past of his late uncle, begs to solicit a continuance of a share of their patronage so generously bestowed on his predecessor.

DON'T LOOK OLD

With advancing years greyness increases. Stop this with Lockyer's Sulphur Hair Restorer, which darkens to the former colour and preserves the apearance. Lockyer's Large Bottles everywhere.

130

Association for the Prosecution of Felons

The annual meeting of the Herts. and Essex Association for the Prosecution of Felons was held at the Bull Hotel on Thursday, May 17th. About thirty sat down to dinner, which was served in excellent style by Mrs. Putt. Several loyal toasts were given. "The Army, Navy and Colonial Forces" were proposed as was "Success to Agriculture".

The business of the annual meeting was transacted and the annual report showed that the Association had commenced the year with a balance of £13 which was now £18. There had been no occasion for prosecution during the year.

The report referred to the loss of the president by the death of Mr. W. H. Lees. A letter of condolence would be sent to Mrs Lees. Another loss to the association was caused by the resignation of their solicitor and treasurer, Mr. Nash-Wortham whose removal from the town had made it necessary. He recommended Mr. W. B. King be appointed to replace him. This was carried unanimously.

Afterwards a few songs were sung and the hat was sent round and £1 1s. was collected which was to be sent to the *Daily Mail* War Fund.

Death of Mr. T. Potter

We regret to announce the death of an old and respected townsman, Mr. Thomas Potter, which took place on Thursday, 24th. The deceased for many years kept the White Hart near the Fish Hill, and during that time, and since, he carried on the business of a pork butcher. He had always, in a quiet, practical way, taken an interest in public affairs in the town and was one of the first Parish Councillors under the arrangements in force before the Urban District Council was formed.

The deceased was the Secretary of the Juvenile Branch of the Independent Foresters' Lodge. He was also a Trustee of the adult branch of the Society and member of the Conservative Club.

The funeral took place at the Additional Church Burial Ground in the presence of a large number of his fellow townsmen. The service was conducted by the Rev. J. Harrison.

Corvus Cornix on Gypsies

Another matter which came up for passing criticism, not only upon its merits, but upon the tendency of the Herts County Council to spend money freely in fees to Counsel, was the proposal to adopt certain Bye-laws respecting gipsy encampments near to dwelling houses and streets. By these Bye-laws, which met with the approval of the County Council, and will be submitted in due course to the Home Secretary, it is proposed to make it an offence on the part of the owner of land, and also on the part of the person encamping, for any tent dweller, squatter, gipsy or other person dwelling in a tent, van, or other similar structure, to so encamp to the annoyance, injury or disturbance of residents in the neighbourhood, within 100 yards of any street or dwelling house. There is a great need for such Bye-laws in many parts of the county, and by their means, if and when adopted, the old standing difficulty of vans on the Warren at Royston could be dealt with and disposed of once and for all.

131

ROYSTON PARISH CHURCH
BAPTISMS

May

13th   Lilian Alice, daughter of James Tuck (Farmer) and Susanna Tuck.

13th   Baden Powell, son of Samuel Darlow (Stableman) and Florence Emma Darlow.

15th   Alice Mary, daughter of Harold Francis John Banham (Solicitor) and Edith Alice Banham.

19th   Eric Charles Warren, son of Charles Warren (Printer) and Maud Warren.

MARRIAGES
None

BURIALS

May

12th   Lilian Harriet Woods, aged 3 years.

14th   John Woods, aged 58 years.

A LETTER TO THE EDITOR

Editor's Comment (We cannot hold ourselves responsible for the OPINIONS expressed by our correspondents.)

The Volunteers Reserve

Sir,

The War office is considering the details of a Volunteer Reserve to be called out in the case of an invasion.

The following would be the general lines:-

(a) Ex-Volunteers of all arms to be eligible.

(b) To be on Regimental lines, i.e., Volunteers to register themselves at the Headquarters of their former unit, or failing this at the Volunteer unit nearest to their permanent place of residence.

(c) No officer or man to be eligible who has not been returned six times efficient within the last ten years.

(d) The maximum age for officers to be 62 years and for men 55 years. On attaining these ages all officers and men will cease to belong to the Reserve.

(e) Each man enrolled will be permitted to fire twenty-one rounds per annum free of charge. All ex-Volunteers fulfilling the above conditions are earnestly requested to send in their names and addresses for registration.

CAPT. AND ADJT. C.M. KENDALL,

Ist (Herts. V.B. Beds. Regt.)

Hertford,

May 2nd, 1900

Other Births, marriages and deaths reported in May

Births

10th   A son to the wife of Barre Goldie, at "North Hall", Royston.

Marriages

24th   Mr. J. T. Freeman and Miss E. M. Chamberlain at the Wesleyan Chapel.

Deaths

11th   Frederick James Giffen, of Reed Mill, aged 75 years at Royston Union.

24th   Thomas Potter, at Market Hill, after a short but painful illness.

HOME REMEDIES

SPORT
Golf

May

5th   Monthly Medal.

17th   Captain's Prize.

19th   Royston v Enfield. Royston 43 Enfield 4.

Cricket

May

5th   Royston Victoria v Cambridge Pelican (on Heath). Royston won.

12th   Royston Victoria v Cambridge Pagans (on Heath). Cambridge won.

14th   Royston v Cambridge Tom-Tits (on Heath). Royston won.

19th   Royston Victoria v Camb. IOU. (on Heath). Cambridge won.

26th   Royston Victoria v Ashwell (on Heath). Royston won.

A MARRIAGE

At the Wesleyan Chapel on Thursday, May 24th, the marriage took place of Mr. J. T. Freeman, clerk at the Royston Post Office, to Miss E. M. Chamberlain, of Queen's Road, Royston. The Rev. T. H. Lomas officiated and a large number of friends and well-wishers were present. The bride, who was given away by her brother, Mr. J. Chamberlain, wore a dress of dove grey trimmed with white satin and a white hat and tips, and was accompanied by Misses M. and F. Chamberlain (nieces), who were dressed in lavender grey and pale blue with hats to match. The best man was Mr. Dyer. Among the useful presents received was a rocking chair from the Royston Post Office staff and a plated teapot from the members of the Wesleyan Society Class.

Kneesworth Street Sunday School Anniversary

As usual the services attracted large congregations. The chapel was made exceptionally bright this year by means of flowers and plants and mottoes. In front of the pulpit, within the communion rail, was a very fine group of flowering plants , flanked by a handsome pair of palms. At the back of the pulpit was the motto, "Hitherto hath the Lord helped us", and on the fronts of the side galleries were the mottoes, "God bless our Sunday School", and "Let the children of Zion rejoice in their King".

The children were placed in the galleries and as usual took a prominent part in the singing of special hymns set to joyous music. The preacher for the occasion was Dr. Rawlings who in the morning, from the incident of Naboth, enforced lessons of character. In the afternoon taking a piece of coal he held the attention of the children while dilating upon the wonders of God's world to be seen in common things; and in the evening he preached to a crowded congregation from the text, "I am the way, the truth and the life".

For the musical part of the services the hymns and music were well selected and heartily rendered by the choir and children under the direction of Mr. Fisher, and evidently enjoyed by the large congregations. The anthems,"The Lord is my Shepherd", and some of the choruses of the hymns were much above the average on these occasions, and added greatly to the interest of the services. The National Anthem was played on the organ at the close of the evening service.

A QUESTION OF TEETH

Old Teeth Bought

Many ladies and gentlemen have by them old or disused false teeth which might as well be turned into money. Messrs. R.D.& J.B. Fraser, of Princess Street, Ipswich, (established since 1833), buy old false teeth. If you send your teeth to them, they will remit you by return of post the utmost value; or, if preferred they will make you the best offer, and hold the teeth over for your reply. If reference necessary, apply to Messrs. Bacon & Co., Bankers, Ipswich.

Rejected

Hundreds of volunteers were rejected for active service through having bad teeth. Unsound teeth mean imperfect mastication, therefore indifferent health. A good digestion cannot be obtained without good teeth. All persons, therefore, with defective teeth should send for the new book on the teeth, (sent gratis and post free) by Shipley -Slipper, the well-known London Surgeon Dentist, 37 High Holborn, London, W.C.

THE COST OF LIVING

JUNE

Three Generations of Soldiers

Royston is able to claim perhaps a unique distinction in this part of the country in having furnished three generations of soldiers from one family. The connecting link is Peter Hoy, roadman. His father was a soldier in the marines, who fought in the War with France in the early years of the century. He fell into the hands of the French after being shipwrecked and was confined in a French prison for two years. The shipwreck happened on New Year's Day, and as that day came round the old soldier would in later years gather his boys round him and tell over again the story of his perilous adventures.

The four sons listened to such purpose to the exciting tales of their father's adventures that all four sons in their turn became soldiers.

One of his sons, Peter, is now employed in the service of the District Council, and saw service in India and was invalided home. Of his five sons, three are soldiers - one in India, and two are at the Front in South Africa - and the other two were only prevented from joining by accidents, which, causing personal injuries, disqualified them from service.

Introducing the Motor Car

There were a number of motor cars and cycles passing through the town on Sunday, Monday, and Tuesday. On the latter day the cars of the Automobile Club which had been on tour in the Eastern Counties, returned from Cambridge and passed through Royston, but at different times and not in a body or procession, as had been anticipated.

Royston Cottage Hospital

The twenty-ninth annual report of the Committee of the Royston Cottage Hospital has been issued this week. In their report the Committee says:

"Mrs. Baker has retired from the position of Nurse-in-Charge, which she had held for nearly 30 years. The Committee raised a fund to ensure a pension for her future maintenance, and the public of the town and district responded generously to the appeal. The fund reached a total of £149 9s. 2d which was mostly invested in a Life Annuity producing £21 7s. 8d.

It was decided to have a qualified assistant nurse as well as a qualified nurse. Your Committee received 100 applications for the posts. The Committee appointed Mrs. Collins and her daughter Miss Collins for these two posts.

Patients in Hospital 1st Jan, 1899, 1 man   1
Patients admitted during the year, women   12
Patients admitted during the year, men   29
Number of Patients treated during the year 42

Death of Mrs A. Porter

The death of Mrs. A. Porter, the wife of the well known fancy shop owner in the High Street, took place on June 7th. Her health had been failing and she had become very infirm of late. The news of her death will be received with great regret and sympathy for the bereaved husband and family. It is not long age that the Mr. and Mrs. Porter had the happiness of celebrating their golden wedding.

At the Workhouse

An Old Couple's Concerns

The Visiting Committee reported the case of a man and woman over 70 years of age in the Workhouse. The man wanted to leave and leave his wife behind, but the Committee did not recommend so exceptional a course, and the Board thought it was not desirable to comply with his request. If he could take his wife he would be at liberty to leave.

Tenders

Tenders were received and accepted as follows:
Bread and flour for the Workhouse
W. South - 4d. per loaf and 24s. per sack
C. Ingrey - 3¼ d. and 19s. (accepted).
Meat - L. E. Clark (Royston), beef and mutton, 5s. 11d. per 14lbs., officers' meat, 7s. 8d. (accepted).
Bread for the out-door poor - No. 1 district, J. E. Lilly 3d. (accepted), No. 2 district, W. South 3d. (accepted), No. 3 district, D. G. Gunnell 4d., J. Wilson 4d. (accepted), No. 5 district, A. Warren 3½ d. (accepted), No. 6 district, A. Wing 3 ¼ d. (accepted).

Resignation of Nurse

The clerk read a letter from Miss Jones giving a month's notice resigning her appointment as Workhouse Nurse.
The resignation was accepted and it was decided to advertise for a successor for the office.

Nurse Wanted

THE GUARDIANS of the Royston Union require the services of a nurse to take charge of the Sick Wards, Lying-in Ward and Children's Nursery at the Workhouse at Royston. Candidates must be single or widows without children.
The salary to be at the rate of £25 per annum with Rations and Apartments in the workhouse and the emoluments for the purpose of the Superannuation Act are valued at £30.
Applications in the candidate's handwriting, stating age and experience, accompanied by copies of recent testimonials, must reach me not later than TUESDAY, the 3rd JULY NEXT.
Selected candidates will have notice when to attend.
By Order,
ARTHUR SHARPE
Clerk to the Guardians.
Union Offices,
Royston, Herts.,
20th June, 1900.

Thoughts on Tom-tits

" A tom-tit is a cheeky little fellow and has been known to build in all kinds of places. But these are advanced times, and if men aspire to electric lights, at least a tom-tit may go in for gas-light in his apartments. So at least, appear to have thought all the tom-tits in Royston. It was discovered on removing the lanterns from the iron pillars in the streets that no less than seven pairs had selected that small hollow space within the top of the pillars as their breeding ground. Here the seven little imps have sat defiantly while the lamp-lighter went his rounds and lit up their small feathered apartments, and here in most cases by daylight and gaslight they sat and hatched out their eggs, and added considerably to the little world of tom-tits."
Corvus Cornix.

The Eclipse of the Sun

In the newspaper of June 1st an eclipse was reported. "The Eclipse of the Sun on Monday afternoon last was seen in this neighbourhood to great advantage. Even those who did not resort to the aid of smoked glass, were able to see through the fleecy haze of cloud which covered the sun during part of the moon's contact, a fairly sharp definition of the shadow, while during the latter part of the contact, a cloudless sky gave the many persons using smoked glass the opportunity of seeing the eclipse very clearly"

THE BOER WAR

The British Flag At Pretoria
Torchlight Procession at Royston

The news of the entry of Lord Roberts into Pretoria reached Royston in a private telegram which was posted soon after mid-day on Tuesday, June 5th, and the Committee formed for the carrying out the proposed Torchlight Procession met on Tuesday evening and decided to carry out the Procession on Wednesday evening. The committee had managed beforehand to secure a large supply of torches, coloured lights, fireworks, &c., and invited decorated cars, cycles, persons in costumes &c., to join in the Procession; an invitation which was responded to with so much readiness and ingenuity that the success of the experiment was assured.

The Priory Grounds (by kind permission of Mr. D. A. Bevan), and the Priory Lane, were the trysting place, inside the grounds for the pedestrians and outside for the larger cars. The general public waited at a distance contenting themselves with glimpses of the curious medley getting itself together - fair ladies and pretty devices in cycles and dresses, masked characters, from nabobs to bushmen in sombreros, and pretty little girls, donkeys and clowns, horses in trousers, and little boys in old soldiers' jackets.

The variety of costumes gave to the Procession something of the character of a masked ball, judging by the remark of one young fellow in the Procession to a friend by the way - "I have had a very nice walk by the side of this young lady, but I haven't the least idea who she is." Probably "she" wasn't at all!

The dresses of the ladies, with and without cycles, who walked in the Procession, presented some charming combinations - white and tri-colour having a prominent place - which were much admired.

A Royston Man Killed At The Front

The news has reached Royston of the death of a Royston man at the Front. *Private W. Day*, 21 years old, of the 2nd Grenadier Guards, eldest son of James Day. He was killed in the action at Senekal, with Rundler's Force, on 28th May.

A pathetic interest is added to the event by the fact that his parents received on the same day, a letter from their son and another from the War Office announcing his death.

In his letter he wrote from the Thabauchu district which had seen some hard fighting. He told of his experiences and discomfort on a mountain 3,500 ft high with Boers on two sides and narrow escapes from Boer shells...... "though the Boers are not so good a shot as they make them to be". He referred to the hardships of half rations and lying on the ground with one blanket covered with white frost. He longed...... "to be with father and have a glass of beer and a piece of bread and cheese. I have not had a wash for five days and not a change of linen since we came off the boat so you know how I feel. But there is a better time coming ..... good day and bless you all".

SCHOOL NEWS

British School

School closed at noon on 1st June for the Whitsun Holiday and reopened on the 6th with an attendance of 151 out of 157.

Miss Clarke was away on the afternoon of the 11th because of sickness and on the same day Nelly Simin was readmitted.

School was closed in the afternoon of the 12th on account of the Band of Hope Treat.

Pupils, Hattie Thompson, and Bertie Bishop, St VII left during the week ending the 15th, leaving 156 on roll.

During the week ending the 22nd Std III had again made 100% in attendance. This class, had as a rule, very regular attendance and the work was in consequence correspondingly good.

National School(Girls)

There was no school on the 4th or the 5th.

The Head was absent from school to attend her brother's wedding and there was a half-holiday on account of two Band of Hope Treats.

Mr. Myers came into school for a few hours at 12 on the 25th.

On the 28th E. Bedwell and J. Gaylor were given leave from school to attend the Annual Sunday School Teachers' outing. To suit the vicar who was to help with a Scripture Lesson, the Secular Instruction would be taken at 9.15 and the Religious Instuction at 11.15.

Charge of Attempted Suicide at Royston

William Burton, tailor, Mackerel Hall, Royston, was charged on the information of Inspector Hart that he did unlawfully take a quantity of deadly poison called oxalic acid, at Royston, on the 14th June, with the intent thereby feloniously, wilfully and of malice aforethought to kill and murder himself.

The defendant said he had been under the Doctor's hands over twelve months, off and on, with pains in his head. At times he had seemed lost and not knowing what he was doing, and had been very low spirited. He had

Dr. Windsor stated he had seen the defendant professionally several times during the past six or nine months, and the chief complaint was that he had pains in the head, and was in a low melancholy state. There was no obvious disease, but he did not seem to improve very much.

The Magistrates retired for a time and on their return the Chairman said that they must send this case to the Quarter Sessions, but as the sessions would not be for some time they would be willing to release him on bail, himself in £5, if he could find someone to be bound in another £5.

Dissimilar Bye-Laws

Samuel Quinton, the Park, Royston, was summoned on the information of P.c. Harry Wright, for a breach of the Lighting Bye-Laws, by driving a carriage in Melbourn Street, Royston, on June 23rd, without a light.

The defendant said when he left the University Arms Hotel, Cambridge, he was informed that he need not have his lamps alight, and as he could see better without them, he was glad not to have them. He did not know that the regulations were different in Hertfordshire from Cambridgeshire and he was very sorry it occurred.

The Chairman said he was aware that the regulations as to lighting in Cambridgeshire were suspended for three months in summer and no doubt it was confusing. Superintendent Reynolds said he did not press the case.

The Chairman said he would have to pay a nominal fine and costs, amounting to 8s.

Drunk and Disorderly

William Hill, a tall middle aged man, using a crutch, was charged with being drunk and disorderly on the highway, at Royston, on May 26th. The defendant said he was guilty. He did not know what he was doing.

P.c. Knight said that on Saturday evening he found the defendant at the Boar's Head Public House, very noisy and refusing to quit, and he had to eject him. He had cautioned him before on the same day when he was in the street exposing a wound.

The Chairman said he would be fined 5s. or seven days in default. The defendant was removed in custody.

Whitsuntide 1900

The Whitsuntide holidays, which had been threatened by almost wintry weather on Friday, were shared in by large numbers of visitors to this district on Sunday and Monday last. The weather on Monday was delightful and there was an unusually large gathering of people on the Heath during the afternoon to witness the cricket match and enjoy the pleasures of the Heath at its best.

A prettier sight has seldom been witnessed on a Bank Holiday than that presented during the afternoon.

The excursions from London brought down many passengers, and a large number of young people home from Saturday to Tuesday swelled the number of people in and about the town during the day.

The Heath Training Ground

A new feature was added to the ground at the west end of the Heath where the race horses do their running, when a new starting gate similar to those used on race courses was put up for the first time. This addition to the ground will enable the trainers to practise starting under similar conditions to those which have to be met with in an actual race.

Suicide on the Line

On Friday, June 15th., an inquest was held at Digswell Lodge Farm, near Welwyn, on the body of a man named John Rogers. He was working at the above farm with a man named Wilson, when he suddenly left, walked on to the G. N. R. railway bridge and jumped down on to the line. Wilson hurried to the spot and found the deceased injured, past recovery and he died shortly afterwards. The deceased's name was not known at the time, but a letter was found upon him from Royston recommending him for employment at the Walkern Brewery. The Royston police were communicated with, and the man identified. The deceased was for a time employed at the Royston Brewery, and will be remembered by some of our readers as "Lord George", a name given to him for his soldierly bearing. He had been seen in Royston a few days before his death. The deceased was 55 years of age.

Flower Service

This annual event took place in the Parish Church on Sunday, June 24th, and proved as interesting as ever to the children of the Sunday Schools, who assembled with their offerings of flowers for the London Hospitals. As the vicar received the offerings at the entrance to the chancel, the children were marshalled round the aisles by their teachers and the choirs sang a series of well known hymns. The flowers were sent to various London Hospitals and the offertory was for the North-Eastern Hospital for Children.

Success Again

A Dog Show under Kennel Club Rules was held at Clacton-on-Sea in connection with the Essex Agricultural Show, when Mr. P. F. Fordham took first and special, two seconds and a third prize in different classes, with his retriever puppy "Crane", bred by himself. He also took first and special, and a second, with carrier pigeons.

Coffee Tavern Company

The annual general meeting of the shareholders of the Royston Coffee Tavern Company was held at the Victoria Restaurant in the High Street on Wednesday evening, June 20th. The Rev. J. Harrison, chairman of the Board of Directors, presiding. The business was of a formal character, and, now that the Coffee Tavern is sub-let, was confined almost to the adoption of the balance sheet. The Directors' report presented was as follows: "The Directors beg to hand you herewith their seventeenth annual report and balance sheet for the year ending April 30th, 1900. The profit on the letting of premises and fittings, &c., is £12 8s. 9d., thus reducing the debit balance to £126 14s., and they have good reason to believe the reduction will in the present year be greater."

On the motion of the Chairman, the report and balance sheet were adopted..

139

ANNIVERSARIES

Wesleyan Sunday School

The anniversary services of the Queen's Road Wesleyan Sunday School took place on Sunday, June 10th and were well attended The preacher was the Rev. H.T. Hooper, one of the Cambridge Circuit Ministers, and an attractive part of the services was the singing by the scholars of especially selected anniversary hymns and music, led by the Choir. On the Monday afternoon and evening the annual tea and public meeting were held in the Chapel. During the evening different speakers gave talks about the role of the Sunday Schools. Several points were made on this subject viz., the Sunday Schools must make the best of the children while young and realise the greatness of the work in which they were engaged; Sunday School teachers should be seven day Christians. They should be "living epistles" all through the week as well as Sunday, as children were very quick to note all their actions. The speakers also called upon parents to show more interest in the teaching of the children.

Baptist Chapel

The anniversary celebrations at the Particular Baptist Chapel were held on Thursday, June 14th, during the afternoon and evening. The weather was fine during the latter part of the day and the congregations included a number of visitors from neighbouring places. Between the two services there was a tea provided at which nearly fifty sat down. Collections were in aid of Chapel funds.

A New Postman

Mr. J. A. Bonnett, who has discharged the duties temporarily for some time past, has been appointed rural postman between Royston, Chishill, Heydon and Chrishall, &c., in place of Mr. T. Baker, who held the office for many years and resigned a short time ago.

John Street Sunday School

The anniversary services and annual meeting of the John Street Congregational Church Sunday School took place on Sunday and Monday, June 17th and 18th. The children had a prominent place in the services, which were bright, attractive, and interesting. The whole end of the Chapel upon and around the pulpit and communion table presented a strikingly pretty picture of brightly coloured flowers and plants, and the children seated in the organ gallery front, added an element of brightness to the scene, which was emphasised by the part they took with the choir in the musical services of the day.

The tea took place in the Schoolroom on Monday and was followed by the annual meeting. A report was presented on the finances and other routine matters. Seven children had entered for the Royston & District Sunday School Union Scripture Examination and had passed, five taking 2nd class certificates, one 1st class, and one 1st prize.

The prizes were distributed and the children were reminded that they should remember that everyone of their acts, words, and thoughts was helping to build up their life and character, bit by bit, just the same as all the great buildings of the world had been built up, stone by stone, little by little, and all the time the design was being developed, until at last the whole plan of the architect was revealed. He appealed to them to take care and form their lives, so that one day they would grow up according to the design of The Great Architect.

TEMPERANCE

Drink - The Campaign for Sunday Closing

On Wednesday, June 13th, a public meeting in support of the Sunday Closing Movement, and the Sale of Intoxicating Drink to Children Bill, was held in the Institute under the auspices of all the Temperance Societies in the town. The chairman, Rev J. Harrison, felt that the legislation would bring great benefit to the country especially in the great centres of population as it was pitiable to see children allowed to begin a habit which too often ended with physical, moral and spiritual ruin.

The speaker, Mr. Durnsford looked upon the two issues as a social wrong and felt a great many publicans would like to see Sunday closing. While a working man agitated for his eight hours a day and the Factory Act provided for a 56-hour week, the average hours at the public houses all over England was 108. The loss in wages for labour by Sunday and Monday drinking was enough to pay for the South African War. For the sake of the long hours and the wastage of Monday through Sunday drinking, he supported Sunday closing. He was of the opinion that Sunday should be a day of rest for the 200,000 people behind the bars and not of toil and the Sabbath should be returned to what God originally intended.

The motion to support the government was passed unanimously.

COUNCIL AFFAIRS

The Building Bye-Laws and the Fleet

The Highways Committee presented a report upon Mr. Beale's plans for cottages in the Fleet. The report stated that on several occasions plans relating to cottages proposed to be erected by Mr. John Beale in the Fleet had been under the consideration of the Committee, and the Committee had been unable to recommend the plan for acceptance through not complying with the Bye-Laws as to air space in front of the buildings.

Mr. Beale had now submitted fresh plans accompanied by a letter stating that Messrs. Phillips had promised him a piece of land on the opposite side of the lane, so that the proper width of road could be obtained, if necessary, without putting back his building line. Upon this the Committee now reported that this proposal would be in contravention of the Bye-Laws. The roadway at the place in question was ten feet wide, so that the new buildings must be set back so as to have seventeen feet in front of them to the boundary of any lands or premises immediately opposite.

Mr. Gimson moved the adoption of the report and Mr. H. Smith seconded. There then followed a lengthy discussion in which Council Member Mr. Goodman said the lane itself was so irregular that by putting the cottages back he would be making for a better frontage and straighten it. They were not dealing with a high road, but simply a blind lane, never taken over by a public authority, and it seemed very questionable whether the Bye-Law in question had reference to such a case as this. It would be throwing obstacles in the way of improving the town, and the renewing of cottages for the working classes.

However, after much further discussion the report was adopted by seven votes to four

Inspector's Report

The Sanitary Inspector (Mr. Webb) reported upon certain cases in which it was complained that urinal arrangements connected with public houses allowed drainage into the surface drains, and that steps were being taken to get defects remedied.

The Chairman remarked that some of the places mentioned had proper accommodation provided, and he did not think the Inspector could visit places unless in case of a nuisance.

Mr. Webb said he did not wish to exceed or to evade his duty. Council Member, Mr. Matthews, thought that if offensive matter got into the surface drain the Inspector was justified in trying to follow it up.

Telephones

At the meeting held on Monday, June 11th, the Clerk read a letter from the Secretary of the General Post Office enclosing a deed authorising the National Telephone Company to erect works to certain towns, but as the powers conferred upon the company by the deed could not be exercised without the consent of the local authorities, they asked for the consent of this Council in respect to the Royston district.

It was understood that consent would be given.

THE UTILITIES

The Water Company and the Roads

At a meeting of the Urban District Council, Mr. Balding said he would like to draw the attention of the Council to the opening of the road on the London Road hill for the purposes of the Water Company. The road was opened some time ago and when the gravel was put back it was left for some time very much about the road, and then after the County Council roadmen had levelled it, the same part was opened again, and now a measuring tank for testing the pumping had been erected on part of the highway, and inside a protecting rail, which in itself was a serious danger to traffic along the road, a pole next the road being placed at an angle not parallel with the road and projecting at one end beyond the rest in a way that was really dangerous.

After some discussion it was directed that the Clerk write to Mr. Rowley, the secretary of the Water Company, on the Subject.

Sale of Water Company Shares

Mr. R. F. Condor, auctioneer, offered for sale on June 13th at the Bull Hotel, Royston, as part of the property of the late Mr. G. J. Chapman, 50 £10 shares in the Royston Water Company, being part of the last issue of additional ordinary shares, upon which the maximum dividend that can be paid is 7 per cent., as against a possible 10 per cent. on the original ordinary share capital. All the shares, sold in 10 lots of 5 shares each, were knocked down at their face value of £10 per share, the chief purchasers being, Mr. W. T. Rowley, Mr. Abbott, and Mr. James Russell.

ROYSTON PARISH CHURCH
BAPTISMS
June
3rd Harold Frederick, son of Frederick Mason (Groom) and Agnes Hannah. Mason.
17th Alexander Barre, son of Barre Algernon Highmore Goldie (Stockbroker) and Bertha Goldie.
17th Harold Alec, son of William Barnard (Labourer) and Caroline Rebecca Barnard.
17th Henry James, son of Henry Woods (Stableman) and Martha Woods.
MARRIAGES
June
None.

BURIALS
June
21st James Humphrey, aged 68 years.

Other deaths reported in June.
8th   Sarah Porter, High Street, Royston, aged 76 years.
15th   Isabel Hollingsworth, Royston Union, aged 72 years.
15th   Lucy Stacey, Royston Union, aged 86 years.

The Water Company Replies

At the Urban District Council meeting on June 11th, the Clerk read a reply from Mr. Rowley in which he stated that he had taken steps to minimize danger and the inconvenience which had been complained of.

ROYSTON GAS COMPANY (LIMITED)

NOTICE IS HERBY GIVEN, That the coupons for the half-year's interest on the 4% Debentures, due on the 1st prox., will be paid upon presentation, less income tax, on and after the 2nd prox., at Barclay & Co. (Limited), Royston Bank .
June 27th, 1900.

SPORT
Golf
2nd   Monthly Medal
        Whitsuntide Meeting. June 2nd, 4th and 5th.
        Winner of "Hill" Gold Challenge Cup - Mr. A. H. Peart
Cricket
June,
2nd   Royston Cricket Club v Victoria Grove (on Heath). Royston won.
2nd   Royston Victoria Cricket Club v Cambridge Rodney (on Parkers Piece). Result - a draw.
2nd   Royston Victoria 2nd XI v Wimpole (away). Wimpole won.
4th   Royston v Victoria Grove. No score reported
4th   Royston NYMS v St . Clements Anchor, Cambs(away). Royston won.
9th   Royston Victoria v Fowlmere (on Heath). Royston won.
9th   Royston Victoria 2nd XI v Melbourn & Meldreth (away). Melbourn won.
14th   Royston NYMS v St Barnabas Youths (on Parkers Piece). Royston won
16th   Royston Victoria v Kings Cross Loco (on Heath). Royston won.
19th   Royston v Leys School (on school ground). Royston won.
23rd   Royston Victoria v Cambridge Liberal Club(on Parkers Piece). Royston won.
23rd   Royston Victoria 2nd XI v Wimpole (on Heath). Royston won.
30th   Royston Victoria v Ashwell (played at Ashwell) Royston won.

OUTINGS

Church Army

On Thursday, June 28th, a pleasant summer outing was organised in connection with Capt. Pegg's Church Army work at the Mission Room. A party numbering about forty was organised, and proceeded in brakes to Wimpole Park. Here, in the beautiful grounds the members of the party enjoyed an ideal picnic, with tea in the open air, and afterwards the free enjoyment of exploring the most delightful Park and woodland scenery, which is just now to be seen at its best. After a very enjoyable evening, the party had a pleasant drive home to Royston.

Temperance Society Treat

The members of the John Street Congregational Band of Hope had their annual outing on Tuesday, June 12th. The party, numbering nearly 100, travelled in wagons and vans to Shepreth. Here by the kindness of the Misses Woodham, the grounds at Tyrells were placed at their disposal, and a delightful afternoon was spent. Tea was provided in the grounds and the workers accompanying the party had the cordial co-operation of the Misses Woodham in carrying out the arrangements. The rest of the evening was spent in games and then followed a pleasant ride home, with a distribution of buns at the end of the journey. The weather was fine and the outing was much enjoyed.

To the Crystal Palace

The members of the Kneesworth Street Congregational Church Choir, following the practice of some years past, went to the Crystal Palace on June 30th and took part in the great Choral Festival in the Handel Orchestra, by the Nonconformist Choir Union, in which choirs from all parts of the country help to swell the great chorus of 4,000 voices. A special programme of high class festival music was rendered, and for this the several choirs had for some months past been rehearsing. The result was a very fine performance and an example of what may be done in the way of improvement of choral music.

The Kneesworth Street Choir on this their tenth year of taking part, were joined by the Barley and Chishill Congregational Choirs, and under the direction of Mr. W. P. Fisher (Royston), and Mr. Chuck (Barley), they had met for rehearsal.

In addition to the festival programme there were many other attractions for the party, including the evening's display of fireworks and the illuminated fountains.

County Volunteers' Prize Meeting

The annual Herts. County Volunteer Competition took place on Friday, June 22nd, at the Runneymede Ranges at Staines. Four of the E Company men went up: Corporal King, Private Stamford, Private R. King and Sergeant-Instructor Clarke. In the Brownlow Prizes, Private R. King took 11th place and £1 prize. In the Staff Prizes, open to Sergeant-Instructors, the first prize of £2 was won by Sergeant-Instructor Clarke, with a score of 30 at 200 yards, standing.

THE COST OF LIVING

JULY
TRIPS AND TREATS

Seaside Outing

The members of Mrs. Newsome's Bible Class connected with the Wesleyan Chapel had their annual outing on Wednesday, July 4th, when they travelled by the excursion to Lowestoft and spent an enjoyable day by the sea. The party, numbering about 30, in charge of Mrs. Newsome, travelled in a saloon carriage and both going and returning had a pleasant journey.

Mrs. Newsome wishes to thank the ladies in the town for their kind help.

Church Choir Trip

The adult members of the Parish Church Choir had their annual summer outing on Saturday, July 21st, when they went to Brighton and spent a most interesting and enjoyable day by the sea there. Reaching Brighton in good time, about 10.30 a. m., they had a long day of about ten hours' enjoyment.

Besides the natural attractions of this popular resort there were some special and interesting attractions in the elaborate programme for the Saturday Lifeboat demonstrations. This included an imposing procession with many emblematical cars, and there was also, besides a water fete, the launching of the lifeboats to rescue a steamer some way out which was supposed to be in distress. These and other attractions made up a very interesting day.

Excursions by Train

On Wednesday, July 4th, 120 people were booked from Royston Station on the excusion to Lowestoft and on Thursday, July 19th, 26 passengers were booked to Skegness.

NOTICE
MRS. PUTT requests the person who has borrowed a Ladder from the Bull Hotel Yard, to return it at once.

British School Trip

On Wednesday, July 4th, a large party of scholars from the British School went for the annual outing organised in connection with the school, the place chosen being Lowestoft. Travelling by the excursion the party, in charge of Mr. Freston, the Headmaster, had a merry time going and returning, and spent a delightful day by the sea, which on such a day afforded no end of attraction to the young people.

Children's Sunday School Trip

Thursday, July 12th, was the children's day in the town, and never since the arrangement of holding all the school treats in the town on the same day commenced, has this interesting fixture been held in more brilliant summer weather. The afternoon was hot, the shade of trees for tea was welcome, and the evening most delightful for the young people and the many parents and friends who joined them in the cool of the evening. Finer balloon ascents have rarely, if ever, been witnessed, and the treats were in every way a great success, marred only in one case by the sudden and tragic death, in the afternoon, of Mrs. Oliver, wife of the caretaker of the Kneesworth Chapel.
[This is reported on later in the month].

The various organisations had the use of different venues: the Church Sunday Schools used the grounds of the Rookery, kindly placed at their disposal by Mrs. Henry Fordham. The Kneesworth Street Congregational Sunday School had the use of the grounds of Yew Tree House, the residence of Mr. F. J. Fordham. The John Street Congregational Sunday School met in the Park Meadows, by kind permission of Mrs. Peebles; and the scholars in the Wesleyan Sunday School had the use of the shady fields up the Kneesworth Street Driftway kindly lent by Mr. G. H. Innes.

The treat connected with the Particular Baptist Chapel was again a very pleasant summer outing and picnic. Driving in brakes, &c., the party numbering between fifty and sixty, met with a very cordial welcome from Mr. and Mrs. A. J. Palmer of Whaddon.

The Mill to the Sea

On Saturday, July 21st, the employees at the Royston Mill of Messrs. T. H. Smith & Sons had their annual outing when they travelled by the excursion to Brighton and spent a most delightful time by the sea.

The Board of Guardians

There was discussion this month about the revaluation of the various parishes in the union. The employment of a professional outside valuer was considered and to that end various tenders had been received. Some members of the committee felt that they could do the job themselves for less cost as had been done twelve years previously at the last valuation when there had been no appeals. The general consensus of opinion was that an outside valuer would be quite unbiased and in spite of an amendment against a valuer being put forward, it was lost by 11 votes to 15 and therefore the matter of a professional valuer would be proceded with.

There had been no applications for the post of Workhouse Nurse even though an advertisement had been placed in the London papers. As there were few people locally qualified for such a post, it was decided to raise the salary offered to £30 and to advertise again in the specialist journals.

The Curate's Fund

On Sunday, July 1st, at the Parish Church the Vicar, Rev. J. Harrison, made a special appeal for this fund. The offertories on Sunday were for the Fund and amounted to £13 0s. 6d., a considerable advance upon last year, but not enough to make up for losses in subscriptions by the deaths of several of the principal subscribers of the past.

Visitors to Royston
Cambridge Cork Club

The members of the Cambridge Cork Club, who have visited Royston Heath for their annual summer outing on previous occasions, came to Royston on Monday, July 2nd. The party drove over in brakes and made their headquarters at the Green Man, where they were ably catered for by Mr. and Mrs. Pickett. During the afternoon the party spent a pleasant time on the Heath in very pleasant weather. Towards evening some rain marred the pleasure of the return journey home.

British Medical Association

The members of the Cambs. and Hunts. Branch of the British Medical Association, with a few invited guests from other Branches, held their annual meeting at the Institute on Thursday evening, July 5th, at which the usual business of the Branch was transacted. About forty members were present.

Business News

The business of Messrs. Samuel Wilkerson & Son, corn merchants, Royston, has been converted into a Limited Company, under the title of Samuel Wilkerson & Son, Limited with a capital of £25,000. The arrangement is quite a private one; the management will be the same as before, and no shares are offered to the public.

Transfer of Licence

The Bench granted transfer of the following licence: The William the Fourth at Royston, from James Jones to John Evans.

A Remarkable Storm

On Monday afternoon, July 16th, a period of most oppressive heat led to a storm of a very remarkable character which passed over the neighbourhood, though not directly over the town, so far as the lightning and thunder were concerned. In the immediate neighbourhood of Royston the storm was more remarkable for the way in which it began. Black masses of thundercloud moved across from the west, southwest, and a terrific storm of lightning and thunder was expected. Just as the storm was about to break there arose a rushing wind which had some very curious effects. A great cloud of dust was seen approaching from the Baldock roadway, and for about ten minutes the town was enveloped in a sandstorm, or duststorm, so dense that the town was in darkness. The great storm cloud had been raised, not only from the dust which lay thick upon the roads before the storm began, but from the soil in the open fields as well, and the whirlwind in passage in some cases tore up plants by the roots. Vivid lightning and heavy rumbling of thunder accompanied the storm, which was much heavier in the west to north side of the district, but in Royston the rain was not very heavy.

Independent Foresters' Anniversary.

The members of the Independent Foresters' Society held their anniversary on Saturday, July 21st, with the usual celebrations, procession, &c. At 3 p.m. the members assembled at the Club Room at the White Horse, and headed by the Royston Military Band, with a handsome banner, paraded the streets, a good number being mounted. Afterwards they marched to the Heath where the afternoon was spent in cricket and other amusements.

At 6.30 p.m. the members returned to the Club Room for the supper, to which a large number sat down, the younger portion of the Juvenile Branch being accommodated at tables in the yard, in charge of Brother Robinson, and the rest in the Club Room upstairs.

Dr. H. R. Archer presided and was supported by Mr. W. Sharpe, president of the Club, and Mr. E. Matthews, secretary.

After an excellent supper, served by Mr. and Mrs. Percy, the Toasts of the Queen, the Prince and the Princess of Wales and the Imperial Forces, were given in appropriate terms from the chair and duly honoured.

Following more toasts and speeches, the President of the Club tendered the thanks of the Society to the host and hostess for providing so well for their comfort, and to the Band and others who had helped to make their anniversary a success.

Musical Successes

At the examination of the Associated Board of the Royal Academy of Music and the Royal College of Music, held at the Academy in June, Miss Olive E. Abbott, pupil of Mrs. Thoulness, at Miss Turner's, "Kingsley," Hampstead, passed in the Higher Division for pianoforte.

Miss Marjorie Goodman, daughter of Mr. T. Goodman of this town, has successfully passed the Pianoforte Playing Examination, Preparatory grade, Trinity College, London, held this month in Cambridge.

Miss Winifred Walker, (pupil of Miss Hagger of Melbourn), youngest daughter of Mr. Robert Walker of this town, has successfully passed the musical knowledge examination, Intermediate division, Honours section, Trinity College, London, held in June. She was also successful in passing the Pianoforte Examination, Intermediate division, Honours section, Trinity College London, held this month in Cambridge.

CRIMINAL ACTIVITIES

Excise Prosecution

George Field, of Redhill, Sandon, was charged at Royston Petty Sessions on the information of H. J. Chapman, Inland Revenue Officer, with killing a hare without having a licence or certificate, at Sandon, on April 30th.

The defendant said his father sent him across the field to shoot a pigeon, and the hare got up in front of him and he did kill it. He admitted that he had no certificate but did not know he was doing anything wrong.

The Supervisor said that this was a case in which the defendant and his father must have known the law and he asked for the higher penalty of £20. Under the Ground Game Act the person occupying the land or some person authorised by him in writing could kill game, though he would still be liable for having a gun licence. It was stated that the land was occupied by the defendant's father.

The Chairman said the defendant had no right to shoot the hare and he would have to pay a fine of 5s. and 7s. costs.

Deserter Gives Himself Up

At the Police Station, on July 19th, *James Charles Dawson,* was charged with being a deserter from the 13th Hussars, at Hounslow, in March last. It appeared that about 12 o'clock on the previous day the defendant went up to Inspector Hart near the Police Station, and said he wished to surrender himself as a deserter from the Army. The Inspector consulted the *Police Gazette* and found the name of a deserter given there, answering the description given by the prisoner who was then detained. The prisoner was now ordered to be sent to St. Albans to await an escort back to his regiment.

Without a Light

Sidney Merry, of Thriplow, was charged at Royston with driving a cart without a light.

The defendant said he went to Melbourn and did not know that he required a light until he saw another man with one and then he got out and led his horse. He was fined 7s. 6d.

Warning to Boys.

At Royston Petty Sessions, *Arthur Pigg, Arnold Day, Walter King,* and *Walter Holloway,* all Royston boys, were charged with obstructing the passage of the foootpath in the High Street, Royston, on June 24th. All the boys pleaded not guilty.

P.c. Gray said that on Sunday, June 24th, at 6.10 p.m., he was on duty in the High Street, Royston. He saw the four defendants playing on the footpath near Mr. Henderson's shop at the Cross. He watched them for ten minutes or more and during that time several people had to get off the path in consequence of the four defendants. The witness went and asked the defendants to come to the Police Station with him. They did so and he took their names and addresses. He had had several complaints about boys playing about on the footpaths. They made a practice of it every Sunday evening. There were others at the Cross but they ran away. The defendants had nothing to say in defence. Inspector Hart said there had been nothing against the boys before.

The Chairman said this was a great nuisance and had been going on a long time and there had been many complaints about standing about on the path at the Cross. They would each pay 5s. including costs, and the Bench hoped the Police would bring forward any other cases that occurred.

A Charge of Damaging Cabbages

At the Police Station on July 19th, *Charles Chamberlain,* labourer of Royston, was charged with damaging with intent to steal six cabbages, the property of John Sussex, in his garden at Royston on July18th, doing damage to the amount of 1d.

Thomas Garner, watchman, employed at the Royston Brewery, said he was on duty on the previous night at 11.15 p.m., in the Briary Lane. He heard a rustling as of cabbages in Mr. Sussex's garden. He then saw a man in the garden, and then the defendant dropped over the wall. He asked him what he was doing, and he said, "What is that to do with you?" Witness questioned him again, and he said he went to sleep there. Witness then handed defendant over to P.c. Knight. He was sober when apprehended.

John Sussex, gardener of Royston, said he lived at the end of the Briary Lane, and had a garden at the back of his house. He there saw six cabbages lying on the ground fresh cut, (the damage was 1d.)

The defendant was ordered to pay 1d. damage, 1s. 5d. fine and 8s. 6d. costs, and was allowed a week to pay.

Police Wanted

The Royston Horticultural Society made application to the Bench for special constables for the Show and Sports on Bank Holiday. They anticipated a large number of people would be present. Last year they had an Inspector and four Constables. This year they had made similar application but in consequence of pressure upon Bank Holiday no members of the force could be allowed for private grounds. Under these circumstances they applied to the Bench to swear in five persons as special constables.

The Chairman said he quite agreed that such assistance was very desirable, but it seemed according to the Act that they could only swear in special constables where rioting or tumult was expected. Dr. Archer said he thought they could not show to the Magistrates that such a thing was going to happen.

Supt. Reynolds, the Deputy Chief Constable, said the police officers stationed in the town would be on duty and available to be called in if any emergency arose in the grounds requiring their presence.

Sudden Death in the Kneesworth Street Schoolroom

A very distressing incident attended the preparations being made in the schoolroom for the children's treat of the Kneesworth Street Congregational Sunday School on Thursday afternoon, July 12th.

Among those engaged in the preparations was Mrs. Lizzie Oliver, aged 30, wife of William Oliver, caretaker of the Chapel. About 4 o'clock she had occasion to go down to the cellar. When Mr. Goodman and Mr. Cane went down shortly afterwards they found Mrs. Oliver lying on the floor apparently in an unconscious, if not lifeless, state. Dr. Windsor was at once sent for but his assistance was of no avail, and the poor woman was quite dead on his arrival. Inspector Hart was communicated with and an ambulance was obtained by means of which the deceased was conveyed to the Cottage Hospital to await an inquest which will be held on Saturday morning, July 14th.

The sad event naturally cast a gloom over the school treat, the arrangements for which had proceeded so far that the young people were on the ground awaiting tea when the sad news reached the ground.

At the inquest, evidence from the post-mortem was presented and Mrs. Oliver was shown to have been a person in good health. However, there had been signs of bruising to the head and a rupture of blood vessels. The bruising could have been caused by a fall or a blow. There was no possibility of foul play or any blow so that the injury must have been caused by a fall either from fainting or otherwise. The foreman said they agreed up on a verdict of death from haemorrhage to the brain as the result of a fall, but how the fall occurred there was no evidence to show.

Casualties in the Street

On Wednesday afternoon, July 4th, just after the close of the market, two casualties occurred in the High Street, one of a typical and the other of an unusual character. At the Cross, a Salvation Army officer cycling from Kneesworth Street into High Street came in conflict with a horse and trap coming from Melbourn Street into Baldock Street and was knocked on the pavement near Mr. Beale's window, but as neither was going fast at the time no great damage was done.

At the top of the High Street near the Chequers a closed carriage containing passengers from the Railway Station was being driven up the street by Mr. Whyman, of Barkway, when the horse fell down at the corner and died suddenly. Another horse was obtained and the dead one was got out of the way of the traffic as speedily as possible.

SCHOOL NEWS

National School (Girls)

E. Bedwell went to London on the 11th.

The 12th was the day of the Sunday School treats and a half-day holiday was granted. On the 18th, it was decided to do Needlework first thing in the morning on account of the great heat in the afternoon.

The Diocesan Inspection was held in the afternoon of the 26th. A half-holiday was granted on the 27th instead of the 26th.

Special Results.

No Present   114

	Division I	Division II	Division III
Old Test.	V.G.	V.F.	G.
New Test	V.G.	G.	G.
Catechism	V.G.	V.F.	G.
Prayer Book	V.F.	G.	G.
Repetition	V.G.	V.G.	V.G.
Writing	G.	V.F.	G.

The British School

It was reported on the 6th that a new record had been made that week in attendance. The % being 99.5. On books 156. Present 155.

On the 12th the register closed earlier than usual in order to allow the school to be dismissed at 11.30 as this was the day for the Sunday School Treat. The school was closed in the afternoon.

On the 13th, the head tried the effect of a slight arrangement of the staff placing Miss Bement in part charge of Standard IV under his supervision and Miss Norman with Standard I.

The 16th brought a new store cupboard to the school and news that Miss Bement was unable to attend school owing to illness. The timetable had to be departed from in several instances during the week in consequence of above. The attendance for the week-ending 20th fell considerably. 9 children had been away all week because of sickness and others had been away on holiday. Overall attendance 90.5%.

The school was closed at noon on the 27th for a half-holiday on account of an attraction in the town.

Miss Bement resumed duties on the 30th and on the 31st the bi-monthly examination took place.

Std. I The writing was exceptionally good and deserving of special mention. Arithmetic was poor and not at all up to standard and carelessness was very apparent.

Std. II & III Work was fairly good on the whole but reading was not so fluent as it might be. Written work was neat. Style was good but very careless indeed and would require special effort on the part of the Teacher whom the Head considered nevertheless worked hard with her classes.

Std. IV This standard, though good on the whole, lacked polish.

The upper standards were very good in all respects (especially the written work of Standard V which deserved great praise) The arithmetic of Standard VI boys was not as good as it might have been. The mental work and class subjects were very well done and showed that the teachers on the whole had worked well.

Concerning Water

A correspondent sent to *The Crow* a regulation about water supply which they felt needed bringing to peoples' attention: "It is not lawful for the owner of any dwelling-house in a rural district to occupy or permit it to be occupied until he has obtained a certificate from the Rural District Council that there is a supply of wholesome water within a reasonable distance of the house sufficient for the use of the inmates for domestic purposes. Public Health (*Water Act 1878*), section 6. Any owner who occupies or permits a house to be occupied in contravention of this section is liable to a penalty not exceeding ten pounds. It is the duty of the Rural District Council to take proceedings against any owner who contravenes the section."

NEWS FROM THE FRONT

The March to Mafeking

The parents of *Private J. Hines* received a letter dated May 20th. Excerpts follow:

"....The march took 14 days....we came across a lot of rebels which we took prisoner, and took their cattle which came in very acceptable as we were rather short on rations........the first we saw of the Boers was on the Sunday. About 5 p.m. we came across very thick bush and bullets were flying round us like hailstones. ...the only thing was to dismount and lay down but we could not see a Boer anywhere....after a bit our scouts found their position and as soon as the guns started they soon shifted leaving a great number of their dead behind..... The order was given that no man should lie down or any horse be unsaddled as we expected to be attacked at any moment......we had nothing to eat or drink and we had no blankets and it was bitterly cold......we moved off to look for water and after a few miles came across a dried up river bed and so we had to dig for water, which we got after digging for two feet...........About 8 miles from Mafeking we came into action with the Boers who ran in all directions...........We marched from 12p.m. until 4a.m. and went straight into Mafeking. Of course most people were in bed and were very much surprised to find us there. How they cheered, and well they might as they had been shut up for seven months living on the food which had been served to them, which I believe was each person 8 ounces oat bread, ¼ lb of horse flesh, ¼ ounce of coffee, ¼ ounce of sugar, so you can imagine how they looked. Also, the fever was very bad and buildings were blown down from the effect of Boer shells."

In Pretoria

Private S. E. Smith, 2nd Lincoln Regiment has written home to his sisters, George Lane, Royston, a letter from Pretoria, in which he says:

"Just a line to tell you we have reached Pretoria, the place we have been wanting to get to for a long time. We arrived about 3 miles off Pretoria on June the 4th and had a fight which lasted from about eleven to sunset and then we went to our camp, and next morning we went nearer to Pretoria, about one and a half miles, and then stopped there till they gave in. Then we went and took over the town, when the Union Jack was hoisted, and then an uproar of cheers went up from the troops and when it was over we went to camp, which is Pretoria Racecourse, where our prisoners were for a long time. The barbed wire round the course is wonderful. There was no fear of their escape, as it was impregnable for anyone to get through. I am very pleased that we have reached the long looked for place which we have been fighting for four months now, and I don't know when we shall shift down country as there are so many troops here, so it will take a long time to get them down country, but never mind as I have got through without a wound for which I think I am very lucky. I think every man should think himself very lucky, as it was not all honey, I can tell you."

Unique Experience

Private E. J. Jarrett, of the Bakery Section, Army Service Corps (formerly at Mr. Lilly's, Kneesworth Street), has written home to his wife and children a letter recording what he thinks may be a unique experience for any private soldier at the Front, viz., in being able to send home a letter written while travelling in a first class carriage while travelling on special service from Winburg to Bloemfontein. Writing of his experiences further, he says:

"We got splendid weather here, but cold at night with 2in of ice on the water in the morning, which makes our teeth chatter a bit, and then hot in the day. I have not heard lately about Arthur, but no doubt he is all right now for they are released by Lord Roberts when he got to Pretoria. We are 1,000 miles up country now, but will soon be on the herring pond again, sailing home to dear old England".

Sickness

Trooper Hart, of the 1st Life Guards (son of Inspector Hart), fell with enteric fever, while accompanying Lord Roberts' force to Pretoria, and has been sent back to hospital at Norval's Point.

Sad Death of Mr Thomas Shell

It is with very great regret that we have to announce the death of Mr. Thomas Shell, late Clerk to the Royston Board of Guardians, and other public bodies, which took place on Saturday evening, June 30th at his home 'Heath View'. It was only in December last that Mr. Shell had resigned his office as Clerk to the Guardians, the Ashwell and Melbourn Rural District Councils, Assessment Committee, and his office as Superintendent Registrar, and had thus only received the superannuation to which he was entitled, for the short period of six months. From that time his health had been failing, and during the last few weeks his illness took a more serious form which left little hope of his recovery.

Mr Shell came to Royston from Wiltshire, 44 years ago, and entered the services of Messrs. Thurnall and Nash, solicitors of Royston, where for 21 years he acted as a deputy to Mr. Thurnall at the Board of Guardians, of which Mr. Thurnall was clerk, and when that office became vacant, Mr. Shell was appointed clerk, a position he held for 22 years. On his retirement the Guardians placed on record their high appreciation of his services, and expressed the wish that he "might live long and enjoy the rest which he had so justly earned by his labours". Mr. Shell had been connected in many ways with all the parochial life of the Royston Union, and was ever ready to give, cheerfully and ungrudgingly, his help in matters of difficulty, often at the sacrifice of valuable time. He had for many years been connected with the John Street Congregational Church, of which he was one of the deacons.

The deceased was 72 years of age, and leaves a widow, two sons, and a daughter to mourn a heavy bereavement and loss in which they will have the sincere condolences of very many friends, and indeed the sympathy of all who knew him. The funeral took place on Thursday afternoon, July 5th. The service was conducted by the Rev. W. Trevor Lewis, pastor of John Street Congregational Church. The coffin, covered with beautiful wreaths, was conveyed in an open car, followed by four mourning coaches in which were the chief mourners. There were also a large number of townspeople and representatives of official bodies who met the procession at the cemetery gates. On Sunday, July 8th, a special In Memoriam Service was held at which suitable hymns were sung. Their deceased brother had been connected with the church for 48 years, 21 of them as a deacon, and he had continually laboured for the good of others and in cheering and encouraging them in their good work. They bade him farewell for the short time until they went to their eternal rest after him, and their prayers would be for God's protection and comfort to the sorrowing relatives left to mourn his loss.

ROYSTON PARISH CHURCH

BAPTISMS

July
5th   Baden Stanley, son of William (Labourer) and Annie Anderson.

MARRIAGES

July
5th   Ernest William Reynolds (Baker) to Kate Draper.

BURIALS

July
24th   Alfred Barnes, aged 20 years.

Other Deaths reported in July

12th   Lizzie Oliver (suddenly) aged 30 years.
13th   John Dellow, Royston Union Workhouse, aged 85 years.
        William Gray, Royston Union Workhouse, aged 81 years.

Sport

Golf

July
19th   Final competition for the Monthly Medal.
21st   2nd competition for the Captain's Prize.
21st   Competition for "China" Cup.

Cricket

July
14th   Royston Victoria v Cambridge Liberals.
        Royston won by 146 runs.
14th   Odsey v Royston Victoria 2nd XI.
        Odsey won by 8 runs.
19th   Royston v Cambridge Camden.
        Royston won by 138 runs.
21st   Royston Victoria v Fowlmere.
        Royston won by 28 runs.

COUNCIL AFFAIRS

A Nasty Smell!!

The Surveyor, Mr. James Smith, reported a block in the sewer near the British School which had caused an overflow at the corner near the cottage at Mr. Bevan's gate near the police station. He proposed a simple remedy which would, he thought, prevent this in future.

Mr. Bevan said the smell from this blocking of the sewer and overflow was very bad and he doubted whether a simple remedy would suffice. There was a very sharp corner near the British School and he was afraid that considerable alterations would be required. After lengthy discussion the matter was referred back to the Highways Committee.

Sanitary Concerns

The Sanitary Inspector, Mr. Webb, presented a report with reference to various sanitary matters, and to a case of scarlatina which was believed to have been imported from a neighbouring parish. He also reported a number of vans on the Warren one night and that they were under observation by the police, complaints being made of the occupants using offensive language.

Private Street Works Act, 1892

At a Meeting of the Urban District Council of Royston, held on the 9th day of July 1900, a Resolution was passed in the following terms, viz:· "That the Urban District Council of Royston do hereby approve the Specification of the works of levelling, metalling, making good, kerbing and channelling Morton Street, and the Plans and Sections of the same: also the estimate of the probable expenses of the works and the provisional apportionment of the estimated expenses among the premises liable to be charged therewith prepared by the Surveyor and this day submitted to the Council."

H. F. J. BANHAM,
Clerk to the said Urban District Council.
Council Offices, Royston, Herts.
19th July, 1900.

Street Lighting in the Summer

The Secretary of the Royston Horticultural Society wrote to the Council stating that complaints were made on the occasion of the above show and sports on the August Bank Holiday last year of there being no lights alight in the streets, and asking the Council to direct that the lamps be lighted that night this year.

Mr. Howard thought that the lighting should be recommenced on the 1st of August instead of the 15th. Dr. Archer and Mr. Titchmarsh remarked that the Lighting Committee were about to consider the question of an earlier date for recommencing lighting. The letter was referred to the Lighting Committee. *[see also article - "On Street Lighting" - page 154]*

Housing of the Working Classes

At the meeting held on July 9th, the clerk read a communication from the Local Government Board on this subject, calling the attention of the Council to their powers under the Housing of the Working Classes Act, with respect to schemes of reconstruction and improvements, especially with regard to insanitary dwellings, and to the provision that in case the local authority made default, the County Council could exercise the powers for them. No action was taken.

CORVUS CORNIX COMMENTS

On Policemen at the Flower Show

The Committee of the Royston Horticultural Society seem to have taken the matter of police arrangements a little too seriously. It seems reasonable enough that if the definite application is made for the exclusive use of a number of police in private grounds, those responsible for the Force should think first of their general duty to the public outside. At the same time it is a mistake to suppose that the general duty does not include, without asking for it at all, some regard for a special occasion when thousands of people are brought together.

The swearing in of special constables for the Flower Show does not appear to be exactly the right remedy. It does not require an Act of Parliament to tell you that the swearing in of special constables is invariably associated with broken heads or the prospect of such incidental discomforts. It is only when such urgent calls for his services arise that special constables' authority would be recognized by all the British public. The British public is apt to be a little pig-headed, and is very hard to convince that one ordinary man's authority is any better than any other, and an amateur constable would be likely to create the friction and arouse the very thing he was appointed to prevent, if suddenly let loose amongst a crowd looking on at such things as bicycle parades, babies in mail carts and rows of nosegays and turnips. Most of the work of keeping order on such occasions as flower shows is committee work, and not law and order from the policeman's point of view. At the same time wherever a crowd is brought together there, of necessity, is involved a considerable element of law and order which the policeman is bound to protect, and consequently the policeman will not be far off if needed. It is probably better policy to assume that a policeman will be on the spot than to make a formal application that he should.

On Volunteers

The increased interest in Volunteers, which has been set in motion by the War in South Africa, has already borne fruit in the field of active service with a private from the City of London Imperial Volunteers being awarded the coveted distinction of the Victoria Cross........ On the face of it, with the immense value of good shooting emphasized by the experience of the War, one would suppose that the entries at Bisley would not have fallen off so much as they have done, even allowing for absent men at the Front. It is a singular comment upon the lessons of the War in South Africa, that at home interest in good shooting, not only at Bisley, but amongst local battalions and companies, seems to be somewhat on the decline. The directions in which a forward movement is being made are just those in which War Office methods have been least successful in the past. The new arrangements for service in Camp will form an experiment which will be watched with interest....... I understand that from the Royston Company, which is just now very strong, 80 men will go into Camp, and chiefly for a fortnight, a fact which shows, at any rate, a loyal co-operation on the part of employers in many cases, where otherwise men could not be spared so long

It was not the parade soldier who won for us the hard fight in South Africa, and for that reason alone one would have supposed that the proposals for Volunteer Shooting Clubs and more local facilities for shooting, would have been received with more favour. At Bisley, only on Tuesday, July 10th, a veteran, who according to War Office Red Tape, is no longer fit for parade, enforced the lesson taught by the Boers, that a man who can do what is most required of him, is sometimes better than the smarter man who can do something that is not so badly needed.

On Street Lighting

The application to the Royston Urban District Council on Monday evening, July 9th, in respect to street lighting towards the end of the summer, raises a question which really deserves consideration upon more general grounds than for the particular day in respect to which the application was made.(See "Street Lighting in Summer" - page 153]

The Council did quite right in asking the Lighting Committee to consider the question generally as affecting the period of "close time", during which the street lamps are not lighted. At present the system is to cease lighting on May 15th and renew the lighting on August 15th. The lighting should be continued a little later and be renewed earlier, with a little more elasticity for dealing with special times of need. At any rate there is no need for the lanterns to be taken away from the lamp posts for so long a period as at present. As to the cost of the extra gas, it is not good economy to deprive the streets of light, if and when public inconvenience is caused thereby.

On Road Taxes

There seems to be quite a recrudescence among local authorities just now of the agitation for taxing cycles and motor cars, on the ground that the owners of these means of locomotion "have now the great advantage of improved highways". The resolution which has been in circulation among and adopted by local authorities, in the district, sets forth that such a tax should be "applied towards the repair and improvements of the highway".

With regards to the merits of the question generally, I suppose the bit of old turnpike philosophy that those who use the roads should pay for them is plausible enough, but in actual practice it is not as simple as it seems. Certainly as regards cyclists there would be hosts of claims for exemption - children, schoolboys, apprentices, and workmen.....................

The bulk of the roads with which cyclists are concerned are, however, roads not under the control of local authorities, and until County Councils take up the question, the cyclist can go on his way untaxed. To his credit he does not "scorch" so much as he did formerly, and bearing in mind the unpopularity of "wheel taxes" in the past, I am inclined to think that when motor car riders learn the same forbearance, we shall not hear much demand for such taxes in the future.

AUGUST

An Old Man Found Dead in His House

The sudden death under peculiar circumstances of an old man known in the town as Charlie Ward, came to light on the morning of Thursday, August 24th. The deceased had lived alone in a cottage at the top of the Black Horse Lane, Barkway Road, and was a well-known figure in the town, and especially at night-time when with feeble steps and bent back he made his way to his cottage where he lived alone. He had been in the habit of going down to the lower end of the town where he had done some odd jobs and earned a little that way. The old man also picked up whatever he came near in the way of rags and bones, and sold them. In this way and through his peculiar life he was looked upon as something of a miser, and though appearing extremely poor, tales of his having money were often circulated, while the condition in which he has been living of late, in regard to health and habitation, have come under the notice of the local authorities.

He was a native of Meldreth and had gone to Australia and made some money whilst there. On returning he bought some property in Bassingbourn which he sold again to considerable advantage. These facts probably gave rise to the tales that he had money.

At the inquest P.c. Knight described finding Charlie lying on the floor of his house with blood on his face, evidently from his nostrils. There was no sign of any disturbance. On searching his clothes, he found several items, money and an order for the Royston Workhouse dated February 1900. The post mortem revealed that the body was well nourished but dark from early decomposition and there were no external marks of violence. The heart was enlarged, flabby and fatty as was the liver. The coroner thought that death was caused by sudden failure of the heart consequent on its fatty condition and if the deceased died very suddenly, which is highly probable, that would account for the early discoloration of the body. The jury returned a verdict according to the medical evidence.

A Rare Sight!

Horses wearing sun-bonnets for protection from the heat have been seen in the streets on the hot days during the present week.

A Leak

The escape of gas at the Cross, which has baffled several attempts to locate it, has at last been discovered in the second or third joint in the main running down Melbourn Street, and has now hopefully been effectually stopped.

HARVEST REPORTS

August 3rd

Wheat cutting, which had begun here and there at the end of last week (last week in July), was very general in this district at the beginning of the week, but was of course suddenly interrupted by the heavy rains on Wednesday morning.

August 10th

The progress of harvest work has been continued during the week under rather unpromising conditions. A large part of the wheat crop on the land at the foot of the hills had been cut last week, and during the present week cutting has been going on above the hills.

August 17th

A very great change has occurred in the prospects of the harvest during the present week.

Towards the end of last week the prospect of getting in the crops seemed very gloomy indeed, but with the fine days on Saturday, Sunday, and still more brilliant summer weather on Monday, the stacking of oats and wheat began in this district and has proceeded.

August 24th

The weather on the whole has been favourable for harvest work during another week, and the fields are showing signs of a fortnight's almost continuous labour. On Wednesday morning about five o'clock there was a heavy rain storm in Royston and the neighbourhood, where for a short time rain fell in torrents, but the ground soon dried up again in the face of a gale of wind, and despite occasional light showers. It was, however, enough to put a check upon harvest work.

Private W. J. Sharp, son of Mr. W. Sharp, York Terrace, Royston, writes from Bloemfontein:

"You will see that we have moved a little further up, we have been here about six weeks. This is not such a bad place. We had 100 men go to the front. They left here for Pretoria by train last Friday. There is only eight or nine of us left here. I am lucky I did not have to go. It is very cold to sleep out at nights; it is cold enough with a tent, much less without one."

" I see by *The Crow*, you had grand doings at the news of Pretoria; in fact in all the papers in England. I wonder when all this is going on if they give one thought of Tommy at the front, laying out in the cold with no tent over him, only a blanket to cover him, and he is dead tired and perhaps no tea; and wakes up in the morning to find his blankets white and stiff with cold, and then the hundreds in the hospital! Well Tommy is not so bad after all, in fact he is everything. What could we do without him?"

"When we came here first it was very sad to see our chums go by in wagon loads of from 8 to 12 on each wagon. They used to be buried from 40 to 50 a day. Thank God it is better now."

Trooper Jack Higgins, servant to Capt. Bell-Smythe, from Pretoria to his father:

"I am very pleased to say this leaves me in the best of health at present...... We have been on the open veldt where there is no such thing as a Post Office. We have been very busy chasing small parties of Boers and have had several engagements with them. The last we had two days ago and we had 6 killed and about 30 wounded. After that we were relieved by General French, and we have come into Pretoria for a rest for ourselves and horses.......Pretoria is a big town and a very pretty one, but the worst of it is we cannot buy very much and there is nothing much coming into town. The people hate the very sight of us, which of course is quite natural. When we are in the streets they stare at us as if we owed them something, but we do not take much notice of them. I have had no letter from anyone this last two months. Our letters and winter clothes were all captured by De Wet and he burned the lot, so here we are in the middle of winter with only summer clothes."

A letter to Miss S. Smith, George Lane, from her brother, of the Lincolnshire Regiment:

"Early in the morning just when the men had finished coffee the Boers opened fire from an inaccessible hill. Out of the confusion which followed there came the quick orders of the officers, and ready obedience. The devoted little band clambered up a kopje and settled themselves to one of those heroic resistances for which the British soldier is famous. The cover they could find was far from adequate, for the enemy fired from a height, but although a groan or a cry every now and again told its tale of death and wounds, still they fought on. The sergeant in charge of the maxim gun brought it up under a hellish fire and merrily joined in the game, and what is more when they were almost surrounded got back his charge to safety, aided by eight volunteers."

"Early in the afternoon the enemy worked round on the left and the the Lincolns knew they were doomed, but there was no sign of despair. Teeth were clenched together, rifles sang out more regularly, but not a word of despondency. A subaltern asked a few men to accompany him to charge the enemy; 15 men spang up, and with glorious courage attempted the almost impossible. Of the 16 who started but two came back. Two natives, armed, came out of the Boer lines and asked a couple of soldiers who were lying on the ground to surrender. "Surrender to you !" was the scornful answer, and both the natives fell dead shot through the head at ten yards distance."

The letter concludes: "We draw the curtain over this scene of heroic gallantry, not without pride, for of the many splendid deeds done by our men in this war, surely the defence of the handful of men will find a prominent place."

The Volunteers

It was reported on August 3rd that a large muster, 90 men, of E (Royston) Company had assembled at the station in command of Captain Cautherley and departed by train for the Shorncliffe Camp, near Folkestone Kent. They were joined on the way by other companies of the Battalion. Most of the men will remain in the camp for a fortnight. There were 520 men of the 1st Battalion assembled in camp in the first week.

As their stay drew to a close later in the month the experience had been one that would be long remembered. In the first place it was the largest encampment of Volunteers ever witnessed, and in the second place the elements afforded the men who made up the citizen soldier under canvas an opportunity of realizing some of the discomforts as well as the attractions which camp life must bring.

COUNCIL NEWS

Public Health

The Sanitary Inspector, Mr. Webb, reported among other matters, a leakage from the sewer which had found its way down the steps into the cave near Melbourn Street. It was found to have been caused by a block in the sewer, which had been removed and the defective part where the leakage occurred had been cemented round and made good.

He also reported that the cowshed occupied by Mr. J. H. Norman in the Mill Road, had been lighted and ventilated as required, but the effectual drainage required had not yet been carried out, although it was some months that the notice was issued. A part had been concreted but it had not yet been finished. On the motion of Mr. Howard, seconded by Mr. Balding, it was resolved that notice be served requiring drainage to be completed within 28 days.

The Back Street Drain

Mr. Goodman said there was one matter arising out of the Surveyor's work which had been complained of and that was the state of the surface drain in the Back Street. Where the channelling had got worn down, stagnant water stood in it and became offensive.

Dr. Balding said that at the last meeting of the Highways Committee the Surveyor had reported upon this matter, and he was directed to take the work in hand in connection with the paving work now being carried out in the Back Street.

The work for the improvement of the paving on the west side of the Back Street, which has been in progress during the last few weeks, has advanced so far that the new tar paving is now completed from Mr. Abbot's gateway up to Mr. Turton's Yard, and granite setts have been laid in the various gateways. The work has been carried out under the supervision of the surveyor, Mr. James Smith.

More Accidents

Mysterious Cause

On Monday, August 27th, a drayman named Alfred Thomas Hoy, a son of Peter Hoy, who lives near the Black Horse, met with rather a serious accident. How the accident happened appears to be rather a mystery. The man was proceeding down Mill Road, on his way to Melbourn with a loaded dray, when it is supposed the dray collided with the wheel of another cart in passing near Mr. Reynold's baker's shop. The man was apparently sitting on the basket usually carried for conveying bottles of spirits, and this slipped and the man fell on his head, probably on to a stone, inflicting a deep wound from which he lost a quantity of blood. The wheel also went over both ankles causing considerable bruising but breaking no bones. Hoy got up and got into the dray again, and was proceeding on his way, when someone noticing the blood running down advised him to go back which he did. Medical aid was procured, and it was found to be a serious case. The man, we learn, is progressing favourably, but very weak from loss of blood.

A Sackable Event !?

A youth named Bright, living in the Garden Walk, and employed at the Brewery, met with an accident and broke his collarbone on Thursday evening, August 2nd, while practising sack-racing for the Sports on Monday.

Dangerous Work

One of the workmen at the Brewery, L. Reynolds, met with an accident this week while cutting nettles at the Malting in the Kneesworth Street, sustaining a very bad cut on the hand.

Places to go on Bank Holiday Monday

Biggleswade Fete.

****

Bassingbourn Flower Show and Sports.

****

Baldock Horticultural Show.

****

Barley Horticultural Show.

****

Barrington, Foxton, Orwell and Shepreth Horticultural Show and Fete at Foxton.

****

Great and Little Shelford, Harston, Newton, Whittlesford & Thriplow Flower Show at Harston.

A Family Jar

Lucy Burton, residing at Mackerel Hall, Royston, was charged with assaulting Frederick Charles Roberts on 25th July. The defendant said she threw things at the complainant after he had struck her because his mother would not let her get at him.

The complainant said he was a painter. About half-past six in the evening he went home, and sat down to eat some bread and butter. The defendant came in and sat down and started jeering him and called him "My darling boy! He will never be any good. He's got nothing in him to be any good". She said that work was no favourite of his, and so on. She kept this on for some time and he said nothing, and at last she broke into abusive language and called him everything not fit to hear. He asked her to go outside if she was going to talk like that. She then got up and said she was not going out for a black-looking.....like him. He was not master of the house. The master was away. He asked her three times to go out and she said she wouldn't. He said he must try and put her out. As soon as he said that, she collared him, put her arms around him and they both went rolling over into an arm-chair and she was just able to reach the items on the table. She then picked up a jar of gooseberry jam and threw it at him, and it struck him on the shoulder, and spilt the jam all over him, and went and smashed on the opposite wall. She threw the plates at him also and they went all over the place. One hit him on the back of the head. She also struck him on the back of the neck with a short piece of wood lying on the table. As soon as he could, the complainant got away and went outside and she followed him and used the most abusive language. A witness then went down the street and spoke to the constable.

Wm. Harradence, a farm labourer, living at Mackerel Hall, said he was in his house when this occurred. He was having his tea and heard the children crying, "...murder this and murder that," and heard plates rattling. He afterwards saw the complainant come out with his coat smothered in jam. He thought it might have been blood at first. He saw nothing of what occurred in the house. It was not fit to go there, and he thought it was about time it was stopped. He paid his rent and had a good home and did not see why he should be disturbed.

The defendant said the complainant was not in the arm chair at all. His mother was between them. She could not get at him or she would have hit him, and so she threw the things at him. She had done all she could for them.

The Chairman said the defendant would have to pay 12s.

Brewer's Licence - The Effects of Spirits???

Mr. James Edward Jarvis, Managing Director of J &. J. E. Phillips, Limited, said he appeared before their worships to ask them to grant to him on behalf of his firm, who are licensed dealers in spirits, a certificate authorising them to take out an additional licence to sell spirits in any quantity not less than one reputed quart bottle. In making this application he might explain that he was not asking for any fresh privileges whatever. The brewery had actually held this licence for nearly twenty years, it being permissible until lately for a brewer, who was a dealer in spirits, to obtain a retail licence by simply making an application to the Excise Authorities and paying 3 guineas. Within the last two or three years the Board of the Inland Revenue had awoken to the fact that they had no power to grant to brewers this additional licence, because a brewery was not a place in which intoxicating liquors are exclusively sold.

The Chairman: You sell grains? (Laughter).

Mr Jarvis confirmed that they sold grains, and it was argued that the sale of the by-products of the brewery, such as grains, yeast and spent hops debarred them from receiving the additional licence without a magistrates' certificate. The Chairman said they had looked into the matter and had no hesitation in granting the licence.

A Case of Desertion

George Ware (26) and *John Hoy (22)*, were brought up in custody charged with absenting themselves from the Royal Engineers without permission. Inspector Hart said at 4 p.m. on the 21st inst., the two defendants came to the Police Station and asked to see the Inspector. They said they wished to give themselves up for running away from the Army. The witness brought them into the guard room where they gave their names and regimental numbers of the A Company, Royal Engineers, stationed at Brompton Barracks, Chatham. He reported to the Deputy Chief Constable, who made inquiry at Headquarters, and received reply that the men bearing the numbers given were absent. P.c. Knight gave evidence of having examined the defendants, and gave the distinctive marks on the defendants.

Both defendants said they were not deserters but absentees without leave.

The Chairman: It is a more polite way of putting it.

Supt. Reynolds: It makes a difference in the punishment.

The Chairman said the defendants would be kept in custody to await an escort back to their regiment.

Annual Licensing Meeting

The Deputy Chief Constable (Supt. Reynolds) in his annual report mentioned the following licensed victuallers proceeded against under the Licensing Act during the year:-

15th November, 1899, James Jones, William Fourth Beerhouse, Royston, permitting drunkeness on licensed premises. Fined £2 and 11s. 6d. costs.

21st February, 1900, Dennis Greenhill, White Bear Public house, Royston, permitting drunkeness on licensed premises. Dismissed.

The Superintendent had no objection to make to the renewal of any of the existing licences.

Case Adjourned

Alfred Chapman, was summoned for using obscene language at Royston. The defendant did not appear, and P.c. Gray, who served the summons, being ill, the case was adjourned for a month.

A WET BANK HOLIDAY

The Sports

The Programme of Sports was not much interfered with by the rain as regards the order of running. Naturally the wet conditions of the ground upset the merits of some of the races, but the entries were so numerous that a great deal of interest was taken on that account alone.

Soon after ten o'clock the grounds were cleared, the bicycle parade formed and the band played an old favourite air into the town, and the public marched with them.

Prize Giving and Report

On Monday evening, August 13th, the prizes gained at the Bank Holiday Show, were presented by Mrs. Bruce-Clarke at the National Schools. On the same evening a meeting of the general Committee was held to receive reports as to the result of this years Show and Sports, and the financial statement. It appears that with the balance in hand, and the year's subscriptions, the Society had, before the Bank Holiday, between £90 and £100 in hand The gate money amounted to a little over £36, and entrance fees and other sources of profit, brought this up to £47. The total receipts amounted to about £145 and the total expenditure amounted to the large sum of £135. Thus balance to be carried forward to next year is only £10. Considering the extremely unfavourable day it is surprising that the gate money should have reached as much as it did, and that the Society, after a heavy expenditure, should have pulled through such a day with any balance at all.

After the Show

The experiment of holding the Annual Flower Show and Sports for Royston and the district on the August Bank Holiday having proved a great success last year, the newly constituted Horticultural Society this year arranged to "go one better," by organizing a more extensive programme, both for the open classes in the Show, and in the way of variety and attractiveness for a popular holiday.

A large amount of preparation had also been bestowed upon the catering department which had severely taxed the workers last year.

The Park Paddocks were again kindly placed at the disposal of the Committee by Mrs. Peebles, and here a track for sports, and plenty of room for show tents and the firework display were available.

With favourable weather there was prospect of a large attendance and a great success. A threatening morning, however, turned into a thoroughly wet afternoon. Commencing about noon, heavy rain fell more or less until five or six o'clock, and, of course, kept many away, and made the work of those taking part in the programme anything but pleasant. Most of the competitors however, braved the elements, even the lady cyclists, and the programme of sports was proceeded with without much loss of time.

The Horticultural Show

The Show cannot be said to have been a large one considering the extent of the schedule, but it included some good things; the cut flowers and table decorations being a special attraction. Competition in the cottagers' classes was not as keen as might have been expected, judging by the number of entries, and in the children's wild flowers, &c., there was little competition.

Special Competitions

Several novelties were introduced in which both ladies and gentlemen could take part. For the ladies' bicycle parade six had entered, and notwithstanding the wet five appeared. Miss Beale, (as Britannia), and Miss Hilda Hoy, (as Winter), well deserved their honours, and for quaintness Miss Putt's sedan chair proved interesting, and Miss Jerard's basket of flowers pretty. The decorated perambulator or mail cart parade was a pretty contest........The illuminated cycle parade was marred by the gale of wind which raged after the rain had ceased, and Miss Hoy had her machine decorations set on fire and she narrowly escaped personal injury. However, enough was possible to show that this would have been an effective display under more favourable conditions.

A Question from Corvus Cornix

Are cottage gardening and the love of flowers declining in this district? It is very significant and a matter of regret that at the local shows all round the district the same state of things had been reported: "a decrease in the entries in the cottager's classes". In the case of the Royston Show, it would almost seem that Royston is not a gardening district at all. I suspect that a large part of the decline is due to the fact that persons who might be expected to take an active part in exhibiting their produce do not set about it in the right way. Instead of beginning in the Autumn in the preparation of the soil and selection of seed, too many gardens are tapped a few days before the show on the chance of there being something to show. As the show grows older, these exhibitors lose heart over their want of success and the prize-winners narrow down to an almost stereotyped circle who do take pains to begin right.

Also there is a little too much formality. If a would-be exhibitor has to walk a mile to make an entry and then the same distance to receive his prize money, it will take a very little to turn the scale between showing and not showing his produce.

ROYSTON PARISH CHURCH
BAPTISMS
August
19th Ernest Roberts, son of Ernest (Painter) and Emily Eliza Blows.

MARRIAGES
August
2nd Harold Warren Miller (Furniture Maker) to Elizabeth Ann Barnes.
4th John Charles Miles (Engineer) to Elizabeth Bowskill
15th George Wright (Butler), to Mary Ann Streather.
21st George Henry Tansley (Gardener) to Rosa Ann Bennett.

BURIALS
August
25th Charles Ward, aged 67 years, at Black Horse Lane, Roryston.
27th Mary Ann Andrews, aged 66 years, at Gower Road, Royston.

Other Births. Marriages and deaths reported in August.
Births
None
Marriages
1st Richard Snatt Trudgett, of Royston, to Florence Edith Dowsett, of Chelmsford, at St. Paul's Church, Haggerston, London.
10th Henry John Clark, of Royston, to Margaret Jane Howell at the Parish Church, Sawston.
Deaths
None

Indian Famine Fund

In connection with the Indian Famine Fund, collections have been made among the schoolchildren attending the National Schools, and have amounted to the sum of 15s., which has been forwarded to the Lord Mayor's Indian Famine Fund.

Havoc

The remarkable gale which accompanied and followed the heavy rain on Bank Holiday, caused discomfort and havoc in all directions. On the Heath after the cricketers had abandoned play the luncheon tent was blown down and completely wrecked, the canvas being torn into ribbons, and in the Park Paddocks after the Show the Catering Committee found it necessary to take down their tent before leaving the ground.

Royston Football Club A. G. M.

The A. G. M. of the Royston Football Club was held on Thursday, August 23rd, at the Victoria Restaurant. Mr. W. C. Titchmarsh presided, and there was a fair attendance of members.

Mr. G. Kelly, Hon Sec., presented the annual report of the Committee. "We have had a very successful season. the First X1 played 21 matches, and of these 11 were won, 6 lost, and 4 drawn........

Our financial position is most satisfactory, we having a balance of £1 14s. 0½ d. on the right side, as against 3s. 2d. last year.

A collection was taken on Football Saturday, and £3 was forwarded to the Secretary of the War Fund.

The thanks of the club are due to Mr. H Stamford as referee and to the Honorary subscribers."

After further discussion concerning fixtures for the next season, a vote of thanks to the Chairman brought the meeting to a close.

The Officers were elected as follows:-
President - Mr John Phillips; Vice-presidents - Mr. D.A. Bevan, Mr J.E. Phillips, Mr. J.H. J. Phillips Mr. R. R. Smith, Mr G.B. Hudson, M.P., Mr C. Warren, and Mr. F.J. Fordham; Captain - Mr. G. Kelly; Vice-Captain - Rev. A. T. Boodle; Hon. Sec. - Mr. F. H. Rudling; Hon. Treas. Mr. W. Ward; Committee - Messrs. S. R. Smith, W. C. Titchmarsh, H. Stamford, J. Dellar, H. Pool, E. Hagger; Captain 2nd X1., Mr. W. Burr.
Other players - E. Chapman, A. L. Berry, E. Amer, R.V. Porter, E. Parminter, C. H. Titchmarsh.
It was decided to enter the Herts. Junior Cup this season....... After some discussion it was decided to change the colours of the club, which have been red and white for a number of years. It was left to the Committee to select the new colours.

Cricket
August
2nd Royston v Past and Present Bishop Stortford Grammar School. A draw.
6th Royston Cricket Club v Cambridge Camden (on Heath). Game abandonded because of weather
9th Royston N. Y. M. S. v Ashwell 2nd XI. Ashwell won by 12 runs.
10th Royston v Hitchin. Royston lost by 12 runs.
11th Royston Victoria v Hitchin Blue Cross. Royston won by 33 runs.
14th Royston v Three Counties Asylum. A draw.
18th Royston Victoria v Mr. R. Fordham's XI. Royston Victoria won by 2 runs.
25th Royston N. Y. M. S. v. Mr. D. Beale's Buntingford XI. Royston won by an innings and 68 runs.

THE BOARD OF GUARDIANS

Appointment of Nurse

The Clerk, Mr. A. Sharpe, reported that of the two candidates for the office of nurse, who had been asked to attend the meeting of this Board, one had written to say that she had obtained another appointment and desired to withdraw her application. The other had written to say that she would attend , but was not yet present.

Mrs. Broughton (of London), the candidate in question, arrived later, and was unanimously appointed to the office at a salary of £30 a year.

Poor Law Administration

The clerk said he had received a circular letter from the Local Government Board on the subject of Poor Law administration, the treatment and classification of the aged poor. It was suggested that the Clerk send a copy to each of the Guardians, and this was ageed to.The Visiting Committee reported that the management of the sick wards by the new nurse (Mrs. Broughton), was found satisfactory. The nurse suggested that flowers would be acceptable for the sick ward.

It was remarked that no doubt the public in Royston and neighbourhood would take note of this suggestion.

Vaccination Returns

The Vaccination Officer, Mr. W. J. Webb, produced a return for the half-year, from July to December 1899. This showed that the number of births during the period had been 189, the number successfully vaccinated being 161, one certificate of exemption, 17 died, 3 postponed by medical certificate, 6 removed to districts the officers of which had been apprized, and one unaccounted for.

Valuation

At the meeting of the Assessment Committee, the subject of the valuing of the Union for Re-assessment was again discussed. 14 tenders had been received and the tender of £876 from the firm of valuers Harding, Low and Harding, was accepted. The clerk would confer with the Valuers and a contract would be drawn up.

Excursions

Bible Class Outing

The members of Miss Stone's Bible Class and friends, making a party of about 30, enjoyed a delightful picnic in Wimpole Park on Thursday, August 2nd, by permission of Viscount Clifden. The pleasure grounds and conservatory were open to the party, and in connection with the Missionary gathering being held, the Mansion was also open for a small charge for the benefit of the Missionary funds. All the party spent a pleasant time and before leaving a hearty vote of thanks was accorded to Viscount Clifden for the use of the grounds. Conveyances were kindly lent by Messrs. G. W. Howard, L. E. Clark, C. Whyatt, G. Pryor and W. Hoy.

Mission Outing

On Thursday, August 2nd, the annual summer outing was enjoyed by members and friends of the Mission at Cambridge, in which Miss Watts is interested. The party drove over from Cambridge in a number of brakes, and on arrival at West Cottage they found every provision made for their comfort; tea beneath the trees in front of the house, followed by other outdoor enjoyments in the grounds or on the Heath &c.

After a very enjoyable time the party drove back to Cambridge.

VISITORS TO ROYSTON

Archaeologists' Visit

On Thursday, August 9th, the St. Albans and Hertfordshire Archaeological and Architectural Society arranged a visit to Royston. Their last visit to the town had been 16 years previously.

After lunching at the Bull Hotel, the party visited the Church where they were joined by the Vicar and Rural Dean, Rev. J. Harrison, who explained the modern changes in the building.

From the Church the party proceeded to King James' Hunting Box, still known as King James' Palace, in Kneesworth Street, where by permission of the present occupier, Mr. H. F. J. Banham, the visitors had every facility afforded to them to inspect the points of interest still remaining of the country residence of James 1 during a large part of his reign.

A visit was afterwards paid to the Cave, the greatest and most unusual curiosity in Royston, and under the direction of Mr. Hardy, the visitors were introduced to the numerous sculptures and their probable meaning pointed out to them.

Visitors and Picnics

During the past week Royston and the neighbourhood have had an unusual number of holiday visitors. The London children made quite a difference to the district, especially in the surrounding villages, but in Royston the enjoyable summer weather of the past week has brought a large number of picnic parties by brakes and cycles, and on some afternoons during the week picnic parties and others were dotted over various parts of the Heath. In many cases the townspeople have taken advantage of the fine weather and enjoyed an open-air tea on the Heath.

Butterflies

The Heath is a favourite haunt of the beautiful little "blues" of the butterfly kingdom, but this year there have appeared some very interesting additions in the pretty "Painted Lady", the handsome "Clouded Yellow", and the still more rare "Pale Clouded Yellow". The last named striking butterfly, the appearance of which has been exceptional in other parts of the country this year, has been met with in abundance on the hot sunny corner beyond the Rifle Butts during the last few weeks, while scores might have been captured in the neighbouring fields of clover on the London Road.

Corvus Cornix on Visitors

The pleasures of country life, even with our changeable climate, have lost none of their attractions, while modern conditions of civilization seem likely to increase the tendency to get away from the crowded centres to the country. It is a significant fact that the tendency now touches all classes of society, from the well-to-do who can afford a country residence, to the children of the poor who feel the stress of pent up city life. " London children" are, in fact, becoming quite an institution as the summer season comes round, in nearly all the villages in this district, and just now they are to be met with all over the countryside, revelling in the new found luxury of roaming about where green fields, berried hedgerows, wild flowers, corn fields, fruit trees, brooks, ponds, country lanes and five-barred gates, take the place of the old cramped life of a London slum. If occasionally their presence is a little too manifest, and the "cheekiness" which is developed in the sordid struggle for existence in the old life, is a little too pronounced, the case is clearly one for a little forbearance on the part of those amongst whom a noisy, roystering contingent, is dropped down. The organisations for sending down these little holiday makers, take reasonable precautions against such risks as the importation of disease &c. The young people's merriment, as they return from our railway stations after their too brief stay in the country, is proof enough that they have made the most of change.

But the pleasures of country life are also bringing every year more people who have business interests in the city, yet like the country best for a home. In this respect Royston and the neighbourhood has made a great advance during the past ten years, a fact which may, I think, be largely attributed to the Heath; a splendid heritage for the town which its inhabitants are only just beginning to appreciate. Some day, perhaps, they will wake up a little more clearly to what might be done to enhance the value of this important element in the growth and prosperity of the town. In the meantime visitors have this year found the natural attractions of the Heath enough in themselves to well repay a visit.

SEPTEMBER

PETTY SESSIONS

A Warning To Cyclists

Harry Greeves, a salesman connected with a 6½d. bazaar, and now at King's Lynn, was summoned by P.c. Reed for furiously riding a bicycle, near the Cross at Royston, on 13th August, to the danger of the public.

P.c. Reed gave evidence to the effect that on the date in question, about 6.45 p.m., he was on duty at the Cross, when he saw the defendant mount his bicycle in Melbourn Street and ride at a furious pace by the Cross into Kneesworth Street without sounding his bell. There were a number of foot passengers about, and the defendant narrowly escaped running into two ladies and some children. The witness called to him to ride slower and the defendant slackened his speed for a second or so, and then went on as furiously as ever to the Railway Station and back. The witness knew where he was going and timed him, and found it only three minutes from the time defendant passed to the time he returned. When the witness stopped him and told him he had ridden much too fast, and to the danger of the public, defendant replied, "I know how to ride a bicycle without you telling me".

The Bench said they considered the case a very bad and dangerous one, and they would inflict a fine of £2 including costs.

Cruelty to a Horse

Herbert Jude, a little lad in the employ of Henry Hunt, farmer, Barrington, was summoned by P.s. Reed for working a gelding whilst in an unfit state, at Royston, on 28th August. The defendant, who was weeping copiously, pleaded guilty.

P.s. Reed said that he saw the horse in Melbourn Road going towards Melbourn with a load of grains. He stopped it and examined it, and found a quantity of sores under the saddle and collar, and on the legs on the off side were several weals , and the horse could hardly walk. He took it into a public-house yard and sent for a veterinary surgeon, who examined it and pronounced it unfit for work, but it could walk slowly home without the cart. The defendant said that the horse had been at work in a binder the previous day, and his master sent him to Royston on the day in question.

To a question from the Bench, the lad now stated that it was his mistress who instructed him to proceed to Royston for the grains.

The Bench said the horse was evidently in an unfit condition for work, but the lad was ordered to take it out and could not well refuse. They would fine him 12s. including costs.

Obscene Language

Alfred Chapman, a bricklayer, of The Warren, Royston, was summoned by P.s. Reed for using obscene language on the Highway, at Royston, on 13th July.

The defendant who is an old offender, did not appear, and a warrant was issued for his arrest.

Drink Again

Charles Sharp, labourer, of Wicker Hall, was summoned for being drunk on the highway, at Royston, on August 10th.

P.s. Reed proved service of the summons, and said the defendant was at work in the harvest field and would be unable to attend.

The Bench said it was an inconvenience for a farmer to spare a man on such a nice harvest day. They would adjourn the case until next sitting.

Charles Sharp, was charged with being drunk, the case having been adjourned from the last Bench day by request of the defendant's wife. The defendant pleaded guilty.

P.s. Reed said on 10th August, about 7.30, he saw defendant near the Sun Hill drunk, and holding on to a fence. He was quiet, but unable to walk, and witness assisted him to his home. The defendant was ordered to pay 2s. 6d.

Domestic Dispute in Black Horse Lane

Mary Evans, of Barkway Street, was charged with using obscene and abusive language on the highway, at Royston, on 31st of August, to the annoyance of the informant, Ann Woods.

The defendant said she was not guilty.

Ann Woods said she was the wife of Walter Woods, and lived at Black Horse Lane, Royston. On Friday, 31st August, she had been in the harvest field and left about half past seven and went for some bread, and then went home. When she got against a neighbour's door in Barkway Street, Mrs. Evans began to call her everything. She used filthy language. She had never been called such filthy names before. The witness told her she was a deceitful woman and it would be more to her credit to keep in her home and wash herself.

The defendant said she was sitting in the cottage and three of them rushed to her cottage and fell into the house. If she did say what she had been accused of saying about the complainant she did not say wrong, for Black Horse Lane was not the same since she had been there. The defendant was ordered to pay 5s.

Inspector Hart said this sort of thing had been going on for the last two years.

The Chairman: It will be as well to keep your eye upon the neighbourhood.

Inspector Hart: I will, sir.

THIS AND THAT

Collapse Through Inhaling Gas

A workman named Thomas Rayment, in the employ of Mr. W.H. Hinkins, met with a peculiar accident on Thursday afternoon, September 20th, while engaged in connecting the old and new gas mains on the London Road. The opening had been plugged in the usual way, but before the work was finished the plugging failed, and let the gas out. While Rayment was holding down over his work it is supposed he must have inhaled a large quantity of escaping gas, at any rate he suddenly became unconscious, and was lifted out of the trench on to the path by the side. Showing no signs of recovery he was carried into Mr. Watson's garden near at hand. There artificial respiration was resorted to, and after a few minutes perseverance with this remedy, he came round, and by the time Dr. Windsor arrived, was able to walk around the garden.

Funeral of a Former Resident

On Friday, September 21st, the remains of the late Mrs. Martin, widow of the Rev. Martin, formerly pastor of the Kneesworth Street Congregational Church were conveyed to Royston and interred, (by request of the deceased), in the Additional Church Burial Ground. The funeral was attended chiefly by relatives and friends.

A Brewers' Supper

On Saturday evening, September 22nd, the workmen employed at the Royston Brewery, J. & J. E. Phillips, Limited, with the members of the office staff had their annual supper at the Green Man, where the Market Room made a convenient rendezvous for a party which numbered between fifty and sixty, and an excellent spread was placed on the tables and much enjoyed. After the supper songs were sung by members of the company and friends, and a very enjoyable evening was spent.

They Came to Royston

On Thursday, September13th, a very large excursion party came up from Cambridge in brakes and wagonettes, &c., and enjoyed a pleasant outing on the Heath and in the town and neighbourhood. The party, which numbered nearly one hundred, had tea in the Market Room at the Green Man, and left for Cambridge about half-past-six.

The Circus Comes to Town

Fossett's Circus paid a visit to Royston on Thursday, September 27th, and after the Bandsmen had paraded in the town, performances were given in the circus on the Warren.

Successful Again

At the Alexandra Dog Show, held under Kennel Club Rules, on September 25th, Mr. P. F. Fordham took three firsts, five seconds and one third prize with his retrievers Time and Crane. The entries numbered 6,000, being the largest show ever held.

Accident in the House

On Saturday evening, September 22nd, Mr. Law, landlord of the Falcon in Melbourn Street, met with a rather serious accident while in the course of his business. He was coming up the cellar steps with his hands full, when his foot slipped and he fell down the steps to the bottom. It was some little time before anyone was aware what had happened, but his groans attracted attention and he was assisted up to the house and got to bed. Medical aid was called in and it was found that Mr Law had fractured two of his ribs.

A Desperate Character

At the Police Station on September 24th, an umbrella mender named *Henry March*, on the road, was brought up in custody charged with being drunk and disorderly on the highway at Royston. It appears that the defendant had, with his wife and children, arrived in Royston about nine o'clock, and having secured lodgings for the night, sallied forth into the streets with an umbrella for sale. He had, however, been drinking freely on the road, and his efforts to do business with his umbrella soon got him into trouble. He went into a number of shops and failing to sell the umbrella abused the tradesmen. In the street his conduct came under the notice of the police who found it necessary to put a stop to his business for that night. Upon that he threatened to "bayonet" the Inspector with his umbrella. On taking him into custody the police found their work cut out. The defendant became desperate and at one time policemen and drunken man were struggling together on the ground. Two or three other men gave a hand and in this way the defendant was got to the Station, his head being cut during the ups and downs of the struggle,. In default of paying a fine he was sent to prison for fourteen days.

AFTER THE HARVEST

ROYSTON FOAL & COLT SOCIETY.
THE
SEVENTH ANNUAL
S H O W

Of Shire and Agricultural Foals, Yearlings and
2-year-olds,Shire and Agricultural Mares, Geldings,
Hunter Brood Mares, Foals, and Hunters.

BUTTER & DEAD POULTRY,

Will be held at ROYSTON
In the Paddock adjoining the Park,
(by kind permission,) on

WEDNESDAY NEXT, SEPTEMBER 12th

Miss ANNIE B. WALKER, from the Dog Kennel Farm
Dairy, Hitchin, winner of many First and Champion prizes
at all the leading Shows in England, will demonstrate on

PRACTICAL BUTTER-MAKING

during the Morning (1 o'clock), and Afternoon (3 o'clock),
and will be pleased to answer questions at any time during
the day.

LUNCHEON and REFRESHMENTS will be provided
on the Ground by Mr. W. L. Saunders, of the Sun Hotel,
Hitchin.

PRICES OF ADMISSION:
From 10.30 o'clock to 2, 1/-: 2 to 4p.m., 6d.

RAILWAY ARRANGEMENTS.

Tickets at a single Fare-and-a-quarter for the Double
Journey, (no less charge than 1s. for an Adult Passenger),
will be issued to Royston from Hatfield, Biggleswade and
Cambridge and intermediate stations. The Tickets will be
available by any ordinary Train on day of issue only.

Corvus Cornix on the Show

The Royston Foal Show was never held under
more pleasant circumstances than on Wednesday
last. It was not only largely attended by landowners
and farmers and those primarily interested in the
Objects of the Society, but it was also graced by the
attendance of a larger number of ladies than has ever
been known before. The only point I heard
complained of was the need for a little more variety
of attractions. "You should have a band of music,
and jumping and driving competitions, and provide
attractions for the large number who attend your
show who are not specially interested in the
particular breed or points in horses." This was the
kind of thing heard again and again on the grounds,
both from ladies and practical business men. The fact
is that The Royston Foal Show has just stepped into
a convenient place at the end of the harvest, when
everybody is ready for a little diversion, and, given
such a pleasant ground as the Park Paddocks, and
such an ideal day as Wednesday proved to be, there
could scarcely be a more agreeable opportunity for
the residents of the surrounding district - farmer's
wives and daughters and others - to foregather.
What I think the Society ought to realize, either
through their own Committee or a supplementary
Committee, is a little more provision for developing
the social side of what is evidently looked upon as a
pleasant rendezvous for the countryside at the close
of the harvest.

Congregational Harvest Services

On Sunday last, September 9th, Harvest Thanksgiving services
were held at the Kneesworth Street Congregational Church, the
evening service being a joint service for the John Street
Congregational Church as well as for Kneesworth Street, the
service at John Street being dispensed with. The friends at
Kneesworth Street had made the interior of the building bright
with flowers and flowering plants, and ferns and corn, of which
there was a handsome group in front of the pulpit, while other
decorative material was arranged on the gallery fronts and pillars,
and the windows. The preacher was the Rev. R. Holme, of
Hitchin, who in the morning took as his text the Parable of the
Sower and of the seed that fell among thorns, and in the evening
a continuation of the same parable. At the morning service the
hymns included, "Come, ye thankful people, come," and at the
evening service, appropriate hymns and an anthem. The services
were largely attended, especially at the evening service, which
was for both congregations. Collections were made for the
Royston Hospital and for Addenbrooke's Hospital, Cambridge.

Wesleyan Harvest Festival

At the Wesleyan Chapel on Sunday, September 16th, the annual Harvest Thanksgiving services were held, and were well attended, especially at the evening service. As is usual on these occasions, the Chapel presented a very bright and suggestive appearance, and much taste and skill had been employed in the decorations.

Collections were made at each service in aid of the Trust Funds. Appropriate hymns were sung at intervals, Mr. Jacob presiding at the organ.

Other Church Affairs
Young Men's Church Association

The Annual meeting of the Young Men's Church Association was held on September 17th, in the National Boys' Schoolroom, the Vicar, Rev. J. Harrison (President) in the chair, when there was a large attendance of members.

During the year games had been played with the Nonconformist Men's Society - football, draughts, and bagatelle; the Association winning all the matches except the first bagatelle match, and a like result attended a cricket match between the two Associations.

The balance sheet showed that the receipts had amounted to £95 5s. 6d., and the expenditure left a balance in hand of £20.

It was resolved that the subscription be raised from 2s. to 2s. 6d. for members over 18, and that smoking be allowed in the Reading Room to members over 18.

A vote of thanks to the Vicar for presiding concluded the meeting.

Church of England Temperance Society

The first monthly meeting of this Society for the autumn was held in the Boys' National Schoolroom, September 20th. The speaker was Mr. G. B. Hardy, of Cambridge, who in the first part of his address referred to drink in connection with home life, and in the second part to the religious obligations for carrying on temperance work. During an interval in the meeting, tea and refreshments were served.

A Presentation.

A presentation to Mr. A. G. Dillistone took place on Tuesday, September 11th. Mr. Dillistone of this town, has recently offered for service to the Church Missionary Society, which offer was accepted. Before leaving for training, the congregation of the Mission Room, at which Mr. Dillistone had been for 2 ½ years an active worker, showed their appreciation of his services by presenting to him a very useful and well-fitted dressing case, a student's Bible and wallet, and a fountain pen. The presentation was made on Tuesday evening, September 11th, at the close of the usual service by Capt. Pegg, in the absence of the Vicar of Royston; Mr. Dillistone suitably responded. At the service Missionary hymns were sung, and Capt. Pegg gave a short Missionary address. Mr. Dillistone left Royston on Wednesday morning to enter on his training career, with the prayers and best wishes for his success from those amongst whom he had worked.

COUNCIL MATTERS

More Lights Wanted

A letter, from Mr. Charles Warren, was read asking that the Council should extend their street lighting to the extremity of the Urban District on the Baldock Road, by placing a lamp at the end of Mr. Nunn's drift-way, the gas main being already laid to that point.

On the motion of Mr. H. Smith, seconded by Mr. Balding, the matter was referred to the Lighting Committee.

Partial Street Lighting

A correspondent had written complaining about the manner in which the street lamps have been lighted in the High Street and other parts of the town when only a part of them were lighted. The correspondent wrote: "I cannot understand why some parts of the town should be lit up and not others, as all ratepayers have to pay."

Surveyor's Report

The Surveyor presented a report of work done during the past month, including an alteration of the opening of the drains so as to avoid recurrences of over-flow near the Priory Lodge corner, the improvement of the surface drains in Back Street on the east side, and the completion of the path on the west side of the same street.

Mr. Matthews said as no mention was made of it in the report he would like to call attention to the cesspool at the end of Green Walk, near his cottages on the Barkway Road. It became a nuisance when there was a storm, and the water leaked through into the cellars of his cottages.

The Chairman: Is not that the natural consequence of building your houses on the top of a pond? (Laughter.)

Mr. Matthews said that was not the cause or he should not have complained. It must be the faulty condition of this cesspool because when in dry weather the Water Company turned their water through the drain for pumping experiments, it came through into the cellars. The matter was referred to the Drainage Committee.

Inspector's Report

The Inspector of Nuisances, Mr. Webb, reported that Mr. Norman had now had his cowshed provided with a concrete floor in accordance with the Bye-laws.

He had accompanied Dr. Annington to cottage premises in Black Horse Lane, upon which the Medical Officer of Health would report to the Council shortly. Bones stored in the Sun yard so as to become offensive, had been visited and they were removed. In consequence of complaints of a nuisance from the keeping of fancy mice - (laughter) - he visited the premises where they were kept and found they were kept very clean, and that there was no reasonable ground for complaint.

NOTICE OF AUDIT
ROYSTON URBAN DISTRICT COUNCIL.

NOTICE IS HERBY GIVEN, that the Accounts of the Royston Urban District Council. and of the officers thereof, for the year ended the 31st day of March, 1900, will be audited by the District Auditor, FRANCIS GASKELL, Esq., on Monday, the 8th day of October, 1900, at 10.15 o'clock in the forenoon, at the Office, at Royston, of the said Urban District Council, when and where any ratepayer, or owner of property, in the above named District may be present, and may make any objection to such Accounts before the Auditor.

AND NOTICE IS HEREBY FURTHER GIVEN, that such accounts will be deposited at the said Office of the Urban District Council, and be open to the inspection of all persons interested for seven clear days immediately before the day of the Audit.

H. F. J. BANHAM, Clerk to the said Urban District Council.
Council Offices, 18th September, 1900.

Corvus Cornix on the Sewers

The Royston Urban District Council finds itself face to face with rather a larger problem than the actual length and cost of extension of sewers on the London Road and the Melbourn Road, which was the occasion of its application to the Local Government Board. Owing to the peculiar situation of the site originally chosen for the outfall, and its nearness to the large number of houses which of late have grown up at that end of town, it was quite expected that the Local Government Board might, on being applied to for the next loan for sewage, look into the general question of its relation to the outfall and the means of disposal of the sewage. The Board has, through its Inspector, called attention to the short time which the lease of the land has to run, and to the need for the Council having the treatment of the sewage in its own hands. But there is the question of providing for the sewage of the houses in Factory Road and the new residential part upon and near the Rock Road, and the larger question of a new outfall possibly being required for taking in this and for carrying the sewage farther away from the town, if its continued growth should render this step necessary.

EDUCATION

SCHOOL BEGINS

British School

School was reopened on the 10th. There was an attendance of 144 out of 154 on books.

Two Upper Standard scholars, Kate Waldock and Arthur Reeves, left and two had been admitted, Reginald James Spence and Dolly Rayment. May Warren left from Standard II. Rose Pulley was re-admitted from the Union.

A Cookery lesson was taken on the morning of September 28th in Lady Dacre's Room under the supervision of Miss Clarke. These lessons were much appreciated by parents and scholars alike and there had been no trouble whatsoever in selling articles made.

National Schools (Girls)

The school was reopened on the 10th with 105 children present out of 115 on the books. None was absent on account of gleaning.

ADVANCE NOTICES OF FURTHER EDUCATION

TECHNICAL INSTRUCTION

CLASSES FOR

DRAWING   Tuesday, October 2nd,
            Commence at 7 o'clock.
JOINERY   Wednesday, October 3rd,
            Commence at 7.30 o'clock to 9 p.m.
WOOD CARVING   Friday, October 5th,
            Commence at 8.15 p.m..

FEES for Artisans: 2/- one subject; 3/- two subjects: 4/- for all three subjects, for the whole course until the end of March.
WOOD CARVING, Monday and Friday. JOINERY, Wednesday and Saturday. Both Classes will be held in Mr Bevan's Room (late Lady Dacre's Room).
DRAWING One Night a week (Tuesday) at Lower Room at Institute.
Drawing Materials, Tools, &c., provided by the Herts. County Council.
All fees must be paid within the first fortnight.
Any persons wishing to join, should give in their names AT ONCE, to the Hon. Sec., A. WALBEY. *Royston, 19th Sept., 1900.*

Corvus Cornix on a New Secondary School.

On the 18th of the month the Cambridgeshire County Council will inaugurate a secondary school for boys and this will give impetus to secondary education. It will provide courses of agricultural science, building trades, and commercial courses of instruction. It will be the first time a County Council has set about providing Technical Education at a day school. This experiment will no doubt be watched with considerable interest, and possibly jealousy on the part of existing institutions. However, the County Council claims that the school is intended to meet the proverbial "long-felt want".

The list of subjects included in the courses of instruction shows a grasp of the necessities of the age in modern education, and, with numerous scholarships offered, the Cambridgeshire County Council is making a bold bid for popularity....... If it should lay itself open to the comment that a public body representing the ratepayers, and spending the ratepayers' money, should not enter into competition with individuals, it will at any rate be able to reply that it is marking out for itself a path along which private individuals have not hitherto gone very far. In fact, the promoters are already able to claim that among the numerous boys entered for the School "not one of them has previously entered secondary school".

TWO INTERESTING SALES

A Freehold Residence for Sale

On Friday afternoon, September 21st, at the Crown Hotel, Messrs. Nash, Son and Rowley offered for sale by public auction, a residence on the Melbourn Road, Royston, known as "Quies Cottage", by the direction of the Rev. T. H. Lomas, who had the house erected some few years ago for his occupation. The residence was described as containing entrance hall, dining and drawing room, lavatory, kitchen, washhouse, three bedrooms, housemaid's closet, bathroom with hot and cold water, and a flower and vegetable garden, the house having a frontage on the main road from Royston to Melbourn and Cambridge and on Green Street. The bidding commenced at £250 and advanced to £395, at which price it was bought by Mr. W. J. Abbott, for Mrs. Ekins, of Cambridge.

An Old Roystonian Takes The Biscuit

by Corvus Cornix

The Paris *Figaro* early in the month gave a special article to one of the foremost British stands at the Paris Exhibition, that of Huntley & Palmer, the famous biscuit makers. The distinguished position taken by them in the Continental trade requires "a clever and insistent introduction," and in this connection it makes a special reference to an old Roystonian, of which the following is a translation: "It is here the place to give the name of the pioneer of these products. It is Mr. Joseph Leete, who, without interruption for 36 years, has travelled all over Europe, carrying with him a provision of these precious biscuits, explaining and enhancing their merits and ending by making their use general. This surprising and indefatigable man, who has represented his firm at all the Exhibitions of Paris, has had the assistance of his son, Mr. Norman Leete, at the present Exhibition of 1900."

Jury Lists

At the Petty Sessions the Overseers and Assistant Overseers for the various parishes in the Division attended and produced lists of persons qualified and liable to serve on Juries in their respective parishes and verified the same on oath.

The Volunteers
Shooting Competition

The Annual Prize Meeting of the local company of the 1st (Herts) Volunteers took place on the Royston Heath Range on Saturday, September 15th in fine weather. The arrangements were made successfully by the Shooting Committee, the targets working without any hitch whatever. The principal prize was the silver Challenge Cup, which must be won by the same competitor for three years in succession before it can become his absolute property. Pte. Stamford had already won it on two previous occasions and therefore a greater interest was taken this year in the final stages.

The new regulation this year of standing at the 200 yard range, and kneeling at 500 yards, affected the scoring considerably, the highest total being 12 points below the previous year. The prize eluded Pte. Stamford and was won by Corporal King with a total of 68 points.

Refreshments were supplied on the ground by Mr. Percy, of the White Horse Inn, a tent being erected near the 600 yards range.

The Board of Guardians
Applications for Testimonials

A letter was received from the porter asking for a testimonial for himself and wife, on his application for a more important appointment.

Miss Hart, the industrial trainer, also asked for a testimonial for her two years' service.

The guardians decided to grant testimonials in both cases.

Defaulting Parishes

A number of parishes were reported as being in arrears with their contributions, and it was decided that they be summoned if not paid in before next Board day.

Contracts for the Workhouse

Meat for the Workhouse, beef and mutton, 5s. 5d. per stone of 14lbs.; officers' meat 7s. 7d. - L. E. Clark, Royston (accepted).
Bread, W. South 4 ¼ d. per 4lb loaf, flour 25s. per sack; C Ingrey 4d. and 23s. (accepted).
Coffins for Workhouse - Carrington Bros. 14s., 7s. 6d. and 5s. (accepted).
Tobacco - H. Brown, 3s. 3d. per 1b.(accepted).
Ale - J. G. Porter 10d. per gallon (accepted).
Coal - S H. Fordham & Co. 25s. 6d. per ton (accepted).
Faggots, 30s. per 120, Straw 20s. per load;
T. Manning (accepted).

A PRETTY WEDDING

The wedding took place at the Parish Church, on Thursday, September 6th, of Agnes Edith Peebles, daughter of the late Robert Davie Peebles and Mrs Peebles of the Park, Royston, and Mr Gerald Cranworth Ince of Brentford.

A very pretty feature in a brilliant scene was the preparation for the event at the Church. At the entrance to the chancel was a charming floral arch, consisting of white flowers on evergreen, phlox and asters on a framework of smilax, while from the centre of the arch was suspended a floral bell of the same materials the clapper of which was of maidenhair fern and orange blossom From the chancel arch to the altar, the passage was lined with palms. (All the floral arrangements and the bouquets were supplied by Mr. John Pigg). Every part of the church was occupied by a large gathering of spectators. As a prelude to the service suitable voluntaries were played by the organist.

The bride wore an Empire gown of cream Liberty satin, trimmed with Brussels lace, soie brillante, veil of embroidered tulle over a wreath of orange blossom and carried a shower bouquet of choice white flowers. The five bridesmaids wore dresses of pale green Roman satin, (made by Whitaker & Co), with fichus of white silk and white muslin hats, and they carried bouquets of white flowers and Empire Fans, the gift of the bridegroom.

After the ceremony the reception took place at the Park and later Mr. and Mrs. Ince left for London, en route for the Isle of Wight where the honeymoon was to be spent. The bride's travelling dress was a fawn-coloured embroidered cloth and toque of mauve silk and wheat ears.

During the afternoon the Church bells continued to ring at intervals in honour of the event.

ROYSTON PARISH CHURCH
BAPTISMS

September
14th   William Henry and Edith Fanny, children of Henry Muncey (Shepherd) and Fanny Muncey.

MARRIAGES

September
6th   George Ince (Barrister) to Agnes Edith Peebles.

BURIALS

September
15th   Anne Elizabeth Hughes, aged 77 years.
21st   Eliza Martin, aged 77 years.

THE FORTHCOMING ELECTION
Corvus Cornix Comments

The General Election, which has come upon the country so suddenly, and is to be carried through so promptly will have certain peculiarities of its own, and it is part of the contest that these peculiarities will apply in a very special manner to the electors in this district. There will for one thing probably be a large number of unopposed returns, and the County of Hertford seems likely to contribute four of them. At any rate, the North Herts. division and Mr. G. B. Hudson's return are not likely to be challenged.

West Cambs. will have more than a local interest. The contest will not only be the renewal of old struggles which have given the victory to either party alternately, but will this time be conducted under very peculiar circumstances. At the 1895 election Mr. Raymond Greene succeeded in winning the seat from Mr. Hugh E. Hoare (Liberal), who in turn won it from the late, Sir Charles Hall (Conservative), and now Mr. Hoare comes forwards to fight the constituency again. But Mr. Greene is away in South Africa and a peculiar character is thereby given to the contest.

More News From The Front

Extracts from a letter from *Private Charles Lawrence*, of the 1st Battalion Suffolk Regiment to his brother Mr. William Lawrence at Wicker Hall Royston dated July 30th from Middelburg. He had been on a march and had done 76 miles in 4 days and were resting. He then goes on to say:

"We are stopping at this place with Generals Hutton and French. I do not think the war will last much longer as we have just heard by telegram that 5,000 Boers have surrendered. We are about 70 miles from Pretoria now. I daresay you saw in the papers about our taking Middelburg. We were cheered by the English men and women. The Boers ran away so fast that we could not get them. They are all cowards; they won't fight but they won't give in, but it will soon be over for them now. It is better weather now, not quite so cold. It is hot in the day time and cold at night. At night we have two blankets, but we sleep on the high hills and no tents, and we have stars to look at. I get on very well but we don't get much to eat. We catch sheep and kill them which is better than when we first came out. I have seen Racher and he wishes to be remembered to you all. He is well, and Giffen has come home, so I suppose he will tell you all the news."

SPORT
Football

The first match of the season took place on September 15th, on Midsummer Common, against Cambridge, the Albert Institute, and the score was a win for Royston 1- 0.
29th September, Royston v Cambridge Rovers (on Heath). Royston won 4 - 3

Cricket

September
1st   Royston Victoria v E. Parminter's XI (on Heath). Royston won.
8th   Royston v. Cambridge Rodney (on Heath). Cambridge won. Last match of season.

At the end of the season the results for Victoria Cricket Club were:
Matches played - 16; won - 10, lost - 1, drawn - 5

Hockey

The meeting for the start of the new season had to be adjourned because too few people had attended.

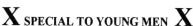

SEASONAL INFORMATION

G. H. INNES & Co.
MARKET HILL,
ROYSTON,
Supply every description of

SPORTING AMMUNITION

Of the best quality at most moderate prices.

WHEAT SOWING
UNDER THE SPECIAL PATRONAGE OF

HER MAJESTY THE QUEEN,
H.R.H. THE LATE PRINCE CONSORT,
H.R.H. THE PRINCE OF WALES,
And Patronised by the principal Noblemen, Landowners,
and Agriculturists in the Kingdom.

DOWN'S
FARMER'S FRIEND.
(CARBOLISED)

Has stood the test of upwards of 60 years, and is acknowledged to be the safest and most effectual preventive of

SMUT IN WHEAT,
BARLEY, OATS, &c.

The Ravages of the Slug, Grub and Wireworm,
and the incursions of Rooks and Vermin.

A Ninepenny Packet is sufficient for Six Bushels of Seed
Wheat, which can be dressed and fit to sow in a quarter-of-
an-hour.

Manufactory: WOBURN SANDS, BEDS.

KILLED
by SANFORD'S RAT POISON, which is said by Farmers and others to be the best ever introduced, as they find the rats dead. Hundreds of testimonials, from Farmers and others. Also Poison for Killing Moles, a New Discovery, answers well. Land infested with these pests can be speedily cleared by using SANFORD'S MOLE POISON. , Price of either of above, 1s. 2d., 1s. 6d., 2s. 6d., 5s., post free, of SANFORD, & SON Sandy, Beds Also Mice Poison for dressing corn stacks. - Sold by Chemists.

G. H. INNES & Co.,
Implement Manufacturers and Agents,
ROYSTON AND HITCHIN.
AUTUMN FARM MACHINERY OF EVERY DESCRIPTION.

Dressing Machines and Corn Screens, Grinding and Ribbling Mills, Ploughs, Harrows,
Cultivators, Corn and Seeds Drills, &c., &c.

TAILORING DEPARTMENT.
C. G. WHITAKER & CO.'S
NEW GOODS FOR AUTUMN & WINTER.

OVERCOATINGS,
SUITINGS
TROUSERINGS,
LIVERIES.

RIDING BREECHES--A SPECIALITY.
PATTERNS AND ESTIMATES ON APPLICATION.
HATS, CAPS, SHIRTS, SCARFS, GLOVES, HOSIERY.

THE CROSS, ROYSTON.

F. H. GIMSON
Ironmonger & Agricultural Implement Agent,
ROYSTON,
Has received a large Consignment of

ELEY'S CELEBRATED SPORTING CARTRIDGES,
LOADED WITH BEST T.S. BLACK **E.C.**, SCHULTZE,
and **S.S. SMOKELESS GUNPOWDER.**
CARTRIDGE CASES, WADS, SHOT,
SMOKELESS AND BLACK GUNPOWDER.
ELEY'S E.B. "NITRO" CARTRIDGES
AND RABBIT CARTRIDGES A SPECIALITY

A. HILLARY'S
GREAT HARVEST SALE
Continuing to the end of September.

GENUINE REDUCTIONS ON EVERYTHING IN STOCK.

BARGAINS IN DRAPERY,
BARGAINS IN MILLINERY,
BARGAINS IN CLOTHING,
BARGAINS IN BOOTS.
SEE THE GOODS & JUDGE FOR YOURSELVES.

HILLARY'S, High Street, ROYSTON.

WHY BE BOTHERED
WITH keeping FERRETS, when for 1s.1d. GAMEKEEPER of 41 years experience will send whole of following REAL GENUINE RECIPES;-
Drawing and Catching Rats in enormous quantities, alive or dead; destroying moles by millions; Bolting Rats or Rabbits from their holes; Drawing Game any distance; compelling Rabbits to lay out for covert shooting; forcing Hens to lay, best on earth; Curing skins; Secret Fishing oils; trapping rabbits, foxes, &c., alive; very valuable dog fanciers' secret to settle any fresh dog so that he will not leave the owner; Carter's Book of Stable Secrets, 1s. 1d. Thousands of unsolicited testimonials. R. Tomson, Frederic Place, Weymouth.

TO BARLEY GROWERS.

MESSRS. J. R. PAGE & SON,
MALTSTERS,
BALDOCK,
OFFER

1st Prize, £15 Silver Cup;
2nd ,, £10 ,, ,,
3rd ,, £5 ,, ,, .

FOR THE MOST CAREFULLY THRESHED
AND SCREENED DELIVERY (not less than
20 qrs.) OF MALTING BARLEY.

The awards will be made March, 1901.

HOCKEY STICKS
Ash Sticks bound handles, made to
regulation size and weight.
3/9 each.
FOOTBALLS.
A good stock at 8/- each.
Sold by WARREN BROS.,
HIGH STREET, ROYSTON

172

OCTOBER
THE GENERAL ELECTION

The Conservatives

WEST CAMBS. PARLIAMENTARY
ELECTION, 1900.

A   MEETING
WILL BE HELD IN THE
ROYSTON INSTITUTE,
ON
Thursday Next, October 4th,
At 8 o'clock p.m.,
IN SUPPORT OF THE CANDIDATURE
OF MR.
W.   RAYMOND
GREENE.

Sir R. Penrose Fitzgerald, Bt.
G. B. HUDSON, ESQ.
AND OTHERS
WILL ADDRESS THE MEETING.

All Electors are cordially invited.

Mr. G. B. Hudson M. P. was the candidate elected to represent North Hertfordshire, on October 3rd, 1900.

MR. W. RAYMOND GREENE,

Meeting at Royston
SPEECHES BY
Sir R. FITZGERALD, M.P. and
MR. G. B. HUDSON, M.P.

This first meeting in Royston during the General Election, in support of the Conservative Candidate Mr. Raymond Greene, was well attended and included a good number of ladies for whom the gallery was reserved.

The Chairman, Mr. Joseph E. J. Phillips, in opening the meeting, said they would agree with him that there was one thing that spoilt the harmony of this meeting and that was the absence of Mr. Raymond Greene. (Applause.) But they all knew that Mr. Greene was away fighting the battles of his Queen and country in South Africa. (Applause), and so was unable to fight his own battles in West Cambs...... He (the chairman) hoped they would return Mr. Greene to Parliament with a larger majority than he had last time. (Cheers) Of course the South African question would take a deal of settlement when Parliament met, and he thought that those who had been in South Africa for so long a time must be able to form a better opinion as to what was necessary to be done, than those who only studied it in the papers. (Hear, hear)

Mr. Hudson spoke about the possibilities of solving the South African question. He was of the opinion that the Conservatives were the only ones capable of bringing about the annexation of the two provinces. The Liberals would not be firm and then all their work and sacrifice of life would have been in vain. Mr. Chamberlain, the most brilliant Colonial Secretary the Country had ever had, had brought about the Australian Federation and if we were to have an Imperial Federation in South Africa no one was more likely to accomplish this than Mr. Chamberlain. Their enemies said they had not been prepared for war but even if that was quite true, they had sent out the 100,000 men that were necessary, at once.

He went on to speak of other issues such as the Agricultural Rating Act, the Workers Compensation Act, Post Office Reforms, and the Vaccination Act. He could not see who would be likely to lead the Liberal Party if it were elected and speculated on the divisions within the party e.g. "Stop the War at any price" and he wondered where Mr. Hoare stood.

Sir Penrose Fitzgerald continued in more detail in the same vein enumerating all Britain's triumphs in conflicts past.

At the end of the speeches, Dr. H. R. Archer said it was a duty they all owed to thank the gentlemen who came over to speak to them. Mr. Hudson was an old friend, but Sir Penrose Fitzgerald was one here for the first time on a Royston platform, and he was sure they were all pleased with the privilege of having listened to him. He had pleaded the cause of an absent man. They had a duty to perform by seeing that Mr. Greene's seat in Parliament was kept warm, and help to support a strong government to settle this great question in South Africa. He proposed a hearty vote of thanks to Sir Penrose Fitzgerald for coming to speak to them that night. (Applause)

Other votes of thanks were proposed and the meeting, which was a very enthusiastic one, then closed with cheers for Mr. Raymond Greene.

North Herts (Hitchin Division)

The nomination of Mr. George Hudson, (Conservative), took place on Tuesday, October 2nd, at the Town Hall, Hitchin.

There were five nomination papers, the nominators and assentors from Royston being as follows:-

Proposer - Joseph Edward Phillips.

Seconder - Herbert Ray Archer.

Assentors - Francis John Fordham; John Goddard Hale, The Rectory, Therfield; Rivers Richard Smith; Robert Walker; John G. Woollard: Joseph Harrison; Harry May, Barley; Ernest Matthews.

Shortly after three o'clock the Deputy High Sheriff, Mr. C. E. Longmore, announced from the steps of the Town Hall, that Mr. G. B. Hudson had been elected Member of Parliament for the Hitchin Division, there being no opposition.

Mr. Longmore said that he was very pleased that Mr. Hudson had been re-elected and hoped that he would continue to represent the constituency for many years as he had done since 1892.

In returning thanks, Mr. Hudson said that he had always done his best for the constituency and would continue to do so and give his support to the present Government in all measures which were for the good of the Empire, of which they were so proud.

MR. G. B. HUDSON, M.P. FOR NORTH HERTS.

MR. HUGH E. HOARE.

The Liberals

Disorderly Meeting

The above meeting was held as scheduled but Mr. Hugh E. Hoare, who was addressing three other meetings in nearby villages, arrived late in Royston. There was a large attendance, the body of the hall being well filled and a large number standing in the doorway whence proceeded no little disturbance and interruption later on in the meeting.

At the outset, the Chairman, Mr. H. G. Fordham, declared that it was the first time the Army had been "brought into a matter of political controversy, and it was unconstitutional to introduce our noble army on one side or the other ..... there was hardly a shadow of difference about the settlement in South Africa, whatever they might think of the way in which the war was begun. The only issue that the Conservatives raised was a suggestion of reform of the Army........ with the experience of the Tories in the past they could not look with much hope for the reform of the Army in the future. They had therefore nothing to look forward to excepting debt and taxation".

Sir Robert Edgecombe enforced the chairman's point of view of changes only likely to come from the Liberals and specially referred to the abolition of the purchase scheme under which an officer could sell his commission, and could only rise by force of money. All newspapers had agreed that in South Africa our soldiers had fought splendidly but had been badly led.

At this point there was a disturbance from people calling out. Sir Robert continued his address and dealt with Home Affairs (Allotments, Old Age pensions and other things which had almost vanished) and the different attitudes of the two parties to agricultural workers and considered "the Union Jack was held up to cover the plaster falling off the walls."

The noisy party in the rear again asserted itself and the speaker sat down with the consolation that some people did not like to hear home truths. The meeting continued in a rowdy fashion, particularly from the young persons in the doorway. After the meeting a noisy crowd of young men hung about the front of the Institute, and on Mr. Hoare appearing he was somewhat hustled and followed as he cycled up Melbourn Street, but there was evidently no intention of violence such as has attended some meetings in this and neighbouring Districts.

The Polling in West Cambs.

In West Cambs. there was a personal note of a peculiar character in the absence of the late member Mr. Raymond Greene in South Africa as Captain in the Imperial Yeomanry. However, during the short time the contest has run, his friends have left no stone unturned in their efforts to make up as far as possible for the personal absence of their candidate.

Polling commenced at 8 a.m. on Thursday, October 11th, and the weather was delightful. The proceedings were quiet except about mid-day and between six and seven in the evening when workmen came in large numbers. Party colours were worn but the display of colours was not as noticeable as at previous elections. Conveyances were in use as usual, and no pains were spared to urge indifferent voters to the poll.

During the morning, Mr. and Mrs. Hoare visited Royston and in the afternoon Sir Walter Greene, M.P. (father of Raymond Greene) and his sister also visited the town.

At Royston, the proceedings from 6 to 8 p.m. became a bit lively. Some hundreds of people congregated in Melbourn Street where the committee rooms were situated. There was a good deal of shouting and cheering among certain portions of the crowd as the last voters came up, but after the close, quiet was very soon restored.

After the Disorder

Letter to the Editor,

Sir,

Kindly allow me through your Paper to express my annoyance at the way my name has been mentioned in respect of the Liberal Meeting held at the Institute last Monday, also to give a most emphatic denial to the reports, that I was there, and that I was the Ringleader. In the first place let me inform my friends that I never left my bed from Saturday midday until Tuesday morning, and secondly, had I been there I should have done my duty as an Englishman and given the speakers a fair and quiet hearing.

Yours respectfully,
ERNEST THAIR.

October 11th, 1900

A similar denial has been received from Mr. J. Coote, Back Street, Royston, who denies that he was ever within 300 yards of the Institute during the time the meeting was held.

RESULT

Raymond Greene(C)	*4,190*	
Hugh E. Hoare (L)	*3,961*	
Majority	*229*	

Corvus Cornix Comments.

The present election has developed here and there in the West Cambs Constituency unpleasant incidents which should afford a lesson to the promoters of public meetings. The immediate object of such meetings before an election is to influence the voters to this or that point of view. The noisy demonstrations seem clearly to point to the desirability of limiting such meetings strictly to electors or at any rate to adults. The large juvenile element allowed to be present at the meetings referred to, immensely aggravated, if it did not altogether occasion, the difficulties under which the speakers laboured. An occasional question is not an unnatural accompaniment of an election meeting, and providing it is not persisted in to the annoyance of the speaker would not be objected to, but when interruption degenerates into mere noisy demonstration from those who have no other part in an election, it becomes a question whether a little discretion might not be exercised by both political parties as to admission to the meetings.

PARLIAMENTARY ELECTION, 1900

TO THE ELECTORS OF THE WESTERN (CHESTERTON) DIVISION OF CAMBRIDGESHIRE

UNIVERSITY ARMS HOTEL,
CAMBRIDGE.

GENTLEMEN,

Allow me to return you my sincere thanks for the honour you have conferred upon my son by re-electing him your Representative in Parliament.

I can confidently promise on his behalf that he will devote himself very earnestly to his Parliamentary duties upon his return from South Africa, and I hope that the experiences he has had, both during the War and his visit to India, may enable him to be of substantial service to the Government in dealing with the important questions which will demand their immediate attention.

My son will, I am sure, continue to realise that he represents the whole Constituency irrespective of Party, but I should be lacking in gratitude if I did not add a word of special thanks to all who have assisted in achieving the victory recorded by West Cambridgeshire today.

I have the honour to be, Gentlemen,

Yours faithfully,
E. WALTER GREENE.

12th October, 1900

HARVEST SERVICES

At The Mission Room

On the evening of Thursday, October 4th, the Annual Harvest Services of the Mission Room commenced with a Service of Song, entitled "Reaping Time." The readings were given by the Vicar, Rev. J. Harrison, and appropriate music was well sung by the choir with the assistance of members of the Church Choir. A solo part was taken by Misses Nellie Onions and Motts, and quartettes by Misses Onions and Motts, Capt. Pegg and Mr. S. R. Smith, Mrs. Harvey Smith accompanying the singing. The offertory was made for the Mission Fund.

At The Parish Church

The Harvest Services at the Parish Church were continued on Sunday, and partook something of the special character of the festival services on the previous Thursday. There was a special service in the afternoon for children, conducted by the Vicar who also preached in the evening. The latter service was a full choral service with special music and anthem as on Thursday. The Vicar preached an appropriate and eloquent sermon. There was a large congregation. and the offertory at the evening service, which amounted to £8 13s. 1d., was for the Royston Cottage Hospital, Addenbroke's Hospital, and the Church Mission Room. At the afternoon service the offertory was for the North Eastern Hospital for Children, London, and amounted to £2 14s.

Prophetic Lectures

The first of a series of four free public lectures on the subject of "The instant coming of our Lord," was delivered in the Institute, on Tuesday evening, October 9th, and will be followed by the remaining three lectures on Tuesday evenings during the next three weeks. The subject as indicated above, embraces "the preparation of His Church to meet our Lord at his coming, and the signs of approaching judgement on those who are unready."

Jumble Sale

A very successful Jumble Sale took place on the evening of Friday, October 12th, in the Kneesworth Street Congregational Schoolroom, in aid of the fund for the new Caretaker's Cottage, recently erected on the site of some older property near the Schoolroom. Gifts of almost all kinds of articles were made, and with a number of ladies and gentlemen to sell and a large attendance to buy, the collection of articles was soon cleared off and about £9 was realised for the object in view.

A Soiree

The annual opening event for the winter session of the Young Men's Church Association took place on Thursday, October 25th, evening at the Institute, and as usual this soiree proved to be a very popular event. As the association has now a very large membership, and the admission to members was free, with a small charge for lady friends, there was a large company present to take part in the dancing, which formed the chief item in the programme of the evening, though hardly so large as the record attendance at last year's soiree. The programme this year contained no outside entertainer, but there was no lack of enjoyment and amusement. In addition to the dancing, there were airgun and other amusements downstairs and a refreshment department. Dancing was under the able direction of Mr. W. Hood as M.C., while Miss M. G. Hinkins proved an efficient pianist.

United

A combined meeting of the Bands of Hope connected with the John Street and Kneesworth Street Congregational Churches was held in the John Street Schoolroom on Tuesday evening, October 23rd, and was well attended. The meeting was one of a series at different centres held for the purpose of hearing addresses from Mr. Fay, with a view to his appointment as agent for the Cambridgeshire Band of Hope Union, similar to the position of Mr. Royds (Uncle Edward) for Hertfordshire. An interesting address was delivered by Mr. Fay, who taking the five senses as a topic was listened to with much interest by the young people present, who at the close demonstrated that they, at any rate, had a good opinion of Mr. Fay. Hymns were sung at intervals, Miss M. D. Titchmarsh accompanying the same.

EDUCATIONAL MATTERS

The British School

During the month of October the arrival and departure of several pupils was reported as was the absence of Arthur Bird who had not attended school for four months due to a "sore head".

On Tuesday, October 16th, school closed at 4.15 for the remainder of the week owing to the Royston Fair.

At the end of the month Cookery lessons were omitted on account of the room being under repair.

On October 30th the bi-monthly exam took place.

Standard I showed great signs of improvement in arithmetic, 26 out of 40 getting 4 sums (including the problems) right, as against 1 out of 39 in the previous exam. The writing too was extremely good and uniform in character.

Standards II & III under Miss Clarke continued to do good work though signs of carelessness here and there are apparent especially in arithmetic. The writing is thoroughly good on the whole; the lines in the exam books being much wider than the ordinary exercise books tend to depreciate the writing a little.

Standards IV, V, VI. VII. as usual passed a thoroughly good exam, Standard V being especially worthy of mention for neat and careful work. Reading throughout on the whole is good. Mental work, object lessons and class subjects have received their full share of attention and signs are not wanting of the good effect these have in the brightness and intelligence of answers given. The school as a whole is well up to standard.

[The only report in October from the National School (Girls) was of the three day holiday for the Annual Fair.]

Royston Evening (Continuation) School

Opened for the Season 1900-1901 on Monday, October 7th, in the National Boys' School-Room under the superintendence of Messrs Attridge and Freston.

Corvus Cornix

What are the causes of the falling attendance at Evening Continuation Schools?

The causes are not altogether connected with the question of age. When the Evening Continuation Schools began upon their present footing, some advanced special subjects were included in the classes and a good number of seniors entered. Then the technical classes ran, in some measure, in competition, the seniors found they could not do everything, and left the Evening Continuation Schools chiefly to scholars just leaving the day schools.

But boys who have just left day school do not, I believe, turn up in large numbers anywhere at evening school. It is unfortunate that it should be so, and parents may well take to heart the advice given by the Rev Joseph Harrison, the writer of the letter, for the question of raising the school age at day schools, and thus making it harder for parents to keep boys and girls at school, may be more dependent upon the effective use of evening schools than parents may suppose.

Evening Continuation Schools

To the Editor of the Herts. & Cambs Reporter

Sir,

As always a warm supporter of night schools, I am distressed to see the great falling off in the numbers attending our Evening Continuation School here, and I am told elsewhere also. It has little more than half the numbers that I have known to be in attendance What is the cause? Twofold I think. It partly rests with the young people themselves who, not unnaturally at their thoughtless age, prefer play to work, bagatelle &c., to arithmetic, grammar and geography &c.. But it rests also with parents and guardians who too often forget that if their boys and girls are to push their way successfully in life they must have an education.

I appeal through your columns to all those who have the well-being of the rising generations at heart, to do their utmost to encourage and insist upon their making use of the educational advantages available. It is all important that they should do so, for what is learnt in the day school is soon lost, unless it is further fixed upon the child's mind as it grows into manhood and womanhood. The day school finished with, the night school should immediately begin. ....

Trusting this letter may be the means of increasing the numbers attending our schools.

I remain, yours faithfully,
JOSEPH HARRISON
Chairman of the Managers of the
Royston Continuation School
The Vicarage, Royston.   *Oct.17th,1900.*

FURTHER WORDS FROM CORVUS CORNIX
A Positive Suggestion

If parents cannot be induced to keep their boys at an evening school during the year or two after leaving day school, there is the more reason for getting hold of him when a lad is entering upon the business of life, and inclined to take up a special subject because he sees for himself that it may be of use to him. It is just at this point that the best work might be done.

In Royston there are two flourishing Young Men's Societies, with a membership of 200 to 300 between them, and rooms open, every evening in the week. I should like to repeat what I have often said in this column, that such a membership should offer a field for educational work for at least some of these members. It is not to the credit of the town to have so much machinery running and yet to have to confess that the educational work is so small. There should be no serious difficulty in such organizations uniting for the support of special classes without in the least affecting their integrity.

TWO WEDDINGS

On Thursday, October 18th at Kneesworth Street Congregational Church, the marriage took place of *Miss Nellie Kingston*, second daughter of Mr. & Mrs. A. Kingston, of Royston, to Mr. Harry Briers of Abingdon, Bucks. The bride, who was given away by her father, wore a cream dress trimmed with chiffon and orange blossom and a cream crinoline hat, trimmed with chiffon and tips and carried a shower bouquet of lilies of the valley. She was attended by three bridesmaids who wore grey dresses with velvet and pearl trimmings and primrose fichus carrying bouquets of yellow and white chrysanthemums.

On Thursday, October 25th, the marriage took place at the Parish Church, in the presence of a number of well-wishers and friends, of *Miss Dorothy Lydia Whitehead*, fifth daughter of the late Mr. William Whitehead, to Mr. Frank Fergusson Edwards of Dartford, Kent.

The bride was given away by her brother and attended by two bridesmaids. The ceremony was conducted by the Rev. J. Harrison and the organist Mr. C. Attridge played voluntaries and a march at the opening and conclusion of the ceremony. During the afternoon the newly married pair left by the 4.54 express for London *en route* for Folkestone for the honeymoon.

TWO VERY EARLY DEATHS
Of a Bandsman

We regret to announce the death at a very early age of 27 years, of Mr. Alfred Richard Wilkins, house painter and paper hanger. He had been for more than eleven years in the employ of Mr. William H. Hinkins, and had very successfully passed a practical examination of the Trade Society. The deceased was also well known, and will be much missed, as an efficient member of the Military Band and the Orchestral Band, and as a player on five dissimilar instruments, but chiefly on the Sarrusophone and the (string) Double Bass. He was the son of Mr. John Wilkins, late of Orwell and now of Royston.

Of Miss Kelly

Much sympathy will be felt with Mrs. Kelly and family, of "Hillside," in the sad bereavement which has just befallen them. Miss Dorothy Mary, eldest daughter of Mrs. Kelly, and grandaughter of the late Mr. Jacklin, visited Scotland recently, and on her return home about five weeks ago, a serious illness ensued, which after the most that medical skill and nursing could do for her, ended in her death on the evening of Thursday, October 4th.

FAIR WEEK

Michelmas Fair

The annual stock and pleasure fair occurred this year nearly as late as it could. The fixture always falls on the first Wednesday after the 11th of October. It is part of the fortunes of the fair keepers that the weather is generally uncertain at this season, and when it rained freely on Wednesday morning the prospects of a fine fair seemed remote and the itinerant vendors looked despondent. By noon, however, the clouds passed away, and a very fine afternoon brought thousands of people into the town. The stock fair, which sometimes is overshadowed by the pleasure fair, was very well maintained. There were a good many horses on the Warren and its vicinity, and among them some really useful animals. Cattle were also very well represented, and the Warren, Barkway Street and the London Road, where the stock fair is usually held, were resorted to by a large number of persons during the afternoon. As for the pleasure fair that was quite up to the average and in some respects was a little in advance of some late years. There were, for instance, more stalls of attractive and respectable appearance than on some occasions, and the many hundreds of young people who flocked in from the villages, found no lack of amusement. The Harris avenue of stalls and their handsome roundabouts were as usual a prominent part of the caterings for the young people, but many other things were there from fortune-tellers to photographers.

Social Evening

In accordance with annual custom in the Fair week, a Social Evening was arranged for the evening of Thursday, October 18th, in the Kneesworth Street Congregational Schoolroom. Organised by the Society of Christian Endeavour, for the young people of both John Street and Kneesworth Street, the evening's amusement included music, recitations &c., and refreshments. There was a very good attendance and a pleasant evening was spent.

THE BOARD OF GUARDIANS

Refusing to Work

James Turner, described as of Darwen, Lancashire, was brought before the magistrate at the Police Station, on Thursday morning, October 4th, charged with refusing to perform his allotted task of stone-breaking at the Workhouse Casual Ward, on the previous day. The case was proved by the Porter, and the defendant had no defence, except that he was not going to break stones on bread and water. He was sent to prison for seven days.

No Drink in the House

The Master of the Workhouse reported that a visitor to one of the inmates had introduced spirits into the House, contrary to the Regulations, a bottle being handed to the person visited.

The Clerk was directed to write to the person in question, informing her that she had rendered herself liable to a penalty by a breach of the Regulations, and to express the hope that she would not do it again.

Resignation of Nurse

At the meeting of the Board of Guardians, the clerk read a letter from Mrs. Broughton, the Workhouse nurse, resigning from her appointment, and asking to be allowed to leave in time to enter upon another appointment on 4th November.

The chairman commented that she had only been there for a fortnight but the clerk said she had arrived just after the August Bank Holiday.

Mr. E. O. Fordham said she was going to one of the best appointments under the Poor Law. It was a misfortune to the Board to lose her services for she was an excellent nurse.

The Board decided to allow her to leave by the date mentioned, and decided to advertise for candidates for the office.

Theft from a Cash Box

On Thursday, October 4th, a theft of money from a cash-box took place at the Crown & Dolphin kept by Mr. F. Chinn, in Kneesworth Street. About ten o'clock in the morning, Mr. Chinn found that his cash-box upstairs had been opened and between £4 and £5 taken. Suspicion at once fell upon a man who had been lodging in the house. It appears that the lodger had, just before the money was missed, gone upstairs for the purpose of a wash, but come down again almost directly, and had at once left the house representing that he was going to the station to see about some goods arriving for him at the station. It is supposed that he not only went to the station, but also by one of the trains then about due. The money was missed shortly after the man had left, but only a part of the contents of the box were taken.

The above sale, on one of the best attended market days for a long time, proved to be an interesting one. There was a large number of persons interested in this breed of small but hardy ponies, some of the foals being so small and wild that they were put into the back of a spring cart under a pig net, and carted home in this way. Very good prices were realised, ranging from about 30s. for the very youngest, up to £9 or £10.

A Well-Deserved Recognition of Merit

The Tailor and Cutter in two recent numbers has reproduced with illustrations, a very able lecture by our townsman, Mr. G. H. Jacob, manager of the tailoring department of Messrs. Whitaker & Co, delivered before the "Tailor & Cutter" Association. The subject of the lecture was "Trousers for Corpulent men," and is illustrated by numerous diagrams showing by clever draughtmanship how the difficulty of putting such a man into a stylish fit may be overcome. The descriptive part of the lecture is lucid and very ably presented, and on the technical points the above journal adds this comment: "It is worthy of the careful study of every member of the tailoring trade. It is full of sound teaching, a model in arrangement and expression, and shows the author to be a man of sound technical knowledge and of considerable literary merit".

THE VOLUNTEERS

Shooting - E Company Recruits' Competition

On Saturday, September 29th, a special shooting competition for recruits who had not taken part in the Challenge Cup Competition recently, took place at the Butts on the Heath, for which prizes amounting to £9 were offered. There was a large number of entries, and the shooting occupied the whole day from 10. 30 a.m.. Some 39 recruits competed, the shooting on this occasion not reaching a very high average, but for the first few places it was very good. Private F. H. Rudling and Private E. Pryor ran close for first place. Private A. Hall who was first at 200 yards with a good score of 27, spoilt his chance at 500 by dropping down to 17. Private E. A. Humphrys also scored 25 at 200 and failed to come off at 500.

Field Day at Hitchin

The members of the E Company, about 50 stong, under command of Capt. Cautherley, with Lieut. Jarvis, went by train to Hitchin on Saturday afternoon, October 20th, to join other Companies of the 1st (Herts.) Battalion Beds. Regiment, in a field day at Hitchin with the Public Schools Battalion. The 1st Herts. men and the Felsted School Boys were a defending force for protecting an imaginary convoy passing between Hitchin and Ippolyts. The attacking force was composed of boys from Haileybury and other Public School boys. The movements took place around and within the Park, and were taken part in by about 600 men.

FIRE AT WICKER HALL

On Sunday, September 30th, about five o'clock, the upper part of the town was thrown into a state of excitement by the reports that the Wicker Hall Cottages were on fire, and when members of the Fire Brigade were seen making for that quarter large numbers of people flocked along the Sun Hill Lane. On arriving at the cottages it was seen that the firemen had got the upper hand of what if left a few minutes later must have been a serious fire. There are six cottages in a row, two others close by these and the beerhouse known as "The Devil's Head," only a few yards away. It was in the midst of this group of cottages that the fire broke out under the roof of the cottage occupied by Mrs. Blows. It seems that a chimney at one of the other cottages had been on fire in the morning, and it is supposed a piece of fire from this fell on to the roof of the cottage in question, and through a hole where the slates were off. The firemen found a long ladder conveniently near at Mr. Stockbridge's stacks and so were able at once to reach the roof and knock in the slates. Next the burning cottages is an old well-house covering a deep well, and here a number of willing hands sent round the wheel of the old well for all it was worth. In this way a few pails of water were available in time to be of service, and their application soon checked the flames. Under the direction of Foreman Course, the members of the Brigade worked with a will, and in less than half-an-hour all danger was over. The roof of the cottage is partly demolished on one side, and the contents of the upper rooms and some of those downstairs by hurried removal were, of course, much damaged. The loss to the owner of the cottage is covered by insurance, but the furniture was not insured.

PETTY SESSIONS

Order for Maintenance

Joseph and William Drayton, of Barley, were summoned by Edwin Davies, Relieving Officer of the Royston Union, to show cause why they should not contribute to the maintenance of their father, John Drayton now chargeable to the Union. Neither of the defendants appeared.

The defendants had been asked to pay 6d. a week each. William Drayton was a carter earning 13s. per week and Joseph, a farm labourer earning 12s. a week and the owner of the house in which he lived. Both defendants were able-bodied labourers and had no young children depending on them. Both worked for Mr. Savill from whom a note was produced that stated that the two defendants were willing to pay 6d. Neither of the defendants had contributed anything hitherto although they had every opportunity of doing so voluntarily.

The Bench made an order for each defendant to pay 6d. a week, but without costs.

No Lights

John Maylin, of Shepreth, was charged with driving a cart without a light in Melbourn Street, near the Cross. The defendant was ordered to pay 8s., including costs.

To make matters worse the same defendant was charged with using obscene language on the highway the same evening whilst driving a cart up Kneesworth Street. He had used bad language to the Police Sergeant and threatened to "run him over". As he had been fined already, he would have to pay 2s. 6d. and the costs would be remitted.

ROYSTON PARISH CHURCH
BAPTISMS
none
MARRIAGES
October
25th Frank Fergusson Edwards to Dorothy Lydia Whitchurch.
28th George Webb to Lizzie Woods.
BURIALS
October
6th Sidney Pretoria Carter, aged 1 month.
9th Ernest Henry Perry, aged 2 years.

Other Births, Marriages and Deaths reported in October

Births
2nd To the wife of George Cautherley a daughter.

Marriages
18th At Kneesworth Street Congregational Church, Harry Briers, of Abingdon, to Elizabeth Eleanor Kingston.

Deaths
25th (ult)James Harradance, of Bassingbourn, at the Workhouse, aged 55 years.
2nd At Mill Road, Albert Richard Wilkins, aged 28 years.
4th At Hillside, Royston, Dorothy Mary Kelly, aged 19 years.

SPORT
Football
October
6th Royston v Baldock(away). Score 3 - 2
27th Royston v Arlesey Town (on the Heath). Result - a draw.

Winners

At the Dog Show held by the Kennel Club at the Crystal Palace Mr. P.F. Fordham took first, second and third prizes with his retriever Crane.

Invalided Home

Among the latest arrivals of soldiers invalided home from South Africa are Trooper Hart, of the 1st Life Guards, son of Inspector Hart, and Private J. Hayes, of the Suffolks, cook at the Royston Workhouse.

£10 Wedding Cake

A claimant has already arisen for the £10 wedding cake offered by Mr. Till to the first C. I. V. (City Imperial Volunteers) married after his return from South Africa. This is Private C. W. Biller, who states that he was invalided home on July 10th, and was married on August 8th. Private Biller is a grandson of Mr. John Biller, an old volunteer of Royston.

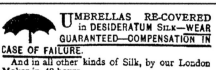
Letters From South Africa

Trooper Hines, of the 11th Dragoon Guards, son of Mr. G. Hines, of Royston, has just written a letter dated Barbeton, September 19th, in which he says:

"I am pleased to say that this leaves me in the best of health. Since I wrote to you last we have got a few more miles up country; in fact we have taken all their land now. They have not a town to call their own, or a place to go for food. In fact I think they are properly beaten now, and it is only a matter of time for them to surrender.....

My officer told me we should be finished by the end of the month. I hope we shall, as I have had enough of this to last me for a while. I want to get home for Christmas and don't want another bout here like the last one we had.......

We are with French's Division now, and to get to this place we had three hard fights, but as usual the Boers made all the running. As soon as we fired a couple of shells into them they ran as if in a race. Thank God, they are done for now. Do not trouble to write to me anymore, as I do not receive any letters. They get lost, I suppose."

From *Private Woodcock* to his parents at the Mount, Royston, dated September 2nd:

"I have got through another stiff fight of four days, but Sunday August 26th was the worst. I had a narrow escape; a bullet struck the heel of my boot..... one went through my slouch hat and I thought I had finished my time but no I am still alive. We were in the thick of it ....pom-poms and shells bursting all over us. There was an officer who said he never saw men go into action the same as we did, every man carrying on as if we were going to a picnic instead of fighting........ We are marching through the mountains now. It is a bit rough I can tell you. I think this was the last place that was made and they did not get time to level the hills, but it is worth seeing the way the railway is laid round the rocks. They have a cog wheel line for the trains to run on. We thought Wonderfontein and Belfast were bad enough but this is worse......I hope you got the Kruger coins I sent you. I posted them on August 1st so you should have them by now."

COUNCIL MATTERS
Sewage Farm

There was much discussion this month about the land on which the sewage farm was situated. The Trustees of the Royston Trademen's Benefit Society were willing to grant a new lease for a term of 31 years at a rent of £46 a year, the Lessees paying all the rates and taxes due. It was proposed that this should be accepted. Mr. Goodman felt that it was a very high rental and the Council ought to consider buying the land. However, it was pointed out by Mr. Gimson that the Local Government Board had held an inquiry, and he thought it would be as well to await their report before renewing the lease or considering purchasing a site. The Board might say that they objected to the system of broad irrigation and were in favour of constructing bacterial beds and then it would not be necessary to have so much land. An amendment was put forward and carried and the whole question was left for further consideration.

Blocked Drains

The surveyor reported certain work done during the month, including the opening of the sewer between the Police Station and the British School, where stoppages had occurred. Pieces of old iron, wet flannel and a quantity of other rubbish were found in the sewer and had no doubt caused the stoppages.

George Lane

Mr. Matthews asked if what was being done in George Lane, putting down the pebbles again, was in accordance with the resolution of the Council......The Clerk read the original resolution which mentioned tar paving or the old paving stone on the sides,

Petrol Licences

The Council decided to renew petroleum licences to Messrs. F. Gimson, G.H. Innes, W.H. Hinkins, A. Humphrey and R. Walker.

First of a Series

The Royston University Extension Society opened the Michaelmas Term of University Extension lectures at the Institute on Wednesday evening, October 17th, with the first of a course of lectures on "Great English Rulers," by the Rev. Dr. Lawrence, Fellow of Downing College. There was a very good attendance. The meeting scheduled for October 3rd was postponed because of the illness of the lecturer.

The Lecturer, before proceeding to his first lecture on Cardinal Wolsey, gave for the benefit of those who might wish to pursue the study of the subjects of the lectures on University Extension lines, an outline of the process of writing papers and accompanying each lecture with a class, either before or after the lecture, for discussion, and of the opportunity of the writers of papers to obtain University certificates, if the courses of lectures could be made continuous, so as to comply with the regulations.........

At the close of the lecture it was put to the vote and decided that the class for discussion should be at 7.30, before the lectures, which will commence at 8 p.m. fortnightly.

National Union of Teachers
Revised Code

The Royston and District Branch of the National Union of Teachers held a general meeting at the National Schools on Saturday afternoon, October 27th, during which, a practical and concise address was given on the working of the Newest Codes, which comes into general operation next year, by Mr. W. C. Lane, of Orwell, followed by a few explanatory remarks by Mr. C. Attridge.

From the general tone of the discussion which followed it was apparent that the teachers were in accord with the Board of Education for giving them a free curriculum in their teaching, and glad to learn that their future school work was to be of a less obtrusive character. There was, it seems, to be free classification in all schools, and the subjects taught beyond the three elementary subjects were to be more directed towards the wants and requirements of the children in their respective districts as regards observations in every-day life and general routine. The *en bloc* payments of the Government Grants instead of the hitherto "piece-meal" instalments was also favourably viewed by the meeting.

Death of a Sweep

We regret to announce the death of an old townsman in Mr. James Rayment, who died on Friday, October 26th. The deceased was well-known in the town and district in connection with the chimney-sweeping business which has been for generations in the hands of the Rayment family. When the agitation took place soon after the beginning of the Queen's reign on the subject of "climbing boys" who were sent up the chimneys, one of the Rayment family was called to give evidence to the House of Lord's Committee. The deceased, who has been all his life connected with the same business, was 69 years of age. He leaves a widow and two daughters The funeral will take place at the Additional Church Burial Ground on November 1st.

Church Missionary Society

The annual sermons on behalf of the above Society were preached in the morning and in the evening at the Parish Church by the Rev. W. St. Clair Tisdale, missionary from Persia. In the afternoon there was a Special Children's Service. Offertories throughout the day were on behalf of the Society. On Monday, October 29th, a public tea preceded the Annual Meeting which was held in the Institute when D. A. Bevan Esq. was in the Chair.

THE BOARD OF GUARDIANS

Appointment of Nurse

The Board had before them three candidates for the office of nurse at a salary of £30 a year and rations. The candidates selected for personal attendance were:- Mrs. Graham, now of London, and late nurse in the Spalding Union; Miss S. J. Brown, late assistant in Todmorden and Chester-le-Street Unions; and Miss Pickett, who wrote from Gower Road, Royston, late nurse in the Blind School, Suffolk.

Miss Brown was proposed and seconded, and on her name being put to the vote her appointment was carried unanimously, and on being called in and informed of her appointment she said she would be able to enter upon her duties on Saturday, November 10th.

Application for an Increase in Salary

The following letter was read from the Master and Matron of the Workhouse on November 21st:-

Gentlemen, - On behalf of the Matron and myself, I beg respectfully to ask the Board for an increase to our salary.

We were appointed as Master and Matron of your Workhouse, 9th of August, 1893, at a joint salary of £70 with rations, &c. This was increased to £100 in January, 1896.

Trusting you will favourably consider our application.

I am, gentlemen,
Your obedient servant,
John W. Wesson.

The Clerk, in answer to questions, said the previous Master and Matron, before leaving, received £125 a year.

Mr. W. W. Clear said they had worked up to that figure after many years service, and when the present Master and Matron were appointed they commenced with the original salary of £70, and afterwards increased it to £100.

The Chairman said he thought they could not consider the question that day. It had better come before them for consideration next Board day.

The Conservative Club

On Friday, November 9th, about 60 members of the Club, sat down to an excellent hot supper provided by Mr. and Mrs. Stockbridge (caretakers). Mr. J. E. J. Phillips, President, was in the Chair. Several toasts were proposed: to the troops in South Africa, the health of the two new members of Parliament for the District, Messrs. Greene and Hudson, and to the Prince of Wales, whose birthday it was. The toasts were interspersed throughout the evening with musical activities.

"The Fifth"

The "Gunpowder Plot," did not create much excitement in Royston on Monday, November 5th. There was an attempt at a 'Guy', more or less reminiscent of the War, but the occasion was chiefly marked by displays of small fireworks by private parties, some in their own grounds and others on the Heath.

The Royston Gold Mines Ltd.

The following is taken from *The Tribune*, published at Nelson, British Columbia. "The transfer of the Royston group of Claims on Morning Mountain by the owners, J. L. Stamford and others, has been completed, and local parties have incorporated a joint stock company with a capital of $1,000,000, to operate the property. The Royston includes the Skene Dow, Nellie, Royston, Barrie and Royston Fraction claims. The new company is known as the Royston Gold Mines Limited, and a small crew of men are already at work on the claims." Mr. J. L. Stamford is the half-brother of Mr. James Stamford of Royston, and will be remembered by many Roystonians.

CHURCH ACTIVITIES

For Men Only

On Sunday afternoon, November 11th, at the Parish Church, an interesting experiment in the first of a promised series of monthly services for men was held. A circular letter had been issued by the Vicar appealing to his brother men, and especially those who lounge away the Sabbath, and in plain, earnest words invited them, "to come and bring a male with you", to a special service for men only at 4p.m. On Sunday afternoon, the subject announced for the address being, "Call a spade a spade." There was a gratifying response at this the first service on Sunday afternoon, when about 80 to 90 men were present. The service commenced with the well known hymn, "All people that on earth do dwell," and the Vicar frankly appealed to them, as there was no choir, to all join in the singing, which they did heartily. A short form of prayer by the curate, Rev. A. T. Boodle, was soon over and then the hymn, "O God our help in ages past," was sung.

The Vicar's address was without a text, but the subject was, broadly, human life, where it has come from and where it is going to. A word of welcome, a brief reference to old associations with places of worship in youth getting dropped before middle age, and then by apt illustration and plain earnest words, was brought home to the audience the tendency to allow all the claims of the higher life, and of God and the hereafter to drift on in a way that not one of them would be foolish enough to do in the affairs of their everyday life. Then by anecdote and illustration was shown the inconsistency of admiring every brave heroic act of self-sacrifice for others in everyday life and forgetting all about the greater love and the greater sacrfice of Him who had bought them with the price of His blood.

The hymn, "Jesu, lover of my soul," was then sung and the Benediction closed an interesting service which was followed with much attention, and was carried out in a manner which may best be described as "brief, bright and brotherly."

Church Sunday School Association

The annual meeting of the above association was held on November 8th, and as usual took the form of an afternoon meeting, model lesson and discussion, tea, and special service, at the Parish Church in the evening. The afternoon meeting was held in the large room of the new Church House which proved very convenient for the purpose. A model lesson was given by a member of the Church of England School Institute and an interesting discussion took place turning more especially upon getting young men to attend a Sunday Class. There was an adjournment to the National Schools where tea was provided. In the evening at 7 p.m. there was a special service at the Church at the close of which the offertory was for the Sunday School Institute Fund.

Second Advent Lecture

On Tuesday evening, October 30th, the fourth of a series of lectures upon the near coming of our Lord was delivered in the Institute. The lecturer reminded his hearers that judgement is frequently mentioned in the Bible in connection with the coming of the Lord. The prophets, Joel and Malachi, wrote of the great and terrible day of the Lord.....The sixth petition in the Lord's Prayer is, "Lead us not into temptation." He had taught them another prayer which most had forgotten. They were told to, "watch and pray always that they may be accounted worthy to escape all those things which shall come to pass and to stand before the Son of Man." He exhorted them to pray this prayer. The speaker announced a further series of lectures to be given on Thursday evenings, commencing November the 8th, at eight o'clock.

Temperance
United Temperance Society

At the monthly meeting of this society held on November 8th, in the Market Hill Mission Room, the Rev. W. Stuart, of St. John's College, Cambridge, spoke on the action of alcohol on the organs of the body, and its injurious effect in impairing the life and character of individuals. Others who took part were Rev. W. T. Lewis, a vocal solo, and Mrs. Keen, recitation. Temperance hymns were sung. Mrs. J. Mason accompanied the singing.

YMCA

The members of the Young Men's Church Association met in the Church House on Tuesday, November 6th and had for discussion " Do sports tend to brutalise?" The Vicar (chairman), Rev. A. T. Boodle, Dr. Archer, and Mr. T. S. Higgins took part in the discussion.

Young Men's Church Association

On Tuesday evening, November 13th, an address was delivered by Trooper Hart on his experiences in South Africa during the Boer War. Dr. Archer briefly introduced the gallant trooper and he began his narrative. Starting from the Modder River he first mentioned the Relief of Kimberley, thence on to Paardeberg, the scene of Cronje's surrender, the fight at Poplar's grove, and thence on to Bloemfontein. Various other places were mentioned, including Winburg, Lindley, Heilbron, Bethlehem and finally Johannesburg, where he was smitten with enteric fever. He then gave a short description of the hospital arrangements of Norval's Point, and considered he owed his life to that institution.

A description followed of his journey from Norval's Point to Capetown Hospital and his subsequent journey home on the 'Kildonan Castle.'

The address was loudly applauded at the end. The Chairman proposed a hearty vote of thanks to the speaker for his address and thought Royston ought to proud of the number of brave men who had left this district to fight for the honour of the Queen and country. Mr. G. F. Phillips seconded, and urged more of the young men to join the service. The Chairman, in supporting the resolution, congratulated Trooper Hart on his safe return, and maintained that when the history of the Boer War came to be written, it would be found to be the greatest feat ever accomplished by any one country in the world. The resolution was carried with acclamation.

Free Church Girls' Guild

On Friday evening, November 9th, an interesting meeting was held in the Kneesworth Street Congregational School-room for the purpose of inaugurating a Free Church Girls' Guild in connection with the Free Churches in the town. These Guilds were being formed in connection with the Free Church Council in places where there was no Young Women's Christian Association for which membership in the Guilds was equivalent. A large number of young girls were present and upwards of 30 gave in their names for membership. A number of ladies who had interested themselves in starting the guild were present and contributed to the interest of the evening by music and recitations &c. Refreshments were also provided. Another meeting would be held later for the formal establishment of the Guild and the election of officers, &c.

Odd Fellows

At the meeting of the Hand of Friendship Lodge of the Ancient Order of Odd Fellows, The Secretary (Mr. R. S. Trudgett) produced the report of the Actuaries upon the quinquennial valuation of the Society's position. The report showed a very satisfactory progress during the previous five years and a surplus of £711 after meeting all liabilities.

The Late Artificial Manure Case

David Barnes, coachman, of Royston, was charged on the information of William Bowskill, that he did commit wilful and corrupt perjury in evidence given by him upon oath at the Hertfordshire Quarter Sessions on June 18th at the trial of the said William Bowskill on the charge of aiding and abetting one Alfred King to commit a felony.

William Bowskill, prosecuting his own case, gave evidence as follows: "I live at Royston, and am a farmer. On the 18th of June last an indictment was preferred against me at the Quarter Sessions at Hertford, for aiding and abetting Arthur King, to steal artificial manure on 25th April, and the result of the trial was that I was found guilty, and sentenced to three months hard labour. My charge against Barnes *(he was earlier a witness for the prosecution)* now is that he gave false evidence as a witness for the prosecution. He swore in the first instance that I handed a bag over the hedge to King, which is false. He swore that he saw me cover up my cucumber frame before I came away in the afternoon; and he further swore that there was no occasion for me to have gone down the drift as he termed it."

After a lot of further discussion and the testimony of various witnesses, the bench retired to consider their verdict and on returning the Chairman stated: "We have considered the case and do not consider the evidence brought before us is sufficient to put Barnes on trial for perjury."

The case was therefore dismissed.

During the hearing of the case the Court was crowded, and a good deal of interest was taken in the case.

Amateur Music Society

The Annual meeting of the members of this Society took place at the Institute on Tuesday evening, October 30th. After the normal business had been transacted it was decided that for the next concert, *The Revenge,* by Villiers Stanford, should be chosen. Practice will, it is understood, be commenced forthwith upon this work. Mr. Fred Dewberry, of Cambridge, will again be the Conductor of the Society.

PETTY SESSIONS

The Institute

On Wednesday, October 31st, the Bench granted a licence, on the application of Mr. James Smith, for stage plays for the Royston Institute, to extend until the end of April, the sureties being Mr. Smith, Mr. Ernest Matthews and Mr. S. Camps.

Trouble with Drink

Charles Sharpe, of Wicker Hall, Royston, was charged with being found unlawfully drunk in Briary Lane, Royston.

The defendant pleaded guilty.

P.c. Arthur Robbins proved finding defendant lying by the side of the road drunk and incapable. He got him home. He was quiet.

The defendant was ordered to pay 6s.

Drink Again

On 11th October *Robert Hepburn,* was charged with being drunk and disorderly on the highway at Royston, The defendant admitted the offence.

P.c. Richard Gray said he saw the defendant at 2.15a.m., on October 11th, lying on the footpath. The witness woke him up, and on the way to his house he used bad language. The defendant was fined 20s.

Without A Light

James Freeman, of Royston, was charged with driving a conveyance without a light, and he said the light was out but had not been out five minutes. P.c. Knight deposed to seeing defendant without a light. The defendant was ordered to pay 8s.

A Musical Evening

A very successful entertainment was given in the John Street Congregational Schoolroom on Friday evening, November 2nd, by Miss Stone's music pupils. There was a crowded audience, and a great variety of items of vocal and instrumental music was provided, and was received with much favour. The songs by a number of the pupils and many of the solos both vocal and instrumental, were well rendered, and numerous encores were called for notwithstanding a rather long programme. The vocal music was accompanied by Miss Stone. There was no charge for admission, but during an interval between the first and second parts a collection was made for the benefit of the Royston Cottage Hospital, the result of which is that Miss Stone has been able to hand over £1 12s. 3d. to the Hospital.

MORE ON THE WAR

Letters from South Africa

Excerpts from *Trooper Hines'* letter to his parents
"Dear father and mother, I again embrace the opportunity of writing a few lines to you. I am very pleased to say this leaves me in the best of health and hope this will find you all the same.

I had quite a happy surprise this morning. I received a letter from you and one from Agnes. Yours was dated July 5th and Agnes' July 28th, so you see I am just as well off as regards letters as yourself. I was pleased to hear you had such lively times at Royston; quite a strange thing for one to hear of Royston being lively. I should very much like to have been there instead of at Mafeking.

It was very amusing to see the Boers run when we entered this place (Barberton), especially one chap in a Cape cart who had £11,000, but General French was a bit too quick for him and snaffled the lot, besides large quantities of stock and stores. I do not know the exact number of prisoners we got here, but judging by the noise they make every night I should say there are a good lot. They sing every night and it is amusing to listen them singing in their Dutch language some words lasting a good half-minute. They sing something about God bless Oom Paul, and when our chaps hear them singing that, you can guess there is a good deal of strong language.

One thing more about this place. There are a good deal of English who are very kind to us and often bring us some nice things; there are also several large gold mines, which of course are not working now.

I think the war is about all over now as far as the fighting line is concerned, and I believe when we do move again from here it will be homewards, at least I hope so."

Excerpts from *Private W. D. James'* letter to his father and mother at Baldock Street, Royston:
"It is hard to be hungry and got money in your pocket and can't get nothing to eat. We are half-starved. We shall be all right when we get to this place, where we can buy something to eat. We haven't got no clothes to wear; they are all torn. We have worn our shoes off our feet and our feet are sore from walking. We were only four miles off of De Wet and we thought we had got him but he got away from us. He sent us notice in that he was going to bombard the place with his big guns and he gave us twelve hours' notice to get the people out. We had to get up in the middle of the night and get into trenches.

I think we shall be home for Christmas. We think we set sail some time in November. I shall be glad when I get home as I am sick of this. I haven't received any paper yet and only one letter which I received on the 28th of September.

Enclosed with the letter is a cutting showing the price which provisions ran up to during the latter part of the siege of Ladysmith-- oatmeal 60/- per 14lbs., condensed milk 10/- per tin, coffee 17/- per lb., eggs 46/- per dozen, fowls 18/6d. each, bottle of jam 31/-, and ¼ lb. of tobacco 60/-."

Tobacco for the Scottish

Private G. Wiffin, of the 1st Scots Guards, has sent home to his mother, Mrs. Wiffin of the Woolpack, Kneesworth Street, to keep for him, an interesting souvenir of the South African War. It is a handsomely designed flat metal box of tobacco, something after the fashion of the Queen's chocolate boxes. These boxes have been presented to soldiers in the Scottish Regiments serving in South Africa by the Scottish Regiments Gift Fund. The box has a gilt lid, at the top is the motto "Frae Scots Tae Scots," and at the bottom "For Auld Lang Syne." A thistle is in the middle, and on one side a lion and on the other the words "South Africa, 1900." The gift is one that has been highly appreciated, and it is worth preserving.

Promotion

Second Lieutenant I. M. M. Phillips, of the 4th (Herts. Militia) Bedfordshire Regiment (son of Mr. John Phillips), Earl's Hill House, has been promoted to Lieutenant.

Local Song Writer

Two patriotic songs, words and music by Arthur Jarman, have been published by Weekes & Co., Hanover Square, Regent Street. Of the first, " The Boys of Dear Old England," a copy has been accepted by Her Majesty the Queen; the second song is entitled "Welcome Home Lads." Mr. Jarman, who is well known in Royston, is also the composer of other popular songs and a Grand March, "The British Heroes."

Royston Nursing Association

The fifth annual report of this Association and the useful work done under its auspices for the year 1899-1900, was issued this month.

"The work of the nurse is steadily increasing and her services more valued than before. During the epidemic of influenza in February last, she was extremely busy, as many as fifteen houses being visited in one morning.

The number of cases during 1899-1900 has risen from 59 to 72, nine of these being maternity cases, and the number of visits from 2,427 to 2,658. The cases included Pleurisy, Rheumatism, Rheumatic Fever, Phthisis, Ulcerated Leg, Abscess, Cancer, Bronchitis, Influenza, Pneumonia, Obstetric, Heart Disease, Burns, Scalds, and Cuts.

The subscriptions have fallen £3, and the committee hope that all their friends will do their best either to increase their own subscriptions or to induce others to become subscribers. The total expenses now amount to £89, and as the subscriptions are only £55, the remainder of the amount required has to be made up by donations; a very uncertain and precarious form of income.

The committee have received, with the greatest regret, notice from Miss Trowsdale that she will be obliged to relinquish her duties in Royston in January next. They cannot speak too highly of her work during the previous two years, and feel that it will be difficult to fill her place. She will be gratefully remembered by all her patients

Many gifts had been given to the Association from residents in the town through Miss Thurnall's exertions viz: a bicycle, a bath chair, a set of clinical thermometers, a steam kettle, clothing and linen, meals, fruit, milk, and beef tea. Further requirements are a water pillow, inhaler, foot warmer, and more linen."

A Letter to the Editor

Sir,

The 5th annual report just issued makes plainly evident the need of larger and more widely extended subscriptions.

It is disappointing to find an Association of admitted value to the town, so ill subscribed that the number of subscribers does not reach one hundred and their annual contributions a trifle over £50 - to meet an annual expenditure of double that amount. The actual balance is 27s. 5d.! which must impose limitations on the "gratuitous" nursing of the sick poor, unless the reluctance of subscribers to provide adequate funds, and of the patients to offer some slight pecuniary recognition can be more successfully overcome in the future than in the past.

The fees for private nursing, though increased, are inconsiderable amounting only to 146 shillings and practically the Association is a charitable institution pure and simple, and therefore must or should regulate its beneficent work proportionately to the amount of reasonably assured income at command.

The necessity for a change of nurse affords the opportunity for adapting to new conditions........ but apart from a hope for more subscriptions and donations the Report is silent upon the remedial measures which need to be taken.

It is conceivable, however, that some would-be subscriber, whilst recognising the duty of providing medical relief and assistance for poorer bretheren, would take a more comprehensive view of the term *nursing* as applied to the sick poor, than flying visits and limited attention convey with as many as fifteen houses being visited in one morning. Also, one cannot feel quite convinced that a nursing system up-to-date and *a la mode* in say London life, is - without adaptation to local needs - the most fitting for a town like this.

For my part I intend to increase my subscription because, in spite of much that seems "pretty folly", I think the Association is so beneficial that with growing experience and consideration for the peculiarities of the place, there would be some encouragement to make it a success.

Yours faithfully,

A SUBSCRIBER, *21st November 1900.*

SCHOOL NEWS

British School

On the 9th, the Head reported that he had to punish Leonard Booth sharply for swearing and insubordination. He had had a great deal of trouble with him on several occasions, and considered, though young, he was a bad lad.

Annie Mabbitt, aged 13, left school on the 12th as she was wanted at home. There were 155 on the register.

During the week ending the 16th, there was a great deal of sickness. 8 children had been away the whole week and several others had been away most of the time.

The Head was absent on the afternoon of the 28th and reported that the 30th was the end of the 4th Quarter.

Expenditure		
Salaries		
1.(a) of Principal Teacher		144. 11. 5
(b) of all other Teachers		123. 17. 0
2 Books and Stationery		14. 1. 3
3. Apparatus and Furniture		7. 12. 0 ½
4. Fuel and Light and Cleaning		13. 15. 3 ½
5. Repairs to Buildings		39. 16. 0
6. Rent (No charge if building held in trust for Educational Purposes.)		
7. Insurance		9. 0
8. Prizes	3. 10. 0	
Bank Interest, Cheque Book, Stamps, Printing	1. 1. 2	
	4. 11. 2	4.11. 2
		396.10. 3

Year ending November 30th, 1900

Income	
1.Grant from Board of Education	£165 14. 3
Fee Grant	78. 2. 6
Additional Grant	80. 0. 0
2. Voluntary Contributions	35. 3. 9.
3. Income from use of Room	2. 0.
Balance on Nov. 30th	37. 7. 9.
	£396. 10 .3.

National School (Girls)

On the 2nd, the Head reported that the roof of the school had given way in several places and a half-day holiday was given so that repairs could be done.

The Vicar took the First Division Scripture Lesson on the 13th. A bad throat kept Miss Higgins away for three days. Mr. A. Barlett, the inspector, paid a visit on the 22nd and there was a half day holiday.

A Letter to the Editor

THE BALDOCK STREET FOOTPATHS.

To the Editor of the Herts. & Cambs. Reporter.

Sir,- May I be allowed through your columns to call attention of the Royston Urban District Council to the deplorable condition of the paths in Baldock Street.

Except for a small bit of paving under the Brewery garden and trees nearest the Cross, laid down last year by the County Council, nothing has been done to the paths since the Urban District Council came into existence three years ago.

Last year rumours of an asphalt path up the south side of this much frequented street, were afloat, but alas! nothing was done. Are we to go through another winter under similar conditions? Last Sunday evening, for instance, the conditions of this particular pathway from the Brewery House to the Briary Lane was wretchedly miserable and a disgrace to the town of Royston. From one end to the other there were continuous puddles of slush and muddy water, and this combined with a dimly lighted street was anything but pleasant to the pedestrians on the way home from public worship. Indeed, close to the Lane referred to, the deposit of mud and greasy clay, which had run across the path and over into the road itself was, to use a mild expression, simply disgraceful.

One is glad to see improvement in both side-walks known as George Lane and Church Lane, but is an important throughfare like Baldock Street, one of the main arteries of the town, to be sacrificed for these?

I do not wish to be thought uncharitable in this matter, but one is wont to ask whether any of our chosen and elected Councillors ever come up this street on a cold, wet, and cheerless night, or ever have occasion to use the paths at all after dark in the winter months? It is a fact that none of the thirteen gentlemen live in this particular street, else methinks there would have been an improvement ere this.

I am, yours faithfully,

BALDOCK STREET RATEPAYER, *October 31st, 1900.*

Corvus Cornix On Numbering Houses.

Should houses in all towns, even small country towns, be numbered? That is a question which came up in a curious fashion at the Royston Urban District Council this month. The Registrar General has to make the arrangements for the Census next Spring and so in seeking the co-operation of the official staff of local authorities, he has also called the attention to the convenience of numbering houses, as a means of facilitating the work of the numerators for the census. But there are other reasons for numbering houses which are of a less temporary character, and also less general in their application. It is an advantage to persons having business calls to make to find the shops and houses numbered, but the need is not of quite the same force to all private houses. The streets in Royston are already named and the Council would probably be doing all that was necessary by requiring numbering in the centre where the shops are.

A Comment from Corvus Cornix

In our local life an English man generally waits until he has some personal discomfort to put up with before he takes enough interest in what is happening around him to grumble at the powers that be. The letter on the pavements in Royston is a case of the *argumentum ad hominem* style of grumbling. There is no question that the state of the footpaths in Baldock Street does require attention, but it is fair to say that its chance of getting attended to does not depend in the least upon whether an Urban District Councillor happens to reside in that particular street, nor does it depend in the least upon the fact that the Council is engaged upon making paths elsewhere. The Urban District Councillor happens to have the power to do what it is doing, but it has no power to do the work referred to in the letter, nor for that matter, work in Kneesworth Street and in theHigh Street which also needs attention. For that work the County Council is alone responsible. Whether the Urban District Council is doing its best to urge on the County Council to do its duty is, of course, another question, and in this connection, the writer of the letter may be right in his complaint. It is not at all creditable that such necessary work should take so long to arrange for and carry out, but negotiations with central authorities are apt to be slow.

University Extension Lectures

The second of these lectures on "Great English Rulers" was delivered at the Institute by the Rev. Dr. Lawrence on Wednesday evening, October 31st. The first lecture had dealt with the early life and times and the domestic policy of Cardinal Wolsey, and now after a class for discussions arising out of the last lecture, Dr. Lawrence proceeded to deliver a lecture on Wolsey's actions in regard to foreign affairs and the latter part of his life, and its famous historic moral......Wolsey served the King rather than the nation and was misunderstood by the people and when he was turned upon by the monarch he had served too well, gave meaning to the words put into his mouth by Shakespeare, "Oh how wretched is that poor man that hangs on Princes' Favours." (Applause)

During the next couple of lectures in November, Dr. Lawrence dealt with the early life training and vicissitudes of Queen Elizabeth, and the national aspect of her life and character, and her prosperous reign.

THIS AND THAT

Prize Dogs

At the Cambridge Dog Show on Thursday, November 1st, Mr. G. W. Howard took second prize in class for Smooth Fox Terriers with "Royston Recorder," and a similar prize in the "Borzois" class with "Royston Statesman." Mr. Howard has had the misfortune to have a valuable wire-haired puppy stolen about three weeks ago which was worth £50. The puppy was kept at Wisbech for him, and was intended for entry in the Cambridge Show.

Mr. P.F. Fordham also took three 2nd prizes in the open classes for retrievers.

Serious Accident to a Stable Lad

A very serious accident happened to one of the stable lads, named Charles Chidgery, in the employ of Mr. Driscoll. He was riding one of Mr Waller's horses on the jumping ground for steeplechase training near G. N. R. line on the Baldock Road, and at one of the hurdles the horse refused to jump and he was thrown and pitched on his head. He was taken up in an unconscious condition and conveyed to the Royston Hospital, where it was found that he was suffering from concussion of the brain. He remained in an unconscious state for a day.

ROYSTON PARISH CHURCH
BAPTISMS
November
3rd   Joan Hunter, daughter of George Sewell (Bank Cashier) and Jane Sewell.
4th   Vera Alice, daughter of John Noades (Labourer) and Alice Anne Noades.
4th   Reginald Frank Hector Seaforth, son of Noah Perry (Soldier) and Ellen Perry.
18th   Albert Wilfrid, son of Wilfrid Dellar (Painter), and Harriet Dellar.
18th   Charles Henry, son of Charles Henry Giffen (Labourer) and Clara Giffen.
MARRIAGES
November
1st   James Munns (Drayman) to Clara Jane Loates.
BURIALS
November
1st   James Rayment, aged 69 years.
8th   Isabella Gertrude Humphreys, aged 56 years.
12th   Robert Norland Howard, aged 46 years.
30th   Martha Whitehorn, aged 4 years.

An Alarming Accident

On Tuesday, November 27th, a serious accident occurred at the Brewery to a man named Edwards, in the employ of J. & J. E. Phillips, Ltd. It appears that he with others had been down in the malting near the Station for a load of malt and was engaged in loading it in Baldock Street, the sacks being drawn up by the chain pulley fastened round the mouth of the sack. He was attending to this part of the work with a man attending to the apparatus above, and was just getting the chain round the sack when the man at the top, before he had been signalled, started the chain upwards with its load. Before Edwards could get his left hand free it was gripped in the chain and he was pulled up with the sack. Hearing his shouts the man at the top appears to have reversed the action just before the double burden had reached the landing, with the result that the man and the sack were run rapidly down. By some misunderstanding the chain began to ascend again before Edwards could rescue himself, and he was taken up some distance again. The result of the severe strain to which his hand was subjected was that his thumb was pulled out, and one of his fingers was broken, besides being bruised in the fall.

A Runaway Horse

A curious, but fortunately not very serious, runaway incident occurred on Tuesday, November 6th, near the Railway Station. A farm horse and cart from Croydon had, it appears, started down the town dragging the heavy, lumbering cart along in rather alarming fashion. On reaching the station yard, the horse, having probably been there before, turned to go in, but just at that moment the railway van was blocking the centre gateway. The horse, therefore, did the next best thing by trying to go through the hand gate for passengers at the side. The gate was smashed by the contact, but otherwise no serious damage was done.

Other Births, Marriages and Deaths reported in November.
Births.
23rd   A son to James Course at Royston.
30th   A daughter to E. W Thair, High Street, Royston
Marriages.
  None.
Deaths
9th.   Mary South , Cemetery Lodge, Melbourn Road , Royston, aged 75 years.
22nd   Thomas Sansbury, of Ashwell, Royston Union, aged 59 years.
27th   George Pymont, London Rd, Royston, aged 73 years.

Living Conditions

Dr. Anningson, Medical Officer of Health, reported at a meeting of the Urban District Council, upon a case of over-crowding in a cottage occupied by Walter Woods and his wife and family in Black Horse Lane - two bedrooms and ten persons, with a 120 feet of air space against the standard requirement of 300 feet. It was reported later that the family had removed to Cambridge.

At the same meeting, the Sanitary Inspector reported on a joint ash-pit for four houses in Market Hill which was in an insanitary state. He was instructed to give notice of the requirements as to cleaning out once a month and to inspect the condition of the ash-pit.

HERTFORDSHIRE COUNTY COUNCIL
TECHNICAL INSTRUCTION
AGRICULTURAL COMMITTEE

A PLOUGHING COMPETITION will take place at the Newnham Hall Farm, Baldock, on Thursday, 22nd November, 1900, commencing at 10 o'clock a.m. Prizes from 30s. to 5s. All entries free. Any person desiring to compete must send his name and address to Neville J. Hine, Esq., Newnham Hall, Baldock, on or before Tuesday, 20th November, 1900.

A. DEAN,
Organising Secretary,
Eastfield, St. Albans

SPORT
School Football

The Victoria House School Football Club played a match with the College School Club at Baldock, on Thursday November 8th. Play was fairly even in the first half which resulted in one point for Baldock. In the second half the home side, with a strong wind in their favour, had the better part of the play, scoring four or five times to the visitors twice. The match ended in an easy win for Baldock.

Football
November

3rd   Royston v. Cambridge St. Mary's(away), Royston for once had some difficulty raising a team and played three men short. Score Cambridge 6 - Royston 0.

7th   The match against Stevenage for the Herts Junior Cup was cancelled by Stevenage allowing Royston into the 2nd round.

24th   Royston 2nd XI v Melbourn 2nd XI (on Heath).
          Score Royston 3 - Melbourn 0

Ladies Hockey
November

3rd   Royston v Perse High School for Girls (on Heath). Royston lost. Score 2 - 3.

10th   Royston v Saffron Walden (on Heath). Royston won. Score 3 - 2.

Police Changes

Some changes in the location of members of the police force have taken place. P.c. Fay of Barkway, having resigned, P.c. Gray, of Royston, has been removed to Barkway to take his place, after three years efficient service at Royston. P.c. Robbins of Hitchin, takes the place of P.c. Gray at Royston.

Winning Birds

At the Crystal Palace Poultry and Pigeon Show held this month, Mr. P. F. Fordham took seven prizes out of ten exhibits, amongst which were two firsts and a special for white carrier pigeons.

DECEMBER

News in Brief

Uncle Tom's Cabin.

The performance of the above, by a travelling company, was held in the Town Hall on Wednesday, December 12th, and attracted a large audience. It afforded a stirring entertainment, which showed that the old story still has a hold on the public mind.

First Aid Lectures

At the Church House on Friday, December 7th, Dr. Archer began his series on First Aid. The series began with a talk, using a skeleton and diagrams, on the framework of the human body and its muscular structure.

Service For Men

At the Parish Church on Sunday, December 9th, the Vicar held the second of his special services for men. There was a very good attendance, including a number who were not regular attendants at the other services.

The Ringers

At the Parish Church on Monday, December 10th, the ringers rang several complete peals of "Bob Singles" on the tower bells, a very creditable performance considering the condition of the bells and the fact that the ringers have only been installed just over six months. The following took part: Rev. Boodle, H. Bonnett, R. Wilkerson, H. R. Smith, A. Wilkerson (Capt.), G. Mowberry.

Lantern Lectures

The Paris Exhibition was the subject of a very able and interesting lecture delivered by Mr. H. G. Fordham at the Nonconformist Young Men's Society rooms on Friday, December 7th, before a crowded audience. The lecturer gave a very instructive lecture upon the chief features of the exhibition - the remarkable beauty of the chief buildings and surroundings, and the lessons to be derived from the different sections - and his description was supplemented by a very numerous and excellent series of views thrown upon the sheet by Mr. E. W. Stone.

The Band

Weather permitting the Band will give their second Open Air Winter Concert at the Whitehall Cross, High Street, from 7.45 to 8.45 on Thursday, December 6th.

University Extension Lectures

The last two lectures of the term in this series entitled "Great English Rulers" were on the subject of the career of Strafford as a Minister of Charles I, who was eventually impeached by the House of Commons and later lost his head.

Chess

A match between the Royston Chess Club and the Cambridge Conservative Club took place on Friday, December 14th in the Kneesworth Street Schoolroom. The result was an easy win for Royston, 16 games to 5.

During an interval in the above programme, the Rev. G. Packer explained that the erection of the caretaker's cottage near the Schoolroom had been an improvement on the old property formerly on the site. It had cost £250 and, as usually happened in such cases, the last £50 or £60 was the hardest to raise. A collection was then made for the above project.

School News

The new school year commenced on December 3rd and the available logbooks spoke of admitting children from the Infant School. The schools closed for Christmas on December 21st.

DRINK - THE CRUSADE CONTINUES

Economically Speaking - Another Point of View

The monthly meeting of the United Teetotal Society was held on Wednesday, December 12th in the Kneesworth Street Church Schoolroom where the speaker was the Rev. Alex W. Pay from the Cambridge Band of Hope Union.

His address referred to the many sides of the temperance question and proceeded to deal with the economic side as affecting trade and wages. Dividing labour into the three classes of productive, neutral and destructive, he classed the manufacture of strong drink with the destructive and proceeded to compare the ratio of wages in the liquor trade with that of other trades, and showed from the Parliamentary Returns that the manufacture of strong drink only meant £7 odd in wages per £100, while other trades ran up to over £50 and averaged £39 out of every £100, which he showed had a remarkable effect upon the number of men employed in a trade in proportion to the capital invested. The Speaker then, with the aid of sample bottles, analytical results showing the proportion of water and alcohol in different kinds of spirits, beer &c, contrasted their small nutritive value with that of the different kinds of food.

Uncle Edward Arrives

On Monday, 10th December, the Church of England Temperance Society held a meeting when Mr. Boyds 'Uncle Edward' of the Hertfordshire Band of Hope, gave one of his popular magic lantern stories with temperance maxims interspersed. The evening meeting was preceded by a meeting for the juvenile members, with whom 'Uncle Edward' is always thoroughly at home.

Calling on Historical Support

An exceedingly able and interesting paper on "Intemperance in Ancient Times and Modern" was read by the Rev. T. H. Lomas, at the meeting of the Society. He dealt with the subject from the point of view of a moderate drinker; an interesting discussion followed.

Drink and the Army

At the regular monthly meeting of the Church of England Temperance Society the speaker was the new secretary of The Ely Diocesan Society, Mr. Isaac Mark. In the first half of his address Mr. Mark referred to the striking advance made by the temperance movement in the Army. (Wellington had found troops too tipsy to be any use in the evening.) Lord Roberts in India had borne testimony to this and abstaining forces now formed one third of the British Army. Lord Roberts considered their abstinence added the equivalent of two battalions to the effective strength of the Indian Army as they were always ready for action. About 7000 members of the temperance movement were now out in South Africa.

After the interval he referred to the beer scare which had happened in his native city of Manchester and the illness and deaths which had been caused through arsenical poisoning. He referred to the attention being given to this subject, and said it was a well known fact that beer was not brewed with malt and hops as of old but with other mysterious compounds. Besides this, temperance advocates had been preaching for years that beer contained poison with a much longer list of victims than the present occasion had produced. In conclusion he reminded them of the signs of encouragement to continue their work, and that France, from whom we did not get much encouagement of late, had taken up this question and the Ministers of Education had issued a circular for the teaching of temperance principles in schools.

Post Office Changes

Mr. J. W. Carter, postmaster at Royston Post Office, has been appointed to the Postmastership at Gainsborough and will enter on his duties there in the New Year. For the first of a long line of Christmases, the public also missed the figure of Abraham Humphrey who retired earlier in the year. Starting in 1868 when the letter delivery was done by himself single handed, he had continued at his post until the same work now requires four or five postmen.

THE MARKET

ROYSTON MARKET
SALE OF CHRISTMAS FAT STOCK
Messrs. NASH, SON & ROWLEY
Will hold a Sale of the above on
WEDNESDAY, DECEMBER 12th, 1900,
when Prizes value **£6 6s. 0d.**
for stock sold at this market will be
offered for
The best pair of Fat Beast
The best pen of 5 Fat Wether Sheep
" " " 5 Fat Hoggets
" " " 5 Fat Pigs
" " " 5 Fat Porkers
" " Fat Pig.
Auctioneers' Offices: Royston, Herts.

Christmas Fat Stock Show

As usual at this show special prizes were offered for the best entries in the several classes, by the Right Hon. Viscount Hampden, Messrs. Foster & Co., Bankers, and by the Auctioneers. The prize winners were as follows:

Best pair of fat beast, (£2), Mr. Hoy. Prices realised £25 10s. and £24 5s.
5 fat wether sheep, (£1 1s.) Mr. G. Duke, (Trumpington). Price realised average 64s.
5 fat hoggets, (£1 1s.), Mr. Ellis Wilkerson. Prices realised 66s. 6d.
5 fat pigs, (£1 1s.), Mr. T. Kestall, (Buckland). Prices realised average 85s.
Best fat pig, (10s. 6d.). Price realised £5 17s. 6d.
5 fat porkers, (10s), Mr. H. Savage. Price realised average 66s.

NOTICE
ROYSTON MARKET

BOXING DAY this year falling on
WEDNESDAY, the ROYSTON CORN
AND CATTLE MARKET
will NOT be held next week.

December 21st. 1900.

No Connection !!!

Mr. J. Evans having left the service of Mr. J. Coote, Fishmonger, &c., of Kneesworth Street, Royston, and set up in the same line of business for himself, Mr. Coote begs to inform the public that the fish stall presided over by Mr. Evans on the Market Hill on Wednesdays (Market Day), is in no way connected with his business in Kneesworth Street, as has been represented.

URBAN DISTRICT COUNCIL
Thoughts on Sewage and Roads

The Highway and Drainage Committee, along with the Medical Officer of Health, visited the present Sewage Farm, where they found the tank clean, and the system of broad irrigation in full operation and acting fairly well. They inspected the surrounding area with a view to ascertaining whether there was any other land near, suitable as a Sewage Farm. They were of the opinion that a piece of land containing about 20 acres adjoining the Coombe's Hole driftway, on the north-east side thereof, would be a suitable site for this purpose and should be acquired by the Council. The sewage would thus be taken further away from the town and with a small expenditure on structural works practically the whole of the piece of land could be utilized for the disposal of sewage and the area would be sufficiently extensive to allow of the system of broad irrigation alone being adopted without combination with any system of treatment of the sewage by chemical precipitation as recommended by the Local Government Board at the present site.

If that field was purchased it would serve the town for a number of years, and in the meantime the present Sewage Farm could be used for the remaining period of the lease. Inquiries would be made into the purchase of the land from the owner (now in New Zealand), and it was anticipated that he would be willing to sell. If it should then become necessary to adopt any other system for sewage disposal, the necessary arrangements could be made on their own land.

The Surveyor submitted a statement of the cost of water for watering the Main Roads within the District during the previous season and of the labour, horse and manual, which needed to be employed. This amounted to £26 6s. 6d. It was decided that the County Council should be asked to contribute the sum of £8 15s. 6d. (being one third of the total cost). The local council was of the opinion that watering the roads helped to consolidate them and reduced wear and tear. They had not made this claim previously but had dicovered that the County Council had allowed something in other districts

Handing over the Institute (Corvus Cornix)

By the simple act of affixing its official seal to the deed of conveyance the Urban District Council of Royston has wound up the mortal coil of Royston Institute in the form in which it has been known to Roystonians for more than 40 years. As in many other places the functions of the older types of Mechanics' Institutes, as such places were called, have been taken up by various agencies each working upon its own lines, and, while doing less solid work than the old institutions stood for, leaving the "Institutes" with nothing but their name. The Royston Institute continued in its moribund stage for several years, without rendering any of its old services to the public beyond the uses of the building, and without any guarantee as to management. Under these circumstances the remaining members and the Trustees have taken the right step in the transfer of the building and its properties and liabilities, to the Urban District Council. The transfer means little as regards the uses of the building by the public except that it will henceforth be held for the public by a representative public body. The first act of the new authority over it has been to strip it of its old name. Under the name of the "Royston Town Hall" it will scarcely be recognisable, but as its chief service to the town will be of that character, it is perhaps the only one by which it could properly be described in future.

ROYSTON TOWN HALL

A POPULAR

ENTERTAINMENT

On behalf of the Funds of the Royston Cricket Club

WILL BE GIVEN ON

THURSDAY, DECEMBER 27th, 1900,

TO CONSIST OF

Vocal and Instrumental Music, Musical Monologue, Humorous Songs and Recitations.

The following Ladies and Gentlemen have promised to assist -
Mrs. Bruce Clark, Miss Violet Peebles, Miss Rose Sanders (Cambridge), Miss Stone, Miss Lily Unwin, (Cambridge), Messrs. B. Bishop, J. Course,
G.E. Green, M.A. (Cambridge), Percy R. S. Piggott (Cambridge), and C. E. Wilkerson.

ADMISSION - Front Seats and First Row in Balcony, (Reserved and Numbered), 1/6; Rest of Balcony and Body of Hall, 1/-; Back Seats, 6d.
Seats under the Balcony, 3d., if space permits, at 7.50.

Tickets of Messrs Warren Bros., up to 8 p.m. Monday, 24th where plan may be seen, or Seats may be booked at the Town Hall, on Thursday 27th, from 2 p.m. to 5 p.m.

Doors open at 7. 30 p.m., to Commence at 8.
Carriages may be ordered for 10 o'clock.

1st (Herts. V. B. Beds. Regt.)
E COMPANY
RECRUITS

There are a few Vacancies for Recruits in the above Company. Any man wishing to join must apply to Sergeant Instructor CLARKE, The Armoury, Royston, before Christmas.

6th December, 1900.   G. CAUTHERLEY.

Relating to Sport

Cricket

An interesting trial is being made upon the cricket ground on the Heath, with a view to improving the state of the wickets in dry weather. At present the pitch has a decided tendency to crumble. On many of the leading cricket grounds in the country experiments of top dressing with special soils have been tried with satifactory results One element in the dressing is a Nottingham marl with the use of which the well-known cricketing name of Daft has been associated, and the other element is a red clay loam obtained from Acton in Middlesex. The mixture has been applied to the part of the ground where the pitch is generally selected.

Hockey

On Thursday, December 6th, a match was played on the Heath, between the Royston Ladies Club and an eleven of Cambridge Ladies. After an interesting game Cambridge won by 1 goal to nil.

Football

December

1st   Royston 2nd XI. v Barrington. Score 1 - 4.
1st   Royston v Camb. Great St. Mary's. Score 0 - 1
Herts. Junior Cup
Royston will play their first match in this competition against Ashwell on Saturday, December 15th, at Ashwell, a Second Round match. The reason for this is that in the First Round when drawn against Stevenage United, the latter scratched. No score was reported.

15th   Royston Reserves v Buntingford (away). Score 1 - 5.
22nd   Royston v Baldock (on Heath). Score 4 - 2.
26th   Royston v Silvertown Athletic (on Heath). The visitors did not arrive.
29th   Royston v Hitchin Blue Cross. No score reported in 1900.

THE BOARD OF GUARDIANS

A Request

At the last meeting a letter had been received from the Master of the Workhouse requesting a rise. There was much discussion about the previous rates for the post and comments about the numbers of inmates. The highest salary that had ever been paid was £125 but there were many more inmates At the moment Mr and Mrs. Wesson were receiving £100. They were appointed in 1893 at a salary of £70 which had been increased in 1896. Mr. E .O. Fordham proposed a rise of £5 each to the Master and Matron. He thought they had fulfilled their duties exceedingly well, and no doubt Poor Law salaries had risen throughout the country, and he thought that they could do no less than grant this small rise There was some dissension and an amendment was put forward by Mr. W. W. Clear, "That the board considers £100 per annum, apartments, rations &c. an adequate salary for the post of Master and Matron of the Workhouse." Speaking in favour of Mr. Fordham's proposal, Mr. Clark thought it would unwise not to grant the rise now proposed and run the risk of losing two good officers by saying they would not entertain their application. The matter was voted upon and the chairman then declared against a rise, carried by 10 to 8.

The Sequel

Later in the month the following letter was received by the Board of Guardians.

> *Gentlemen, - On behalf of the Matron and myself, I beg respectfully to ask the Board for a testimonial as to the manner in which we have discharged our duties during the 7½ years we have been respectfully Master and Matron of the Workhouse.*
> *Your obedient servant,*
> *J. W. Wesson.*

They did not think it was a resignation but Mr. Clear said he supposed they were making an application for something elsewhere. He moved that a testimonial be granted, for he thought they had served the Board well. The motion was seconded.

Christmas
At the Workhouse

The pleasures of Christmastide were shared as usual by the inmates of the Workhouse, in the form of a substantial dinner given by the Guardians and various gifts by other friends. Tradesmen, and other townspeople, provided many treats such as fruit, nuts, tobacco, sweets, ale and toys. Coffee and bread and butter for breakfast paved the way for dinner. This consisted of roast beef, roast pork, roast mutton with vegetables, plum puddings and a supply of beer. The dinner took place in the Dining Hall which was very prettily decorated with evergreens, mottoes, lanterns, and a striking display of artificial flowers &c., and no pains were spared by the Master, Matron and staff to carry out the annual event worthily.Tea time found the table again laden with a plentiful supply of tea, cake and bread and butter. In the evening social pleasure reigned supreme, the women and children in games, the men singing the old songs of long ago. The inmates numbered 97 and all of those who could were present in the Dining Hall while those too sick to attend were served in the sick wards.

Winter Fuel
(Corvus Cornix Comments)

The Royston Board of Guardians will have before them at their next meeting the question of making an extra allowance to persons receiving out-door relief during the winter months, owing to the high price of coals. The proposal is one which has been adopted in other Unions, and has so much to commend it that it is not likely to meet with a different reception in this case. It may be said that even apart from the higher price of coals this year, there is a great difference between winter and summer, and that the allowance for the out-door poor cannot possibly go so far in cold weather as in warm. To the old and infirm, warmth is life, and with coal at 1/8 or 1/9 a cwt., as it is in the outlying villages, how the aged manage to keep a home going at all upon the small pittance received from the Guardians is a problem which most of us would not care to face. The need may not be equally great in all cases, but where a home is dependent, or chiefly dependent, upon the slender income of "parish pay" for food and firing, there can be no doubt as to the course the Guardians should take on a question of this kind.

The Annual Sale

The sale for the Sower's Band juvenile workers for the Church Missionary Society took place at the Town Hall on Thursday afternoon, December 20th, under the superintendence of Mrs. Rivers R. Smith, Miss Kate Cautherley, and a number of other ladies. At the stall of work done by the Sower's Band the members of the Band assisted, but this was by no means the only attraction.

The most interesting variation from previous years' programmes was the Cake Competition, in which prizes were offered for the best made and baked fancy, iced and plain cakes. There was a refreshment department with cosy little tables dotted about the Hall, and a Christmas Tree was lighted at dusk and a Magic Lantern Story provided downstairs for the children.

On Christmas Opening (Corvus Cornix)

The peculiar problem of how to arrange the Christmas holidays when Christmas Day falls on Tuesday, as it does this year, has, I understand, been occupying attention in Royston as elsewhere. Obviously it is a great convenience to shop assistants desiring to go home to friends at a distance, and also to shopkeepers themselves, who may wish to go out at Christmas, to be able to include a Sunday and a Christmas Day both within the holiday. This could, however, only be done by closing on Monday, which for most trades and especially the provisioning trades, would be almost out of the question. In Royston, an arrangement is being made to close an extra day after Christmas - on the Thursday following Bank Holiday. This will give three clear days, and, as Thursday is an early closing day and business is not very brisk immediately after Christmas, the extra day will probably cause a trifling loss of business.

A Case of Nostalgia??

(Comments on Christmas Past by Corvus Cornix)

The "Christmas Numbers" which were issued some weeks ago had not, in their contents, any very pronounced setting of Father Christmas in the old time fringe of hoar frost, with family parties coming home through the snow. All that seems to have happened long ago, and we are now living in an age when Christmas numbers are made up in the summer and issued in the Autumn. Whether Christmas can be quite the same to an Englishman without trace of frost and snow, as it used to be may be an open question, for in these days of much travel Englishmen spend Christmas in all sorts of climates; and to a large part of our Colonial friends Christmas is always associated with heat rather than cold. Still we have hardly got accustomed to the change yet, and there is a fine field for some of our publishing firms with the courage to stand aside from the insane race of modern times to be first even if it is not best, and give us a genuine Christmas number of good seasonable pictures and stories, issued fresh in Christmas week when the cards and compliments begin to get into circulation A mild flabby Christmas with only dog-eared literature lying about, is not so inspiring as the old before we began record breaking. For those who can wait, however, there are always good things in store, and for those who go about their Christmas preparations in the old-fashioned way, and make the most of the next two days much may be done to give the accustomed season its wonted joy and gladness.

Christmas at the Parish Church

Christmas was as usual heralded at the Parish Church on *Christmas Eve* with a short Carol Service, conducted by the Vicar. The carols were sung by the Sunday School Choir, with the assistance of the members of the Church Choir. After a short prayer, the service took the form of an outline of the nativity story in the carols sung and short selections read from the New Testament.

The Church bells ushered in *Christmas Day* when special services were held. There was an early celebration of Holy Communion at 8 a.m. The morning service was appropriate to the day. The Vicar preached a sermon for the day and its lessons and made pointed reference to its special character as the last Christmas Day of the Century. There was another celebration of Holy Communion after the morning service and another short service at 4 p.m. The Church was decorated with much taste and was of a seasonable characer - chiefly holly, red berried and variegated, ivy and other evergreens.

Boxing Day Treat

On the evening of Boxing Day a very interesting and enjoyable gathering took place at the British School in connection with Mrs. J. Mason's Market Hill Mission. About 200 parents and children were entertained to tea by Mr. and Mrs. Mason at 5.30pm, the large room presenting a busy and animated scene. After tea a programme of music was enjoyed for about an hour, and then followed an interesting item for the young people. A Christmas tree, laden with many coloured "fruit", was stripped to the delight of the children, some 67 of whom received presents from its branches. The distribution of presents being over, the large company enjoyed themselves with games &c., until 10p.m. when the company broke up, with many thanks to their entertainers, who had spared no pains to provide an enjoyable evening.

CHRISTMAS PURCHASES

203

EXTRACTS FROM THE CROW'S CHRISTMAS MISCELLANY

PUZZLES AND JOKES
HOW TO TELL A PERSON'S AGE.

Among many ingenious schemes for telling a person's age this is one of the easiest and best. Let the person whose age is to be discovered do the figuring. Suppose, for example. if it is a girl, that her age is fifteen and that she was born in August.

Let her put down the number of the month in which she was born and proceed as follows:

Number of month...8
Multiply by 2..16
Add 5...21
Multiply by 50..1050
Then add her age, 15..1065
Then subtract 365, leaving..700
Then add 115..815

She then annouces the result 815, whereupon she may be informed that her age is fifteen and August, or the eighth month, is the month of her birth.

The two figures to the right in the result will always indicate the age and the remaining figure or figures the month the birthday comes in.

This rule never fails for all ages up to a hundred. For ages under ten a cipher will appear prefixed in the result, but no account is taken of this.

******

AN ARITHMETICAL MYSTERY (1).

Thirteen commercial travellers arrived at an inn, and each desired a separate room. The landlady had but twelve vacant rooms but she promised to accomodate all according to their wishes. So she shewed two of the travellers into room No. 1, asking them to remain a few minutes together. Traveller No. 3 she shewed into room No. 2; traveller No. 4 she shewed into room No. 3; traveller No. 5 into room No. 4; traveller No. 6 into room No. 5, and so on until she had put the twelth traveller into room No. 11. She then went back to where she had left the two travellers together, and asking the thirteenth traveller to follow her, led him to No. 12, the remaining room. thus all were accomodated. Explain the mystery.

******

SOME GOOD ANAGRAMS

The pith of a good anagram is that it should in some way relate to the meaning of the original word:

Astronomers.............No more stars, or, Moon starers.
Impatient.................Tim in a pet.
Punishment..............Nine thumps.
Matrimony..............Into my arm.
Revolution...............To love ruin.
Sweetheart..............There we sat.
Telegraphs..............Great helps.
Parishioners............I hire parsons.
Radical reform.........Rare mad frolic.
Presbyterian............Best in prayer.
Misanthrope...........Spare him not.
Catalogue................Got at a clue.
Elegant...................Neat leg.

******

CURIOUS CHANGES (2)

1. Remove the head and tail of a bird of passage, reverse the remains and they will become putrefaction.
2. Remove the head and tail of a certain species of fish, reverse the remains and you will have a fight.
3 Remove the head and tail of a small animal, transpose the remains and you will find a French coin.
4. Remove the head and tail of a bird with a long bill, reverse the remains and you will see a short, pointed piece of wire with a head.
5. Remove the head and tail of a bird that feeds upon fish, reverse the remains and you will discover metal in its fossil state.
6. Remove the head and tail of a wading bird, leave the remains as they are and you will be rewarded by finding affection.

******

THE DICE GUESSED UNSEEN

A pair of dice being thrown, to find the number of points on each dice without seeing them: Tell the person who casts the dice to double the number of points on one of them and add five to it; then to multiply the sum produced by 5, and to add to the product the number of points on the other die. This being done, desire him to tell you the amount, and having thrown out 25, the remainder will be a number consisting of two figures, the first of which, to the left, is the number of points on the first die, and the second figure to the right, the number on the other. Thus: Suppose the number of points of the first die which comes up to be 2 and that of the other 3. Then if to 4, the double of the points of the first, there be added 5, and the sum produced, 9, be multiplied by 5, the product will be 45; to which if 3, the number of points on the other die, be added 48 will be produced, from which, if 25 be subtracted, 23 will remain, the first figure of which is 2, the number of points on the first die, and the second figure 3, the number on the second die.

******

ANSWERS TO PUZZLES
(1) No. 13 was the traveller shewn into Room No. 1. No. 2 traveller is still unaccounted for.

(2) 1. S-tor-k. 2. S-wor-d. 3. M-ous-e. 4. S-nip-e. 5. H=ero-n.
6. P-love-r.

NUTS TO CRACK
A Transposition (1).

A gentleman who was paying his addresses to a lady, at length summoned up sufficient courage to ask if they were agreeable to her, and whether he might flatter himself with a chance of ultimate success. The lady replied, "Stripes!" telling the gentleman to transpose the letters so as to form out of them another word, which word was her answer. The reader who can find out the word need never fear being nonplussed by a lady; those who cannot must either persist till they overcome the difficulty or may give up all thoughts of wooing.

******

INSERTIONS (2).
If only I were there:
1. A heavenly body would be a means of ascending.
2. A quick motion would be a shower.
3. A human being would be the principal one.
4. A heavy stick would be a necessity for a fisherman.
5. A means of keeping cool would be to desire.
6. At a great distance would be pleasant to look at.
7. A beautiful fowl would be a country lover.
8. The front rank would be proud.
9. An undulation would become to dispense with.
10. Stout would become a decree.
11. A small piece of ground would be a fold.
12. Downcast would become mentioned.
13. To peruse would become a piece of money.
14. A crossing place would become an inlet.
15. To be able would become a Bible character.
16. A liquid would become a servant.
17. Insane would become a female.
18. A musical term would become earth.
19. Human beings would become manner.
20. A large company would become to lift.
21. A shallow, open vessel would become suffering.
22. An attitude would become a regulating power.

******

BROKEN WORDS (2)
Example: Break a pardon and make a preposition and to bestow; answer, for-give.

1. Break a bird, and make to fold over and part of an army. 2. Break to perform to excess, and make above and a division in a drama. 3. Break one of the same name, . and make to nominate and purpose. 4. Break a name somtimes given to an emigrant, and make a colour and a musical instrument. 5. Break the end, and make part of a fish and verb. 6. Break delight, and make part of the head and a case of boxes. 7. Break a familiar piece of furniture, and make observing and a brittle substance. 8. Break the pole star, and make burdens and a sailor. 9. Break a Grecian theatre, and make a short poem and upon. 10. Break to separate chaff with wind, and make to gain and the present time.

When these words have been rightly guessed and written one below the other, the initials of the first column of words will spell the name of a famous poet, and the initials of the seccond the name of a famous American statesman and soldier.

****

ROMAN ARITHMETIC (4)
Example: Subtract five from a frolic and leave a spool. Answer: Revel-v=reel.
1. Subtract five from sin and leave frozen water.
2. Add four to a pronoun and make a bee's home.
3. Divide a squirming fish by ninety and get a word meaning to surpass.
4. Add one hundred to a fastening and get a timepiece.
5. Subtract ten from part of a wheel and get a drink.
6. Subtract six from the second King of Israel and get his father.
7. Add two hundred to a personal pronoun and get a word meaning to happen.
8. Subtract nine from sixty and get a pig's home.
9. Subtract six from a neighbourly call and get a word meaning to be seated.

******

ANSWERS TO PUZZLES
(1) Persist.

(2) 1. Sta(i)r. 2. Ra(i)n. 3. Ma(i)n. 4.. Ba(i)t. 5. Fa(i)n. 6. Fa(i) 7. Swa(i)n. 8. Va(i)n. 9. Wa(i)ve. 10. F(i)at. 11. Pla(i)t 12. Sa(i)d. 13. Co(i)n. 14. F(i)ord. 15. Ca(i)n. 16. Wa(i)ter. 17. Ma(i)d. 18. So(i)l. 19. M(i)en. 20. Ho(i)st. 21. Pa(i)n. 22. Po(i)se.

(3) Broken Words: 1. Lap-wing. 2. Over-act. 3. Name-sake. 4. Green-horn. 5. Fin-is. 6. Ear-nest. 7. Looking-glass. 8. Loads-tar. 9. Ode-on. 10. Win-now. Longfellow, Washington.

(4) Roman Arithmetic: 1.V-ice. 2. H-IV-e. 3. E-XC-el. 4. C-lock. 5. A- X-le. 6. Da-VI-d. 7. O-CC-ur. 8. S-IX-ty. 9. VI-sit.
****

CONUMDRUMS
1. My *first* is a society, my *second* a recluse, my *third* a part of the ear, and my *whole* is intended to amuse.
2. My *first* is nimble, my *second* innumerable, and my *whole* fatal.
3. What part of speech is "no," with two bits of fun added to it?

ANSWERS.
1. Co-nun-drum. 2. Quick-sands. 3. No-un.

Contaminated Beer

A report appeared in the press during December, which though it did not directly concern Royston touched upon their lives in a small way. A number of people in the North of England had been affected by arsenical poisoning due to beer being manufactured from impure ingredients and substitutes for malt and hops and indeed some had died. Many thousands of gallons of beer had been destroyed. The matter found itself the subject of much discussion in Parliament and a number of other places. Concerned speakers stated that the the British people were entitled to be safeguarded against substitute materials and the subject was a matter for intervention by Parliament. They called upon the Government to pass a Pure Beer Act in the next session.

It was widely reported in *The Crow* and advertisements appeared in the newspaper from local brewers assuring their customers that their beers were manufactured only from pure malt and hops and guaranteeing them free from injurious ingredients and at a temperance meeting in the town the facts were used as ammunition against drinking. The Board of Guardians received a letter enclosing a copy of the resolution for a Pure Beer Bill which had been sent to every Board of Guardians in the country. The Guardians felt it was not really part of their business and that although they supplied beer to the inmates of the workhouse, they did not suppose that any brewers in the area put anything in their beer but malt and hops. It was resolved that the communication lay on the table.

ROYSTON PARISH CHURCH
BAPTISMS
December
16th Harold Guy, son of Arthur Sharpe, (Clerk to Guardians), and Jane Elizabeth Sharpe
16th Ethel Elizabeth, daughter of George Harradance (Labourer, Bassingbourn) and Jane Harradance.
16th Edward, son of George Carr (Malster) and Susannah Carr.
23rd Rose Macdonald, daughter of William Henry King (Basketmaker, London), and Edith Elizabeth Jane King.
23rd Muriel Stamford, daughter of Ernest William Thair (Hairdresser) and Ada Mary Thair.

MARRIAGES
December
1st Hugh Alexander Ross (Artist) to Kate Rawlins
10th Robert Kingston (Sheepdealer) to Edith Flora Kingston (Publican).
26th William Reid (Grocer's Assistant, London) to Selina Forster Kingsley.

BURIALS
December
3rd George Pymont, aged 73 years.
13th Emmeline Lizzie Percy died on 9th at White Horse Inn, Melbourn St, aged 18 months.

Other Deaths reported this month
3rd Sarah Sell, beloved wife of Joseph Sell at West Terrace Royston, aged 65 years.
15th John Abraham Baker, at Mill Road, Royston, aged 61 years.
22nd Thomas Barnes, at the Union Workhouse, Royston, aged 81 years.

Drunk and Disorderly

A man from London was brought up in custody at the Police Station for being drunk and disorderly in the High Street and Market Hill. He had been knocking drunkenly at the door of Camps & Co.'s boot shop. Inspector Hart was sent for and found the defendant lying very drunk on the ground near " The Plough" with a crowd of children around him. He was using bad language and continued to do so all the way to the Police Station. The Magistrates fined him 10s. including costs or 7 days hard labour. As he had no money he went to prison by default. He apologised and said he was all right when sober.

The Final Words on 1900
Corvus Cornix

The last Christmastide of the Century has come and almost gone, without bringing us more than a passing breath of traditional Christmas weather. Those who like to see a bright, crisp, bracing Christmas must have felt somewhat elated when on Sunday morning they woke to find what was practically the first frost of winter. However the change came only too soon and left us with the roses and chrysanthemums in the gardens and bats flying abroad in the evening, and indicated one of the mildest Christmastides of the Century. By the way, it seems that the two Christmastides of 1800 and 1900 have been singularly alike. The 25th December, 1800, was mild and damp, though slightly colder than this one, but the two ends of the two centuries were singularly alike in this one particular of the weather - the most constant friend that the Englishman has. But in all else the two Christmastides are as far asunder as the poles.

Before another issue of this Paper makes its appearance the 19th Century will have run its course and we shall have reached the end of a hundred years which has no parallel in the history of the world. The advent of steam power and electricity, or rather of appliances for their practical application to the needs of daily life, would have been sufficient of itself to have placed the 19th Century before all other centuries that have been. This, however, was but the prelude to a host of discoveries and inventions by which art and science have altered the whole character of the environment of human life. It has been a century, a very wonderful century, of emancipation all along the line of human life, not only in this country but in most civilised countries; a century of clearing away old obsolete forms of obstruction, and of opening up the blocked channels along the highway of life, facilities of communication on the highways, on railways, on the ocean, through the telegraph, the telephone, and the penny post - all these were but the flood-gates through which many other things became possible. A hundred years ago men were tied hand and foot in many ways we can hardly realize today. As soon as these hindrances, domestic, social, and political were removed, men were free to act and to put into practice many intimations of a better way which had occurred to their fathers as theories, impossible of realization in the then state of mechanical science. In the space of a hundred years we have moved forward into a different world and we can let the century go with gratitude rather than regret.

BIBLIOGRAPHY

A Brief Look at 1900
The Story of Britain, Sir Roy Strong (Hutchinson, 1996).
Chronicle of the 20th Century (Dorling Kindersley, 1995).

Poverty, Health and Essential Services
Poverty and the Workhouse in Victorian Britain, Peter Wood (Alan Sutton, 1991).
The Cottage Hospitals 1859-1900, Dr. Meyrick Emrys Roberts (Tern Publications, 1991).
The Story of Hertfordshire Police, Neil Osborne (Herts. Countryside, 1969).
Victorian Things, Asa Briggs (Penguin, 1990).

Education
History of English Education from 1760, A.C. Barnard (U. L. Press, 1961).
The Victorian Schoolroom, Trevor May (Shire Publications, 1994).
The Victorian and Edwardian Schoolchild, Pamela Horn (Alan Sutton, 1989).

Getting About
The Dawn of Motoring - How the Car came to Britain, Erik Johnson (Mercedes Benz
    (UK) Ltd., 1986).
The Raleigh Book of Cycling, Reginald Short (Peter Davis 1975).

After Work
Victorian Britain Through The Magic Lantern, Steve Humphreys (Sidgwick and
    Jackson, 1989).
Old Gramophones and other Talking Machines, Benet Bergonzi (Shire Publications, 1991).
History of Royston Golf Club, Helen Allsop, Harry Hainsworth, Angela Tinston
    (Cortney Publications, 1992).
Royston Inns and Public Houses (Royston and District Local History Society, 1990).
The Hertfordshire Regiment:An Illustrated History, J. D. Sainsbury (Castlemead
    Publications, 1969).

Working in Royston
The Rise and Fall of the Victorian Servant, Pamela Horn (Alan Sutton.1990).
Labouring Life in the Victorian Countryside, Pamela Horn (Gill and Macmillan, 1976).
Royston in Old Picture Postcards, Vols. 1 & 2, F. J. Smith (European Library, 1983).
History of Royston, Alfred Kingston (Warren Bros., 1906).
20th Century Royston,The First Fifty Years, Frederic Sillence (Cortney Publications 1993).

MAP OF ROYSTON
At the Turn of the Century

The attached map is part the Ordinance Survey (1903) Map - Second Edition.
This map was made up of Cambridgeshire SW - Sheet LVIII and Hertfordshire - Part of Sheets IV & V.

[Cambridgeshire was surveyed in 1885 and revised in 1901; Hertfordshire was surveyed in 1876 and revised in 1896-1897]

Scale - Six Inches to one Statute Mile or 880 Feet to One Inch.

– – – – – – – –   County Boundary

. . . .   Parish Boundary

This map shows how the town was gradually developing outwards from the centre. This was a common factor in most towns and continues to this day.

Price of map - 1/6 net.(7½p)

A full copy of the map is to be found in Cambridgeshire Record Office.

CORVUS CORNIX

208

umul

—